TEXTUAL DYNAMICS

OF THE PROFESSIONS

Textual Dynamics of the Professions

HISTORICAL AND CONTEMPORARY

STUDIES OF WRITING

IN PROFESSIONAL COMMUNITIES

EDITED BY CHARLES BAZERMAN

AND JAMES PARADIS

THE UNIVERSITY OF WISCONSIN PRESS

The University of Wisconsin Press
114 North Murray Street
Madison, Wisconsin 53715

3 Henrietta Street
London WC2E 8LU, England

5   4   3   2   1

Printed in the United States of America

Library of Congress Cataloging-in-Publication Data

Textual dynamics of the professions : historical and contemporary
studies of writing in professional communities / edited by Charles
Bazerman and James Paradis.
404 pp.   cm. — (Rhetoric of the human sciences)
   Includes bibliographical references and index.
    1. Discourse analysis.   2. Technical writing.   3. Business
writing.   4. Professions.   I. Bazerman, Charles.   II. Paradis,
James G., 1942–   III. Series.
P302.T455   1990
808'.0014 — dc20
ISBN 0-299-12540-4   90-50079
ISBN 0-299-12594-7 (pbk.)   CIP

CONTENTS

CONTRIBUTORS

John Ackerman coordinates Business Writing and teaches at the University of Utah. His research interests are in the connection between writing and disciplinary learning. He is coauthor of *Reading to Write: Exploring a Cognitive and Social Process* (Oxford University Press, forthcoming).

Charles Bazerman teaches at the Georgia Institute of Technology, where he directs degree programs in rhetoric and technical communication. His interests are in theory of writing as a social activity and the rhetoric of science. He is author of *Shaping Written Knowledge: The Genre and Activity of the Experimental Article in Science* (University of Wisconsin Press, 1988). His textbooks include *The Informed Reader* and *The Informed Writer*.

Carol Berkenkotter teaches rhetoric and composition at Michigan Technological University. Her early studies of audience-related composing strategies have led to an interest in the situational contexts of writing and academic genres. She has published essays in *Research in the Teaching of English, College Composition and Communication, Rhetoric Review,* and *Journal of Advanced Composition* and has completed the textbook *College Contexts for Reading and Writing.*

Amy J. Devitt teaches at the University of Kansas, specializing in composition theory and in the English language. Her publications include *Standardizing Written English: Diffusion in the Case of Scotland, 1520–1659* (Cambridge University Press, 1989).

Stephen Doheny-Farina teaches technical communications at Clarkson University. He has published on a range of issues related to writing in nonacademic settings and has recently edited *Effective Documentation: What We Have Learned from Research* (MIT Press, 1988).

Jeanne Fahnestock teaches rhetoric and writing at the University of Maryland at College Park. She is coauthor of *The Rhetoric of Argument* and has published articles in *College Composition and Communication, Written Communication,* and *Science, Technology, and Human Values.* She is now working on a book on the rhetoric of science.

Contributors

Barbara A. Fennell teaches linguistics and German at North Carolina State University, where she also coordinates the minor in linguistics. Her main research interests are in Germanic and English sociolinguistics.

Cheryl Geisler teaches rhetoric and composition at Rensselear Polytechnic Institute and directs the Writing Intensive Program. She has published articles on academic conversation in *Written Communication, Rhetoric Society Quarterly,* and *Rhetoric Review,* and is coauthor of the textbook *Arguing From Sources: Exploring Issues Through Reading and Writing.*

Carl G. Herndl teaches English at North Carolina State University, and has published on corporate and technical writing. He is currently writing about postmodernism and ethnography, and about the implications of Marxist critical theory for writing research.

Thomas N. Huckin teaches discourse analysis, advanced expository writing, and technical writing at the University of Utah. He enjoys doing context-sensitive linguistic analyses of written texts, written genres, and "rules of good writing." He is coauthor of *Technical Writing and Professional Communication* and has published articles in *Research in the Teaching of English, Written Communication, Linguistic Analysis, Visible Language,* and other journals.

Lucille Parkinson McCarthy teaches literature and writing at the University of Maryland, Baltimore County. She has published articles about students writing in academic settings and has coauthored a book on the psychiatry of handicapped children.

Carolyn R. Miller teaches at North Carolina State University where she coordinates the M.S. in Technical Communication. Her primary research interest is the rhetoric of science and technology, on which she has published several theoretical and critical essays. She is also coeditor of *New Essays in Scientific and Technical Communication.*

Greg Myers is a lecturer in Linguistics at the University of Lancaster, Lancaster, England. He has recently published a book of case studies, *Writing Biology: Texts in the Social Construction of Scientific Knowledge,* and he is now working on a study of the discourse of the computational linguistics and AI research communities in Britain.

James Paradis teaches technical communication at the Massachusetts Institute of Technology. His primary scholarly interests are the rhetorical history of science and technology and science and literature in Victorian culture. He has consulted extensively as an expert witness on the role of manuals in the social construction of technology. His publications include *T. H. Huxley: Man's Place in Nature* and numerous essays in journals and volumes. He is coeditor of *Victorian Science and Victorian Values* and *Evolution and Ethics* (Princeton University Press, 1989).

Les Perelman is an Assistant Dean and Coordinator of the Writing Requirement at the Massachusetts Institute of Technology. Trained in medieval literature and rhetoric, he is interested in historical relationships between the social function of discourse and the concurrent formulation of rhetorical theory. He has coedited *The Middle English Letter of Alexander to Aristotle* and has published articles in *College English, The Writing Instructor,* and *Neophilologus.*

Robert A. Schwegler teaches courses in rhetoric and composition in the English Department at the University of Rhode Island. His research currently focuses on the ways cognition, disciplinary constraints, and ideology shape readers' perceptions and evaluations. He has published articles in *College English, Freshman English News, Journal of American Folklore,* and *The Writing Instructor.* Among his textbooks are *Patterns in Action* and *Patterns of Exposition.*

Marie Secor teaches at Penn State University, where she has also served as director of the Penn State Conference on Rhetoric and Composition. She has published essays in *College Composition and Communication, Pre/Text, Rhetoric Society Quarterly, Philosophy and Rhetoric,* and *Written Communication,* and she is coauthor of *A Rhetoric of Argument* (2d ed., McGraw-Hill) and *Readings in Argument* (Random House). She is interested in rhetorical history, theory, and analysis, and is doing further studies on the rhetoric of literary argument and on style.

Linda K. Shamoon is Director of the College Writing Program in the English Department at the University of Rhode Island where she teaches courses in rhetoric and composition and in the teaching of writing. In addition to articles in *College English, Freshman English News,* and *The Writing Instructor,* she has published a textbook, *Think/Write: A Guide*

Contributors

to *Research Writing Across the Curriculum* and is the author of a forth-coming text on reading and writing in the disciplines. Her current research focuses on the connections between gender and argumentative style in undergraduate writing.

Ann Harleman Stewart, Visiting Scholar in the American Civilization Department at Brown University, has taught linguistics and writing at Rutgers, the University of Washington, Dartmouth, and MIT. Her schol-arly work includes *Graphic Representation of Models in Linguistic Theory* (Indiana, 1976), *Ian Fleming: A Critical Biography* (Twayne, 1989), and many articles on language and style. She has received fellowships from the Guggenheim, Fulbright, and Rockefeller foundations and currently holds the Rhode Island State Arts Council Literature Fellowship.

Gail Stygall teaches rhetoric, composition, and English language linguis-tics at the University of Washington. She has published articles in *The Journal of Basic Writing* and *The Journal of Teaching Writing*. She is cur-rently at work on a book examining the language theories invoked in judicial decisions.

James P. Zappen teaches at Rensselear Polytechnic Institute. He has pub-lished articles on rhetoric and scientific communication in numerous journals. He is also editor of the State University of New York Press series Studies in Scientific and Technical Communication.

TEXTUAL DYNAMICS

OF THE PROFESSIONS

INTRODUCTION

The Interactive Text

The studies developed in *Textual Dynamics of the Professions* concretely elucidate the broad abstraction that writing is social action. Writing is more than socially embedded: it is socially constructive. Writing structures our relations with others and organizes our perceptions of the world. By studying texts within their contexts, we study as well the dynamics of context building. In particular, by understanding texts within the professions, we understand how the professions constitute themselves and carry out their work through texts.

This view that texts are dynamic, causal entities in the social environment rejects some assumptions common in modern criticism. Textual analysis typically isolates texts from their social and intentional origins. The trained literary critic who attributes specific authorial purposes to creative works is accused of perpetrating the "intentional fallacy." The view that texts are independent of authorial purpose and social origin, the outgrowth of postwar literary criticism, associates texts with artistic creativity. The enduring Romantic thesis of self-transcendence in the act of creation promotes the kind of vigorous attention to textual detail that vastly enriches — and complicates — the reading of authors of the literary canon, whether Shakespeare, Melville, Austen, or Dickinson. On the other hand, concepts of textual independence tend to ignore the profound material basis of all texts, while discarding as inconsequential those texts that have manifestly functional purposes.

The illusion of the self-sustaining text is maintained, surely, by the abstraction of the library as a repository of "literature" and "knowledge." Book-objects, removed from the social tangle of their textual origins, are grouped alphanumerically in classes of subject, genre, language, historical period, and discipline. Exegetical traditions associated with the library retain their identifications with these abstract categories. In the library interior, always reminiscent of the chapel or cathedral, the text exists in a timeless, contemplative silence, away from the secular compromises of daily human transactions. We are thus conditioned to associate the text and all its attendant acts with academic remove. This hieratic removal overintellectualizes the notion of text and stigmatizes the worldliness of the literature of transactions. The social functions of texts, and how texts manage those functions rhetorically, have rarely been considered fit subjects for serious scholarship.

In the workplace, be it academic, white collar, or blue collar, we are met with texts whose functions are unfamiliar in the realm of polite letters or the library. Yet these texts have almost certainly had as great an impact on our modern culture and concepts of reality as the literary canon. These texts are the transactions that make institutional collaboration possible; they are the means by which individuals collectively construct the contexts out of which intellectual and material products emerge. In the pragmatic worlds of these specialized work communities, text is a force that transforms human physical and conceptual limits. The discourse of social transactions is typically functional, material, and purposive. Yet, it still exploits all the underlying rhetorical resources of language. Its dynamics are the dynamics of all texts. Textual analysis thus yields us important new avenues into this social realm, as we see text constructing versions of reality. The textual autonomy associated with the library fails in the workplace, where textual dynamics are a central agency in the social construction of objects, concepts, and institutions.

Exploring Textual Dynamics

The studies developed in this volume are concerned with exploring the textual side of social construction. The phrase "textual dynamics" refers to the idea that written discourse is produced by a complex of social, cognitive, material, and rhetorical activities; in return, written texts dialectically precipitate the various contexts and actions that constitute the professions. These activities, as the studies of this volume show, yield to several modes of analysis, borrowing from writing pedagogy, rhetorical studies, literary theory, linguistics, cognitive studies, sociology, and historical analysis. This methodological diversity, however, converges upon a striking subject matter well outside the traditional domain of textual analysis.

In these essays, we see how the shifting configurations of written discourse that people create to address their immediate social needs actively shape psychological, social, political, physical, and even fiscal realities. Out of provisional clusterings of people, activities, and language emerge highly organized professions of great social consequence. Once established, professions maintain their organization, power, and activity in large part through networks of texts. As these professions increasingly form the framework of modern existence, their texts set the terms of our lives. The better we understand the textual dynamics of the professions, the better we can appreciate the world we have made and continue to make through text. This effort to locate the place of self and society in the world, by means of examining the role of text in constructing that world, is one of the traditional tasks of the humanities.

Themes of the Dynamics

We have grouped the studies of this collection into three closely related themes identified as (1) textual construction of the professions, (2) the dynamics of discourse communities, and (3) the operational force of texts. These distinctions are largely matters of emphasis, since several of the essays might conceivably be collected under all three categories. On the other hand, the themes help to focus attention on three important aspects of text in the professions. The first is the important role texts play in profession-building. This process is seen in the rigorous manner in which textual forms and definitions impose structure on human activity and help to shape versions of reality. The second cluster of essays focuses on this process from the transactional standpoint of various discourse communities, as their members attempt to locate the tools of consensus. In this section, we see the enrollment activities of profession-building and profession-maintenance at work. The third group of essays explores texts as they give rise to actions. The emphasis here is on the powerful role texts assume in shaping the daily actions of individuals and the rather far-ranging social consequences thereof. These three themes by no means exhaust the possibility of our subject matter, but they do illustrate the crucial role texts play in our social constructions of reality.

TEXTUAL CONSTRUCTION OF THE PROFESSIONS

The essays in the first section of this collection explore the ways in which texts help shape professional perspectives of human experience. Textual construction is an essential part of this process, giving shape and stability to the versions of reality located in the subject matter. In Charles Bazerman's introductory essay, for example, Joseph Priestley's historicizing of discovery is viewed as a textual means of consolidating the scattered productions of natural philosophers into a stable and progressive knowledge structure. Priestley's rhetoric of science coordinates texts in order to promote a new kind of social interaction. Priestley's rhetorical problem is similar to that Greg Myers finds in the review article: to give order to the past, so as to establish a shared present that will be the basis for coordinated work in the future. In "Stories and Styles in Two Molecular Biology Review Articles," Myers compares two apparently different review articles from the same period to show how molecular biologists

James Darnell and Francis Crick use the device of plot to weave diverse scientific papers into two stories of professional progress. Others, he argues, are thus encouraged to shape their own research in a manner that continues the narrative. This temporal structuring of the labor of the many also accommodates important social themes of progressive inquiry that drive the ideological machinery of the sciences.

In an illuminating contrast to the first two studies, Jeanne Fahnestock and Marie Secor explore a number of rhetorical conventions that constitute available means of persuasion within literary criticism, organized around topoi that often seek to demonstrate textual complexity. This testimonial rhetoric reinforces value systems and is, in this respect, less like the modelling process of the rhetoric of professional research than the ceremonial rhetoric of the self-reinforcing religious community. Criticism, serving epideictic functions, praises and blames texts in ways that reinforce a particular moral attitude toward the world, thereby giving pleasure to members of the literary community.

The textual harnessing of human social energies to support institutional versions of reality is seen in a more general context in the studies of Ann Harleman Stewart and Les Perelman. Stewart examines some of the textual dynamics by which the business professions constitute an academic subject matter that has some claim to extra-academic reality. In "The Role of Narrative Structure in the Transfer of Ideas," she demonstrates how the ordering of events in case studies, deliberately left unresolved, imparts a calculated heuristic quality to the materials by appealing to the reader's psychological need for closure. As the reader is pulled in to help construct "plot," causal elements are inferred from temporal circumstances. Perelman, using a historical example, likewise explores the textual channeling of social energy. In "The Medieval Art of Letter Writing," he considers how textual formulae contributed to institutional self-definition at a time when ecclesiastical authority was rapidly expanding and consolidating in medieval Europe. The formal rhetorics of letter writing, the _ars dictaminis_, he argues, enabled a new religious bureaucracy both to constitute itself and to control social practice by fixing and thus stabilizing a variety of common secular transactions. By such means, rhetorical forms set standards for the structuring of human relations.

To conclude this first section, James Zappen reviews some of the ways in which nineteenth-century ideological implications are lodged in rhetorical practices. In "Scientific Rhetoric in the Nineteenth and Early Twentieth Centuries: Herbert Spencer, Thomas Huxley, and John Dewey," he examines the role of rhetoric in the ideological construction of social discourse. These ideologies mainly concern the relations of science and society. Spencer and Huxley, he argues, follow rhetorical models that subordinate science to the service of society; Dewey gives rhetorical authority to organized science and, in the process, subsumes society within science. This essay explicitly considers a theme that underlies all the studies in the volume: how communities establish themselves as distinctive through their discourse practices and how they then relate to other communities that lie outside their domain.

THE DYNAMICS OF DISCOURSE COMMUNITIES

The second section of the collection shifts the emphasis to the activities of social construction by examining how discourse communities rhetorically structure and maintain their interests. These essays emphasize the discursive process as a means of inducting or enrolling outsiders into an insider's views and commitments. In the first two essays, for example, we see how the learning of discursive models guides the process of enrolling individuals into certain professions. Cheryl Geisler's study "Toward a Sociocognitive Model of Literacy: Constructing Mental Models in a Philosophical Conversation" examines the strikingly different ways in which novices and experts construct their respective discourses in the subject of philosophy. The norms of professions, she suggests, are embodied, to a considerable extent, in the specific discursive models recognized by individual practitioners. These schema, which are based on actual philosophical debates, furnish trained philosophers with models that help them structure the content of their reading, as well as to construct their own written discourse. Novices, lacking professional schemata, respond in intuitive, idiosyncratic ways to the claims in their readings. Geisler's study is supported in the findings of Berkenkotter, Huckin, and Ackerman in "Social Context and Socially Constructed Texts." This study examines ways in which writers exploit generic rhetorical structures to impose the specialized perspective of an interpretive community upon a subject matter. The authors examine the changing rhetorical strategies in the introductory section of a student's papers as the student becomes enrolled into a research community. The student increasingly uses professional context-setting devices invoked in specialized terms, problem statements, and research linkages that constitute a plausible disciplinary model.

The use of rhetorical models to enroll novices into professions with their specific conceptual commitments is examined in yet another respect by Schwegler and Shamoon in "Meaning Attribution in Ambiguous Texts in Sociology." Based on interpretive models followed by specialized discourse communities, the authors construct the presuppositions upon which academicians critique student papers. Textual criticism is shown to be part of the dynamic by which novices are enrolled into the conceptual and rhetorical order that embodies the commitments of a profession. Sociologists reading student papers invoke discipline-specific structures as a means of locating the ambiguities of student texts and then suggest rhetorical remedies to the student. In these classical educational processes, textual criticism serves to socialize the novice, who accepts rhetorical goals identified with accepted professional goals. As textual insufficiencies are revealed to student authors, students are introduced to the rhetorical framing and manipulating techniques associated with the professionalization of subject manner.

The rhetorical complexities of enrollment into discourse communities are seen in the failures traced in Gail Stygall's "Texts in Oral Contexts: The 'Transmission' of Jury Instructions in an Indiana Trial." Stygall locates the limits of induction in the classical courtroom predicament, where jurors — typically novices to the legal professions — are enlisted into the specialized discourse community of the courtroom. In effect, we see a boundary between two discourse communities, where jurors, accustomed to the demotic discourse of transactions that are socially representative, are introduced to the hieratic discourse of legal specialists, who use language to construct specialized legal conventions. Different rhetorical agenda are pursued. The jury instructions ostensibly attempt to induct novices orally into an unfamiliar discourse community that is precipitated around written courtroom processes. But the rhetorical agenda of the instructions answer less to juror needs, than to the legal maneuvers of lawyers and judges.

THE OPERATIONAL FORCE OF TEXT

In the final section, we explore the dynamics of how texts, originating within specialized discourse communities, can profoundly influence a wide range of common social activities. Such texts do not follow the rhetorical models of formal professional research, although they invoke the authority of expertise to make their general recommendations. Thus, we come to another dimension of textual dynamics different from the *construction* and *enrollment* activities of parts 1 and 2: an *operational* mode where the expertise originating within the more narrowly defined research processes is rhetorically transformed into broader terms of socially operative texts that guide human actions. These texts constitute the transactional domains, where the hieratic discourse of expertise is converted to the demotic discourse of everyday practice.

Examples of how texts and human actions are interdependent are often found in failures. In "Text and Action: The Operations Manual in Context and in Court," James Paradis examines the interconnections among different social worlds in the literature of product instructions. This literature — a vast, largely submerged, body of informal texts — furnishes the discourse by which the products of expertise are converted to the terms of human actions. Paradis explores how instructions for a publicly marketed tool serve to mediate between the world of technologists and manufacturers and the everyday world where tools are employed. Using the courtroom as a complex forum that brings together several worlds, Paradis explores how these submerged texts are socially legitimized in tort law and the concept of liability.

Rhetorical disjunctions also lie at the heart of the next two studies, in which failures in the deployment and commercialization of technology are the consequences of actions based on texts. In "Understanding Failures in Organizational Discourse: The Accident at Three Mile Island and the Shuttle Challenger Disaster," Herndl, Fennell, and Miller explore the rhetorical basis for social disaster in two well-known technological incidents. Analyzing document clusters on formal linguistic, pragmatic, and argumentative levels, they find that within the same "discourse community" managers and engineers familiar with different argumentative resources defined problems in different ways. Arguments had difficulty being sustained across these social groupings, resulting in different actions being perceived as appropriate to the same set of circumstances. Similarly, in "Creating a Text/Creating a Company," Stephen Doheny-Farina looks at the textual basis for the financing and development of a new software corporation. Through interviews and text analysis, he traces the role of a text — a proposal — in initiating the activities of numerous investors, university faculty, students, administrators, and software engineers to capitalize and staff a new company. The proposal, a rhetorical idealization with the theme of investing in high-tech and "the future" has severe shortcomings as the material basis for the activities of everyday corporate reality. These shortcomings ultimately lead to the company's failure.

In the final two studies, socially operative texts materially shape the activities of specialists, whose discourse governs two very fundamental social realms: taxes and mental health. Amy Devitt examines the discourse of tax accountants, a community that stands between the legal system and everyday financial matters. In "Intertextuality in Tax Accounting," she shows how tax codes shape human financial activities on a massive scale. Tax documents are bound in a textual system that serves to translate the activity of finance into legal representations. Hence, the tax code, providing an intertextual reference point for all tax-related documents, furnishes the basis for diverse institutional activities. In "A Psychiatrist Using *DSM-III*," Lucille McCarthy locates another example in which text is profoundly involved in the creation of social reality. The world of mental phenomena is regulated by texts. She finds in the American Psychiatric Association's taxonomy of mental disorders (known as *DSM-III*) a charter document that substantially influences the rhetoric of mental health in standard psychiatric clinical reports on individuals. On the basis of interviews, observations, and text analysis, she argues that the taxonomy provides the framework for psychiatric diagnosis, as well as for its subsequent clinical practice, research, and fiscal-institutional arrangements. Hence, the taxonomy constructs at many rhetorical levels the realities that guide the actions of the psychiatric world in which individual mental health is mediated.

Conclusion

The multiplicity of textual activities revealed in the studies of this volume suggests that we live in a very complex rhetorical world indeed. We consistently find texts functioning to consolidate professional interests, enroll novices into the professions, and direct human activity with far-ranging social consequences. The world, on the other hand, cannot be reduced to the rhetorical domination of a powerful monolithic discourse of science and technology, as is sometimes feared. While professional discourses may hold much influence over many aspects of our lives, they provide varied enough voices to maintain a robust rhetorical environment and keep the forces of reductionism at bay. And they provide enough of a rhetorical challenge to require our best efforts at understanding them.

PART ONE

TEXTUAL CONSTRUCTION

OF THE PROFESSIONS

1

HOW NATURAL PHILOSOPHERS

CAN COOPERATE

THE LITERARY TECHNOLOGY

OF COORDINATED INVESTIGATION

IN JOSEPH PRIESTLEY'S

HISTORY AND PRESENT STATE

OF ELECTRICITY (1767)

CHARLES BAZERMAN

> *Cheerfulness and social intercourse do, both of*
> *them, admirably suit, and promote the true spirit*
> *of philosophy.*
> (2:164)

Recent studies of the rhetoric of science have emphasized the competitive struggle played out through scientific texts. Scientific publications are seen as persuasive briefs for claims seeking communal validation as knowledge (Latour and Woolgar; Knorr-Cetina). Moreover, individual texts have been seen as part of a negotiation process among competing interests that may result in statements of knowledge different than those proposed in the initiating texts (Myers; Collins; Latour). During these struggles authors draw on many extratextual resources (social, economic, intellectual, and empirical) which are deployed in the text

Charles Bazerman

(Collins and Pinch; Callon, Law, and Rip; Rudwick). Only after communal acceptance do these claims take on the appearance of irrefutable truths stated with objective authority transcending the urging of an author (Latour).

Genres of scientific writing can be seen as recurrently successful rhetorical solutions to the persuasive problem of advancing claims within an empirical research community. Communally persuasive forms of representing empirical experience and structuring compelling arguments upon that experience have resulted in claims appearing to be proven knowledge, except to those who know of the local struggles. The standardization of textual form has helped to regularize and focus the struggle of scientific writing, even while it has served to hide that struggle (Bazerman, chap. 2).

Nonetheless, an older tradition has considered scientific activity as more than competitive play. Scientific communication has most often been conceived of as part of a cooperative endeavor. The charter myth of this tradition is Sir Francis Bacon's description of Salomon's House in *The New Atlantis*. Here Bacon describes a cooperative bureaucracy of thirty-six field researchers, reviewers of the literature, experimenters, experimental designers, theorists, and applied technologists. Bacon anticipated no particular communication difficulty in this cooperative project, beyond the general linguistic problem of the four idols. Later in the seventeenth century, this cooperative, bureaucratic model inspired a number of organizational decisions of the French Royal Academy and the British Royal Society. However, personal interests and disagreements soon tore at the fabric of such an untroubled plan, and a communication system which facilitated and structured disagreement took shape over the next century (Bazerman, chap. 3).

Despite the systemic competitiveness of modern science, when we remove ourselves from the daily hand-to-hand combat of scientific argumentation, we can perceive large patterns of cooperation and the communal construction of a shared knowledge. This knowledge is not dictated by a single text or monumental figure (whether God, Aristotle, or Newton), but is advanced (sometimes slowly, sometimes rapidly, sometimes spasmodically) through the joint endeavors of large numbers of people. Not only are little details filled in and puzzles worked out within static paradigms, but major novel findings appear and are absorbed, theories are modified and replaced, and knowledge moves in startling and unanticipated directions. To be persuaded of the overall cooperative pattern of scientific work, one need only contemplate the remarkable changes currently being wrought and absorbed by diverse researchers in "hot" areas such as superconductivity, fundamental forces, viral biochemistry, and neural physiology. Indeed many modern commentators of science make cooperation an essential component of scientific activity and communication (Merton; Ziman; Garvey).

The Puzzle of Cooperation

Noticing that cooperation seems to occur, however, does not let us know how it happens, nor why the cooperation should seem to be as enduring and fundamental as it appears to be in science. Persuasion and cooperation as we know from political and other familiar everyday realms are uncertain and fragile phenomena. Beliefs seem to change rapidly, alliances fall apart, and cooperation often needs to be cemented by laws, money, and coercion. If even the degree of cooperation we manage in everyday affairs remains beyond our full comprehension, how can we begin to account for the much more remarkable cooperation evident in scientific work, a cooperation which seems to span religions, philosophies, national boundaries, and centuries? However, until we have as concrete, detailed accounts of the microprocesses by which cooperation and coordination occur as we do of competitive processes, cooperation and coordination may only appear to be value-laden suppositions rather than actual social activities. This chapter, accordingly, offers a microanalysis of the cooperative mechanisms of one eighteenth-century text that was self-consciously constructed to foster cooperation and that foreshadows a number of features of modern scientific papers. This analysis reveals the many levels on which coordination needs to be achieved through language and the tension which needs to be maintained between cooperation and competition, codification and originality, if communal endeavor of science is to move forward.

Certainly early science did not seem to achieve the cooperative complexity and coordination of contemporary science, despite Bacon's high hopes. Rather than building on one another's theories, authors were as likely to attempt to supplant each other's claims. Authors rarely constructed claims that explicitly integrated a wide range of the claims of others. Even the Baconian hopes for an appeal to the facts did not lead to philosophic harmony, as facts themselves became a matter of dispute. Within this atmosphere, local cooperation was only created by the dominance of strong individuals who set the national theoretical terms and research agendas, supported by institutionalized power; Newtonianism and Cartesianism, although occasionally communicating in individual ad hoc circumstances, more often fired salvos across the English channel (Bazerman, chap. 4).

While science remained small, with relatively few results to coordinate and few compelling challenges to the hegemony of the brilliant works of early giants, such ad hoc cooperation as existed through unsystematic familiarity with each others' works from travel, correspondence, and publications was perhaps adequate to carry the communal work of science forward. The emergence of societies and journals helped create regular forums for communication among scientists and organize the communication practices (Bazerman, chap. 5); however, as natural philosophic findings proliferated in the eighteenth century, cooperation had to be explicitly achieved within the substance of the communications. Textual mechanisms needed to be developed to coordinate the work and emerging perceptions of researchers widely dispersed temporally, geographically, and theoretically.

Joseph Priestley's 1767 book _The History and Present State of Electricity_ explicitly takes up the challenge of fostering cooperation among the growing number of electricians and drawing new participants into this emerging research community. Besides expressing concern for the benefits of joint work, the book employs many textual mechanisms that integrate past, present, and future work in the field. Through a comprehensive review of the literature Priestley establishes the corpus of communal experience and organizes it around problems and principles that define an evolving state of knowledge and research agenda. A list of generalizations emerging from that communal history provides a common knowledge base for continuing work; a discussion of the major theories sorts out the conceptual meaning of research; a list of open issues suggests directions for research; and a historical review of the development of apparatus and practical suggestions for construction provide a common material basis for generating phenomena to be investigated. Besides trying to establish coherence and focus within a research front emerging from a shared understanding of past work, Priestley is concerned to draw new researchers into the communal project, so he provides practical suggestions for carrying out experiments and a series of amusing experiments to attract and train neophytes. Finally he provides narratives of his own work to demystify the process of investigation and to provide exemplars of work that might be carried on with only humble means. With our current, limited knowledge of the development of textual features of scientific writing, we cannot unequivocally credit Priestley with invention of the textual devices he employs nor can we trace a direct line of evolution to current cooperative literary practices.[1] Yet Priestley's thoroughgoing interest in fostering coordinated work of an extensive community offers a striking starting point for examining the complexity of cooperative textual machinery that has developed to coordinate the voluminous and undeniably competitive work of contemporary science.

Priestley and Eighteenth-Century Electricity

Electricity by the mid-eighteenth century was a proliferating area and presented much that could use coordination. The modern study of electricity is usually dated from William Gilbert's *On the Magnet* (1600), which includes one chapter on the attractive power of rubbed amber, known since classical times. Gilbert noted a number of other substances that showed a similar property. During the seventeenth century a few items were added to the list of electricals, various theories were presented to account for the phenomenon, and electrical repulsion was noticed for the first time. At the beginning of the eighteenth century, however, the invention of the electrostatic generator made possible the discovery and investigation of such phenomena as luminosity, sparks, shocks, conduction, induction, and the difference between two varieties of electricity. The improvements of these machines and the 1745 invention of the Leyden jar (the modern condenser) permitted experiments with charges of increasingly great power; medicinal and lethal effects were noted. By 1750 Benjamin Franklin had presented evidence of the equivalence of lightning and electricity, setting off a series of investigations into atmospheric electrical phenomena. Electricity was literally exploding across the mid-eighteenth-century natural philosophic scene.[2]

Although Joseph Priestley (1733–1804) had an interest in natural philosophy during his own education and early career as dissenting minister and schoolmaster, he did not actively pursue scientific studies until the mid-1760s when Matthew Turner, his colleague at Warrington Academy, offered a course of lectures in chemistry (Schofield, 8). Priestley was to achieve his greatest fame in this area through the discovery of oxygen in 1774. Nonetheless, electricity and not chemistry provided the subject of Priestley's first investigations and publications.

We do not know exactly when Priestley began to work on electricity, but by late 1765 on a trip to London he arranged an introduction to Franklin and several other prominent electricians to gain their support (see

Charles Bazerman

the letter from John Seddon to John Canton in Schofield, 14). Franklin encouraged him in his plan to write a "history of discoveries in electricity," and helped arrange for the requisite books (Priestley, *Autobiography*). Franklin, John Canton, William Watson, and Richard Price remained his correspondents, mentors, and benefactors over the next year as he wrote *The History and Present State of Electricity*.

The first, longer half of the lengthy book (432 of 736 quarto pages in the first edition) is a detailed history of all investigations and discoveries in electricity from the time of the ancients to his day. In its synoptic command, attention to empirical details in the literature, and its open-ended attitude, it can be seen as one of the earliest versions of the modern genre of review of the literature.

The second half of the work, not indicated in any of Priestley's early plans, consists of seven additional parts: a list of general properties of electricity then known; a discussion of the history of electrical theories including a detailed comparison of two major theories; some general considerations on the current state of electrical research and a series of queries to direct future work; descriptions and directions for constructing electrical machines; a set of procedural advice (or practical maxims) for those wishing to carry out electrical experiments; directions for carrying out entertaining demonstration experiments; and a description of his own new experiments on the subject. As the first half may be designated the history, this latter half may be said to be the "current state of electricity." Much of this material is presented in no other previous work on electricity. Although today we might find the various kinds of materials presented in this latter half in a variety of places, ranging from children's activity books through advanced textbooks, equipment manuals, and research journals, we are not likely to find them all under the same cover.

Doing Natural Philosophy by Doing History: Priestley's Philosophic Framework

Although this odd mixture of things may appear to be a neophyte's grab bag, talking about everything he sees with little sense of design, such lack of design is unlikely, for each part of the book is introduced by several pages of explicit description and rationale for the literary procedures that follow. Moreover, at Warrington Academy Priestley had regularly delivered a series of lectures on oratory and criticism (eventually published in 1777) as well as a course of lectures on the theory of language (printed privately in 1762). He was a self-conscious user of language, and his procedures in *The History and Present State of Electricity* are consistent with his teachings on rhetoric (see Moran).

His rhetorical practices, moreover, are a self-conscious attempt to realize his millenarian vision of human progress. Particularly relevant here is his understanding of the role of historical discourse in increasing human wisdom, for it is a history of electricity that he tells and it is as participants in a historical process that he addresses his readers.[3]

As instructor at Warrington Academy since 1761 he had been delivering a series of lectures on history (later published in 1788). In these lectures he argues that the study of history "strengthens the sentiments of virtue" by showing us the characters of the many kinds of humans and "improves the understanding" by extending our experience. In particular, study of the history of natural philosophy presents edifying portraits "of genius in such men as Aristotle, Archimedes, and Sir Isaac Newton, [which] give us high ideas of the dignity of human nature, and the capacity of the human mind" (120).

Moreover, the history of natural philosophy increases our individual empirical experience by attaching us to a community of experience. Priestley declares, "the most exalted understanding is nothing more than the power of drawing conclusions, and forming maxims of conduct, from known facts and experiments, of which necessary materials of knowledge the mind is wholly barren" (108). Understanding is based on experience to form the proper associations.[4] But each individual is limited, so only through history can we come to share in the experience of others. For "the improvement of human kind and human conduct, and to give mankind clear and comprehensive views of their interest, together with the means of promoting it," Priestley felt "the experience of some ages should be collected and compared, that distant events should be brought together" (108). Natural philosophy gives order to the accumulated human experience, so that we may then choose wisely about our lives and improve the human condition.

Priestley himself seemed to have a strong synoptic grasp of history revealed in his invention of the historical time line. Using the bar graph for the first time to represent historical duration (Funkhouser), Priestley published in 1765 an extremely popular *Chart of Biography*, which went through over fifteen editions by 1820, and in 1769 an equally popular *Chart of History*, which also had at least fifteen editions by 1816 (Fulton, 6–7). By this now-common technique he was able to give graphic shape to the sweep of history. This sense of the sweep of history is essential to the vision of the *History of Electricity*. Moreover, he reveals an open-ended attitude toward the historical process by leaving a blank space at the far end of the *Chart of History* for the reader to fill in the developments of the last decades of the eighteenth century. Again this open-ended sense of the historical process imbues the electricity book. He does not pretend that electrical knowledge is complete and history ends with his account. Rather he views electricity as an evolving practice and investigation, caught at a present moment or state of development and leading into an unknown future.

Priestley's concern for progressive historical improvement of life is founded in his millennial theological positions concerning the perfectibility of man led by a benevolent deity (see Hiebert; Laboucheix; McEvoy) and consonant with his radical politics, including support of both the American and French Revolutions (see Crosland, "Image"; Fruchtman; Kramnick; Priestley, *Autobiography*).[5] In his writings on education, Priestley turns this concern into a practical program of training young men for a life of worldly activity to replace the purely clerical education common at his time (*An Essay on a Course of Liberal Education for Civil and Active Life*, 1765). Natural philosophy has an obvious place within such a theology, politics, educational plan, and progressive view of history. Natural philosophy reveals the benevolence and wisdom of God's plan and offers humans a way to participate actively in the fulfillment of that plan.[6]

Within these theological, historical, educational, and rhetorical contexts, Priestley's aim for his account of electricity becomes clear: to further the communal work of electrical investigation. The preface to the first edition of the *History and Present State of Electricity* keeps returning to the theme of how this history and others like it may advance the progress of science; for example, "once the entire progress, and present state of every science shall be fully and fairly exhibited, I doubt not but we shall see a new and capital aera commence in the history of all sciences" (1:xviii).[7] Later he states even more directly, "To quicken the speed of philosophers in pursuing this progress, and at the same time, in some measure, to facilitate it, is the intention of this treatise" (2:53–54). Moreover, in a simplified version published the year after (1768), he reveals his plan comprehensively: "My principal design was to promote discoveries in Science, by exhibiting a distinct view of the progress that had been made hitherto, and suggesting the best hints that I could for continuing and accelerating that progress" (*Familiar Introduction*, v).

A History of Natural Philosophy: Part 1

The first step in this project of furthering the communal work is to gather together the accumulated experience of electricity by natural philosophers. As Priestley comments in the preface to the first edition, "At present, philosophical discoveries are so many, and the accounts of them are so dispersed, that it is not in the power of any man to come to the knowledge of all that has been done, as a foundation for his own inquiries. And this circumstance appears to me to have very much retarded the progress of discoveries" (1:vii). Although this comment may be familiar in the twentieth century, it represents an attitude not generally reflected in natural philosophic texts before this time. Generally references to the work of others was perfunctory, if present at all, and little attempt was made to make systematic sense of the previous literature. Often the writers seem unfamiliar with relevant published work. Franklin, in the distant colonies, presents an extreme example; he began his work with only the aid of a popular summary of contemporary work published in the *Gentleman's Magazine*. Even after he became familiar with a wider range of work, his publications rarely mentioned any historical work and gave only passing mention to the work of his contemporaries.

The most extensive discussion of the electrical literature Priestley had seen before writing his history was the four-page bibliographic appendix to Desaguliers' 1742 forty-eight-page pamphlet, *A Dissertation Concerning Electricity*, which elaborates and gives citations for items mentioned in the main text. A more extensive German summary of the literature and annotated bibliography by Daniel Gralath did not come into Priestley's hands until after the first edition had been published; Priestley used Gralath's work to revise the second edition.

Priestley took very seriously the task of gathering the accumulated experience of prior electricians. He insisted on reading, wherever possible, the original texts of all his predecessors. Much of Priestley's correspondence in this period concerns his attempt to obtain rare volumes (Schofield), and he apparently incurred large expenses in this regard (see Crosland, "Practical Perspective"). In the bibliography of his book he also requests his readers to send him volumes he has not yet seen.

To establish the immediate connection between the sources and his retelling, he footnotes with specific page references each text quoted, summarized, or discussed. About half of the pages of the historical section have at least one reference note and some have as many as five or six. Except for secondary format differences, Priestley follows modern footnote practice. He also includes a bibliography of all items on electricity he had heard of (sixty-three items in the first edition and seventy-five in the second and ensuing editions) and also notes the volumes which he had consulted (thirty for the first edition and forty-three for later editions). In addition, a detailed index identifies where each author is discussed.

In giving such care to identify sources he emphasizes that he is writing a history of natural philosophy embodied in publications rather than a Baconian natural history of the phenomena themselves. Priestley comments, for example, on Franklin's *New Experiments and Observations on Electricity*: "Nothing was ever written upon the subject of electricity which was more generally read and admired in all parts of Europe than these letters. There is hardly any European language into which they have not

Charles Bazerman

been translated" (1:192). The history of electricity is in part the history of the appearance and circulation of texts which carry accounts of experiences. The experiences are not separable from the people who encounter them nor from the texts in which accounts are transmitted.

Historical Consciousness within Progressive Knowledge

This historical awareness of the evolving human accounting for natural phenomena allows him to treat earlier findings within historically appropriate knowledge, while still using later developments to comment on, evaluate, or interpret the findings.[8] Typically, we see Priestley's historical awareness of the current state of knowledge in his discussion of Boyle's work: "We should now be surprised that any person should not have concluded *a priori*, that if an electric body attracted other bodies, it must, in return, be attracted by them, action and reaction being universally equal to one another. But it must be considered, that this axiom was not so well understood in Mr. Boyle's time, nor till it was afterwards explained in its full latitude by Sir Isaac Newton" (1:8).

He even includes material that was by his time considered in error, so as to make the account of communal experience complete. Although sometimes he labels the discredited results as delusions, elsewhere he presents them with no comment, and in other places as productive challenges. His account includes so many cases of at first implausible results later accepted as common knowledge that he is chary to exclude any result. Discredited theories are respected for their appropriateness to the state of knowledge in their times and their heuristic value for new discoveries.

Where results evoked controversy and troubled attempts at replication, he gives accounts of the processes by which the community came to pass judgment, as when J. A. Nollet travels to Italy to investigate claims about the medicinal effects of an electrical device and becomes "convinced that the accounts of cures had been much exaggerated" (1:187). Priestley then recounts other unsuccessful attempted replications, including some performed "in the presence of a great number of witnesses, many of them prejudiced in favour of the pretended discoveries; but they were all forced to be convinced of their futility, by the evidence of facts" (1:187). He comments, "After the publication of these accounts properly attested, every unprejudiced person was satisfied, that the pretended discoveries from Italy and Leipsick, which had raised the expectation of all electricians in Europe, had no foundation in fact" (1:188). Priestley describes judgment as being passed by the accumulated experience, which is recorded and circulated in a sequence of documents.

Specific Accounts and General Claims

In the attempt to represent fairly the experience and thinking of previous electricians, Priestley offers lengthy accounts, staying self-consciously close to the original presentations. Rarely is any publication given less than a full paragraph's discussion and often several pages are devoted to describing crucial findings. In both the preface and in passing he shows self-conscious awareness of the responsibilities and difficulties of accurate summary and he often quotes at length, sometimes for more than a page at a time. In the preface he comments "that I might not misrepresent any writer, I have generally given the reader his own words, or the plainest translation I could make of them" (1:x). And throughout he explains and justifies any liberties he takes with the text or the chronology.

Priestley's discussion of each electrician is built on specific empirical experiences or experiments which that individual was the first to notice or verify. These are recounted in sufficient detail for the particular event to be pictured, and in a number of cases to be replicated. Further, Priestley seems to have replicated many of the experiments he recounts. He explicitly notes the few cases when experiments present practical obstacles for replication, such as the need for unusual, costly, or sensitive apparatus.

A description of one of Francis Hauksbee's experiments is typically particular yet concise, relying as it does on the familiarity of typical apparatus and general procedures.

> Having tied threads round a wire hoop and brought it near to an excited globe or cylinder, he observed, that the threads kept a constant direction towards the center of the globe, or towards some point on the axis of the cylinder, in every position of the hoop; that this effect would continue for about four minutes after the whirling of the globe ceased, and that this effect was the same whether the wire was held above or under the glass; or whether the glass was placed with its axis parallel, or perpendicular to the horizon.
>
> He observed, that the threads pointing towards the center of the globe were attracted and repelled by a finger presented to them; that if the finger, or any other body, was brought very near the threads, they would be attracted; but if they were brought to the distance of about an inch, they would be repelled, the reason of which difference he would not seem to understand. (1:10)

Specific observations are the core of the account, but they are introduced and punctuated by discussion of experimental procedures and followed by a brief discussion. By such accounts of experiments Priestley makes available a vicarious experience of essentially all the significantly novel experiments performed by all electricians to that point in time and opens up the possibility of actual repetition of the experiments.

These accounts of experiences are not, however, presented as isolated events. Priestley organizes the experiments around general principles of electrical behavior. The Hauksbee experiment described above is preceded by statements classifying the experiment at two levels of generalization, with Priestley's italics emphasizing the significant general concepts: "I shall first relate the experiments [Hauksbee] made concerning *electrical attraction and repulsion. . . .* The most curious of his experiments concerning electrical attraction and repulsion are those which shew the direction in which these powers are exerted" (1:19–20).

Moreover, he presents series of experiments as coherent sequential investigations into particular phenomena, so that one experience seems to lead to the next according to the dictates of rational investigation. The Hauksbee experiments quoted above are immediately followed by further experiments to explore attraction and repulsion phenomena. This sense of a coherent program is extended beyond the work of individual researchers to be used as an organizing device for the work of many researchers. He imposes a rational shape to communal work, which by this gesture becomes a communal research program. Such generalizing coherence, naturally enough, appears at the head of chapters and sections, such as at the beginning of section 9: "Electricians, after observing the great quantity of electrical matter with which clouds are charged during a thunderstorm, began to attend to the lesser quantities of it which might be contained in the common state of the atmosphere, and the more usual effects of this great and general agent in nature" (1:421).

At times, the coherence of a communal program is identified through a fundamental problem being investigated, rather than through the phenomena discovered, as at the beginning of section 2: "One of the principal desiderata in the science of electricity is to ascertain wherein consists the distinction between those bodies which are conductors, and those which are non-conductors of the electrical fluid" (1:241). As we shall see in considering the later section on desiderata, the concept of research question is to Priestley an important device for organizing current work and helps project the discipline into the future. And even in this historical part, such open questions can be used to make sense of and evaluate work already accomplished. The opening of section 2 quoted just above continues:

> All that has been done relating to this question, till the present time, amounts to nothing more than observations, how near these two classes of bodies approach one another; and before the

period of which I am now treating, these generalizations were few, general, and superficial. But I shall now present my reader with several very curious and accurate experiments, which, though they do not give us intire satisfaction with respect to the great desideratum above mentioned; yet throw some light on the subject. (1:241)

Overall the book presents a progressive historical account of increasing knowledge, organized around the accretion of general principles that give order to the accumulated experience. This textual structure does require some chronological adjustments and conceptual relabelings. Priestley admits his imposition of an after-the-fact logic on events, such as commenting that his accounts of Hauksbee's experiments are "related not exactly in the order in which he published them, but according to their connection. This method I have chosen, as best adapted to give the most distinct view of the whole" (1:19). Moreover, as mentioned previously, he makes connections between earlier observations and later-developed general principles. Although such anachronistic use of generalizations may offend modern historiography, it does give order to prior empirical experience and establish broad empirical grounding to current generalizations. By creating an account of all prior experiences using current generalizations, yet remaining close to the original experimental particulars, Priestley demonstrates the general force of his generalizations. In a late chapter, Priestley even goes back to examine ancient Roman accounts of phenomena that only since the time of Franklin could have been considered electrical. This procedure, later articulated by Pierre Duhem as "saving the phenomenon," ensures that the history of experience is not ignored when new concepts are developed. This is also the historical standpoint of contemporary reviews of the literature that use current concepts and research questions to make sense of the previous work in the field.[9]

Despite the organizing power Priestley finds in his contemporary concepts, he does not discard those experiences that do not fit under any concept or contradict current categories. To make room for anomalous and aconceptual material Priestley vigorously uses the category of *miscellaneous* both at the end of chapters and as full chapters, as in the "Miscellaneous Discoveries of Dr. Franklin and his Friends in America During the Same Period" and the final chapter of the historical section, "Miscellaneous Experiments and Discoveries Made Within This Period."

Because he believes in the power of anomalies to reveal new truths, he carefully notes them. In introducing his discussion of tourmalin he remarks, "This period of my history furnishes an entirely new subject of electrical inquiries; which, if properly pursued, may throw great light upon the most general properties of electricity. This is the *Tourmalin*: though, it must

Charles Bazerman

be acknowledged, the experiments which have hitherto been made upon this fossil stand like exceptions to all that was before known of the subject" (1:367).

Codification and Access to Ordered Experience

In the collection, representation, and codification of all recorded experience of electrical phenomena, Priestley has made accessible and given order to the communal empirical experience. By rescuing from obscurity early and unread work and showing that work consistent with following work and contemporary concepts, he draws a wider range of participants and experience into the cooperative effort of coming to terms with nature. Moreover, in making the previous work available, intelligible, and experienceable (vicariously or in actual practice) to his readers, he enriches each person's experience and provides a common base of experience and knowledge for all new participants in the field. All electricians will now know and have contact with essentially the same range of experience, with whatever local additions they might have access to or create themselves. With the history of the field available and codified, and all participants knowing the same thing, work may then proceed more rapidly, efficiently, and cooperatively. Throughout the history Priestley had noted as admonitory examples just those instances where lack of access, ignorance of previous work, or lack of shared assumptions led to duplication of effort or unnecessary conflict.

The shared history Priestley presents has not reached conceptual or empirical closure. He indicates the open questions, the anomalies, and the incompletely understood phenomena. In the preface he promises to provide updates on future research (as is provided in the second edition and as a separately published pamphlet). Last-minute prepublication addenda were also included in both first and second editions. The third edition had only limited revisions, for Priestley promised to write a *Continuation to the History* — a promise never fulfilled. Even more significantly, the latter half of the book points to an open-ended future by establishing the shared basis for continued work and offering practical guidance for further experiments. Priestley presents the extensive history of the first half as only a necessary prologue to the ongoing practice of knowledge creation.

General Propositions and Observable Knowledge: Part 2

The product of history, as Priestley tells it, is emergent principles which order the accumulated experiences. In part 2 of the book,

Priestley abstracts these generalizations in a seven-page "series of propositions comprising all the general properties of electricity." These propositions describe the observable effects of electricity, rather than present ontological statements about the nature of electricity itself.

The propositions are largely cast in terms of generalized experimental events: for example, "It is the property of all kinds of electrics, that when they are rubbed by bodies differing from themselves (in roughness or smoothness chiefly) to attract light bodies of all kinds which are presented to them" (2:4). Accordingly many statements begin with "if" clauses to indicate the generalized experimental conditions that may be experienced by all observers. "If an electric shock, or strong spark pass through, or over the belly of a muscle, it forces it to contract as in a convulsion" (2:9). Even the occasional existential statement is elaborated in generalized operational experimental terms: "Electricity and lightning are, in all respects, the same thing. Every effect of lightning may be imitated by electricity, and every experiment in electricity may be made with lightning, brought down from the clouds, by means of insulated pointed rods of metal" (2:10).

The succinctness and generality of these claims is to Priestley a sign of the advance of knowledge: "For the more we know of any science, the greater number of particular propositions we are able to resolve into general ones" (2:2). Since these propositions are not a priori projections, but rather inductive generalizations, they compose an order created out of accumulated experience. The ability to find encompassing propositions of increasing generality indicates understanding of more powerful and fundamental principles of phenomena.

Nonetheless, the propositions presented by Priestley, although generally following a sequential expository order, are not tightly organized around a single account of the nature of electricity, although such an account might have led to even greater succinctness, as Priestley notes (2:2). They are largely disjunct statements about separately observable phenomena, with only a few logical connectives. Priestley is very careful to distinguish these general propositions which may be separately observable by all electricians from any coherent account of what electricity might be, for in his time that was only a matter of theoretical speculation about unobservable matters.

By establishing a succinct codification of what is currently known, generally agreed to, and observable, Priestley clarifies the extent of shared knowledge. This brief, yet comprehensive, list allows for coordination of continuing work, recognition of novelties and anomalies in new observations, rapid socialization of neophyte electricians into the current state of knowledge, and easy reference. The list of propositions thus serves the functions of both the modern handbook and the modern textbook. Furthermore, by separating those statements which are generally agreed to be empirical truths from uncertain theories, Priestley allows for a differentiation of discussion in ensuing work. He does not propose a unitary system of knowledge, as Newton does where general theory appears inseparable from representation of empirical experiences, so that the theorizing is made invisible and denied (see Bazerman, chap. 4). Rather he establishes agreement on the level at which all can agree and focuses debate on less certain matters. Thus he not only codifies the existing knowledge, but codifies the levels and manners of discussion. He provides literary technology first for coordination of areas of agreement by slowing down the communal ascent up the ladder of generalization (as Bacon cautions the individual researcher to do) and second for domestication of conflict by limiting the arena of disagreement.

Historicizing Theory: Part 3

Having historicized experience and discovery in the early parts of his work, Priestley historicizes theory in the third part. Theories, as Priestley presents them, historically precede knowledge. Theories, which he uses interchangeably with hypotheses, help frame experiments and lead to newly observed phenomena, but they themselves are not substantiated knowledge. When the hypothesized phenomenon is made observable through experiment, it passes out of the realm of theory into the realm of operational knowledge. As Priestley states in his introductory comments to part 3:

> Hypotheses . . . lead persons to try a variety of experiments, in order to ascertain them. In these experiments, new facts generally arise. These new facts serve to correct the hypothesis which gave occasion to them. The theory, thus corrected, serves to discover more new facts, which, as before, bring the theory still nearer to the truth. In this progressive state, or method of approximation, things continue; till, by degrees, we may hope that we shall have discovered all the facts, and have formed a perfect theory of them. By this perfect theory, I mean a system of propositions, accurately defining all the circumstances of every appearance, the separate effect of each circumstance, and the manner of its operation. (2:15–16)

At the end of investigation, then, theory changes from a conjecture about causes to an empirically based operational account.

Theories, then, are useful but uncertain and historically bounded accounts. They are heuristic. Discussion of theories leads to difficulties only because investigators present their hypotheses as general truths and become too attached to them. Thus they do not allow the replacement or modification of theory in relation to new findings, nor do they admit new hypotheses that would serve as heuristic for new discoveries. Priestley found this attachment to speculative theories particularly rife within electricity because, "As the agent is invisible, every philosopher is at liberty to make it whatever he pleases, and to ascribe to it such properties and powers as are most convenient for his purpose" (2:16).

In his own account of electrical theory, Priestley adopts several literary methods to identify the limited and transient utility of theories and to decrease his own and the reader's attachment to any particular theory. He describes the historical state of knowledge out of which each theory arises and which it is meant to account for, identifies the new findings that the theory led to, and finally presents the empirical results the theory could not adequately account for. Unlike the timeless presentation of general propositions, theories are given a specific time and place. Moreover, Priestley casts theories aside after they have played their role in the generation of empirical truths and have been made obsolete by further discoveries.

Priestley adopts this historical attitude even to theories viable in his own time, including his favored account: Franklin's theory of positive and negative electricity. Priestley discusses how Franklin's theory provides a satisfactory account of a number of phenomena, especially that of the Leyden jar—the phenomenon which the theory was first developed to explain. But he also discusses a number of phenomena for which the theory remains inadequate, such as the influence of points and the electrification of clouds. Moreover, he points out that the theory is in a state of flux, being subject to modification by a number of electricians. On the other hand, he finds that the ability of this theory to incorporate findings and ideas from previous theory very much in its favor, as it does not abandon collective experience. Finally, although Priestley ends this chapter with a panegyric to Franklin, the quality he praises most is Franklin's diffidence about his own theory and his just "sense of the nature, use and importance of hypotheses" (2:39), which attributes more importance to the facts produced than the general accounts.

The most significant feature of Priestley's presentation of theories is that the chapter on his favored theory is followed by an almost equally long chapter on a contending theory to which he also attributes great utility. Priestley comments, "I shall, notwithstanding the preference I have given to Dr. Franklin's theory, endeavour to represent [the theory of two electrical fluids] to as much advantage as possible, and even to do it more justice than has yet been done to it, even by Mr. Symmer himself" (2:41). After an extensive summary of the theory he points out certain phenomena for which this theory appears useful and plausible, in some instances providing less-tortured accounts than Franklin's single-fluid theory. Like Franklin's theory, Robert Symmer's theory offers no inconsistency, but lacks insight into certain phenomena. Priestley then modifies the theory to answer the chief objection made to it and comes to the conclusion that the theory is consistent with all available evidence. Priestley cites another electrician, Cigna, granting Franklin's theory the upper hand because of its overall greater simplicity, but no final strong judgments are made. The section ends with Priestley inviting readers to communicate "any other theory, not obviously contradicted by facts" (2:52).

Thus even while maintaining a favored theory, Priestley manages to distance himself from it and develop a dispassionate method for discussing and evaluating competing theories. Not only does his tone and literary method allow for modification and theory change, it separates the advocacy of theory from the discovery of facts, even while recognizing the dialectical connection between fact and theory. His mode of discussion diffuses the argumentative gap that results from theory differences, allows cooperative research on the level of general propositions, and offers an orderly procedure for discussing and evaluating theories. He offers a means for communal theory development and modification short of total replacement. Finally, by reducing the status of theory, he reduces the stakes in theory wars.

"A Great Deal Still Remains to be Done": Part 4

To Priestley, the codification (or gathering together and conceptual organization) of prior work only served to highlight the incompleteness of our communal electrical knowledge. In the first three parts—the history, the general propositions, and the theory—he is at pains to point out what issues are left open, what is unknown, what is puzzling. One of the great dangers he finds in the individual's adherence to a single theory is that the individual may feel that electricity has been solved and therefore find little motivation to extend researches. Such is his accusation against Nollet (2:25). Systematic codification, to the contrary, identifies specific areas needing investigation and unsolved research problems (or desiderata, as Priestley calls them).

To make these incompletenesses even more visible, and therefore to guide future work, Priestley gathers them together in the middle chapters of section 4, in the form of "queries and hints," following on the exhortation to continuing research of the opening chapter. These queries and hints are presented as lists of questions. Questions, even while they invite unknown answers, constrain the form of the answers. A series of questions can set an agenda for communal work and provide a framework for comparing competing answers.

Priestley's questions are set under various headings corresponding to phenomena identified and elaborated in the previous work. Under each heading, the opening questions tend to be the more fundamental questions, which are then elaborated more specifically in the following questions. For example, the "Queries and Hints Concerning Excitation" begins with a fundamental question of structure, moves to elaborating phenomena, and then specific experiments:

> What is the difference, in the eternal structure of electrics, that makes some of them excitable by friction, and others by heating and cooling?
>
> What have friction, heating, cooling, and the separation after close contact in common to them all? How do any of them contribute to excitation? And in what manner is one, or the other electricity produced by rubbers and electrics of different surfaces?
>
> Is not Mr. Aepinus's experiments of pressing two flat pieces of glass together, when one of them contracts a positive and the other a negative electricity, similar to the experiments of Mr. Wilcke concerning . . . ?

By explicitly mentioning recent and ongoing work in relation to open questions, Priestley identifies common problems that can draw researchers into a common endeavor and sets an example of public discussion of unresolved work. Rather than leaving the workshop of the various researchers closed until the individuals are ready to present a claim substantiated by a public demonstration of a successful experiment, he invites the entire community to share in open discussion, drawing hints from each other. Furthermore, he invites others to present their open questions, for

> Many persons can throw out hints, who have not leisure, or a proper apparatus for pursuing them: others have leisure, and a proper apparatus for making experiments, but are content with amusing themselves and their friends in diversifying the old appearances, for want of hints and views for finding new ones. By this means, therefore, every man might make the best use of

his abilities for the common good. Some might strike out lights, and others pursue them; and philosophers might not only enjoy the pleasure of reflecting upon their own discoveries; but also upon the share they had contributed to the discoveries of others. (2:60–61)

Publicly shared questions help coordinate the work of many hands and help further the incomplete ideas of many minds. As that work goes forward, questions are answered, discarded, or change. Questions, like theories, are historically bounded. Priestley comments that his questions may likely soon appear "idle, frivolous, or extravagent" (2:58), and he makes a number of emendations in the second and third editions, eliminating some questions and adding new ones. He clearly has the idea of a moving research front composed of evolving problems, and he wishes to establish a textual means of communally articulating the current state of questions.[10]

To Priestley, the advancement of electrical knowledge also depended on coordination with other forms of knowledge which bear on the investigations. The closing section of part 4 discusses the other branches of knowledge which electricians ought to become familiar with: in particular the studies of chemistry, light and colors, atmosphere, anatomy, mathematics, mechanics, and perspective. His inclusion of mechanics and perspective recognizes that research is an empirical and social practice. The philosopher who wishes to explore new phenomena must be able to construct new philosophical machines, and the philosopher who wishes to share his findings by publication must be able to draw precisely.

Mechanical Coordination: Part 5

Since Priestley recognized that the advance of electrical knowledge was dependent on the advance of machines, he felt the need to engage electricians in mechanical construction. In the historical first part of the book he often pointed out the importance of machinery to specific discoveries. Here in the fifth part he summarizes the historical progress of machinery to codify and coordinate the state of the art. Machines provide the originators with access to new phenomena, but even more they provide the entire community of electricians access, for reproduction of machines allows reproduction of phenomena. Shared machinery makes possible shared experiences and cooperative investigation of the phenomena generated and displayed by the apparatus. Moreover, to maximize communal development the best machinery and principles of construction should be made available. Finally, to coordinate work, you must coordinate apparatus, so that investigators are making claims concerning the same things.

Therefore, explanations of the principles of the machines and specific guidelines for the construction of the most effective machines are important to a coordinated experimental science. Priestley devotes about twenty pages to the description of guidelines for the construction of electrostatic generators, metallic points, batteries of Leyden Phials, and electrometers. Just as there are open questions about electrical phenomena, there are open questions about the optimum designs: for example, "It has not yet been determined by electricians what kind of glass is the most fittest for electrical purposes" (2:91). He then devotes another dozen pages to discussing the advantages and disadvantages of particular machines developed and used by various investigators. The mechanical descriptions are supported by illustrations.

As indicated by an advertisement accompanying the *Familiar History* of 1768, Priestley himself engaged in the construction and distribution of electrical machines. (For further discussion of the importance of mechanical practice in Priestley's work, see Schaffer.)

The Increase of Empirical Experience: Parts 6 and 7

Access to machines does not guarantee successful, copious, and progressive results. People must use those machines and use them correctly. Experience has been the traditional teacher of successful experimental practice, but in parts 6 and 7, Priestley aims to expedite successful experience for neophytes, so that they will produce more results more rapidly.

Part 6 is devoted to "Practical Maxims for the Use of Electricians," describing the craft knowledge that Priestley has gained through his own experience. He hopes to make the path of young electricians less arduous, for "it is in the interest of science in general, that everything be made as easy and inviting as possible to beginners. It is this circumstance only that can increase the number of electricians, and it is from the increase of this number that we may most reasonably expect improvements in the science" (2:119). What follow are fifteen pages of homely craft advice and warnings, such as "A little bees wax drawn over the surface of a tube will greatly increase its power" (2:120). And "let no person imagine that, because he can handle the wires of a large battery without feeling any thing, that therefore he may safely touch the outside coating with one hand, while the other is upon them. I have more than once received shocks that I should not like to receive again" (2:132). Such advice currently is conveyed in laboratory manuals and other training documents. But as Collins forcefully argues, much craft knowledge remains inarticulate and certainly unpublished, so it is learned, if at all, directly over the laboratory bench.

In this same spirit of introducing neophytes into experimentation and ultimately increasing the communal experience, Priestley offers in part 7 directions for performing "The Most Entertaining Experiments Performed by Electricity." He opens this part with an enthusiastic account of the delights and wonders of simple experiments: "What can seem more miraculous than to find, that a common glass phial or jar, should, after a little preparation (which, however, leaves no visible effect, whereby it could be distinguished from other phials or jars) be capable of giving a person such a violent sensation, as nothing else in nature can give . . . and this shock attended with an explosion like thunder, and a flash like that of lightning?" (2:135). Moreover, he encourages would-be experimenters by suggesting that these effects, although entertaining, are far from trivial: "So imperfectly are these strange appearances understood, that philosophers themselves cannot be too well acquainted with them. . . . It is possible that, in the most common appearances, some circumstance or other, which had not been attended to, may strike them; and that from thence light may be reflected upon many other electrical appearances" (2:136).

Thirty pages of detailed instructions follow on how to carry out experiments involving explosions, shocks, flashes of light, ringing bells, dancing dolls, puppets with hair standing on end, and gunpowder. They are all described with much enthusiasm for their amusing qualities. Such descriptions now are reserved for children's introductions into experimental sciences of the "Scientific Tricks You Can Do" genre, with much of the same motivation: recruitment of the young into science. Priestley well understood that no communal research program will prosper without the personnel to carry it forward.

Extending Knowledge: Part 8

In the last part of the book Priestley presents his own experiments, developed out of his replications of experiments in the literature. In a sense he presents himself as the ideal reader of his account of the history and present state of electricity, using the text as a foundation for new activity.[11] Moreover, he presents his new work as an example of the dynamics of knowledge, that the history of natural philosophy is open-ended and that new work proceeds out of old. This message of continuing, coordinated work outweighs the specific findings that Priestley presents; he comments that his method of presentation is "less calculated to do an author honour as a philosopher; it will, probably, contribute more to make other persons philosophers, which is a thing of much more consequence to the public" (2:165).

Priestley's new experiments are arranged according to topics first raised in the historical chapters. Moreover, he continually refers to the literature and private correspondence with other electricians. He opens sequences of experiments with comments such as he found certain of Beccaria's experiments not quite adequate (2:232), or that he had certain doubts about an aspect of Franklin's theory (2:184), or that there was a matter of dispute among electricians (2:201). Similarly he indicates obtaining materials (e.g., 2:308) and ideas for experiments from other electricians (e.g., 2:187). In addition, he reports corresponding with them about procedures (e.g., 2:179). Finally, he compares his results with those of others (e.g., 2:273–76). In such repeated cross-reference to the work of others he follows modern practice rather than the practice of his contemporaries.

Yet, although he embeds his accounts in the literature and indicates his constant interaction with the rest of the community, he does not present his work as necessarily occupying a fixed or stable place in the literature, as is often the case in modern articles, where one uses the literature as a matrix around the new claim to assert its centrality, meaning, and solidity (see Swales and Najjar; Dudley-Evans). Priestley presents his work as part of an ongoing and unsettled process. The starting place in the literature does not fix where the investigation ends up nor is the opening hypothesis (derived from the literature or by analogy with other reported phenomena) necessarily the final one confirmed or denied. He presents his research as a mode of dialectical discovery which sometimes ends in a strong claim, but more often does not. Sequences of experiments are left off with unresolved questions or invitations to others to continue the work.

Priestley called this discovery path form of presentation an analytical argument and believed it was more deeply persuasive than the prooflike argument which supports a claim asserted at the opening of the essay, which he called the synthetic argument. In analysis you could carry your reasonable audience down the same path of experience and reasoning that led you to your conclusions rather than coercing belief through a constraining set of arguments. Intellectual coordination would come from a more complete sharing of the research experience (2:166–67; see also Priestley, *Lectures on Oratory*; Moran; Lawson).

Additionally, he felt that this analytical method would aid others in their investigations by indicating all the false leads and mistakes. Others could avoid these mistakes, find meanings in details that did not seem so significant to the original investigator, and take advantage of the full range of thinking. Moreover, such naturalistic accounts would demystify the research process for neophytes so that they would be less intimidated to take up their own researches.[12] He, in fact, criticizes Newton for hiding his thinking process, with the result that we hold the man too greatly in awe to follow in his footsteps:

> If a man ascend to the top of a building by the help of a common ladder, but cut away most of the steps after he has done with them, leaving only every ninth or tenth step; the view of the ladder, in the condition in which he has been pleased to exhibit it, gives us a prodigious, but an unjust idea of the man who could have made use of it. But if he had intended that any body should follow him, he should have left the ladder as he constructed it, or perhaps as he found it, for it might have been a mere accident that threw it in his way. (2:167-68)

Priestley's ladders, as presented in over two hundred pages, are many, but few get far off the ground. He presents the different lines of investigation sometimes as having strict logical direction, with each hypothesis or problem suggesting a new experiment and the results suggesting a new problem or hypothesis. Yet he rarely concludes in any statement of great certainty or generality. At other times the sequencing of experiments seems weaker as accidental observations set the sequence in motion with no strong direction. Priestley ends such sequences just by varying the experiment to see if he can find any leads. In this vein, he comments at the beginning of the sequence of experiments on circular spots:

> In the courses of experiments with which I shall present the reader in this and the following two sections, I can pretend to no sort of merit. I was unavoidably led to them in the use of a very great force of electricity. The first appearance was, in all the cases, perfectly accidental, and engaged me to pursue the train; and the results are so far from favouring any particular theory or hypothesis of my own, that I cannot perfectly reconcile many of the various phenomena of any hypothesis. (2:260)

This sharing of wide-ranging, but imperfectly accounted for, experience leads to a diffuse presentation, where few forests emerge from many trees. Priestley here does not even have the ordering potential of retrospective categories, as he did in the historical account. As I have noted elsewhere (Bazerman, chap. 3), this kind of discovery account gained popularity in *Philosophical Transactions* at just about this time (possibly led by Priestley's enthusiasm for it), but it did not last until the turn of that century. Although it allows for sharing of open-ended work and recognition that the truths of natural phenomena cannot be directly and self-evidently read from individual experiments, it seems to have been too equivocal in its message for the codification necessary for the coordination of continuing work. A century earlier Newton had also used a discovery narrative in his "New Theory of Light and Colours," but he had found it insufficiently persuasive to forestall serious controversy. In order to compell assent he developed the prooflike form of argument which Priestley criticized him for (Bazerman, chap. 4).

Modern scientific articles have found a solution for codifying the research which combines compelling assertion in the fashion of Newton with a recognition of the evolving character of the literature and the communal investigation in the fashion of Priestley. By asserting claims within a constructed matrix of the literature, modern articles attempt a kind of rolling codification. They typically pretend their claims are already accepted and integrated into a literature reconstructed in the article introduction (see Berkenkotter, Huckin, and Ackerman, chapter 8 of this volume). The body of the argument then appears to act as an irrefutable inductive proof, although the value and meaning of both the literature and the current investigation may be far from settled within the knowledge-validating research community. In this manner, each new article takes part in the sorting out of knowledge claims even as they are proposed.[13]

Conclusion: The Dilemma of Large Cooperative Endeavors

In forging a way of talking about science that would coordinate the work and experience of many, while not holding them accountable to any a priori or individually conceived theory, Priestley was attempting to create a broad-based science open to all who wished to respect and extend the common experience. This project was founded on his radical theological, philosophical, and political beliefs. He believed democratic participation and open-ended negotiation of phenomena would lead to discovering the true accounts of nature, encompassing the experience of all humankind. He understood that such an endeavor must be coordinated on many levels, from experimental findings to machine construction to research problems. But he desired that codification emerge only from the shared wisdom, experience, and responsible negotiation of humanity, excluding none of the verifiable variety of life. His well-worked-out philosophy and sociology of science relied on his developing an appropriate rhetoric of science that would facilitate cooperation and coordination of current communal empirical investigation while respecting the experience embodied in the history of science.

Priestley was partly successful in creating rhetorical means to assert codification yet still to keep the door open to the full range of experience. To avoid the cultural amnesia of codification of history, Priestley stays close to the literature, which he attempts to reproduce with some historical sensitivity and copious detail, even where it does not fit into his contemporary categories. Codifications of present activities of theorizing, experimenting, and machine construction, Priestley treats as useful but temporary accounts, to be rewritten as events progress. Codifying the future, however, is trickier; it can shut down the open-ended processes of experience and discovery by enforcing a closed system of bureaucratic definition of what can and should be done. Yet not codifying the future strongly enough leads to an uncoordinated proliferation of actions of little meaning — an open end that unties the threads of the past drawn together in the present moment. This is a rhetorical problem that Priestley had not yet solved, although many of his rhetorical techniques for dealing with past, present, and future have been used in scientific writing since his time.

Perhaps the most important consequence of the rhetorical dynamics put in motion by Priestley is a form of discourse directed at an inward-facing community concerned with shared research problems and developing a communal experience. He creates textual means for researchers to look toward each other to create a common knowledge. In support of this prototype discipline, Priestley also offers textual means of recruiting and socializing new participants into the communal project.

What Priestley perhaps undervalues, however, are individual assertion and competition within the coordinated communal activity. In eschewing individual glory in the name of the communal advance, in letting all into his unsettled workshop, and in refusing to pretend to certainty in the face of historical flux, Priestley has inadequately allowed for the hypothesizing force of science that has allowed individuals to assert bold leaps of knowledge and then to await to see if the world lives up to their educated intuitions. Priestley creates a machinery for benign cooperation, but that machine also has seemed to need the drive of agonistic struggle, to help force claims up the ladder of generalization and power. Despite Priestley's amiable sociability, science has maintained an important role for aggressive assertion of theories, embattled competition, and Nobel Prizes. In fact, these have become part of science's sociability.

Nonetheless, the coordinating mechanisms of the kind Priestley advances are precisely what make the agonism more than a war of all against all. These mechanisms have given order to the accumulating corporate experience and have provided common assumptions, comparable terms, and similar empirical procedures with which to advance the shared work. Priestleyian codification has created an evolving and contingent — but at any moment predominantly stable and communally recognizable — playing field, upon which focused and fruitful struggle can take place.[14]

NOTES

This essay was supported by released time granted by the Dean of Liberal Arts and Sciences, Baruch College. I also thank Rachel Laudan, John McEvoy, Michael Moran, Greg Myers, Simon Schaffer, and Harriet Zuckerman for their comments and criticisms.

1. Rachel Laudan's current investigation of early histories of science may reveal more about the textual tradition out of which Priestley was writing (private communication).

2. J. L. Heilbron's standard modern history of electricity to 1800 affords fewer than sixty pages to seventeenth-century developments, but devotes about one hundred and eighty pages to the two-thirds of the eighteenth century that preceded Priestley's publication.

3. Unexplored in this essay is how Priestley's vision of history and the historical progress of knowledge fits in with developing enlightenment attitudes toward history and the accumulated wisdom of the human race. Encyclopedism in its direct French and modified British forms are of course relevant here. Also unexplored are the roots of Priestley's ideas of cooperative communities, which may have their foundations in radical Puritanism of the seventeenth century.

4. Priestley's psychology is explicitly Hartleyian associationist in both *A Course of Lectures on Oratory and Criticism* and *The History and Present State of Electricity*. See also the introduction to the modern edition of the former by Vincent Bevilacqua and Richard Murphy. In light of Priestley's view of empirical natural philosophy it is important to emphasize the role Priestley sees for experiences in forming associations. Associations are for him not just arbitrary connections among mental representations. Progress (and thereby fulfillment of the divine plan) comes for Priestley from the incorporation of empirical experience of the world into the set of mental associations and the readjustment of those associations so as to be harmonious with and useful for the ordering of the experience. Increasing empirical experience becomes, for him, a moral duty. This is a curious theological variant on Fleck's observation that modern science is characterized by the active pursuit of passive constraints.

5. Laboucheix reconciles Priestley's radical politics and progressivism with his theological and physical determinism by examining Priestley's dynamic view of materialism, necessity, and decision making, which creates the opportunity for human intelligence to understand and abstract the laws of nature, so that humans may accommodate themselves and live in harmony with those principles that determine their existence.

6. Priestley, by associating natural philosophy with a life of action to be pursued by males in fulfillment of a divine plan and then by framing the study of natural philosophy within a corresponding male educational system, furthers the gender-coding of human action in Western culture. There are consequences here for genderization of rhetoric as well as the more general genderization of society, but both these issues must remain beyond the scope of this essay. I would, however, point out that the cooperative technology fostered by Priestley differs significantly from the forms of cooperation involving acquiescence and subordination often stereotypically gender-coded as female. Priestly also notes certain characterological correlates of the philosophic activity he promotes for men: "Nor is the cultivation of piety useful to us only as men, it is even more useful to us as philosophers: and as true philosophy tends to promote piety, so a generous and manly piety is reciprocally, subservient to the purposes of philosophy" (*History of Electricity* 1:xxiv).

7. Page references throughout will be to the third edition of 1775 (in two octavo volumes), which is available in a modern reproduction (New York: Johnson Reprint, 1966), instead of the first edition of 1767 (a single-quarto volume), available only in the original. The texts of the two editions (and the intermediate second, 1769) are in most details the same, except for updated information, presented largely through whole paragraph insertions describing more recent work and a few deletions of research questions which have been superseded. The later fourth (1775) and fifth editions (1794) follow the third in all respects. A French translation in three volumes (1771) follows the first edition, and a single-volume German translation follows the second.

8. Hoecker examines in greater depth the tension between Priestley's historical sensitivity and his progressive vision of divinely inspired historical development.

9. However, Priestley's history does differ from modern reviews of the literature in its comprehensiveness of coverage, historical extensiveness, and detail of reportage. In part this may be because modern findings usually occur within highly codified systems of knowledge, practice, and questions. Thus new findings usually come presorted into categories, as elaborated in introductory review sections; only novel, unexpected, or anomalous work stands out and calls for attention. Otherwise most findings simply confirm or elaborate the already codified system. Reviews of literature necessarily focus on those unusual details that raise questions, and are selective about the many reports that only add "more gory details." Only revolutionary new claims need to go back to examine the entire file of gory details to reinterpret them consistent with the novel concepts and new questions, and even the reinter-

pretation may be carried on through translation of large groups of material under general headings. Priestley, on the other hand, was creating the codification which made sense of the extensive history. He was first putting the material into conceptual categories, although the concepts had been emerging through the entire period he examines. On the modern review article, see Myers, chapter 2 of this volume.

10. In listing questions he varies a practice used a century earlier in the early *Philosophical Transactions* and then early in the century by Newton in the *Opticks*. In the early *Philosophical Transactions*, however, these questions were aimed at gaining specific data from world travellers who could report back on life forms, geologic and astronomical phenomena, and cultural knowledge from far corners of the earth. The list of questions for travellers were not set as research problems so much as specific informational requests. The respondents were asked to cooperate in providing useful information, but they were not invited to participate in a research front. Newton, on the other hand, used his queries as ways of asserting his beliefs on topics about which he thought he had certain answers but about which he did not have compelling arguments. To Newton there was no research front, only settled issues, imperfectly proven. The questions are often in the coercive form of "Is it not true that . . ." The form of cooperation he sought (and often obtained among the Newtonians) was acquiescence to his suggestions. Priestley here, however, phrases his questions as genuinely open invitations to cooperative investigation.

11. The process of writing the book was indeed his apprenticeship into the community of electricians, introducing him to the literature, machines, experiments, and active investigators. For a discussion of the relation between reading, activity, and writing in the formation of working scientists' knowledge and plans, see Bazerman, chap. 8.

12. In this impulse he anticipates Medawar by two centuries.

13. Huckin has noticed in some fields an increased emphasis on the news-value of articles, at the expense of the empirical argument. This carries the sometimes useful fiction of rolling codification one step further. If the pretended codification leads the actual evaluation by too great a distance, however, consequences may go beyond problems in examining the claims of each article to a disorganization of the communal knowledge which allows coordination of work.

14. In Fujimura's terms, by creating means to allow alignment of disciplinary and individual work, Priestley has made possible the identification of doable problems within modern science, against which the individual may assess his or her own resources.

BIBLIOGRAPHY

Bacon, Francis. *The New Atlantis.* London, 1627.
Bazerman, Charles. *Shaping Written Knowledge: The Genre and Activity of the*

Experimental Article in Science. Madison:University of Wisconsin Press,1988.

Callon, Michel, John Law, Arie Rip, et al. *Mapping The Dynamics of Science and Technology*. London: Macmillan, 1986.

Collins, Harry. *Changing Order: Replication and Induction in Scientific Practice*. Beverly Hills: Sage, 1985.

Collins, Harry, and Trevor Pinch. *Frames of Meaning: The Social Construction of Extraordinary Science*. London: Routledge and Kegan Paul, 1982.

Crosland, Maurice. "A Practical Perspective on Joseph Priestley as a Pneumatic Chemist." *British Journal for the History of Science* 16 (1983): 223–38.

Crosland, Maurice. "The Image of Science as a Threat: Burke versus Priestley and the 'Philosophic Revolution.' " *British Journal for the History of Science* 20 (1987): 277–307.

Desaguliers, Jean Theophile. *A Dissertation Concerning Electricity*. London, 1742.

Dudley-Evans, Tony. "Genre Analysis: An Investigation of the Introduction and Discussion Sections of MSc Dissertations." In *Talking about Text*, ed. Malcolm Coulthard. Birmingham, Eng.: English Language Research, 1986: 128–45.

Franklin, Benjamin. *Experiments and Observations on Electricity*. London, 1754.

Fruchtman, Jack. *The Apocalyptic Politics of Richard Price and Joseph Priestley: A Study in Late Eighteenth-Century English Republican Millennialism*. Philadelphia: American Philosophical Society, 1983.

Fujimura, Joan H. "Constructing 'Do-able' Problems in Cancer Research: Articulating Alignment." *Social Studies of Science* 17 (1987): 257–94.

Fulton, John F. *Works of Joseph Priestley, 1733–1804: Preliminary Short Title List*. New Haven: Yale University School of Medicine, 1937.

Funkhouser, H. G. "Historical Development of the Graphical Representation of Statistical Data." *Osiris* 3 (1937): 269–404.

Garvey, William D. *Communication: The Essence of Science*. Oxford: Pergamon Press, 1979.

Gilbert, William. *De Magnete*. London, 1600. Tr. P. F. Mottelay. New York, 1893.

Gralath, Daniel. "Geschichte der Electricitaet" including "Electrische Bibliothek." Naturforschende Gesellschaft, Danzig. *Versuche und Abhandlung* 1 (1747): 175–304; 2 (1754): 355–460; 3 (1757): 492–556.

Heilbron, J. L. *Electricity in the 17th and 18th Centuries*. Berkeley: University of California Press, 1979.

Heibert, Irwin A. "The Integration of Revealed Religion and Scientific Materialism." *Joseph Priestley Scientist, Theologian, and Metaphysician*. Lewisburg, Pa.: Bucknell University Press, 1980.

Hoecker, James J. "Joseph Priestley as a Historian and the Idea of Progress." *Price-Priestley Newsletter* 3 (1979): 29–40.

Huckin, Thomas. "Surprise Value in Scientific Discourse." Paper delivered at the Conference on College Composition and Communication, Atlanta, Ga., 1987.

Knorr-Cetina, Karen D. *The Manufacture of Knowledge: An Essay on the Con-

structivist and Contextual Nature of Science. Oxford: Pergamon Press, 1981.

Kramnick, Isaac. "Eighteenth-Century Science and Radical Social Theory: The Case of Joseph Priestley's Scientific Liberalism." *Journal of British Studies* 25 (1986): 1–30.

Laboucheix, Henri. "Chemistry, Materialism, and Theology in the Work of Joseph Priestley." *Price-Priestley Newsletter* 1 (1977): 31–48.

Latour, Bruno. *Science in Action*. Milton Keynes, Eng.: Open University Press, 1987.

Latour, Bruno, and Steve Woolgar. *Laboratory Life: The Social Construction of Scientific Facts*. Beverly Hills: Sage, 1979.

Lawson, C. "Joseph Priestley and the Process of Cultural Evolution." *Science Education* 38 (1954): 267–76.

McEvoy, John G. "Electricity, Knowledge, and the Nature of Progress in Priestley's Thought." *British Journal for the History of Science* 12 (1979): 1–30.

McEvoy, John G. "Joseph Priestley, Scientist, Philosopher and Divine." *Proceedings of the American Philosophical Society* 128 (1984): 193–99.

Merton, Robert K. *The Sociology of Science*. Chicago: University of Chicago Press, 1973.

Moran, Michael G. "Joseph Priestley, William Duncan and Analytic Arrangement in 18th-Century Discourse." *Journal of Technical Writing and Communication* 14 (1984): 207–15.

Myers, Greg. "Texts as Knowledge Claims: The Social Construction of Two Biology Articles." *Social Studies of Science* 15 (1985): 595–630.

Priestley, Joseph. *Autobiography*. Teaneck: Fairleigh Dickinson University Press, 1970.

Priestley, Joseph. *A Chart of Biography*. Warrington, 1765.

Priestley, Joseph. *A Chart of History*. London, 1769.

Priestley, Joseph. *A Course of Lectures on Oratory and Criticism*. London, 1777. Ed. V. M. Bevilacqua and R. Murphy. Carbondale: Southern Illinois University Press, 1965.

Priestley, Joseph. *A Course of Lectures on the Theory of Language and Universal Grammar*. Warrington, 1762.

Priestley, Joseph. *An Essay on a Course of Liberal Education for Civil and Active Life*. London, 1765.

Priestley, Joseph. *Familiar Introduction to Electricity*. London, 1768.

Priestley, Joseph. *Lectures on History and General Policy*. Birmingham, 1788.

Priestley, Joseph. *The History and Present State of Electricity*. 2 vols. London, 1767, 1769, 1775, 1775, 1794. Paris, 1771. Berlin, 1772. New York: Johnson Reprint, 1966.

Priestley, Joseph. *Selections from his Writings*. Ed. Ira V. Brown. University Park: Pennsylvania State University Press, 1962.

Rudwick, Martin. *The Great Devonian Controversy*. Chicago: University of Chicago Press, 1985.

44

Charles Bazerman

Schaffer, Simon. "Priestley's Questions: An Historiographic Survey." *History of Science* 22 (1984): 151–83.

Schofield, Robert E. *A Scientific Autobiography of Joseph Priestley: Selected Scientific Correspondence*. Cambridge: MIT Press, 1966.

Swales, John, and Hazem Najjar. "The Writing of Research Article Introductions." *Written Communication* 4 (1987): 175–91.

Ziman, John. *Public Knowledge*. Cambridge: Cambridge University Press, 1968.

2

STORIES AND STYLES

IN TWO MOLECULAR BIOLOGY

REVIEW ARTICLES

GREG MYERS

The comments on the writing of review articles scattered in library journals and handbooks for writers of scientific articles stress the practical importance of reviews for the scientific community: pointing out that they collect, select, order, and interpret the huge outpouring of scientific reports, putting relevant findings and generalizations in a form useful to researchers outside the immediate group working on a problem.[1] But the comments also betray a certain uneasiness about the lack of originality in the genre, if only by insisting again and again on this originality.

> A scientific paper worth submitting to a journal must describe previously unpublished work. A *review* article will, of course, discuss previously published scientific work; its originality lies in the discriminating selection of material for comment and in the author's assessment of the current state of research on the topic under review. (O'Connor and Woodford, p. 4)

This issue is a problem because the one characteristic that the handbooks agree defines a review article — which can be interpretive or merely bibliographical, short or long, popular or specialized, in a review journal or a report journal — is that it does *not* report original work. So what does it do?

I will argue that the writer of a review shapes the literature of a field into a story in order to enlist the support of readers to continue that story. At any moment in the development of a field, the past has a canonical shape, recorded in the historical introductions of textbooks, in citations of "classic" articles, in eponymous terms. But the present is still a scattering of articles reporting various results with various methods aimed at various immediate problems. That's why classic research papers (see, for

Greg Myers

instance, those collected in Taylor) are often so hard to relate to the discoveries with which they are now associated; they are phrased in terms of immediate problems, while we understand the discovery in terms of a history leading to current work. The review selects from these papers, juxtaposes them, and puts them in a narrative that holds them together, a narrative with actors and events but still without an ending. It draws the reader into the writer's view of what has happened, and by ordering the recent past, suggests what can be done next.

The other crucial rhetorical feature of a review is its style, particularly the persona the writer presents in relation to the readers outside his or her specialty that he or she wants to influence. The author may want readers to accept the author's claim or use it in their own work, as in a research report. But a review may have a more subtle persuasive goal; it may define and present the whole topic so that readers see it in a certain way, as moving in a certain direction, so that it relates to them. And if they see themselves as part of a line of work, if they see the problem as their problem, they contribute to the power of its proponents (see Latour). But the influence does not all travel one way, from writer to audience.[2] The discovery of this broad audience is also a rediscovery of the topic. In a specialized research article, the writer can take for granted certain assumptions and methods, knowing that any competent specialist reader will also take these ideas and methods for granted, and will be looking for what is new, the claim. In a review article, it is just these assumptions and methods that must be brought out and put into an apparently logical order.[3] The writer can make sense of his or her field as a whole because he or she sees it from outside, with these readers, and has to ask the always risky question, "So what?"

Francis Crick suggests the importance of this two-way relation in his response to Horace Freeman Judson's interview question about a symposium paper Crick gave in 1957. The historical accounts of this period suggest Crick's paper had an influence on the development of research at the time, changing the way researchers saw current research (for instance, in his discussion of the Central Dogma) and enlisting support from experimentalists in their plans for future work (to test the Adaptor Hypothesis).[4] What is interesting about Crick's comments, whether one accepts them as historically accurate or not, is that he chooses to present himself as finding his ideas only in response to the need to state them to a symposium audience, to a general audience of biologists outside his usual circle.

> But you realize that what one was called upon to do for that
> symposium was to write a review article. To write a review article
> you had to put your ideas down on paper. You then express
> ideas which you hold but you didn't know you *held*. (Judson, 337)

Stories and Styles in Two Molecular Biology Review Articles

The Rhetorical Situation

We can see the shaping of the field and the interaction with readers by close analysis of the stories and styles of reviews. I am going to compare two reviews on the same topic. One is James E. Darnell Jr.'s 1978 *Science* article, "Implications of RNA-RNA Splicing in Evolution of Eukaryotic Cells," which I take as fairly typical in its story and style. The other — Francis Crick's "Split Genes and RNA Splicing" — is atypical in many ways; it appeared in *Science* four months later. This article was written more than twenty years after the 1957 symposium paper, but Crick's reviews still have an important role in shaping the field.

My argument is that both articles show the rhetorical problems and purposes at work in review articles. Since Darnell's article is much more like most reviews, it might seem that I could illustrate my point with just one text. But my argument will be stronger if I can show that this explanation of the relation between form and function applies even to texts that would seem to be atypical. Jonathan Potter and Margaret Wetherell make this methodological point in their introduction to discourse analysis:

> If the proposed functional analysis is correct it ought to make sense of *both* the pattern regularly found in the data and the exceptions. That is, the analyst must predict that there will be special features of the organization of the exceptions which allow them to fulfill the required function in some other way. (69)

I am arguing that both the apparently odd text by Crick and the more typical text by Darnell can be explained as ways of telling a story about the past that shapes the future.

The form of Darnell's review presents the various results as offering a choice between two rival stories. But the style of Darnell's article plays down any sense that he is attempting to enlist support for his own view; the reader takes his view as the result of an apparently logical, impersonal process. Crick's article, on the other hand, seems to have no story at all. But gradually we see that he is focusing attention on the process of sorting out findings, rather than on the result; he is enlisting support, not for a claim, but for a way of formulating claims. For Crick's persuasive purpose, the impersonality of Darnell's article (and most other reviews) would be inappropriate. Instead he uses an informal style, as if inviting the reader to join a discussion among molecular geneticists.

One reason for these differences in style is that the two writers are famous for different things and thus have different rhetorical problems. Darnell has the rhetorical problem of an experimentalist using his lab's experimental results without wanting to seem to promote them. Crick has the rhetorical problem of any theoretician, sorting through the research on split genes when he himself hasn't done any of the research.

Greg Myers

Darnell is one of the more heavily cited researchers working on RNA processing, the director of a large laboratory at Rockefeller University (which has a distinguished tradition in molecular biology), and author of a number of reviews and popularizations. An article that might serve as representative of the work of Darnell's lab is their contribution to the 1977 Cold Spring Harbor Symposium (the meeting where split genes were first discussed). In it they summarize several years of work that showed that in adenovirus 2, a DNA virus infecting human cells, the RNA that is first produced must be processed to produce the messenger RNA (mRNA) that codes for the protein. At the same symposium, other researchers announced the discovery of split genes. As we will see, Darnell knew of the discovery but planned his group's paper to stress a related but distinct issue. Whether Darnell's work is presented as part of the discovery of split genes or as another line of work depends on how reviews present it. Readers might see this *Science* article as a chance to hear an experimentalist relating a range of experimental reports to a highly speculative topic. But because he is known to be involved in the field, they might also be alert for any sign that he was using this format to promote his own experimental work.

Thanks in part to Watson's *The Double Helix* and to a number of histories, including a recent television movie, Crick is one of the most publicly known biologists of our time. His most famous papers — besides the 1953 article with James Watson that proposed the double-helical structure of DNA, and the 1961 article with a team at Cambridge that showed the triplet structure of the genetic code — include several reviews. These were usually written originally for symposia, conference keynote addresses, or lectures, and often, like the 1957 symposium paper I have mentioned, introduced large concepts which have since entered the textbooks. Crick did not, like Darnell, contribute experimental results to split genes research, so he could hardly be accused of plugging his own work. The rhetorical danger is that some readers might see him as playing around with other people's data, without offering anything of his own.

To understand Darnell's and Crick's contrasting approaches to a review on split genes, we need to try to reconstruct what the field would have looked like when they were writing in the late 1970s.[5] Both articles refer to recent dramatic developments in the field that are the reason for commissioning the reviews; Crick mentions the specific meeting where the discovery was announced.

> By the time of the annual Cold Spring Harbor Symposium, in the summer of 1977, it was clear that there was something very strange about the arrangement of the genes in several mammalian viruses, and for this reason it seemed highly likely that some

chromosomal genes would also be in several pieces. This has since been found to be the case. (Crick 264)

At the conference to which Crick refers, groups of researchers from both MIT and the Cold Spring Harbor laboratory announced that parts of the genes on the adenovirus DNA were separated by strings of DNA that didn't appear on the messenger RNA (these intervening strings were later termed *introns* by Walter Gilbert). Previous work on cells without nuclei (*prokaryotes* such as bacteria) had led biologists to assume that the code on the DNA would correspond directly to the code on the mRNA and on the protein. The discovery with viruses (which use the cell's own mechanisms) suggested that cells with nuclei (*eukaryotes* such as those in yeasts, mice, rabbits, chickens, and humans) process the RNA in a much more complex way than had been thought.

Both Crick and Darnell were at this Cold Spring Harbor conference. Since we are interested in the persona Darnell chooses to project, it is important to ask how his own work on adenovirus RNA is related to the work he would review. Darnell gives this account of how he presented his work in relation to the discovery of splicing.

> I knew about the two splicing papers before they were presented at CSH that Friday (I think) night. We purposely did not go ahead to discuss any of that in our CSH paper but rather featured the point that all our evidence taken together compelled the view that large hnRNA [heterogenous nuclear RNA — large strands of various lengths found in the nucleus during infection] was the mRNA precursor. . . . This . . . is one of the reasons why the splicing evidence (in the form of EM [electron microscope] pictures) was so readily accepted as a biochemical fact. (Pers. com., 13 November 1987)

In this account, Darnell's work did not show split genes, but provided evidence that suggested a reason for splicing — to trim precursor molecules. (Some news articles, e.g., those of Sambrook and Schmeck, present Darnell's work in relation to the discovery in this way.) His decision not to refer to the other papers at the conference shows an awareness of the need to place his work effectively, so that it is neither subsumed in the new developments nor separated from them.

Starting in September 1977, reports began to appear, from researchers who had been at the Cold Spring Harbor conference, confirming that genes were split, not only in the viruses infecting eukaryotic cells, but in eukaryotic cells themselves. The data piled up as researchers, using the new sequencing techniques and the new recombinant DNA techniques, quickly found introns in a very wide array of eukaryotic genes. These reports came so fast that in 1977 and 1978 the situation was hardly stable from one month to the next; what was pure speculation in June was news in September and by February 1978 it was a piece of knowledge that could be indicated with just a note. Brief reviews of the adenovirus work appeared in the news columns of *Science* (Marx) and *Nature* (Sambrook) even before papers from the Cold Spring Harbor Symposium could appear in *Cell* and *PNAS*. In 1978 and 1979, the first large-scale review articles on what was now called "split genes" could already list several hundred articles — while apologizing for leaving so many out (see Abelson; Breathnach and Chambon).

One effect of all these reviews taken together was to create "split genes" as a topic. To see this effect, we have to distinguish the view of the field by outsiders such as science journalists (or myself), for whom the field is a series of events and distinct topics, from the view of those working in the field, for whom topics are defined by the daily work of research. No laboratory set out to study split genes; they set out to study RNA transcription units, or cell differentiation, or the generation of diversity in the immune system, or processing controls on genetic expression. And no lab continued to study "split genes" afterward; they study protein domains, or molecular evolution, or self-catalyzing RNA. One of the discoverers of splicing in adenovirus 2 RNA comments that the discovery, which is so important in popularizations and in reviews, soon became just a working fact for the researchers themselves. "The discovery of splicing was a singular event in a fairly large scientific field of research and it was so rapidly incorporated into the conceptual and experimental activities of the community that the fact of the discovery was soon ignored" (Phillip Sharp, pers. com., 21 April 1987). The topic "split genes" arises as reviews and popularizations relate all these separate research programs around what can be called one phenomenon. This is not to say that the first researchers did not see the implications of their findings — they certainly did — but that it took the synthesizing activities of other researchers to make "split genes" a basic problem and to make the evolution of splicing a central issue.

These reviews have another social function, one that may seem unscientific to nonscientists: they encourage speculation. Crick and Darnell are searching for the constraints that further research, after the discovery, puts on possible scenarios for the evolution and function of the introns. The scenarios that remain after their sifting suggest further ways of designing and interpreting experiments that have led, for instance, to evidence for a once speculative notion, the "recruitment" of protein domains in primitive nucleic acids. As Crick puts it in his review, "This gap in our knowledge [concerning the origin of split genes] does not deter speculation, and for good reason, for such speculation may suggest interesting ideas and perhaps give us some general insight into the whole process" (268). Seen this way, speculation is not some imaginative flight tolerated in the last sentences of a research report; it is a crucial part of many reviews, for it focuses on the ending, the future work that will give the story its shape.

Plot and Story

The first problem for a writer like Darnell or Crick would be just reading and sorting out a great mass of papers, and then finding a way of parcelling out between forty and four hundred citations in some logical pattern. It can be a highly controversial matter who is mentioned, in what order, and what is said about them. It is not just that those who are omitted will be annoyed; those who are included will almost certainly find their work in a different context from that in which they themselves would put it. This is a problem of rhetoric, not just of mechanics. There is no template for the structure of a review article, no Introduction-Methods-Results-Discussion in which one can fill in the blanks. One handbook suggests this template is still useful.

> If you have previously written research papers and are now
> about to write your first review, it might help you conceptually
> if you visualize the review paper in terms of the research paper,
> as follows. Greatly expand the Introduction, delete the Materials
> and Methods (unless original data are being presented); delete the
> Results, and expand the Discussion. (Day 96)

But this is not very helpful advice, because the review writer cannot, as in a report, organize the introductory review to lead up to the work reported, or organize the concluding discussion to show its possible importance; one cannot make one's own work the focus.

Although review articles do not follow the Introduction-Methods-Results-Discussion format of research reports, there are certain regularities related to the social function of the genre. Since they must appeal to a broad audience, the introduction usually defines a topic and stresses the importance of recent work on it. The conclusion usually presents the prospects for research in the near future. In between the statements are arranged in some larger narrative. It may be useful, in analyzing this narrative, to introduce here a distinction drawn in literary criticism between plot and story.[6] *Plot* is the order of events as presented in the text. So, for instance, in Poe's "The Purloined Letter," Dupin and his friend the narrator are talking in Dupin's rooms, the police chief comes in and describes a case, time passes, and later Dupin explains the case to his friend. *Story* is the supposed chronology of events behind the plot: the queen

Greg Myers

is having an affair, the minister picks up her letter, the police search his residence without success and appeal to Dupin for help, Dupin visits the residence twice, recovering the letter and substituting his own letter for it, and finally Dupin explains the case to his baffled friend. The plot of a review article is what gives it a surface organization, often a complex table of headings and subheadings; it follows the chronology of the reader's experience of reading. The story is the underlying narrative it aims to convey, with a different chronology following some actors — molecules, biologists, methods, views — constructed in the article. (Perhaps in some scientific discourse the underlying structure is not chronological — but as far as I know it always is in biology.) I make this distinction between plot and story to bring out a difference between Darnell's article and Crick's. Although the plots of the two articles are similar — they move from the discovery of split genes to the evolutionary implications — the underlying story of Darnell's work takes the organisms as its subject, while the story of Crick's article is about the scientists themselves.

The *plot* of Darnell's article is summarized in the introduction.

> Acceptance of the hypothesis that, in eukaryotes, "spliced" mRNA molecules are frequently formed from non-contiguous sequences raises several interrelated questions: Why, when, and how in evolution did the divided genes arise? What function is served today by having genes remain divided? (1257)

To simplify, the plot has to do with research and argument among scientists:

> Recent experimental results cause a shift in thinking.
> Researchers present two views of when divided genes arose.
> One can propose two ways divided genes aid evolution.
> Researchers present evolutionary reasons for the retention of divided genes.
> Research strategies will change as a result.

The *story* of Darnell's article involves a new account of evolution in which the common ancestor of prokaryotes and eukaryotes would have had a splicing system, and the prokaryotes would have evolved by eliminating it.

> This article explores the idea that the complex of biochemical reactions that result in mRNA formation is the chief evolutionary basis that sets eukaryotes apart from prokaryotes. Further, the key evolutionary step is the ability of eukaryotes to utilize contiguous information in DNA. (1257)

So the story has to do with eukaryotic organisms:

> Eukaryotes and prokaryotes arose from a common ancestor.
> Eukaryotes maintained split genes while prokaryotes eliminated them.
> Eukaryotes were able to use split genes to their advantage in evolution.
> Eukaryotes keep divided genes today.

The various parts of the plot, the various sections of the article, all contribute their bit to this underlying story, this new account. The implications of this story for the practices of biologists become clear only in the last paragraph. If eukaryotes didn't evolve from prokaryotes, and use different processing mechanisms, then experimenters can't assume prokaryotes are models for the eukaryotic cell; they have to do everything all over again with eukaryotic cells. To readers who had done all their work on prokaryotes, this could be seen as a threatening view. As we will see in discussing style, Darnell is careful to present it, not as his view, but as the logical outcome of the comparison of two interpretations of the available evidence.

A similar skimming of the headings of Crick's article suggests that the plot moves from the experimental data to broader and broader speculations, from sections on the problem in general, to the extent of genes, the kind of molecules affected, and the length of the introns, to the mechanism of splicing, to evolutionary and taxonomic questions. The basis of his plot is to start with statements of facts that seem quite scattered, presented as if in simple lists — lists, say, of which genes have been found to have introns, or of how many introns various genes have, or of which sequences have been determined to date. When one does see very broad general ideas emerging, they emerge in such an offhand way that one might overlook them. The lack of order indeed is the order; we seem to follow the wanderings of the author's train of thought, but we are being led from specifics to some large evaluations of existing hypotheses and comments on what to look out for in the future.

Crick too mentions the adenovirus findings, but he presents them as an event in the world of researchers. His story involves, not genes, but ways of thinking about genes. Instead of presenting two views that sum up the field, he admits in each section the confusion into which the field has been thrown and then attempts to reestablish order with some tentative generalizations, always with a tension between the need for some clarity and the need to leave possibilities open. This focus is apparent in both his opening with the event at Cold Spring Harbor (the audience astonished, the researchers eager to take on the new problem) and in

Greg Myers

his closing comments on researchers' reactions to the shift the field has undergone.

> There can be no denying that the discovery of splicing has given our ideas a good shake. It was of course already surmised that the primary RNA transcript would be processed in some way, but I do not share the view sometimes expressed that splicing is only a trivial extension of our previous ideas. I think that splicing will not only open up the whole topic of RNA processing, which had become somewhat bogged down before splicing was discovered, but in addition will lead us to new insights both in embryology and in evolution. What is remarkable is that the possibility of splicing had not at any time been seriously considered before it was forced upon us by the experimental facts. This was probably because, looking back, we can see that there was no experimental evidence to suggest that such a process might be taking place, at least for mRNA. Lacking evidence we had become overconfident in the generality of some of our basic ideas. (270)

The take home message about relying on prokaryotic models is much the same as that in Darnell's article. But Crick steps back to look at the change in perceptions required by the new results. He presents a story that could almost be a folk tale, beginning with false security, which tends to stasis ("the whole topic . . . had become somewhat bogged down") and then to the discovery "forced upon us." Finally he reaffirms the significance of the event, while others doubt it. The problem for him is not just evaluating the evidence, but evaluating the response of various researchers to the evidence, figuring out how the community works. Though his earlier articles tend to end on an optimistic note, foreseeing rapid advances, the 1979 article I am discussing here ends by throwing some cold water, saying that the rapid progress on split genes should not obscure the difficulties with transcription, where "we badly need additional breakthroughs." We will see later how this story was interpreted by one journalist.

Analysis of plot and story focus our attention on the level of events. On the level of sentences, one way reviews relate the order of statements — the plot — to the order of narrated events — the story — is through a characteristic verb structure. Both Crick and Darnell follow the sort of verb sequence John Swales (in *Aspects of Article Introductions*) has found to be typical of article introductions. Darnell's article, for instance, begins with a present perfect verb, implying a series of events leading up to and including the present moment:

> For some years evidence *has been accumulating* that messenger RNA (mRNA) formation in eukaryotic cells is substantially different and more biochemically complex than in bacteria (1–4).

Then it continues with present-tense statements giving the knowledge that the new research takes as given:

> At the 5' terminus most eukaryotic mRNAs from yeast to man *contain* a modified methylated structure called a "cap."

The move to past tense at some point signals the story of the work of the researchers, a narrative of human events contingent on techniques, luck, genius, or institutional organization.

> This very unexpected conclusion *came* first from work on adenovirus mRNA's.

The return to present tense signals the new state of knowledge.

> The only primary RNA transcript that can be detected from the regions of the spliced late mRNA's *embraces* all the spliced regions as well as all the major mRNA regions.

There are two types of past tense in Darnell's article, the past of particular events in laboratories last year (as in the example here) and the past of evolutionary events "1.0 to 1.5×10^9 years ago." Both types of past tense signal stories, and the present tense signals a return to the level of present knowledge, the level of the organization of the paper. Crick also follows this basic sequence.

> I have spoken as if splicing only occurred in the processing of mRNA, but we already know that at least two other species of RNA *are spliced*. Indeed, one of the earliest discoveries *was* that some of the transfer RNA (tRNA) molecules in yeast are spliced, although their introns are fairly small (9, 10). More recently, two groups of investigators *have isolated* a crude enzyme preparation that will perform the operation in a test tube (11, 12). (265)

As with Darnell, the past tense signifies events in human history ("one of the earliest discoveries was"), the present tense signifies truths about nature ("two other species of RNA are spliced"), and the present perfect focuses attention on recent research that is directly relevant to the present ("recently . . . groups of investigators have isolated"). Both sequences allow a two-level chronology, as if in a complex novel with frame tales, flashbacks, and flash forwards.

Besides this verb structure, there is a structuring feature of reviews so obvious that it may be overlooked: the disposition of footnotes. Citations are the point of a review article. Darnell's article has a reference for nearly every statement, except for some summary statements and hypotheses, 72 references in all, so that the pattern of the article is an alternation between the claims of the cited texts and the comments of the review, or the general statements of the review and the details in the cited texts. Although Crick cites more than a hundred articles (he even apologizes at the end that because of lack of space, "References have been kept to a bare minimum"[7]) his text is not organized around the references as Darnell's is. Most of the references Crick does give occur in densely packed paragraphs of survey between paragraphs that explore ideas with few references. So, for instance, in the important (and often cited) section on the possible ways split genes could evolve, he refers to only a few articles; most of the notes refer to personal communications, Crick's own articles, or his own comments on various points. For Darnell the citations support each step of a complex argument. For Crick they are just the first step from which he begins his own thinking.

Styles

The persuasive power of a review arises, not just from the apparent coherence of its story, but from its ability to enlist readers, to make them see their own work as part of this ongoing project. To do this, the article sets up a relation between the writer and the reader, creating a persona for the writer and making some assumptions about the knowledge and responses of the reader. I am going to look at some striking stylistic differences between these two articles in terms of differences in rhetorical stance. Persona is complicated in both articles because the authors speak for several points of view. Darnell divides the field at the moment into two "views" that are compared in one impersonal voice; the reader watches the demonstration. Crick seems to present a more personal voice, but it would be more accurate to say that he presents several voices in contrasting styles; the reader is invited to participate in the discussion. Similarly, the syntax and cohesion in Darnell's article suggest the impersonality of the reader-writer relation, while everything in Crick's article suggests an interaction between people.

We can see the differences in persona in the opening sentences of these two articles. Darnell begins:

> For some years evidence has been accumulating that messenger RNA (mRNA) formation in eukaryotic cells is substantially different and more biochemically complex than in bacteria (1–4). (1257)

The author, though he cites himself, remains in the background; the subject of the main clause, *evidence*, relates to what I have called his plot, while the subject of the subordinate clause, *mRNA formation*, relates to what I have called his story. We are asked to read the article because impersonal evidence requires a change in impersonal theories.

Crick, as we might expect from what we have seen so far, has an unusual opening:

> In the last two years there has been a mini-revolution in molecular genetics. When I came to California, in September 1976, I had no idea that a typical gene (1) might be split into several pieces and I doubt if anybody else had. (264)

The first sentence makes the same moves as Darnell's opening to attract the attention of other biologists, mentioning a new development with broad implications. But the second is oddly personal, in its use of *I*, in its orientation in personal time (*When I came to California* rather than *For some years*), and in the offhand comment on the rest of the molecular genetics community. We are asked to read this article because an important theorist has had his ideas shaken up.

The persona Darnell presents is both assertive (because he has a claim to make) and carefully impersonal (because he does not want to present it as just his own claim). The phrasing throughout shows how important it is for Darnell, as for most scientific writers, to keep a carefully impersonal surface even where, or especially where, there are personal commitments and choices underneath. His account begins with the Ad2 work, summarized in some detail, and the Ad2 work begins with his own lab's work on transcription units (footnotes 9, 12, and 13).

> This very unexpected conclusion came first from work on adenovirus mRNA's. Late in adenovirus type 2 (Ad2) infection a series of at least 13 individual mRNA molecules (8, 9) were found to contain sequences from non-contiguous sites on the adenovirus genome (10, 11). That each of these "mosaic" mRNA molecules comes about by RNA-RNA "splicing" or "ligation" was inferred from studies on the synthesis of Ad2 specific RNA in the nucleus of the infected cells (12, 13).

He does not say in the text that he is referring to work in his lab; he could just as well be writing about someone else, and one must comb the notes to see that he had any role in this research at all. There are, of course, no references to his personal experiences or responses, except for the one mention of a "startling" post-transcriptional event (which implies someone to be startled). Other people are omitted too; there are no names in the article (with one exception), so everyone is reduced to a footnote number.[8] The depersonalization is not just conventional; it helps deal with the problem of his presenting his own lab's findings in what he sees as the most effective context without seeming to blow his own horn.

The depersonalization also helps in presenting controversy. The two views around which Darnell organizes his plot are not attributed to anyone, though it would have been possible to find names on which to hang them; each is presented entirely by a depersonalized "view."

> A contrasting view for the origin of divided genes is that . . .
> This view denies an intermediary role in evolution to . . .
> According to this view, the separated DNA segments . . .
> In this scheme, where RNA-RNA splicing is held as basic . . .

It is usual to introduce one's own hypothesis as one of several alternatives, the others of which are then vanquished. But it may be unusually cautious to keep stressing the hypothetical nature of the belief in every sentence. (When Darnell and Doolittle reviewed the work of the field in *PNAS* eight years later, they did give names and citations for the two views. But I would argue that the device of identifying two views worked differently then; in 1978 they were *creating* two views as a way of putting forward a claim; by 1986 there really were two established views, with extensive literature on each side.)

Although Darnell's presentation is carefully impersonal, in Crick's article, one is immediately aware of a strongly personal, colloquial, spoken voice.

> I have been so rash as to say, more than once, that we might expect between 10 and 100 different enzymes; but that was pure guesswork. The number could be as low as two.

But as one reads on one can hear, not just the voice of Francis Crick, given special privilege as an eminent biologist, but two voices. The flow of the text breaks into a kind of dialogue between the Crick who speculates and the Crick who reports, between the Crick who gives "an overall view of the present position" and the Crick who gives "some general ideas and a few remarks about future work." We can hear two voices in the contrast between the bold statement in

> In a higher organism a gene has, if anything, more nonsense than sense in it.

and the cautious qualification that follows

> These preliminary estimates are necessarily very insecure.

The cautious voice is like a critic restraining the more colorful statements. But it is not just that Crick talks to himself; he talks to others in the field too. There are actual comments from other researchers in the text:

> Gilbert has pointed out to me . . .
> A reasonable guess, as supposed by Tonegawa . . .

Personal communications like these have a special status in the text; they get a name and a comment, while citations of published work just get a footnote number, as in Darnell's article. Another dialogic device is the use of notes that comment on the text, 17 of them, functioning as asides that respond to but are not part of the main thread. So, for instance, this statement is followed by a note qualifying it:

> Thus, one should not invoke some selective advantage occurring only in the future unless this is likely to happen within a time comparable to the time needed to remove the intron (63).
>
> 63. Not all inserts now present need to have a function. For all we know a fair proportion of them may be sitting there, doing nothing, and simply waiting to be excised or deleted.

The sense of back and forth comment is strengthened by the contrast between the style of the text and the even less formal style of the note. Here the anthropomorphism of *sitting there* is part of a comic style. He replaces the textbook voice and authority of a paper like Darnell's with the sort of license granted to ideal discussion after a conference paper. This is an article with a mug of beer in its hand. Suggestions are thrown out and followed up, half serious guesses are allowed, what is known is ticked off in citations and what isn't known is ticked off in questions. So the result is not as personal to Francis Crick as it seemed from the opening sentence of the article or the more brash speculations; rather, he plays, and allows us to play, the typical molecular geneticist in the audience of these reports, turning over the new findings, looking for something interesting to do.

Crick's article differs from Darnell's more typical review article in several features: Crick's shorter than usual sentences, his less complex syntax, and his preference for cohesion by replacement and substitution rather than by repetition and conjunction. These stylistic differences can be related to differences in rhetorical strategy, if we think of them as indicating the kinds of readers the two articles imply.

Crick's tendency to use short sentences and Darnell's to use long sentences may seem to be matters of personal or editorial taste, but these choices also have rhetorical implications. One can take this sentence from Darnell's article as typical not only of his style but of the style of many reviews.

> For example, although the genetic code is universal (or nearly so) and the machinery for protein synthesis is quite similar in pro- karyotes and eukaryotes, the tRNA molecules for specific amino acids — even including initiator tRNA (37, 38), and ribosomal RNA's (rRNA) (35, 36, 39) — bear little resemblance even between

Greg Myers

> lower eukaryotes and prokaryotes while there is considerable
> sequence overlap between various eukaryotic tRNA and rRNA
> molecules.

The reason this sentence is so complex is that it both makes a statement and incorporates all the objections that might be raised or attitudes that might be held by readers. The basic statement here is that *the tRNA molecules for specific amino acids bear little resemblance between eukaryotes and prokaryotes*. This statement is modified by two assertions that broaden the statement:

> (1) that even initiator tRNA is included (the readers must expect resemblance here—perhaps because this tRNA codes for a processing function common to all translation), and
> (2) that even lower eukaryotes (which the reader might expect to be closer to prokaryotes) are included.

There are also three assertions that put the statement in the context of the current state of disciplinary knowledge, making it more surprising, more worthy of the reader's attention:

> (3) the comparison at the end, to the sequence overlap within eukaryotes, of tRNA and rRNA,
> (4) the observation at the beginning that the genetic code is universal,
> (5) and another observation at the beginning that protein synthesis is similar.

Then in almost every statement there is some qualifying adverb or adjective that makes the statement more cautious:

> (or *nearly* so)
> *quite* similar
> *little* resemblance
> *considerable* sequence overlap

And at the beginning there is a phrase telling us to take this whole thing as just one example of the striking differences between prokaryotes and eukaryotes. Such complex sentences are appropriate to Darnell's task of constructing two clear views of the evidence. In this case, even if one does not know what a particular sentence is saying, one can see the argument has two—and only two—sides. Each piece of evidence is incorporated in a way that acknowledges implicitly the initial skepticism of the implied holders of the other view.

It is not so much the average length of Crick's sentences that makes them seem short compared to Darnell's, as the apparent baldness of some of their assertions and the way they follow each other with only implicit connections.

> 47. Where are split genes to be found? 48. So far, they have only been noticed in eukaryotes. 49. If they were common in prokaryotes (the bacteria and the blue-green algae), they would almost certainly have been discovered earlier. 50. We cannot yet say categorically that they do not occur in prokaryotes but it certainly seems unlikely that they do. 51. They are common in eukaryotic viruses. 52. Indeed, that is where their importance was first realized, but an interesting distinction exists. 53. They have only been found in DNA viruses that occur in the cell nucleus (2) or in RNA retroviruses which have a DNA nuclear phase (16). 54. Split genes have not so far been discovered in viruses that exist only in the cytoplasm of a cell. (265; sentence numbers added)

The short sentences, parallel assertions in similar forms (*they have been noticed, they were common, they are common, they have been found*), seem to cry out for some conjunctions and subordination. But a closer look shows a back-and-forth movement between statements on the distribution of split genes (sentences 48, 51, 53, 54) and statements about the research on them (49, 50, 52). The direction of argument becomes clear only gradually; the point emerges at the end of a series of steps ("All this would suggest that the phenomenon of splicing is correlated with the existence of a nuclear membrane") instead of being given at the beginning, as in the passage from Darnell. The style assumes the readers can put these statements together, can themselves see the relations as they develop.

If we compare the two authors' cohesive devices, we see that Darnell prefers conjunction and repetition, while Crick prefers replacement and substitution (see Halliday and Hasan for terms). The difference in effect is hard to describe, since we have only a hazy understanding of how cohesion works, but it seems that, again, Darnell's prose suggests logical demonstration, while Crick's suggests a more open-ended process. For instance, in the paragraph from which I took the sample sentence about prokaryotes and eukaryotes, Darnell starts most sentences with logical connectors.

> 44. Both prokaryote[s] and eukaryotes existed at least 1.0 to 1.5×10^9 years ago (34, 35), and studies to date provide no evidence of sequential prokaryotic to eukaryotic evolution (35–37). 45. *For example,* although the genetic code is universal (or nearly so) and the machinery for protein synthesis is quite similar in prokaryotes and eukaryotes, the tRNA molecules for specific amino acids — even including initiator tRNA (37, 38), and

ribosomal RNA's (rRNA) (35, 36, 39) — bear little resemblance
even between lower eukaryotes and prokaryotes while there is
considerable sequence overlap between various eukaryotic tRNA
and rRNA molecules. 46. *Furthermore*, even in yeasts, which are
among the least complex eukaryotic organisms, some tRNAs are
formed from a precursor tRNA by the removal of fifteen to twenty
nucleotides from the middle of the tRNA sequence (26–28), with
subsequent RNA-RNA splicing. 47. *Likewise*, there is little evidence
of any overlap between prokaryotes and eukaryotes of primary
amino acid sequences even for similar proteins *although*, it must
be admitted, there has been very little work done on which such
comparisons can be made (37, 40, 41). 48. *Thus*, there is at present
no evidence of a "core" or residue of prokaryotic genes that are
still present within a now expanded set of eukaryotic genes.
(1258; sentence numbers added, connectors in italic)

The whole passage would make some sense even if one didn't know what
prokaryotes and eukaryotes were, because every relation is explicitly
marked. In sentence 45 the shift to a specific piece of evidence is marked
by *for example*. (And we have already seen that this long sentence is full
of internal conjunctions.) The next two sentences are marked as continuing the same line of evidence with the conjunctions *furthermore* and *likewise*. The *thus* in the last sentence marks it as ending this line of evidence.
(In this case, the argument is complicated by the fact that it is based on
negative evidence — demonstrating that certain correlations that should
hold if eukaryotes descended from prokaryotes do not in fact hold.)

Besides using conjunctions, Darnell repeats words and phrases, so the
reader can identify the same topic in each sentence. The repetition in sentence 44 serves to repeat a topic from the previous paragraph, which then
continues through the paragraph:

> 44. sequential prokaryotic to eukaryotic evolution
> 45. little resemblance even between lower eukaryotes and
> prokaryotes
> 47. little evidence of any overlap between prokaryotes and
> eukaryotes
> 48. "core" or residue of prokaryotic genes

Such repetition allows the reader to follow the main point through a series
of difficult sentences. The constant topic is part of what gives the sense
of exhaustive argument to Darnell's style. As we will see, the substitution
of a word ("this") for a phrase has a different stylistic effect, and also reflects a different pattern of topics.

Despite this complexity of this paragraph, anyone could sit down and produce an outline of it, or of the whole article. The extremely, even ponderously tight cohesion seems to be designed to lead the reader through the argument, even at the cost of overloading some sentences with embedding and loading each paragraph with conjunctions and repetition. The article could end with Q.E.D.

If close cohesion is characteristic of Darnell's style, Crick's style is characterized by apparent gaps that can only be filled by a reader with some knowledge of the field. I see this loose cohesion as another device for involving the reader in the discussion. The use of lexical replacement and substitution seems to demand more from readers than Darnell's logical conjunctions and repetitions, but it has the effect of including them, implicitly, in the set of intended readers, those familiar with this semantic network. For instance, consider the links between sentences in this passage.

> 120. What is the actual *mechanism* of splicing? 121. At the moment any ideas must necessarily be largely speculative. 122. One would certainly expect at least one *enzyme* to be involved, if not several. 123. In the case of *tRNA* from *yeast*, an *enzyme* activity has been found by two groups, as was mentioned above, although it has still to be purified (11, 12). 124. It is not completely obvious that such a *mechanism* would require a source of *energy* since two phosphate ester bonds need to be broken whereas one (or possibly two) have to be made. 125. On balance, one would suspect that *energy* might be required if only because the process must be an accurate one. 126. Preliminary evidence indicates that the enzyme appears to need *adenosine triphosphate* (ATP) (11). (266; repetition and lexical replacement in italic)

One can construct a reader for this article based on the knowledge Crick assumes in connecting one clause to another, one sentence to another. So, for instance, sentences 120 and 122 are held together if one connects *mechanism* and *enzyme*. Sentences 125 and 126 are linked here only if we connect *energy* and *adenosine triphosphate*. Sentences 127 and 128 (not shown here) are linked by a contrast between *tRNA* and *mRNA*. On the basis of repetition we can also provide the connections suggesting a relationship of hypothesis and confirmation between 122 and 123 and an adversative relationship between sentences 124 and 125.

While Darnell maintained a constant topic by repeating key words in each sentence, Crick tends to move from topic to topic through substitution (such as the pronoun "this" substituting for a previous statement).

> 103. Let us now consider in more detail the arrangement of introns and exons. 104. The *first thing* we notice, from the very

> limited experimental data at present available to us, is that a
> chromosomal gene only produces a single protein (45), whereas a
> stretch of DNA in a virus may produce more than one protein,
> depending on which way the primary transcript is spliced. 105. I
> adopt the attitude that in most cases *this* is because viruses are
> short of DNA and, by various devices, their limited amount of
> DNA is made to code for more proteins than would otherwise be
> possible. 106. We can see *this* even in prokaryotic viruses . . .

In these sentences, the *first thing* substitutes for the whole statement that
is to come, while the *this* in sentences 105 and 106 each refer back to the
whole statement of the previous sentence. The effect of substitution is
different from that of repeating the whole phrase or a variant on it, as
Darnell might do. It is unusual in a scientific article to do this so much,
and the use of the device may be part of what makes Crick's style seem
so informal. Crick's choices of cohesive devices are consistent with the
creation of a sense of discussion, as Darnell's cohesive devices are consistent with his emphasis on the logical resolution of two views.

Melting into the Stream of Knowledge

I have argued that these articles tell stories that try to
enlist readers in a particular view of the present and future of the field.
Now, almost ten years later (a long time in molecular genetics), we have
some idea of how the field did develop. The articles themselves have become parts of other provisional histories of the field. We can see how these
and other reviews might have influenced the course of research, both in
articles that specifically cite them and more generally in changes in the
discourse of the field.

The usual way sociologists gauge the influence of a text is by tracing
citations and perhaps examining their contexts (see Swales, "Citation
Analysis"; Cozzens). A review is typically cited often, but not for long;
in its brief time, it may be read by many more researchers than any
experimental report. Darnell's and Crick's articles are both cited a great
deal (for instance, in 1980, 39 times for Darnell and 80 for Crick),[9] but
random checks of the contexts of these citations suggest they are cited
in somewhat different ways. Darnell's article is nearly always cited in relation to one issue, the views of evolution he proposes, while Crick's is cited
for a variety of general ideas and specific phrases. I would suggest that
these different citation histories result in part from the different stories
the two articles present. As we have seen, Darnell organizes a complex
series of narratives around one story of how evolution could have oc-

curred. In Crick's article, the underlying story of the shaking up of the research field is not so easily summarized. The styles of the articles may also have something to do with the way they are cited, for Darnell's strategy of presenting two impersonal "views" means he is easily assimilated into one line of the literature, while Crick's personal and informal style means he can make a number of quotable phrases and intriguing remarks.

We can find an example of a typical citation of Darnell in a recent article:

> As has been suggested [cites Darnell, Doolittle, Blake, and Reanney] the split gene organization may have been present in the original ancestral cells, with only the . . . present day prokaryotes and lower eukaryotes having lost their introns under selective pressure. (Michelson et al., 6969)

The issue of whether introns were introduced in eukaryotes or eliminated from prokaryotes has continued to be a focus of research, with new information of various sorts relating to one side or the other of the debate (so, for instance, the Michelson article is interpreting the sequence of the gene they study in terms of this issue). When Darnell is cited for this, he is always cited with one or more of a cluster of other articles. Sometimes, as in his own later articles and Doolittle's (and one they coauthored), his position is presented in contrast to that of the researchers who saw introns as being introduced between prokaryotes and eukaryotes. More often, articles with all sorts of speculations are cited together, just to show that the issue has received considerable attention.

> The problems of the origins of introns, and the possible evolutionary advantage of the split gene organization have been the subject of intense speculation (11, 122–129). Although we have very little chance ever to answer the basic question of whether the split gene organization is the most primitive one and whether present-day bacteria are "streamlined" cells, there are a number of observations that are relevant. . . . (Breathnach and Chambon, 359)

Only rarely is Darnell's article cited for one of its more detailed claims. In another passage from Michelson's article, he is cited for his argument on why split genes are preserved.

> While the original amino acid sequence homology of the common nucleotide binding domain would be eliminated over time as point mutations accumulated, the similarity in the arrangement of exons encoding this domain would be preserved by the relatively

infrequent occurrence of precise intron loss, at least in the
genomes of higher eukaryotes (ref. 30, see below).

But such specific credits are hard to disentangle from the many similar
arguments made at the same time. There was a general convergence on
evolutionary issues, and in this case the fact of convergence matters more
than who said what first. As Crick says about evolution in his review,
"I've noticed that this question has an extraordinary fascination for almost
everyone concerned with the problem" (269).

Crick's article, too, is most often cited as part of this cluster of discussions of evolutionary issues. Many of the citations of Crick's article in
more specialized articles refer to specific claims, but usually these turn
out to be the claims of others that he is just evaluating. So, for instance,
Wallis, writing in 1980, cites Crick after a reference to "AG, a base sequence found almost universally at the 3' end of an intervening sequence,"
but this does not imply that the idea was Crick's—it was based on
Chambon's work, and Crick just gives a good short account of it. As late
as 1984, Crick is cited by Levenson for the statement that the "intervening sequences . . . may be larger than the coding region itself." This is
not Crick's own idea, but again he does put this in a striking phrase ("In
a higher organism a gene has, if anything, more nonsense than sense in
it"). Interestingly, he seems to be frequently cited for the term "exon
shuffling" (Darnell is cited for this too). This is Crick's way (I believe he
coined the catchy phrase) of describing one of the proposals in an article
by Gilbert. Crick is also frequently cited for the proposal that "these genes
have evolved from already distinct exons, each coding for a different
structural domain." This too is proposed in Gilbert's article. That so many
articles cite Crick for this does not necessarily indicate any confusion about
the source of the proposal, but just sends the reader to Crick's more
evaluative and comparative treatment rather than to Gilbert's rather com-
pressed and sometimes cryptic first statement.

Of course, Crick is also cited for interpretations that, as far as I know,
appear for the first time in his review. When Chambon cites his discussion of the mechanism of splicing, it may be because his comment on the
ambiguity of the splicing sequence ("an interesting point which is perhaps
not immediately obvious") is not made in other reviews. Abelson takes
Crick's guess about the number of enzymes as worth repeating: "Francis
Crick estimates (182) that there are more than ten but less than one hundred RNA splicing enzymes, which seems a good guess" (1059). Crick's
treatment of possible scenarios for the origin of split genes is also different from that in other reviews of the time.

Several popularizations quote Crick's review, partly because he has a
striking way of putting things, and partly because he is Francis Crick.

Stories and Styles in Two Molecular Biology Review Articles

Marcel Blanc, writing in *La Recherche*, starts by quoting the first two sentences of the article, so that the estimation of "l'un des pionniers de cette discipline moderne" indicates the importance of split genes. Then Blanc presents the area in terms of a controversy between the old guard, like Crick, who try to adapt this discovery within the framework of earlier molecular biology, and somewhat younger researchers like Gilbert who see it as revolutionary.

> In a way that is typical in the history of sciences, the new genera-tion of researchers involved in the discovery are inclined to see it as a revolution, while the attitude of certain pioneers of the discipline, as Francis Crick shows in this *Science* article, is to try to make these "new facts" fit in the old theory, while making some concessions. (My translation)[10]

I do not agree with this way of dividing up the participants, but I can see how Crick's article, by telling a story about the responses of researchers, and by ending, as we have seen, with some cold water, could be useful to a journalist trying to construct his own provisional history of the field.

Reviews may also relate to texts that do not specifically cite them. Taken together, they can make or reflect changes in the discourse of the field. They can do this just be defining problems in general terms, rather than in terms of a specific program of research. For instance, all the research articles are illustrated, usually with electron micrographs, schema, and maps showing the structure of one gene or set of genes. Crick's review article is the first, I believe, to start with a very simplified illustration that shows split genes in general terms, without reference to any particular case. And in the text, he begins by laying out "The Basic Problem," not by relating one particular line of research to others. It is a crucial step in the making of a concept, like Walter Gilbert's naming of the excised portions as "introns" (in "Why Genes in Pieces?") confirming (what had perhaps already been implied) that these sequences were entities to be studied rather than just stuff between the expressed sequences to be studied. Similarly, after the introductory survey, Darnell writes, not about *E. coli* or adenovirus or rabbit beta-globins or chicken ovalbumin, but about prokaryotes and eukaryotes in general.

Another sign of this process of generalization is Crick's and Darnell's reflection on the basic terms of split genes research. A note in Crick's second sentence points out that, with this discovery, the term *gene* be-comes problematic:

> Throughout the article I have deliberately used the word "gene" in a loose sense since at this time any precise definition would be premature.

Greg Myers

Then he digresses from his explanation of the problem to discuss Gilbert's new terminology of *introns* and *exons*, going on in a note:

> There are two main difficulties. . . . Nevertheless, used judiciously, the two words are undoubtedly useful. I imagine some committee will eventually decide on a wholly logical terminology.

This care with terminology reflects Crick's concern with examining the underpinnings of the theoretical framework. Darnell shows the same awareness by putting every new term or slightly colloquial expression in cautious quotation marks.

One bizarre kind of influence may come simply from giving a name to a notion so that it can be discussed. This explains why Crick's article is sometimes cited for something he explicitly said he wasn't talking about. A year after it, Leslie Orgel and Crick published one article, and W. F. Doolittle and Carmine Sapienza another, on the topic of "Selfish DNA." In introducing this topic, Doolittle and Sapienza say that "Dawkins, Crick, and Bodmer have briefly alluded to it" (601). But the mention by Crick in the 1979 article is really very brief. After criticizing the fallacy of "evolutionary foresight," he says, "This problem should not be confused with the related phenomenon of a particular stretch of DNA spreading within the genome, the case of 'selfish DNA.' " But he doesn't talk about what selfish DNA is. Apparently there had been enough informal discussion of this idea in Crick's circle to make it worth addressing in this offhand way, but the idea did not yet have the general currency it has today, which allows the phrase to be used without explanation or citation. This odd use of Crick's article brings us back to the basic difference between his style and Darnell's. It is characteristic of Crick's influence that it should be personal, that a phrase and a suggestive, offhand remark would be cited later; his earlier reviews also contributed a number of striking phrases and broad generalizations to the field. In the same way, it is characteristic of Darnell's work that his influence should be inseparable — and that he should want it to be seen as inseparable — from the influence of other researchers exploring similar ideas at the time. These different kinds of influence reflect two sides of the same strategy of enrollment (Latour 118); the successful researcher must both have allies to carry out the program and have his or her individual contribution to this program recognized. Crick's article illustrates the importance of attribution of credit, while Darnell's illustrates the importance of allies, but both illustrate the same process that is essential to either text having an influence. As I said in introducing Crick and Darnell, the importance of the exception is that it too can be explained in terms of the function of the review article, the use of the past to shape the future.

Recently there have been several retrospective articles that look back at these articles that looked forward; for instance, Gilbert summarizes the research related to his short review in "Genes in Pieces Revisited," and Darnell and Doolittle review research related to their 1978 articles in "Speculations on the Early Course of Evolution." These articles show that much experimental research — sequencing new genes or identifying new biochemical processes or defining a whole new taxonomical kingdom — has pursued just those evolutionary problems laid out in the review articles of 1978 and 1979. But this correlation leaves open the question of whether reviews actually shape future research or whether they just give convenient citations for points of view that are established in the discourse in other, less formal ways. One example will show how the reviews figure as justification for a new line of investigation. P. Senapathy recently published a statistical analysis of available sequences, and he introduces his project with a reference to Darnell and Crick and the various reviews of the late 1970s.

> The origin and function of eukaryotic introns has been an enigma since their discovery and there have been contrasting discussions — whether the introns were introduced when eukaryotic genes evolved from more ancient prokaryotic intron-less genes or whether the primitive single-celled eukaryotes were the most ancient to evolve with introns (5-9). . . . This paper presents a hypothesis for the origin of introns based on statistical analyses of codon distributions in DNA sequences from data banks. . . . (2133)

Now it may be that evolutionary questions are never far from the mind of any biologist. But it may be that a series of reviews by some of the best-known figures in the field made it easier to focus an introduction, like Senapathy's, on these very broad issues, rather than on more narrowly defined issues. There are always plenty of alternative contexts. Whether reviews do shape the field, or merely seem to shape it by reflecting other social interactions, the subsequent development of research along the lines laid out in the reviews shows that they did not just sum up past research; they created a story that continued into the future.

My own aim parallels that of the genre I am describing: I want to enlist other textual analysts in an incomplete project, to get them to do broader and deeper studies of review articles and of what is usually considered "secondary" literature. Traditional sociologists and historians of science have focused on experimental reports as the key scientific texts. This is partly a reflection of the traditional concern with matters of priority and the roles of individuals in discovery — a desire to find the real beginning. But if we are interested in the social construction of science rather than in individual credit, we need to look at some of the other, later textual forms, such as reviews, news articles, textbooks, and popularizations.

Greg Myers

Perhaps we look for the original form of each idea because the notion that there is no original form is deeply unsettling. As Max Delbruck remarked in his Nobel Prize address, science involves the dissolution and reconstruction of textual forms.

> While the artist's communication is linked forever with its original form, that of the scientist is modified, amplified, fused with the ideas and results of others, and melts into the stream of knowledge and ideas which forms our culture.

Literary critics have begun to look beyond the "original form" of artistic communications to the "stream of knowledge" of which they are a part. Analysts of scientific texts, too, need to look more closely at the textual forms in which the original communication is modified, amplified, fused, and melted.

NOTES

My thanks to J. E. Darnell, Jr., for his comments on and corrections of an earlier draft, and to Tony Dudley-Evans of the English Language Research Department of the University of Birmingham, and to his postgraduate seminar on genre, for their discussion of an earlier version of this paper.

1. For articles on the review article form, see Eugene Garfield; A. M. Woodward; and J. A. Virgo. For representative handbook and style guide comments, see M. O'Connor and F. Peter Woodford; Robert Day; and Janet S. Dodd.

2. This view of reviews is supported by Charles Bazerman's comments (now in *Shaping Written Knowledge*) on how the writing of a review article shaped the thinking of the physicist Arthur Compton.

3. For instance, when I write an article for other researchers within the specialty of social studies of science (such as "Texts as Knowledge Claims"), I can assume a commitment to relativism, and a methodological interest in showing the variability of accounts. When I review work in the field for readers in other disciplines (as in "Writing Research and the Sociology of Scientific Knowledge"), I have to define *relativism* and *accounts* in other terms, and I have to make explicit the assumption that the possibility of variable accounts supports the relativistic interpretation of knowledge, thus raising the question of whether the assumption is correct. And of course I have to show why people who are not immediately involved with this research—such as writing teachers—should invest their time and effort in understanding and applying it.

4. For accounts of the influence of Crick's 1957 review, see Horace Freeland Judson (a huge, readable, *New Yorker*-style account with wonderful interviews), Franklin H. Portugal and Jack S. Cohen (a more academic account), John Gribbin (an interesting example of popularization, but sometimes odd in the slant on details), and, perhaps the best introduction for absolute

beginners, the comic book *DNA for Beginners* (Rosenfeld et al.). Pnina Abir-Am has a detailed critique of the historiography of molecular biology that is relevant to the problem of "influence."

5. This account assumes that the reader knows some textbook facts about genes: that genes are instructions for protein production encoded in the base sequence of DNA molecules; that one strand of the DNA double helix is copied onto complementary single-stranded messenger RNA in a process called transcription; that this mRNA then goes to the ribosomes, where transfer RNA reads each triplet of bases and lines up the appropriate amino acid, forming a protein in a process called translation. These processes were elucidated by research on bacteria (prokaryotes), particularly *Escherichia coli*, in the 1960s and 1970s. Work on the much more complicated cells with their DNA in nuclei (eukaryotes) was hampered by a number of technical difficulties until new techniques were developed in the mid-1970s.

I have analyzed other texts about split genes in "Making a Discovery," and in an unpublished conference paper comparing two *News and Views* articles, "Scientific Speculation and Literary Style." Neither of these are historical articles. For popular histories of split genes research, see the article in *Scientific American* by Pierre Chambon, or the article in *La Recherche* by Antoine Danchin and Piotr Slonimski. It should be noted, for those who (like me) know science only through the studies of historians and sociologists, that this episode, though dramatic, and though often described as a "revolution," was nothing like the kind of revolution Kuhn describes. RNA splicing could be accounted for within the basic principles of molecular genetics. Nor does it seem to have been a particularly controversial topic; though there were different views about mechanisms, about evolutionary sequence, and other issues, all the researchers seem to have accepted one interpretation of the adenovirus experiments very quickly (what it was like at the symposium I don't know). This is partly because the interpretation put on their results by the CSH and MIT groups enabled other groups, working on hemoglobin, immunoglobin, and ovalbumin, to make sense of results they had been trying to interpret (for a sense of this response, see Chambon, "The Molecular Biology of the Eukaryotic Genome Is Coming of Age").

6. The plot/story distinction, and its variants, have entered Anglo-American literary criticism through Russian Formalism and the structuralism of Gérard Genette and Roland Barthes. There are many introductions in English, the most useful of which, for me, remains Fredric Jameson's *The Prison-House of Language*. Seymour Chatman's *Story and Discourse* discusses these distinctions in detail, and the first chapter of Peter Brooks' *Reading for the Plot* provides references to more recent studies. Note than E. M. Forster's distinction between plot and story in *Aspects of the Novel* is different from the distinction I am following.

7. It may well be that Crick's choices of what to ignore, or to restrict to a mention, are significant. When he leaves out most of the work on viruses and immunoglobulin, he presents his omission as a problem of space, but it also means he does not have to give much attention to claims for a "multiple-choice" gene.

8. The one exception to Darnell's impersonality is the mention of W. F. Doolittle's name in the text and a brief discussion of his paper in a note. The note explains why he might be a special case requiring personal recognition:

While this manuscript was being prepared, a note appeared in _Nature_ (London) [272, 581 (1978)] by W. F. Doolittle which proposes the same general premise as this article — that splicing and "genes in pieces" is representative of an early phase of cell evolution. Doolittle then goes on to advocate . . .

Darnell gives a name where it is a question of adequately acknowledging the priority of another article. He seems to be bending over backward to give full credit to Doolittle, while also stressing that he himself had the idea independently. (My paper "The Pragmatics of Politeness" comments on such acknowledgements.)

9. While neither Darnell's article nor Crick's article is among the author's most cited papers, they were both cited a great deal from the time of their publication until 1982, and both have continued to be cited some since then.

	Darnell	Crick
1979	16	21
1980	39	80
1981	34	76
1982	29	40
1983	19	24
1984	7	21
1985	13	24
1986	11	12

The first citations take them as the most current review articles, cited with the first reference to splicing, split genes, or introns, so that the reader can catch up ("For review, see . . ."). But they are still cited long after they could have been current, for instance, after Breathnach and Chambon's long review in 1981, and after masses of new data relevant to the evolution of split genes had been published. This suggests that they both have some appeal that the other, more up-to-date reviews didn't have. It is interesting that most of the earlier citations are in _Cell, Nature, PNAS,_ and _Science,_ the most prestigious places for breaking research in molecular biology. Later citations are more often in review journals and journals of fields outside molecular biology (Crick was even cited in an anthropology review), perhaps suggesting that those at the core of the nucleic acid research soon began citing more recent reviews.

10. "De manière caractéristique dans l'histoire des sciences, la nouvelle génération de chercheurs à l'origine de la découverte penche pour le bouleversement; tandis que l'attitude de certains pionniers de la discipline, comme Francis Crick le montre dans cet article de _Science,_ est d'essayer de faire rentre les 'faits nouveaux' dans la théorie ancienne, tout en faisant des concessions" (897).

BIBLIOGRAPHY

Abelson, John. "RNA Processing and the Intervening Sequence Problem." *Annual Review of Biochemistry* 48 (1979): 1035–69.

Abir-Am, Pnina. "Themes, Genres, and Orders of Legitimation in the Consolidation of New Scientific Disciplines: Deconstructing the Historiography of Molecular Biology." *History of Science* 23 (1985): 73–117.

Bazerman, Charles. *Shaping Written Knowledge: The Genre and Activity of the Experimental Article in Science*. Madison: University of Wisconsin Press, 1988.

Blanc, Marcel. "Une mini-révolution en génétique moléculaire." *La Recherche* 103 (September 1979): 896–98.

Breathnach, Richard, and Pierre Chambon. "Organization and Expression of Eukaryotic Split Genes Coding for Proteins." *Annual Review of Biochemistry* 50 (1981): 349–83.

Brooks, Peter. *Reading for the Plot: Design and Intention in Narrative*. Oxford: Oxford University Press, 1984.

Chambon, Pierre. "The Molecular Biology of the Eukaryotic Genome Is Coming of Age." *Cold Spring Harbor Symposium Proceedings* 42 (1977): 1209–34.

Chambon, Pierre. "Split Genes." *Scientific American* (April 1981): 48–59.

Chatman, Seymour. *Story and Discourse: Narrative Structure in Fiction and Film*. Ithaca: Cornell University Press, 1978.

Cozzens, Susan. "Comparing the Sciences: Citation Context Analysis of Papers from Neuropharmacology and the Sociology of Science." *Social Studies of Science* 15 (1985): 127–53.

Crick, F. H. C. "On Protein Synthesis." *Symposia of the Society for Experimental Biology* 12 (1958): 138–63.

Crick, Francis. "Split Genes and RNA Splicing." *Science* 204 (1979): 264–71.

Crick, F. H. C., Leslie Barnett, S. Brenner, and R. J. Watts-Tobin. "General Nature of the Genetic Code for Proteins." *Nature* 192 (1961): 1227–32. Rpt. in Taylor, ed.

Danchin, Antoine, and Piotr P. Slonimski. "Les gènes en morceaux." *La Recherche* 155 (May 1984): 616–26.

Darnell, James E., Jr. "Implications of RNA-RNA Splicing in Evolution of Eukaryotic Cells." *Science* 202 (1978): 1257–60.

Darnell, James E., Jr. "Variety in the Level of Gene Control in Eukaryotic Cells." *Nature* 297 (1982): 365–71.

Darnell, James E., Jr., and W. F. Doolittle. "Speculations on the Early Course of Evolution." *Proceedings of the National Academy of Sciences* 83 (1986): 1271–75.

Darnell, James E., Jr., R. Evans, N. Fraser, S. Goldberg, J. Nevins, M. Salditt-Georgieff, H. Schwartz, J. Weber, and E. Ziff. "The Definition of Transcription Units for mRNA." *Cold Spring Harbor Symposium Proceedings* 42 (1977): 515–22.

Day, Robert. *How to Write and Publish a Scientific Paper*. Philadelphia: ISI Press, 1979.

Delbruck, Max. "A Physicist's Renewed Look at Biology: Twenty Years Later (Nobel Lecture)." *Science* 168 (1970): 1312–15.

Dodd, Janet S., ed. *The ACS Style Guide: A Manual for Authors and Editors.* Washington: American Chemical Society, 1986.

Doolittle, W. Ford, and Carmen Sapienza. "Selfish Genes, the Phenotype Paradigm and Genome Evolution." *Nature* 284 (1980): 601–3.

Fleck, Ludwik. *The Genesis and Development of a Scientific Fact.* 1935. Trans. Fred Bradley and Thaddeus J. Trenn. Chicago: University of Chicago Press, 1979.

Garfield, Eugene. "Reviewing Review Literature, Part 1. Definitions and Uses of Reviews." *Current Contents* (4 May 1987): 3–8.

Garfield, Eugene. "Reviewing Review Literature, Part 2. The Place of Reviews in the Scientific Literature." *Current Contents* (11 May 1987): 3–8.

Gilbert, Walter. "Why Genes in Pieces?" *Nature* 271 (1978): 501.

Gilbert, Walter. "Genes in Pieces Revisited." *Science* 228 (1985): 823–24.

Gribbin, John. *The Search for the Double Helix: Quantum Physics and Life.* London: Corgi, 1985.

Halliday, M. A. K., and Ruqaiya Hasan. *Cohesion in English.* Harlow: Longman, 1976.

Jameson, Fredric. *The Prison-House of Language.* Princeton: Princeton University Press, 1972.

Judson, Horace Freeland. *The Eighth Day of Creation: The Makers of the Revolution in Biology.* London: Jonathan Cape, 1979.

Latour, Bruno. *Science in Action: How to Follow Scientists and Engineers Through Society.* Milton Keynes: Open University Press, 1987.

Levenson, Robert, Vincent Racaniello, Lorraine Albritton, and David Housman. "Molecular Cloning of the Mouse Ouabain-Resistance Gene." *Proceedings of the National Academy of Sciences (USA)* 81 (1984): 1489–93.

Marx, Jean L. "Gene Structure: More Surprising Developments." *Science* 199 (1978: 517–18.

Michelson, A. M., C. C. F. Blake, S. T. Evans, and S. H. Orkin. "Structure of the Human Phosphoglycerate Kinase Gene and the Intron-Mediated Evolution and Dispersal of the Nucleotide Binding Domain." *Proceedings of the National Academy of Sciences* 82 (1985): 6965–69.

Myers, Greg. "Making a Discovery: Narratives of Split Genes." In *Narrative in Culture,* ed. Christopher Nash. London: Routledge and Kegan Paul, 1990.

Myers, Greg. "The Pragmatics of Politeness in Scientific Articles." *Applied Linguistics* 10 (1989): 1–35.

Myers, Greg. "Text as Knowledge Claims: The Social Construction of Two Biologists' Articles." *Social Studies of Science* 15 (1985): 593–630.

Myers, Greg. "Writing Research and the Sociology of Scientific Knowledge." *College English* 48 (1986): 595–610.

O'Connor, M., and F. P. Woodford. *Writing Scientific Papers in English.* Oxford: Elsevier, 1975.

Orgel, L. E., and F. H. C. Crick. "Selfish DNA: The Ultimate Parasite." *Science* 284 (1980): 604–7.

Portugal, Franklin H., and Jack S. Cohen. *A Century of DNA: A History of the Discovery of the Structure and Function of the Genetic Substance.* Cambridge: MIT Press, 1977.

Potter, Jonathan, and Margaret Wetherell. *Discourse and Social Psychology.* Beverly Hills and London: Sage, 1987.

Rogers, John. "Genes in Pieces." *New Scientist* (5 January 1978): 18–20.

Rosenfeld, Israel, Edward Ziff, and Borin Van Loon. *DNA for Beginners.* London: Writers and Readers, 1983.

Sambrook, Joseph. "Adenovirus Amazes at Cold Spring Harbor." *Nature* 268 (1977): 101–4.

Schmeck, Harold M., Jr. " 'Nonsense' in Gene is Prompting New Thoughts On Man's Origin." *The New York Times* (3 November 1981), C1.

Senapathy, P. "Origin of Eukaryotic Introns: A Hypothesis Based on Codon Distribution Statistics in Genes, and Its Implications." *Proceedings of the National Academy of Sciences* 83 (1986): 2133–37.

Swales, John. *Aspects of Article Introductions.* Birmingham, Eng.: Aston University, 1981.

Swales, John. "Citation Analysis and Discourse Analysis." *Applied Linguistics* 7 (1986): 39–56.

Taylor, J. Herbert, ed. *Selected Papers on Molecular Genetics.* New York and London: Academic Press, 1965.

Virgo, J. A. "The Review Article: Its Characteristics and Problems." *Library Quarterly* 41 (1971): 275.

Wallis, M. "Growth Hormone: Deletions in the Protein and Introns in the Gene." *Science* 284 (1980): 512.

Woodward, A. M. "Review Literature: Characteristics, Sources, and Output in 1972." *Aslib Proceedings* 26 (1974): 367–76.

3

THE RHETORIC OF

LITERARY CRITICISM

JEANNE FAHNESTOCK AND

MARIE SECOR

In the ongoing debate about the nature of literature and literary theory, there has also been an emerging interest in the nature of literary argument itself. Cary Nelson's 1976 article "Reading Criticism" was a controversial first step toward self-consciousness about the critical medium. Nelson argues that criticism is "more personally motivated than we usually assume" by analyzing the ethos of critics like Bloom, Brown, and Kenner (802ff.). Wayne Booth's *Critical Understanding* (1979) raises questions about the "accuracy, validity, and adequacy of interpretive approaches" (32–33), questions that can easily be turned on literary argument itself. And in the same year, Richard Levin published a critique of trends in the interpretation of Renaissance drama that uncovers some of the basic but rarely articulated assumptions about what constitutes a "reading," a piece of interpretive literary criticism (see esp. pp. 2–5, where he lists ten conceptions "frequently employed and seldom discussed"). The final chapters of Stanley Fish's *Is There a Text in This Class?* ("What Makes an Interpretation Acceptable?" and "Demonstration vs. Persuasion: What Makes an Interpretation Persuasive?") point toward a rhetoric of literary argument. Jonathan Culler's pursuit of the conventions of literary competence can be seen as a search for the conventions of literary argument; the convention of thematic coherence, for example, might also be described as the need for a coherently argued thesis. More recently (and more cynically), Terry Eagleton has defined literary theorists, critics and teachers as "not so much purveyors of doctrine as custodians of a discourse" (201).

Literary criticism selects, processes, corrects and rewrites texts in accordance with certain institutional norms of the "literary" — norms which are at any given time arguable, and always historically variable. For though I have said that critical discourse has no determinate signified, there are certainly a great many ways of talking about literature which it excludes, and a great many discursive moves and strategies which it disqualifies as invalid, illicit, noncritical, nonsense. Its apparent generosity at the level of the signified is matched only by its sectarian intolerance at the level of the signifier. (203)

A study of these "institutionalized norms," these field-dependent constraints on the published interpretation of literature falls naturally under the domain of rhetoric. And such a rhetoric of literary criticism would have the same aim that all rhetorical criticism has: understanding the available means of persuasion. The means of persuasion available to a literary scholar, however, will not be definable without some methodology, some even more prior set of assumptions about what we are looking for and how we might know when we find it — not an easy program and one not likely to be achieved in the opening gambit of a single essay. Nevertheless we would like to open the search.

We have begun our search for the rhetoric of literary argument by examining a set of articles published in a selection of journals of established reputation, not limited to the work of one author or circle; most of the journals were not even limited to one period, although we confess a bias of interest toward the nineteenth century and toward fiction. We aimed for a variety of subjects, but avoided articles on literatures other than English and American and textual studies that depend on physical evidence. Beyond that we followed no conscious principle other than synchrony: the articles we read were all published betweeen 1978 and 1982. A larger selection might produce some differences in emphasis, but even though the scale of our study is small, we think the articles we read show enough similarity in assumptions, manner, and argumentative methodology to warrant some tentative observations about the nature of literary argument. At least, we would like this essay to be construed as an invitation to further study, refinement, and correction. We who are so quick to identify the conventions employed by the literary figures we study should also be aware of the rhetorical constraints under which our own discourse operates.

One caveat is in order. Our study is not empirical, despite the fact that we draw conclusions after examining a group of essays. It is, rather, deductive, since we will begin with some assumptions about argument, as widely held as possible, which we then test against a body of evidence, as representative as we could make it, on the way to some conclusions, as tentative as they must be.

We can probably begin with the assumption that most of the critical articles published in literary journals are intended as arguments whose

Jeanne Fahnestock and Marie Secor

authors have aimed to win intellectual conviction from their readers. That is, they consist of discursive techniques that aim "to induce or to increase the mind's adherence to the theses presented for its assent" (Perelman and Olbrechts-Tyteca, 4). Though it appears that the gesture in many literary studies is that of informing rather than persuading, the distinction between the informative and the arguable is often more of degree than of kind, residing as much in the perception of the reader as in the material. As Stanley Fish has pointed out, presenting content as informative rather than challenging (by using phrases such as "there can be no doubt") is a natural rhetorical gesture to this end (339). Still literary criticism, whatever its strategy, remains argumentative in its purposeful support of claims and in its attempt to gain its audience's adherence.

Once we acknowledge the status of literary criticism and interpretation as argument, our next procedural step must be to adopt a method to facilitate the rhetorical analysis of literary articles. Our method of analyzing literary arguments is drawn from Aristotle, Cicero, Toulmin, and Perelman and Olbrechts-Tyteca. It would be immodest to call it a synthesis; it is more a mélange of the analytical points on which they are compatible.

1

We can reasonably begin by looking at the kind of issue or question that is at stake in an argument, that is, its stasis. According to Cicero (21–35), the first two stases deal with issues of fact and definition. Arguments in the first stasis establish the existence of a subject and arguments in the second characterize it. An answer to a question about existence or definition will take the form of a categorical proposition, and all such arguments will hinge on definition.

We identified four argumentative issues or stases in our selection, each one requiring its own structure of support. An article by Blanche Gelfant supplies us with an example of a first-stasis argument in "Sister to Faust: "The City's Hungry Woman as Heroine" (1981); Gelfant calls our attention to the existence of a Faustian heroine who hungers for knowledge and experience, a heroine previously overlooked in American fiction. To put her thesis in terms of a crude paraphrase, "This is what a Faustian heroine is, and we find her in x, y, and z." Robert Merrill supplies us with a second-stasis argument in "Another Look at the American Romance" (1981). He argues that *The Scarlet Letter* should be redefined as a novel rather than as a romance. Such first- and second-stasis arguments require definition of the predicated term — in Merrill's argument, "novel" and "romance," and in Gelfant's, "hungry heroine" — and evidence linking the subject terms, the works under scrutiny, with the carefully defined predicate. For example, once definitions of "novel" and "romance" are in place, definitions which must both work in the argument and strike scholarly readers as plausible, Merrill must present evidence from *The Scarlet Letter* itself to earn for the text its classification as novel. Similarly, Gelfant's task, once she has constructed a convincing definition of "hungry heroine," is to gather examples under the term, distorting their individuality as little as possible, to show that such a character does indeed exist.

Arguments about existence or definition can take the form of comparisons. These are nothing more than arguments for two categorical propositions brought into juxtaposition, since to say that two works or characters or theses are similar is to argue that both can be characterized in the same way. Or, one step up in complexity, a comparison argument can show that one subject has more and one less of a certain quality. If, to take an example from Thomas J. Embry's allusion-sleuthing article, "Sensuality and Chastity in *L'Allegro* and *Il Penseroso*," "Il Penseroso" is comparable to "Comus," it is because each individually shows Milton's preoccupation with chastity.

We would distinguish another stasis not separately identified by classical rhetoricians, one questioning cause (Fahnestock and Secor, 1985). Answering causal questions has, for the most part, attracted literary historians rather than critics. To establish persuasively how the preoccupations of an age or a life inform a work, how manuscript history or publishing habits affect an individual text or genre, or how one work influences another directly or indirectly, requires causal argument. An example in the set we examined is Anne Falke's " 'The Work Well Done that Pleaseth All': Emanuel Forde and the Seventeenth-Century Chivalric Romance," which argues, among other things, that Forde's prose fictions derive from medieval verse romances. To argue causality convincingly requires more than pointing out a similarity between two things succeeding one another in time; the agency of connection, the links uniting cause and effect, must be forged as well. Agency in Falke's argument would be the availability of a medieval verse model for the seventeenth-century writer.

Arguments in the next stasis attempt to answer questions about the quality or value of the subject under discussion. Such evaluation arguments use the structures of both categorical and causal arguments to establish a credible judgment about the value of a literary work, about whether it deserves labels such as "great," "classic," "important," "impoverished," "failed," or "incoherent." Such an evaluation argument shows how the work under consideration either meets or fails to meet a standard that a par-

Jeanne Fahnestock and Marie Secor

ticular scholarly audience would accept. This standard can be constructed from the effects the work has brought about (e.g., *Uncle Tom's Cabin* was an important novel because of its historical impact), but it is more often a set of formal criteria. Thus it is a commonplace to claim that *Middlemarch* is a "great novel" because of its moral seriousness, its verisimilitude, its thematic resonance, its complex but balanced structure. Among the articles we examined, Paul Sherwin's *"Frankenstein*: Creation as Catastrophe" evaluates Mary Shelley's novel negatively for not living up to its opening, for descending to domestic melodrama, and for failing to provide a "liberating verbal space."

2

We found that categorical propositions (i.e., existence and characterization arguments) appeared most frequently in literary criticism. Indeed much of what we call interpretation amounts to support for categorical propositions classifying, characterizing, describing, or defining an author, an individual text, or a group of texts. Thus to do a Freudian or new historicist or Marxist or feminist reading of a text is to claim categorically that "x work has y qualities" or that "x can be described as y" or that "x is really a y." As we pointed out, to make such an argument requires a careful adjustment of definition and evidence.

We can best illustrate what we mean by looking at several examples in detail. Robert Merrill's attempt to reclassify *The Scarlet Letter* is admirable for its clarity of purpose; no one can read it and fail to grasp what it is trying to do. Merrill amply demonstrates that critical consensus has labeled *The Scarlet Letter* a romance.

> For the moment, let me say that the word [romance] must signify, besides the more obvious qualities of the picturesque and the heroic, an assumed freedom from the ordinary novelistic requirements of verisimilitude, development, and continuity; a tendency towards melodrama and idyl; a more or less formal abstractness and, on the other hand, a tendency to plunge into the underside of consciousness; a willingness to abandon moral questions or to ignore the spectacle of man in society, or to consider these things only indirectly or abstractly. (383)

To remove *The Scarlet Letter* from this category and place it in the category of the novel, as Merrill intends, could be done in either of two ways. First, the arguer could set up disjunctive definitions of novel and romance as the only possible classifications for prose fiction. Then to take *The Scarlet Letter* out of the category of romance would automatically place it in the category of novel; if it is not one, it must be the other. Or the arguer could avoid the problem of defending a perfect disjunction (virtually impossible anyway) by positing a definition of novel that rivals in fullness and precision Chase's definition of romance. This definition must obviously be made to fit *The Scarlet Letter* yet still be acceptable as a general definition of the novel. That is, it cannot be so narrow that it would fit only *The Scarlet Letter*.

In pursuing his argument, Merrill seems to mix these alternative techniques. He spends most of his time showing why *The Scarlet Letter* does not necessarily fit Chase's definition of romance (e.g., because it is tragic, because it contains only one minor supernatural occurrence). But he does not establish the novel/romance pair as a disjunction, though he seems to come close to assuming a disjunction, nor does he set forth a full and authoritative definition of "novel." The closest he comes is to say that realism, and by implied extension, the novel, explores "the impact of experience on individuals," but this simple attribute (which could apply equally to "'Tis' Pity She's a Whore" or "Michael") cannot balance the weight of Chase's definition of romance. Merrill's argument, then, may not rigorously support its thesis, though it does call into question for its intended audience the usefulness of the presumption that *The Scarlet Letter* should automatically be labeled a romance.

Arguments for categorical propositions can also founder when the definition of a crucial term, or the term itself, shifts in mid-argument. Something of this sort happens in Susan Wolfson's article, "The Speaker as Questioner in *Lyrical Ballads*." Wolfson wishes to demonstrate that a pattern of question and response pervades Wordsworth's ballads, a pattern which culminates in the unexpressed questions submerged and ultimately controlled in "Tintern Abbey." The questions in Wordsworth's earlier ballads ("The Thorn," "We Are Seven," "Anecdote for Fathers") are present for everyone who can see a question mark, but there are none of this obvious sort in "Tintern Abbey," and to find unexpressed questions requires a redefinition of what a question is.

In order to carry on her argument and to include evidence from "Tintern Abbey," Wolfson must extend the definition of "question" so that the word becomes interchangeable with some more or less tangentially associated terms — "qualifications," "hesitations," "perplexity," "doubt," "uncertainty," and "restraint." She wants to associate words that describe what is being said with a mode of expression — the question (in terms borrowed from speech act theory, which Wolfson does not use, to associate an underlying speech act with a certain surface form). Wolfson's argument depends on her readers first accepting this extension of the semantic field of the word "question" and then on their accepting linguistic evidence for the existence of such doubts, hesitations, and thus unexpressed questions in the poem. But there is an unheralded enlargement of the territory included under the term "question." It spreads to cover evidence such as lacunae, the repetition of "this" and "these" as "unvoiced questions about possible differences," and the phrase "I would believe" as an indication of a "tentative tone," "a conditional utterance expressing more a wish than an actual conviction." Why "more a wish" rather than equally or less than a wish? "I would believe" could just as easily express determination as tentativeness. But Wolfson's stretched definition of what constitutes a question presumably did not trouble her intended audience.

The evidence offered in a categorical proposition argument should usually be typical in both number and kind of the subject term. Thus, to take a deliberately simple example, someone who argues that "most mid-Victorian novels are polemical" must offer representative examples of novels that fit both the categories "mid-Victorian" and "polemical." One or two would presumably not do, and historians might expect the evidence to include both famous and little-known novels. Or, in an argument characterizing one work, the evidence must be typical in the sense that it represents a reasonable portion of the text, or at least does not exclude any significant proportion of it. An argument, for instance, that economic motives predominate in *Emma* could not be sustained by examples of monetary metaphors and word choices taken from a single chapter. Indeed we often judge the validity of an interpretation by how much of the text it can account for.

Among the articles we read, the quantity and typicality of the evidence were rarely defended. We might take as an example Arnold Weinstein's "The Fiction of Relationship," whose thesis is that the novel has gradually learned to depict, realize, express, and give form to loving relationships. Weinstein's definition of the abstraction "relationship" is as encompassing and open-ended as his selection of six illustrative examples to represent all of Western fiction for the last three hundred years is minuscule. Although his examples were carefully chosen to represent three cultures and three centuries, they can in no way bear the weight of the generalization. Nor does Weinstein pretend that his selection is anything but arbitrary: "To be sure my deck is stacked and small," he writes (5). But even after this disarming concession, Weinstein goes on to deal from his stacked deck anyway. If his essay persuades — and we do find it eloquently persuasive — it is not because of the representativeness of his evidence.

If it is difficult to defend generalizations characterizing texts or groups of texts, it is even more difficult to defend value judgments as arguably intersubjective rather than as matters of personal preference. To convince another reader that a work is a "classic," or simply worth the time it takes to read it, requires appealing to shared criteria of what has value in literature. These criteria certainly change over time, and writers are promoted or demoted from the canon of major works (definable operationally as works included in undergraduate or graduate literature curricula). To complicate the matter, the criteria that are explicitly identified may not be the ones that are actually operating as the basis of the value judgment. When we say, for instance, that a work is admirable for its richness, for its complexity, for its truthfulness to experience, we may simply mean that it lends itself to discussion in familiar terms.

No one who finishes Paul Sherwin's pyrotechnical essay on Mary Shelley's *Frankenstein* can doubt that it is the negative evaluation of the novel that its title, "Creation as Catastrophe," suggests. However, the criteria by which Sherwin reached this judgment are by no means explicit in the article which consists of two carefully elaborated and then refuted readings of *Frankenstein*'s opening chapters — one classically Freudian and one personally psychoanalytic. Given the article's conclusion, Sherwin apparently assumes that the novel fails because these rococo readings cannot be sustained much beyond the scene of the creature's creation; thus he complains late in the essay: "Frankenstein has become just another Gothic hero-villain, a tiresome neurotic whose presence impoverishes the larger portion of the work that bears his name" (898). Such a judgment presupposes that a work is valuable to the extent that it sustains a particular reading or a consistent interpretation; that is certainly a defensible assumption, or has been until recently.

A problem arises, however, when we try to make a work sustain an individual reading and evaluate it negatively when it cannot. *Frankenstein* obviously breaks under the weight of Sherwin's interpretive strategies. But why judge the work by those particular standards? The arguer who wants to show the failure of a work because it cannot sustain a particular reading ought first to establish that the attempted reading is the justifiable standard of judgment. Such justification is easier for a positive evaluation than for a negative one, since the successful application of a criterion justifies using it. Most readers will accept such pragmatic support for a standard, even though the resulting argument is essentially circular: if a particular reading yields a positive evaluation, it must be the right one — because it yields a positive evaluation. But if a standard is going to produce a negative evaluation, it may need to be defended against charges of irrelevancy. We would not, for example, judge a Shakespearean sonnet defective because it lacks a tragic sense of history or More's *Utopia* deficient because it never sensitively portrays an individual psychological crisis. Similarly, Sherwin's argument becomes problematic because he never defends his criteria of judgment. The considerable persuasive impact of the article derives from other sources.

Jeanne Fahnestock and Marie Secor

3

So far we have been pointing out that literary arguments often do not make explicit certain structurally predictable elements — the definitions, causal linkages, comparisons which derive from the stases and common topoi of classical rhetoric. Arguers in all circumstances and in all disciplines draw upon these common topoi, but they are not self-consciously exploited in the arguments in our selection. Yet while purists might find these arguments deficient, literary scholars probably would not find them unconvincing; certainly editorial readers for the journals they appeared in did not. In other words, though literary arguments may seem flawed when viewed from a distance and by a field-independent standard, they can still be compelling to the audiences for whom they were intended. To identify the sources of their appeal, we must remember that these arguments exist in a particular field, a unique rhetorical situation; they are acts of communication directed at a special audience in a particular kind of forum, and as such they have their own characteristic procedures. Just as political oratory, pulpit homilies, and even advertising copy exploit a limited set of rhetorical possibilities, so also does literary criticism employ a definable repertoire of persuasive tactics to achieve communication in its well-defined environment.

Classical rhetorical theory can account for the persuasiveness of arguments in unique rhetorical situations by invoking the special topoi. The special topoi are warrants that Aristotle and later rhetoricians identified, to supplement the common topoi, as most useful in particular persuasive situations (see Toulmin).

We would like to extend this notion of the special topoi to contemporary literary argument and suggest that literary scholars have their own distinctive sources of argument, their own special topoi which they employ when constructing arguments and applaud when reading them. Like the Aristotelian special topoi that appeal to shared values and shared perceptions, these special literary topoi invoke the shared assumptions of the community of literary scholars, and at the same time create that community. We maintain in fact that appeals to these special topoi make literary arguments convincing to their intended audience. The writers in our sample all draw on them in one form or another, whether consciously or unconsciously; they are assumptions underpinning other arguments, sometimes formally invoked, sometimes glancingly referred to, rarely explored. Yet once they are identified, we recognize in them the nature and value of the critical endeavor.

The most prevalent special topos of literary argument appears in many forms, but we can nevertheless group its manifestations under the general heading "appearance/reality" (Perelman and Olbrechts-Tyteca, 415–

19). This dissociation can stand for all those occasions when the literary article is structured by a dualism, the perception of two entities: one more immediate, the other latent; one on the surface, the other deep; one obvious, the other the object of search. We might even claim that the appearance/reality topos is the fundamental assumption of criticism, since without it there would be no impetus to analyze or interpret literature.

Thomas Embry provides the first and perhaps simplest allotrope of the appearance/reality topos when he argues that "L'Allegro" and "Il Penseroso" (and beyond them Milton's attitude to sensuality and chastity) cannot be adequately assessed until a reader recognizes their allusive density. The poems have been taken at face value as pro and con presentations of two ways of life, but Embry argues that the sensuality "L'Allegro" presumably advocates is seriously undercut when the original context of one of the poem's allusions is identified. For example, the "checkered shade" that is so alluring in "L'Allegro" acquires a sinister meaning when the reader acknowledges its source in *Titus Andronicus*, where the phrase "checkered shadow" occurs in a seductive speech. Thus the apparently innocent is really corrupt, the poem's surface meaning altered when the reader brings to it a new dimension of awareness. Whether any reader but Embry has ever noticed these allusions (and he does not argue that Milton was aware of them), and whether these allusions from negative contexts are the only ones recoverable, is less important than the topos represented by the allusion-seeking endeavor: that of turning the two-dimensional, flat linguistic surface of a poem into a three-dimensional house of allusions.

We seldom see the appearance/reality dichotomy as clearly articulated as it is by Michael Steig, who frankly acknowledges his preoccupation "as a critic and a person" to be "the search for hidden meanings," which are the "meanings that really matter to us" (323). When Steig searches for hidden meanings in Kenneth Grahame's apparently innocent tale for children, *The Wind in the Willows*, he probes with the tools of psychoanalytic, biographical, and reader-response criticism. Not surprisingly, he finds erotic depths underlying two passages in a fantasy which, its author claimed, was "clean of the clash of sex" (321). Thus what appears to be a childhood idyl is in reality tinged with the author's sexual preoccupations. Although Steig makes a case for the sexual connotations he uncovers, he does not distinguish between finding and constructing a reality, or worry over the possible difference. Obviously, what appeals to the intended audience is less the magnitude and nature of the discovery than the familiarity of the pursuit, the search for a reality behind appearance — and a sexual reality at that.

The prevalence of the appearance/reality topos further suggests that we cannot discuss texts without using spatial metaphors. The very notion of appearance versus reality translates immediately into images of a surface

Jeanne Fahnestock and Marie Secor

with something underneath, of solids that can be probed, of layers that can be peeled away to reveal deeper layers. These metaphors, and the word choices they inspire, probably reveal as much about how the mind works as they do about literary discourse; psychologists have pointed out that our ability to abstract is informed by our experience of a three-dimensional world. Thus it is not surprising that most of the authors in our sample rely on spatial metaphors.

We find another highly sophisticated allotrope of the appearance/reality topos in Carr and Knapp's "Seeing through *Macbeth*," which invites us to pass "through" the text of the play, "through" performances of the play, "through" pictorial representations of these performances by Zoffany and Fuseli, and even "through" centuries and layers of criticism to some under-lying psychological and social truthfulness that the text as a classic em-bodies. To take just one manifestation of this "seeing through," Carr and Knapp claim that Zoffany's portrait of Macbeth emphasizes his "inner conflict" in a way that readers of literary criticism will find familiar.

Speaking of characters as having depth is a commonplace of the rhet-oric of literary criticism, but the appearance/reality topos pervades more than the discussion of character in this article. Carr and Knapp carry spatial metaphor to a baroque height when they interpret *Macbeth* by interpret-ing a painting which interprets a performance which comes full circle to interpret the play. Zoffany's print suggests to them an emblematic ar-rangement of Macbeth, Lady Macbeth, and the eighteenth-century audi-ence as a paradox of the Apprentice (Macbeth) torn between Industry (Lady Macbeth) and Idleness (the audience, not depicted in the print). Thus the two-dimensional print stands for a three-dimensional tableau whose third dimension is supplied by the interpreter; this whole gazebo is then set into the play to represent its inner meaning. Such an interpretive methodology is unimaginable without spatial metaphor to create a locus for a reality behind appearance.

When critics use a literary text as a document of intellectual or social history, they invoke the appearance/reality topos by using spatial meta-phors to suggest reaching through or behind the textual façade to a hid-den reality. Thus a text can function as a scrim between the stage of real history and the audience/reader on the other side. This scrim may be opaque to a contemporary audience who can observe only its surface features, but it becomes transparent to a reader with historical perspec-tive who sees the social reality through it. Thus Frank Whigham, in "The Rhetoric of Elizabethan Suitors' Letters," looks through the "conspicuous expenditure of words" (868) in sixteenth-century business letters to find their "real message," their place in the network of fawning and patronage that defined the Elizabethan power structure.

If the appearance/reality topos is everywhere, "everywhereness" is its own topos as well. One of the most persuasive endeavors that a literary scholar can engage in is to find something (a device, an image, a linguistic feature, a pattern) that no one else has seen—and to find it everywhere. Thus the perception of one set of doubles in a novel is interesting, but the perception of fourteen pairs of doubles is impressive. Ubiquity reinforces the initial perception, and as readers of literary arguments and partakers of the literary topoi, we are convinced and delighted by the ingenuity which points out a repeated form. And the less obvious the repetition, the more convincing.

The ubiquity topos comes in two forms: either the critic finds many examples of the same thing, or he finds one thing in many forms, up and down a scale of grandeur and abstraction. George Wright uses both forms of the ubiquity topos in his "Hendiadys and *Hamlet*." First, with a scrupulous attention to detail, Wright finds the same rhetorical figure, hendiadys, everywhere in *Hamlet* (66 times to be exact) as well as precisely counted appearances of it in other plays. But in *Hamlet* the double figure of hendiadys is doubly ubiquitous: this verbal linking of uncoordinated words in a coordinate structure (e.g., "the perfume and suppliance of a minute") resonates in doublings of characters, of plots, of themes, of images, and of "all relationships, familial, political, cosmic, and even artistic" (179). And more than a simple duplication, the doubleness of *Hamlet* represents not joining but disjunction, an appearance of harmony which masks disunion. Thus Wright places the ubiquity topos at the service of the appearance/reality topos, and we might even say that the more than normally powerful appeal of Wright's article (it was judged the year's best in *PMLA*) results from its "hendiadytical" union of two powerful topoi.

We find ubiquity everywhere, but another topos is the more elusive object of the critic's search: the prized unification of apparently irreconcilable opposites in a single startling dualism—the paradox. Critics seize upon paradoxical joinings with special delight. In the articles we examined, we found paradoxes at every level, from passing oxymorons (e.g., "formless form," Sherwin, 896) to the very thesis of the article. Thus Carr and Knapp notice that Zoffany's portrayal of Macbeth and Lady Macbeth depicts them as they "both advance toward and recoil from each other, their mutual attraction and antipathy held at equilibrium," and they combine their methodology and its result in their last paragraph: "So, paradoxically, because of the layers of mediation we have used, Macbeth seems to confront us directly . . ." (846). Similarly, Michael Steig begins his discussion of *The Wind in the Willows* with a paradoxical observation, derived from Freud, that "heimlich" became long ago a virtual synonym for "unheimlich": "Thus that which is of the household is familiar and pri-

Jeanne Fahnestock and Marie Secor

vate, even secret, and paradoxically, strange and forbidden" (305).

What is the appeal of the paradox? Why does this violation of Aristotle's first law of thought surprise and delight us with the impression of discovery and insight that accompanies its formulation? One answer may be that the precise verbal form is itself the attraction, making it seem possible to impose an apparent unity on disparate elements and thus provoke wonder. So the production of paradox may both serve the intellectual content of the argument and be an aesthetic end in itself, demonstrating the cleverness of the critic. Appropriately, the paradox is the only topos that is also a rhetorical figure, one particularly attractive to the language-conscious literary scholar.

Another special topos, one which particularly reveals shared values between critic and audience, is an assumption of despair over the condition and course of modern society which we shall call the *contemptus mundi* topos. "Modern" may be defined as any time from the Renaissance to the present, depending on the article. Critics seem to expect a woeful nod of tacit agreement whenever they mention the alienation, seediness, anxiety, decay, declining values, and difficulty of living and loving in modern times. Consequently, works which directly express such despair are highly valued. But even more indicative of the appeal of this topos is the search for unresolvable tensions and shadows in literature that at face value seems optimistic. Thus critics find sinister meanings in the fantasies of Lewis Carroll, darkness in the poems of W. S. Gilbert, cynicism in the novels of Jane Austen, and cruelty in the comedies of Oscar Wilde, while at the same time they do not write about literature which is sunny.

Among the articles we examined, the *contemptus mundi* topos functions as a touchstone of shared value. It is especially strong in Arnold Weinstein's "The Fiction of Relationship," which identifies forces of darkness and despair closing in on the warm and loving partners he has searched out in twentieth-century fiction. As his article advances through the centuries, he complains that the world outside becomes more and more hostile to human relationships. Similarly, according to Blanche Gelfant, hungry heroines, whose search for knowledge has positive value, all fail, all succumb to a prevailing social mediocrity that thwarts their quest for fulfillment. Still another manifestation of this topos appears in Susan Wolfson's darkening of "Tintern Abbey," in her reluctance to credit the poem's positive assertions as anything other than "pious platitudes." The unspoken assumption in her article is that doubt and uncertainty somehow make the poem more profound and more valuable to contemporary readers. Finally, Max Byrd's elegantly argued "Johnson's Spiritual Anxiety" applies one of our century's most famous definitions of "angst," Tillich's "spiritual anxiety," to Samuel Johnson's eighteenth-century occasional prose. In none of the articles we examined did we find any work praised for optimism. Literary scholars may be quick to rebut that "it is not us, but the world that casts shadows"; such a perception may show the strength of this topos.

The *contemptus mundi* topos is thematic. A more formal topos is the paradigm, an elucidation of a structure in a literary text that is often imitated in the structure of the literary argument as well. As we use the term, a paradigm is an arrangement of verbal concepts in opposition or congruence; it is, in other words, a kind of template fitted over the details of a literary text to endow them with order. Literary scholars seem to create paradigms in two ways: microstructurally and macrostructurally. In the first method, they find a microparadigm, a small structural unit in the text, which becomes the center of ever-larger concentric applications. Thus in his article on *The Tempest*, Stephen Miko identifies the limits of Prospero's magic in the play and extends them into a "metaphor for the powers and limits of Shakespeare's own imaginative world and, by not too forced an extension, art in general" (9). This particular extension, from work to author to art itself, is a critical commonplace, perhaps even a topos in its own right. To claim that any work of art is really about art itself confers dignity reciprocally on both artist and critic.

In the second method, scholars find a macroparadigm, a recognizable set of relationships drawn from the world outside the literary text, and then detect its avatars in a particular genre or work. This method often enables a scholar to bring together many apparently diverse works under a single definition. Martha Vicinus, for example, borrows a paradigm of class struggle to create a generic definition of melodrama as a portrayal of the victory of the powerless over their oppressors without disturbing the social structures that make them powerless to begin with (note that this paradigm is also a paradox). She finds this macroparadigm worked out in many Victorian novels and plays, thus supporting, somewhat circularly, her original thesis. Similarly, William Greenslade in his essay on *The Ambassadors* sees the late nineteenth-century boom in advertising and journalism congruent with forces at work in the novel, the large social reality writ small in the individual text. All articles that find an Oedipal complex in a particular short story, or a Jungian archetype in a drama, or Lacanian "others" everywhere, apply macroparadigms. And, as we might expect, deconstructionists are continually surprised and disappointed by their inability to make a paradigm stick.

Ultimately all the topoi we have discussed reduce to one fundamental assumption behind critical inquiry: that literature is complex and that to understand it requires patient unraveling, translating, decoding, interpreting, and analyzing. Meaning is never obvious or simple for, if it were, the texts under scrutiny would not be literature and therefore would not

Jeanne Fahnestock and Marie Secor

be worthy of unraveling, interpreting, decoding, etc. Obviously, here we stumble on an endless circularity in literary criticism, the characteristic which creates the complexity which justifies it. We are led to ask, "Do we have literary criticism because literature is complex, or is literature complex because we have literary criticism?" We cannot resolve this circularity; we can only point to its existence.

This assumption about the complexity of literature informs every aspect of the articles in our sample. We found no articles praising the simplicity of a work, or its transparency, or its uncomplicated optimism, or the ease with which meaning is plucked from its surface. Instead, the critics we looked at justify their endeavor by finding complexity in the ways represented by the special topoi. Thus reality is always more complex than appearance, surfaces by definition have underlying depths, the multiplying vision of ubiquity complicates perspective on a text, paradoxes turn unities into nodes of tension, the *contemptus mundi* topos creates discomfort with a decaying world, and paradigms, which ought to simplify by creating structure, actually complicate by disclosing previously unsuspected relations.

All these versions of complexity seem to originate in the critical reader's perception of contrast or similarity in a text. Often the associations aroused in a reader by a single word will vary either among its separate uses in a text or between its use in the text and in the reader's understanding. Thus within the same text, a single word like "persuasion" may seem to be used in different senses; so the critic sets out to find a more complex order of meaning that will unify all those senses (see Swanson). Or the reader will find similarities between apparently unlike elements and so postulate another order of meaning, not self-evident, to account for surface differences, thus creating levels of meaning and hence complexity. The job of the critic is to turn this perception into an arguable claim, and to do that the special topoi are invoked.

Literary argument also seems to demand that the critic make one more choice: where to locate complexity. One obvious residence for complexity is the author's psyche where complexities of various kinds, conscious or unconscious, can be said to exert pressure on a text. Thus the unresolved tensions in an author's life (discovered by biographical scholarship) account for unsatisfactory resolutions in his work. Or complexity may be located in the times in which the author wrote, all ages being ages of transition filled with dialectic tension. Or the locus of complexity may be in the form of the work, prior to or irrespective of the author's intentions. Thus authors must to some extent intend the conventions of a chosen genre, no matter how much they may wish to undermine or defeat them. More recently the locus of complexity has moved either to an interaction between the reader and the text or to the reader alone, particularly the educated, critical reader.

The special topoi identified above are by no means a definitive or complete listing of all the possible loci for literary argument. They are a rough sketch, a first outline of uncharted territory. Our formulation of them is meant to be suggestive rather than final: further reading will undoubtedly suggest refinements, variations, additions, overlappings. Such flexibility in the special topoi is to be expected since the set of discipline-specific assumptions to which arguments appeal and from which they are generated are bound to evolve over time.

4

From one point of view the special topoi are the logos of literary arguments and are thus the very constructs which enable scholars to operate on literature. But from a rhetorical point of view the locus of all the topoi is the interaction between arguer and audience, between logos and ethos. In other words, to invoke the topoi of paradox, appearance/reality, ubiquity, paradigm, *contemptus mundi*, and complexity serves to announce one's membership in the community of literary scholars who in turn will listen most attentively to the speaker with such credentials. Thus the special topoi inform the logos and constitute one manifestation of the ethos projected in a literary argument.

Other manifestations of the literary arguer's ethos are somewhat obvious but worth mentioning briefly. Certainly the critic must demonstrate familiarity with the subject matter and the work of other critics in a particular field. To do so is patently part of the logos, but it serves ethos as well. An early paragraph or footnote in a literary argument will often survey the scholarship behind a particular essay. But ethos may be conveyed more subtly in the allusive density of an article, in glancing references to this critic or that work. In fact, we seem to prize the very casualness that reaches out to a wide range of knowledge and pulls it into significance, creating the ethos of an alert and well-stocked mind.

A literary arguer's ethos also depends not just on what is said but on the vehicle of its saying. It is only appropriate that literary scholars convey their ethos through the artistry of their language, demonstrating virtuosity with the very medium they analyze. And if we take elaborateness as a sign of mastery, we can see how the complexity topos affects language as well as content. Thus a significant number of the articles we examined are very hard reading; simply parsing the predication out of

Jeanne Fahnestock and Marie Secor

a sentence often requires an analytic attack little short of diagramming.

Such complexity of language, which enhances our perception of an author's subtlety and hence ethos, frequently appears as metaphor. Such metaphors are not merely ornamental; they are in fact the very vehicle by which the argument is framed in language. We would even suggest that without the juxtaposing of semantic fields achieved by metaphor, literary argument could hardly be carried on.

For at the level of language, interpretation may be seen as paraphrase. That is, any interpretation selectively recapitulates a text using terms from another semantic field. Turning to metaphor ourselves, we can call this linguistic activity "reading in another register." Here is an example of how it is done. Stephen D. Cox quotes the entire Blake poem "A Little Boy Lost" and then follows with a condensed paraphrase: "A child pointedly asserts his right to a mild form of egoism, and he is murdered for doing so" (302). Cox has here translated a twenty-four line poem into one sentence, using words like "egoism" from the register of psychoanalysis, "mild" from the register of reader evaluation, and "murdered" representing an ethical categorization. Thus what looks like bald restatement is actually an interpretation of the poem. Later on in his article, Cox describes and refutes other interpretations, each of which defines its own register: "Some of his commentators regard the Little Boy as a rationalist, and some as a visionary; some believe that he is conversing with a human father, and some that he is praying to a divine one" (308). Presumably reading in the rationalist register would paraphrase the poem using words associated with rationalism, the visionary reading with words from the semantic field of mysticism. The third version would select words characterizing human dialogue, the fourth divine colloquy, and so on.

At the level of word choice then, an interpretation is a metaphorical paraphrase juxtaposing a text with the lexicon from a chosen semantic field. The challenge in such an undertaking is to use words from the two domains without straining their meanings beyond the audience's recognition while at the same time accounting for a representative proportion of the work under scrutiny. To succeed at such a delicate balancing act is to project an ethos of elegant linguistic mastery. Occasionally the difficulty of the process shows up in mixed metaphors, odd predications, and tortured phrasings. Take the following three examples as representative of linguistic strain:

> Down by the river the previous afternoon the real relations between Chad and Madame de Vionnet have floated into Strether's pastoral frame.

> The magic lore that creeps into the play is capable of causing embarrassment both to those who prefer the notion that they all

just dreamt the tempest and the transportations and those who say magic is magic, usually invoking John Dee and insisting that at least it's white.

One resource of interpretation, then, would be to unpack what is implied in the illustration, scrutinizing each implication to understand its latent content in the image and in the submerged layers of Shakespeare's text.

All three of these sentences bring together words from semantic fields that refuse to converge. In the first example, we are asked to imagine "real relations" floating into a frame — and a pastoral frame at that. Thus an abstraction concretely moves into what we assume is a perceptual frame, but the modifier "pastoral" makes it generic as well. The second example personifies magic lore as creeping and causing embarrassment, and it ends with the allusiveness of private responses. And the last tries to make its point by combining in one sentence three metaphors for the hidden: we can unpack what is packed, actualize what is latent, and retrieve what is submerged, but it is hard to comprehend how all three can be done at once. All these metaphoric usages invoke confused images rather than clarifying ones, so the language breaks down, at least briefly, and the critic's ethos may suffer too, depending on the audience's degree of tolerance.

Most of the time, however, scholars of the word use words with precision and even flair, thus contributing positively to their ethos. Often, indeed, the language of the article mirrors the language of the literary text it discusses. Notice, for instance, the Johnsonian ring of Max Byrd's prose in the following sentence: "This author and Pope, perhaps, never saw the miseries which they imagine thus easy to be borne" (370). And surely Paul Sherwin can command as much élan as any Romantic stylist: "To Walton, however, belongs the burden of the mystery as he watches this self-destroying artifact vanish into darkness and distance and contemplates a catastrophe at the Pole" (883). Such stylistic virtuosity contributes powerfully to persuasiveness in the rhetorical situation of the literary argument.

5

So far in the rhetorical analysis of literary argument we have found that appeals to the special topoi and to a certain metaphorical paraphrasing and artistic use of language are dominating features. The predominance of these features suggests the unique rhetorical function of such arguments. Aristotelian rhetorical theory offers three basic forums or purposes for rhetorical discourse: forensic, deliberative, and epideictic. At first these categories of civic discourse seem to have little connection

Jeanne Fahnestock and Marie Secor

with the world of scholarly argument. Literary arguments are not obviously concerned with legislative or judicial decisions, and they seem far from platform speeches praising victorious athletes. But in a broader sense Aristotle's categories are relevant. Literary arguments do judge past performances, they do imply future policies (which works to teach), and, most important, they do the work of epideictic discourse: they create and reinforce communities of scholars sharing the same values.

When we place literary argument in the epideictic or ceremonial mode, our understanding comes into focus. Ceremonial rhetoric affirms the shared values of a community and harmonizes new insights with what is already believed. It is a subtly ritualized form of communication, and as ceremonial rhetoric literary argument has much in common with religious discourse. Reading a literary argument, especially a good one on a familiar text, may be like hearing a sermon on a familiar theme. What is preached may not be really new, but it is brought home to us with an appropriate elegance, a liturgy of citations, special topoi, and carefully constructed ethos.

This comparison with religious discourse may be more than a passing metaphor. Literary criticism also keeps alive a traditional set of texts by subjecting them to continual exegesis, and literary scholars constitute a body of believers who welcome new members into their sect. There are, however, many doctrinal controversies among believers, many disputes about the canon, even to the point of reform movements and recusancy.

Finally, like any system of religious belief, literary criticism addresses the great metaphysical questions about the nature of reality, of humanity, of life, of society, of God. The articles we read raised large questions about matters of philosophic interest to their authors and intended readers: to what extent can faith encompass doubt? (Wolfson); how can literature express the desires of the weak? (Vicinus); how can art portray the complexity of creation? (Sherwin); how can human love be sustained? (Weinstein); and how can the intellectual hungers of women be satisfied? (Gelfant). Criticism may locate such questions in the literature it selects for discussion, but they are not therefore of less significance for the scholars who identify them and the audiences they address.

None of this emphasis on high seriousness or didactic content seems to take any account of pleasure as the end of literature; at least none of the articles we read ever mentioned the beauty or pleasing effects of the works under scrutiny, even of admired works. Yet the pleasure principle is not absent in criticism, just as it is not absent in religion. We might say it is simply transferred from the literature to the criticism, from the dogma to the ritual. For surely no activity could consume so much time, attention, and energy were it not in itself a pleasure.

Thus in the absence of other compelling systems of belief, literature and literary criticism can be a religion that we go to for the reaffirmation of values, for a sense of community, for intellectual stimulation — for all that religion can supply. The fulfillment of such human needs gives pleasure. Here then may be the best explanation for the ceremony of literary criticism. The process of discovering paradigms, paradoxes, ubiquitous elements, complexities, realities behind appearance, and our disdain for this world must be in itself a pleasure.

BIBLIOGRAPHY

Booth, Wayne. *Critical Understanding: The Powers and Limits of Pluralism.* Chicago: University of Chicago Press, 1979.

Byrd, Max. "Johnson's Spiritual Anxiety." *Modern Philology* 78 (1981): 368-78.

Carr, Stephen Leo, and Peggy A. Knapp. "Seeing through Macbeth." *PMLA* 96 (1981): 837-47.

Cicero. *De Inventione. De Optimo Genere Oratorum. Topica.* Loeb Classical Library. Cambridge: Harvard University Press, 1949.

Cox, Stephen D. "Adventures of 'A Little Boy Lost': Blake and the Process of Interpretation." *Criticism* (Fall 1981): 301-16.

Culler, Jonathan. "Literary Competence." In *Reader-Response Criticism: From Formalism to Post-Structuralism*, ed. Jane P. Tompkins. Baltimore: Johns Hopkins University Press, 1980.

Eagleton, Terry. *Literary Theory: An Introduction.* Minneapolis: University of Minnesota Press, 1983.

Embry, Thomas. "Sensuality and Chastity in *L'Allegro* and *Il Penseroso*." *JEGP* 77 (1978): 504-29.

Fahnestock, Jeanne, and Marie Secor. "Toward a Modern Version of Stasis Theory." In *Oldspeak/Newspeak: Rhetorical Transformations*, ed. Charles W. Kneupper, 217-26. Arlington, Tex.: Rhetoric Society of America, 1985.

Fahnestock, Jeanne, and Marie Secor. "The Stases in Scientific and Literary Argument." *Written Communication* 5 (October 1988): 427-43.

Falke, Anne. " 'The Work Well Done that Pleaseth All': Emanuel Forde and the Seventeenth-Century Popular Chivalric Romance." *Studies in Philology* 78 (1981): 241-54.

Fish, Stanley. *Is There a Text in This Class?* Cambridge: Harvard University Press, 1980.

Gelfant, Blanche. "Sister to Faust: The City's Hungry Woman as Heroine." *Novel* 15 (1981): 23-38.

Greenslade, William. "The Power of Advertising: Chad Newsome and the Meaning of Paris in *The Ambassadors*." *ELH* 49 (1982): 99-122.

Levin, Richard. *New Readings vs. Old Plays.* Chicago: University of Chicago Press, 1979.

Manley, Lawrence. "Concepts of Convention and Models of Critical Discourse." *New Literary History* 13 (1981): 31-52.

Merrill, Robert. "Another Look at the American Romance." *Modern Philology* 78 (1981): 379-92.

Miko, Stephen J. "Tempest." *ELH* 49 (1982): 1–17.

Nelson, Cary. "Reading Criticism." *PMLA* 91 (1976): 801–15.

Perelman, Chaim, and Lucie Olbrechts-Tyteca. *The New Rhetoric: A Treatise on Argument*. Notre Dame: University of Notre Dame Press, 1969.

Schauber, Ellen, and Ellen Spolsky. "Stalking a Generative Poetics." *New Literary History* 12 (1981): 397–413.

Schulman, Samuel E. "The Spenserian Enchantments of Wordsworth's 'Resolution and Independence.'" *Modern Philology* 79 (1981): 24–44.

Sherwin, Paul. "*Frankenstein*: Creation as Catastrophe." *PMLA* 96 (1981): 883–903.

Steig, Michael. "At the Back of *The Wind in the Willows*: An Experiment in Biographical and Autobiographical Interpretation." *Victorian Studies* 24 (1981): 303–23.

Swanson, Janice Bowman. "Toward a Rhetoric of Self: The Art of *Persuasion*." *Nineteenth-Century Fiction* 36 (1981): 1–21.

Toulmin, Stephen. "Logic and the Criticism of Arguments." In *The Rhetoric of Western Thought*, ed. James L. Golden, Goodwin F. Berquist, and William E. Coleman, 391–401. 3d ed. Dubuque: Kendall Hunt, 1978.

Vicinus, Martha. "'Helpless and Unfriended': Nineteenth-Century Domestic Melodrama." *New Literary History* 13 (1981): 127–43.

Weinstein, Arnold. "The Fiction of Relationship." *Novel* 15 (1981): 5–22.

Whigham, Frank. "The Rhetoric of Elizabethan Suitors' Letters." *PMLA* 96 (1981): 864–82.

Wilson, W. Daniel. "Readers in Texts." *PMLA* 96 (1981): 848–63.

Wolfson, Susan Jean. "The Speaker as Questioner in *Lyrical Ballads*." *JEGP* 77 (1978): 546–68.

Wright, George T. "Hendiadys and *Hamlet*." *PMLA* 96 (1981): 168–93.

4

THE MEDIEVAL ART OF

LETTER WRITING

RHETORIC AS

INSTITUTIONAL EXPRESSION

LES PERELMAN

Classical rhetoric, from the early Greek Sophists to Cicero and Quintilian, was solely concerned with oral rather than written discourse. In particular, most rhetorical treatises were almost completely limited to three specific types of speeches, each linked to three respective institutions: deliberative to the public assembly, epideictic to the public ceremony, and forensic to the law courts. Although these three forms accurately reflected the social responsibilities incumbent upon a free male of a Greek *polis*, they continued to dominate rhetorical theory long after the institutions that created them had either ceased to exist or had undergone fundamental changes. Thus deliberative rhetoric was taught both in schools and by tutors all during the period of the Roman Empire, even though the function of both the Roman Senate and local assemblies became severely limited, possessing relatively little actual power except in some specific local matters (Kennedy, *Art of Persuasion*, 22). Similarly, forensic rhetoric continued to be taught in Carolingian schools, despite the fact that the imperial law courts for which it was designed had vanished hundreds of years before.[1]

Although the writing of letters was common during the classical period, it never became a formal subject of discussion until its inclusion as a brief appendix in the fourth century A.D. rhetoric of C. Julius Victor. During the Middle Ages, however, the written letter became a central concern of rhetorical theory. Medieval society, in general, and medieval political structure, in particular, were not primarily urban. Consequently, unlike

97

Les Perelman

the classical *polis*, communication could not usually be conducted through oral, face-to-face encounters. Furthermore, as medieval ecclesiastical and secular bureaucracy grew, the earlier medieval collections of official and legal formulae proved insufficient to meet the administrative needs of institutions that functioned primarily through letters.

As a consequence, beginning in the eleventh century, there arose a whole genre of theoretical works concerned with the form and composition of the official letter, the *ars dictaminis*, or "art of letter writing." Although these works drew from classical rhetorical texts, they modified the earlier theory to meet both the ideological requirements of medieval institutions and the practical requirements of the epistolary form. They became, in a sense, an early prototype of the modern handbook on effective business writing. Moreover, the teaching and application of these manuals became almost universal in literate medieval culture, and the form and style they dictated became present in almost all types of letters, from the official pronouncements of popes to the letters of students.

The development of letter writing as a distinct and formal branch of rhetorical and political study was itself the product of historical circumstance. First, from A.D. 476 most of the area that had comprised the Western Roman Empire found itself ruled by monarchs who were nearly all illiterate. Educated Romans and churchmen had to be able, in the words of Cassiodorus, to speak and write the king's own words in the king's own presence (Murphy, *Rhetoric in the Middle Ages*, 197). Furthermore, the depopulation of urban centers that accompanied the breakup of the Roman Empire and the lack of any central capital for the Frankish monarchy made written communication one of the only mechanisms of control available to the Merovingian kings. Sending a letter, however, was an extremely expensive and unreliable undertaking. Since there was no regular postal service, each letter cost the services of the messenger hired to carry it, and complaints on the unreliability of professional couriers antedate contemporary complaints about the postal system by at least a millennia. One result of the expense and uncertainty connected with letter writing is that letters, especially letters in the early Middle Ages, became almost solely the domain of political and ecclesiastical discourse, giving them a more permanent and public character than they had either in antiquity or in more modern times (Constable, *Letters* 2:2–24).

Consequently, the institution of the Chancellor or Arch-Chancellor, chief of the *cancellarii* or scribes, evolved during the reign of the early Merovingian kings. The chancellor, rather than attached to a specific place, was a part of the king's household and moved with the king in his constant peregrinations between royal estates. From the reign of Louis the Pious, the post was held by a bishop, who, by virtue of the office, became the chief judicial and administrative secretary of the emperor. Soon almost all great officers and corporate bodies in Western Europe, both secular and ecclesiastical, employed a chancellor to supervise the production of official correspondence.

In the early Middle Ages, many of the letters were simply derived from prototypes that covered the majority of situations in which a written letter was needed. These collections of *formulae*, standardized statements capable of being duplicated in different circumstances, appear to have been quite common during the Merovingian period (Murphy, *Rhetoric*, 199), and a number of collections have survived (Giry; Zeumer). Essentially, these letters were similar to the blank forms of legal documents that attorneys still use today. A form from about A.D. 650 donating land to a monastery and then allowing the donors to use the gift during their lives without having to pay taxes on it — a practice that until recently was still a common method of tax avoidance in the United States — demonstrates the contractual and legal nature of such "letters":

> I, (name), and my wife, (name), in the name of the Lord, give by this letter of gift and transfer from our ownership to the ownership and authority of the monastery of (name), over which the venerable abbot (name) presides, and which was founded in the honor of (name) by (name) in the county of (name), the following villas (name), situated in the county of (name), with all the lands, houses, buildings, tenants, slaves, vineyards, woods. . . . We do this on the condition that as long as either of us shall live we may possess the aforesaid villas, without prejudice to the ownership of the monastery and without diminution of the value of them. . . . After the death of both of us, the aforesaid villas with any additions or improvements which may have been made, shall return immediately to the possession of said monastery and the said abbot and his successors, without undertaking any judicial process or obtaining the consent of the heirs. (Thatcher and McNeal, 345-46)

However, as the complexity of medieval political and administrative life grew, the form book was unable to provide documents that could cover all situations. As Murphy notes, "Even five hundred or a thousand *formulae* would probably not be enough to provide for the diverse demands of even a minor principality" (*Rhetoric in the Middle Ages*, 202).

The Development of the *Ars Dictaminis*

The solution, a rhetorical art specifically devoted to official correspondence, the *ars dictaminis*, developed in the eleventh century at the ancient Benedictine abbey of Monte Cassino, partially at the

Les Perelman

embryonic universities of Bologna, Salerno, and Pavia, and at the newly created Papal Chancery. Accompanying this new theory of composition was the appearance of a new genre of rhetorical manual, also called *ars dictaminis*, or, collectively, *dictamen*. Some scholars have attempted to attribute the creation of this new rhetorical genre to a specific individual and to a specific place. In the nineteenth century Ludwig Rockinger argued that the *ars dictaminis* was invented by Alberic of Monte Cassino (d. 1105) at the abbey, which was the first center where the genre was studied. In the 1950s Franz-Josef Schmale maintained that the genre originated with Adalbertus Samaritanus in Bologna between 1111 and 1118. However, in the late 1970s, William Patt offered convincing evidence to demonstrate that the *ars dictaminis* arose out of a widespread tradition which had been developing over centuries. Instead of asking "Who invented the *ars dictaminis*, and where?" he asserts, we should ask, "From what sources did this develop and by what process?" (135–36).[2]

One institution that directly influenced the development, formalization, and popularization of these conventional rhetorics of letter writing was the Papal Chancery. During the pontificate of John XVIII in the early eleventh century, the supervision of the production of letters passed from the office of the Librarian to a new official with the Frankish title of Chancellor, who, like his imperial counterpart, was personally attached to the ruler and traveled with him. The influence of the usages of the Frankish court on papal administration is also illustrated by the adoption in this period of the practice of writing papal documents in the imperial court hand, Caroline Minuscule, rather than in the older Roman Curial hand (Poole, 57–60).

The pontificate of Leo IX (1049–1054) firmly established the titles, forms, officials, and handwriting of the Imperial Chancery within the Papal Court (Poole, 67). By greatly increasing the output of papal correspondence, Leo IX, a cousin of the Emperor Conrad II, instituted a fundamental and lasting change in the nature of papal administration. The rise of centralized monarchies and the beginnings of the modern nation states of Western Europe in the eleventh century are paralleled in the reorganization of ecclesiastical government during the same period. Just as secular monarchs were developing administrative tools to lessen the power of feudal lords and impose royal authority upon them, so the revolution begun by Leo IX aimed to subordinate the power of local bishops to the absolute authority of the pope (Southern, 170). Leo's revival of papal authority was largely effected through three instruments: the system of papal legates (ambassadors endowed with papal authority), frequent church councils, and a virtual explosion of letters from the papal chancery. As Southern notes, "the two main characteristics of medieval government, whether secular or ecclesiastical, were these: the ruler was a dispenser of benefits, and he was a dispenser of justice" (111). Through legates, councils, and especially through an efficient chancery generating various types of papal correspondence, the papacy was able to dispense both benefits and justice more efficiently.

Papal letters became divided into two distinct categories: *Privileges* and *Letters*. Privileges were the instruments of a grant or confirmation of rights, property, and jurisdiction to churches and religious houses. Privileges were, in actuality, title deeds, and as such were carefully saved by their recipients as something of great value. Like modern deeds, such forms were highly conservative and tended to maintain the forms of Curial *formulae*. Privileges were indicated by two specific pictorial devices: the Rota, an amplified Cross in a circle with some writing in each quarter and a biblical quotation around the circumference, and the Monogram, which, adapted from the imperial monogram, appeared on the right hand of the document as a compression of the greeting *Bene Valete* (Poole, 105).

The pontifical letter was the instrument of the pope's administrative and judicial acts and was classified as *Tituli*, or Letters of Grace, and *Mandamenta*, or Letters of Justice (Poole, 115). *Tituli* were documents by which the pope granted or confirmed rights, licenses, or indulgences, conferred benefices, promulgated statutes, or decided points of canon law. Frequently, they fulfilled the same purpose which had in earlier times been effected by the Privilege.

Mandamenta, on the other hand, conveyed the pope's administrative orders concerning some specific issue, such as injunctions, prohibitions, appointment of commissioners, as well as the mass of official correspondence on both political and administrative matters (Poole, 117). At the beginning of the twelfth century, the number of *Mandamenta* issued by the chancery increased dramatically. To allow the bulk of these documents to be written and sealed by relatively low level chancery clerks, a standardized form, *in forma communi,* was developed from preexisting theories of letter writing and rhetoric in general. These standardized forms of papal letters, in turn, provided crucial models for the development and standardization of the *ars dictaminis*.

There is, however, even firmer evidence from which to infer a close connection between the rise of the Papal Chancery and the development of the formal teaching and practice of the art of letter writing. As mentioned previously, Alberic of Monte Cassino is credited with the first extant treatise on *ars dictaminis*. Alberic's pupil, John of Gaeta, served as papal chancellor for thirty years (1089–1118), before becoming Pope Gelasius II in 1118. Moreover, it was during this period that papal correspondence began to exhibit the *cursus*, an elaborate system of prose rhythm, that was often included as part of the *ars dictaminis*. A century later, Albert of Morra, the author of a dictaminal work that emphasized the cursus, the *Froman Dictandi*, was also chancellor to three successive popes and then became pope himself as Gregory VIII in 1187 (Poole, 79).[3]

Although the chancery was originally a secular invention, it was the papacy that refined that office and the techniques for the performance of its function: the efficient production of administrative letters, including the development of a standardized style of letter writing. In addition, the standardization of the forms of the official letter implicitly validated both the institutions and the institutional assumptions in which the discourse took place. In particular, as we shall see, the standardized form reinforced notions of social hierarchy, causing a writer not to ask first, "What am I going to say?" but instead, "What is the rank of the person to whom I am writing this letter?"

This standardized form for official correspondence grew to become a necessary component of the expansion of both the ecclesiastical and secular bureaucracies. As Denholm-Young notes (27), from the time of Innocent III, the system spread to almost all the chanceries of Western Europe, becoming the rule not only in the Imperial Chancery, but also in the chanceries of the bishops and princes of Germany, and the kingdoms of France, Sicily, Aragon, Castile, and, eventually, England.

Although the *ars dictaminis* was originally taught in monasteries and by independent teachers of rhetoric (*dictatores*), by the mid-eleventh century there was a sustained interest in the *ars dictaminis* in the schools of Pavia, Orleans, and Tours, and in such southern German monastic and cathedral schools as Bamberg, Speyer, Tegernsee, and Regensburg (Patt, 145). Because the teaching and practice of letter writing offered one of the few opportunities for access to the seats of power, the ecclesiastical and secular chanceries and courts, it soon became a regular part of the curriculum in cathedral and monastic schools, and later was taught in universities all over Europe. Although rival schools existed — very early on in the tradition, one Bologonese teacher not in religious orders urges his readers to "spurn the harsh, thorny, insoluble *dictamina*" of a monkish rival (Adalbertus, 51) — the basic content of teaching remained fairly constant. Quite possibly the stability of the form of the *ars dictaminis* was partially due to its being a practical art with real and ongoing connections to fairly conservative institutions such as the Papal Chancery. Because these institutions would tend to resist change in the way they conducted their business, we would expect that the rhetorical art which was primarily concerned with teaching individuals how to write within these institutions would exhibit comparatively little variation from teacher to teacher.

As stated earlier, however, the theory and practice of the art of letter writing did not arise *ex nihilo*, nor did it come into existence like Athena, fully grown and armored. Similar to the other institutions of the Middle

Ages, it did not appear as a new phenomenon at all, but as a continuation of classical culture. Although the *ars dictaminis* was responding to changing institutions and changing discourse situations — the growth of secular and ecclesiastical bureaucracies and the concomitant rise of bureaucratic forms of discourse — it did so by adapting one of the Middle Ages' most revered legacies from antiquity, classical rhetoric, particularly parts of Cicero's *De Inventione* and the *Rhetorica ad Herennium*, a work incorrectly attributed to Cicero throughout the Middle Ages.

The transition between the received forms and conventions of classical rhetoric and the emergence of the new rhetorical forms particular to the *ars dictaminis* is best illustrated by an examination of one of the works of Alberic of Monte Cassino, the eleventh-century monk generally credited as a founder of the genre. A teacher and scholar of the classical rhetorical texts at the oldest monastery in Western Europe, Alberic was perfectly situated to begin the teaching of a rhetoric of the official letter. From references in the monk's works to his discussions with his students, Murphy concludes "that Alberic's school at Monte Cassino was actively engaged in discussing the nature of letters" (*Rhetoric in the Middle Ages*, 207). Furthermore, the late eleventh century was the period of Monte Cassino's greatest political and ecclesiastical influence. Its abbot was the overlord of an extensive territory and bishop of several dioceses, and the most powerful of its abbots, Desiderius (1059–1086), was himself a man of letters and in 1086 became pope as Victor III.

At about the same time as the accession of Victor III to the papacy, Alberic wrote the *Flowers of Rhetoric (Flores Rhetorici)* also known as the *Glory of Composition (Dictaminum Radii)*.[4] Although much of the work emphasizes traditional rhetorical elements that are ignored by later dictaminal authors, it also provides a clear indication of what parts of classical rhetoric the new genre retained and expanded and what parts it discarded. It shows how rhetorical theory moved from the Ciceronian emphasis on the logical and legalistic dimension of a specific topic, the *logos*, to the elements concerned with the specific relationship between the writer and reader, *ethos* and *pathos*.

After an ornate introduction, Alberic presents Isadore of Seville's four-part division of a speech: *exordium, narratio, argumentatio,* and *conclusio.* This classification, of course, is a reduction of the seven-part division found in *De Inventione* and the six-part division of the *Ad Herennium.* Alberic then briefly explains the purpose of the *exordium*, the introduction, by quoting Cicero's famous dictum that it is to make the audience "well-disposed, attentive, and receptive" (36).[5] His treatment of the narration is equally brief and also equally derivative from Ciceronian rhetoric, largely consisting of a division of narrative into "high," "middle," and "low" forms. As we shall see, the use of this specific Ciceronian division is almost

Les Perelman

omnipresent in dictaminal works, although the exact form of their application varies widely. Alberic's treatment of argumentation is once more, abbreviated:

> Next comes the argument, which has a place in the course we would follow if we intend to strengthen our own position and weaken the position of our adversary. Yet it is important to note that this approach is not always and everywhere called for, but only when the subject in hand is one to which serious objections might be raised. . . . (*Flowers*, 139)

What is remarkable about Alberic's discussion of argument is not what he says, but what he doesn't say. Although he adapts parts of the *Ad Herennium* and *De Inventione* throughout the work, especially in his treatment of rhetorical figures, he ignores most of their discussion of techniques of argumentation, particularly the extremely lengthy discussion in both works of the theory of *status*, the complex discovery procedure designed to identify the specific issue or issues underlying any argument.

At this point, however, Alberic's work exhibits a feature particular to the emerging genre of the art of letter writing. Without having yet discussed the *conclusio*, he begins again to consider in order, the various parts of the letter, but he starts not with the exordium, but with a new element distinct from it, the *salutatio*. Although salutations usually consisting of the sender's name and the name of the addressee were a fairly common and fixed element in the classical letter, they had never before been included as an item of discussion in a rhetorical treatise. Alberic fits his discussion of the salutation into the received mold of the Aristotelian triad of speaker, subject, and audience, of *ethos, logos*, and *pathos*:

> First we must consider the identity of the sender and of the person to whom the letter is sent; we must consider whether he is noble or common in rank, a friend or an enemy, then what kind of person he is and of what background. The next consideration is the thing dealt with: is it a just or unjust matter, and is it serious or minor? Next the writer should ask himself what attitude he wishes to project: proud or humble, harsh or forgiving, threatening, flattering, stern, or that of a trusted friend. (*Flowers*, 138)

While this passage seeks to develop a rhetoric particular to the form of the letter, it still looks back to the traditional formulations of classical rhetorical theory designed for the law court and public assembly, of a rhetorical practice presupposing the need for persuasive discourse among equals. As we shall see, the treatment of the salutation expands to become the single largest topic in dictaminal teaching, recreating and redefining rhetorical theory to reflect both the social reality and the social ideology of the institutions in which it existed.

The rest of the *Flowers* has little to do with the specifics of letter writing, consisting instead of a discussion of some of the rhetorical figures of thought and diction listed in book 4 of the *Ad Herennium*, the major source of rhetorical tropes throughout the Middle Ages. There is, however, another extant work of Alberic's which bears on our subject: "The Outline of Composition" (*Breviarium de dictamine*). Unfortunately, of the three parts of the work, only two have been edited.[6] Furthermore, the preface clearly indicates that the work is not to be taken as a treatise in itself, but is meant as a supplement to oral discussion and other texts (Rockinger, 30). While the second and third parts are only tangentially related to letter writing, the first part of the text is clearly a discussion of the *ars dictaminis*. Although the treatment still lacks several of the structural elements that characterized later manuals, it does possess some of the major features of the genre. Alberic states that the beginnings of letters, that is, the salutation and the exordium, can be constructed in a variety of ways (33), and he gives a fairly long series of example salutations, a practice that becomes one of the most predominant features of subsequent treatises on letter writing. The next section, a discussion of the construction of papal Privileges and how they differ from other documents, provides further evidence for the connection between the development of the *ars dictaminis* and the continuing expansion of the Papal Chancery under Alberic's student, John of Gaeta.

Although Alberic does much to make letter writing a separate rhetorical discipline, his treatises are relatively unsystematic compilations of various elements of classical rhetoric haphazardly applied to the specific task of composing official epistles. The *Lessons in Letter Writing (Precepta dictaminum)* of Adalbertus Samaritanus, on the other hand, is a work that, in both theoretical and practical terms, is entirely devoted to the writing of letters. Completed by 1115 (Constable, "Structure," 254), this work delineates the rules for salutations in great detail. Adalbertus, for example, seems to be the first to establish the rule that in a salutation the name of the more exalted person precede that of the inferior.

Adalbertus explicitly divides letters along the traditional Ciceronian threefold scheme, calling the high style, the "exalted" (*sublimis*), the middle style, the "medium" (*mediocris*), and the low, the "meager" (*exilis*). As Constable points out ("Structure," 254), his division is not based on the styles themselves, as with Cicero or Alberic in the *Breviarium*, nor is it based on the subject matter, like Alberic's division of narratives. Instead, Adalbertus uses the relative social position of the writer and reader as his central criterion:

> Exalted letters are written from a lesser person to a greater one
> and are called exalted for two reasons. It ascends from an inferior
> to a superior and it is comprised of three characteristics: 1) flattery
> in the beginning, 2) the cause of the flattery in the middle, and
> 3) a request at the end. (33)

Similarly, the meager style is written from a superior to an inferior and
is called meager, according to Adalbertus, because it descends from the
superior person to the inferior one and only contains the single feature
of a request or a command. Finally, the medium style is called such because it neither ascends or descends and thus belongs between the other
two types. In addition, it contains two features: one instance of flattery
and a request.

Although the rest of Adalbertus' work consists primarily of sample
salutations and sample letters, his taxonomy continues to develop the
dictaminal obsession with social rank. Whereas classical rhetoric always
appeared, at least, to give precedence to logical argument as a means of
persuasion, the rhetorical theory of the *ars dictaminis* seems to recognize
hierarchical social relationships as the principle element of communication, reflecting a fundamental change in both rhetorical practice and the
social organization which underlies it. In contrast to Ciceronian rhetoric's
presupposition of communication among equals and its consequent reliance on persuasion, the medieval arts of letter writing presuppose a world
of hierarchical social relationships and thus reflect the bureaucracies which
created them. The chanceries, both imperial and papal, owed their very
existence to the respective secular and ecclesiastical hierarchies in which
they existed. Their function was not to convince, but to command, to
dispense benefits, and to execute judgment.

Although the emphasis on developing a coherent scheme for analyzing
and classifying both salutations and letters as a whole remains a constant
feature of these works, the exact models and the terminology vary greatly.
Some subsequent reworkings of Adalbertus, for example, reverse his distinctions, as does this taxonomy of letters from an unedited mid-twelfth-
century compilation cited by Constable:

> As there are three orders of persons, so there are three principal
> types of letters: humble, middling and exalted. A humble letter is
> one sent by a humble person, such as oxherds, cobblers and
> tanners and others who have no lower order beneath them. An
> exalted letter is one sent by an exalted person, as by a pope or
> emperor. An exalted person is one than who there is no higher
> dignity, as is the pope in ecclesiastical affairs [and] the emperor in
> secular affairs. A middling person is one who is between exalted
> and humble, such as tetrarchs, kings, marquises, counts, dukes,

archbishops, captains, vavasors, vidames, and others who are between exalted and humble. ("Structure," 255)

Thus the determinant for classification of letters is no longer the relative social position of the writer and reader, but only the social position of the writer. With the further evolution of the genre, the exact distinctions within these taxonomic systems remained fairly fluid, although the three-part division was always maintained, with the noted exception of Peter of Blois ("Structure," 260).

As the twelfth century progressed, the number of dictaminal works increased. Two in particular — *The Principles of Prose Letter Writing (Rationes dictandi prosaice)* of Hugh of Bologna (c. 1119–1124) and the anonymous *The Principles of Letter Writing (Rationes dictandi)* (c. 1135) — helped to establish in Bologna a basic doctrine, what Murphy calls the "Bolognese 'Approved Format'" (*Rhetoric in the Middle Ages*, 224–25). A modified version of Murphy's table comparing the format presented in *The Principles of Letter Writing* with the Ciceronian six-part oration provides a vivid illustration of the movement of the *ars dictaminis* away from a rhetoric of persuasion toward a rhetoric of personal relationship:[7]

Table 4.1. Comparative Structure of Ciceronian and Dictaminal Rhetoric

Ciceronian Parts of an Oration	Bolognese "Approved Format"
1. Exordium	1. Salutation
	2. *Captatio benevolentiae*, securing of good will.
2. Narrative	3. Narrative
3. Division	(Omitted)
4. Proof	(Omitted)
(Omitted)	4. Petition, presentation of requests
5. Refutation	(Omitted)
6. Conclusion	5. Conclusion

Ciceronian Referential Rhetoric versus Dictaminal Phatic Rhetoric

Closely connected with the Ciceronian division of the oration is the Aristotelian communication model of speaker, subject, and audience. Each part of the Ciceronian oration is normally directed at one or at most two of the Aristotelian elements. Thus, the *Exordium* is primarily aimed at the audience, while the division is associated primarily with the subject. The Aristotelian model, however, while extremely useful, is limited and static. Each point of the triad is presented as sufficient in itself. Thus, in the Aristotelian model *pathos*, appeal to the interests and emotions of the audience, is presented as a mode of development completely distinct from *ethos*, appeal to the authority and character of the speaker, even though the two actions are often completely intertwined. For example, a defendant in a court of law can sometimes produce pity in the jury simply by convincing them of his or her naïveté.

In the twentieth century, Roman Jakobson expands Aristotle's paradigm into a more dynamic model by transforming the concepts of speaker, audience, and subject, into addresser, addressee, and context, and adding the additional elements of message, contact, and code. This expanded model provides a richer theoretical framework on which to establish the essential difference between Ciceronian and dictaminal rhetoric. To Jakobson, each of his communicative elements has the corresponding language function given in table 4.2:

Table 4.2. Jakobson's Communication Model

Element	Function
Addresser	Emotive
Addressee	Conative
Context	Referential
Message	Poetic
Contact	Phatic
Code	Metalingual

Although we could simply state in Aristotelian terms that the rhetorical stance implied in the Bolognese format is more oriented toward the audience than it is toward the subject, Jakobson's scheme provides us with a much more precise terminology by which to define the essential differences of the two rhetorical practices. In particular, we can characterize Ciceronian rhetoric as transmitted through *De Inventione* and the pseudo-Ciceronian *Rhetorica ad Herennium* as primarily referential, concerned with contexts and subjects external to the specific relationship and specific linguistic interaction between addresser and addressee. While classical theories of persuasion and their subsidiary constructs of the enthymeme and example are often concerned with both the emotional state and unstated assumptions held by an audience, classical rhetoric, especially in the abridged form by which it was transmitted in the Middle Ages, had as its central goal persuading an audience to take a specific position about some matter external to the immediate relationship of addresser to addressee.

The rhetorical practice outlined in the standardized Bolognese format of the dictaminal manuals, on the other hand, can be characterized as primarily Phatic, concerned with establishing and maintaining the communication channel, "to attract the attention of the interlocutor or to confirm his continued attention." (Jakobson, 92)

In fact, the elements of the classical oration omitted in the "Approved Format" are precisely those that are most concerned with the referential function of communication, the concentration on the external subject encoded in the message. Cicero in *De Inventione* (1.22.31) defines *Partitio*, Division, as taking:

> . . . two forms, both of which greatly contribute to clarifying the case and determining the nature of the controversy. One form shows in what we agree with our opponents and what is left in dispute; as a result of this some definite problem is set for the auditor on which he ought to have his attention fixed. In the second form the matters which we intend to discuss are briefly set forth in a methodical way. This leads the auditor to hold definite points in his mind, and to understand that when these have been discussed the oration will be over. (63)

Although Cicero's definition includes the auditor, it is only in terms of enhancing the auditor's comprehension of the subject matter at hand, and thus the central function of the division is clearly referential. Similarly, his proof and refutation coincide with what Jakobson defines as referential language functions. Cicero defines proof in *De Inventione* (1.24.34) as, "the part of an oration which by the marshalling of arguments lends credit, authority, and support to our case" (69), and refutation (1.42.78) as, "that part of an oration in which arguments are used to impair, disprove, or weaken the confirmation or proof of our opponent's speech" (123). Reflecting the primarily forensic tradition from which they derive, both *De Inventione* and the *Ad Herennium* devote the largest part of their discussion to the various forms and types of effective arguments for any given case, that is, to the theory of *status*.

Of the three remaining elements of the Ciceronian oration, both the narrative and the conclusion contain referential and nonreferential elements. The narrative, according to *De Inventione* (1.19.27), "is an exposition of events that have occurred or are supposed to have occurred" (55), and thus clearly refers to an external context. Cicero goes on, however, to give three species of narration: (1) narratives directly related to the principal subject of the oration; (2) narratives tangentially related to the subject and told to attack an opponent, make a comparison, or amuse the audience in a way connected with the subject; and (3) narratives unconnected with the subject but told for amusement. In terms of Jakobson's model, then, the first type of narrative is purely referential; the second type can be viewed as referential, conative, in that it seeks to produce a specific effect on the addressee, and poetic, in that the message is functioning for its own sake; the third type is purely poetic. Similarly, the three parts of the Ciceronian conclusion, the summing up of the important points of the argument, the development of hostility in the audience toward an opponent, and the arousing of pity and sympathy in the audience, contain both referential and conative functions.

The only element of the Ciceronian oration that is primarily phatic, that is, whose main focus is on the actual contact between the addresser and the addressee, is the *exordium*. Cicero's famous definition of its function to make the audience "well-disposed, attentive, and receptive" (*Inventione*, 41) clearly indicates the *exordium*'s phatic function. Although making the audience "well-disposed" may also involve the conative function, "attentive" and "receptive" confirm that the primary function of this element is to establish and maintain the communication channel between the addresser and addressee.

The phatic and conative functions of language dominate almost all the elements of the "Approved Format" of the anonymous Bolognese *Principles of Letter Writing*. As mentioned previously, the function of the classical *exordium* is divided into two separate parts, the salutation and the securing of good will. "The Salutation," states *The Principles*, "is an expression of greeting conveying a friendly sentiment not inconsistent with the social rank of the person involved" (7). Thus the function of the salutation is primarily phatic; it is only referential in that it conveys specific information about the relative and absolute social ranks of the writer and addressee.

As with most dictaminal works, the discussion of the salutation occupies the largest part of the *Principles of Letter Writing*, in this particular case almost half of the entire work and slightly more than half if we include the accompanying section on "The Securing of Good Will," with which it overlaps. Among its many prescriptions are fairly rigid rules for referring to the writer and the recipient:

> . . . we must consider carefully how to place somewhere in the
> Salutation some additions to the names of the recipient, above all,
> these additions should be selected so that they point to some
> aspect of the recipient's renown and good character.
>
> Now, if we want to add something to the names of the senders,
> let it at least be made suitable, since it should be chosen to indi-
> cate humility and certainly not pride. . . . for example, if it is a
> clerk or someone of ecclesiastical status, he should always be
> titled thus: "Johannes, clerk" or "deacon" or "bishop" or "abbot,"

"although unworthy" or "undeserving" or "sinful." In secular positions or offices, of course, it is not necessary for it to be done in this way, if we say for instance "N——, friend of the Tuscans," or "N——, Duke of Venice," or "Marshall of Tusca," and the like. (*Practice*, 8).

The treatise then goes on to state some other considerations necessary to formulating a proper salutation. A letter writer, for example, must consider whether the letter is for one person or several. Additional considerations include, of course, the relative social position of the author and recipient. As in other manuals, if the recipient of is of higher rank, his name should precede that of the sender. Another important factor mentioned is knowledge of the exact titles and terms associated with each rank. The author also includes a one-sentence statement that the subject matter should be examined, "so that the writer may fashion the salutation with words suitable and prescribed according to it" (10). The consideration of subject matter is briefly alluded to again at the end the long discussion of salutations in reference to how a salutation would be modified in a letter of reprimand. Between these two references to subject matter, however, are hundreds of lines of edited text giving examples of salutations from an emperor to a pope, their respective universal salutations, salutations of lay clergy and monks among themselves, salutations of ecclesiastical prelates to their subordinates, salutations among nobels and princes, salutations of the lower nobility among themselves, salutations of the lower nobility to their subordinates, salutations from a teacher to his student and from a student to his teacher, and salutations from parents to their children and children to their parents.

The next part of the "Approved Format," the *captatio benevolentiae*, the Securing of Good Will, is defined as a "certain fit ordering of words effectively influencing the mind of the recipient" (16). Five ways of securing good will are then briefly mentioned: (1) the author of the letter humbly stating his achievements, duties, or motives in writing the letter; (2) further praise of the recipient; (3) the author both stating his achievements and praising the recipient; (4) reference to the relationship between the author and recipient; or (5) reference to the subject (18–19). For *exordia* to hostile audiences, a short and oblique reference is made to the "indirect approach," *ephodos*, a technique explained in great length in both the *Ad Herennium* and *De Inventione*. The author concludes the discussion of the securing of good will by stating that much of this function is actually performed in the salutation and presents even more sample salutations.

The discussion of the narrative is extremely brief, stating that it should be short, that some narratives only narrate one incident and others recount several different events, and that narratives can be divided into those that narrate the past, those that narrate the present, and those that narrate the future.

Like the discussion of narrative, the discussion of the petition is fairly limited and perfunctory in its division of petitions into several species. Underlying this classification, however, is a scheme that once again reinforces the primacy of social hierarchy and personal relationships over any notion of reasoned argument. *The Principles of Letter Writing* gives nine classes of petition: supplicating (*deprecatiua*), explicating (*preceptiua*), threatening (*conminatiua*), inciting (*exhortatoria*), encouraging (*hortatoria*), admonishing (*ammonitoria*), advising (*consultoria*), censuring (*correptoria*), and the absolute *absoluta*, which is defined as "when we ask that something be done in none of these ways, but only by indicating it directly" (19). In the terminology of speech act theory, the petition is clearly what both Searle (13) and Bach and Harnish (47–49) term directives, and what Searle defines as "attempts . . . by the speaker to get the hearer to do something." Some of the types of petition are clearly distinct. Supplicating, for example, presupposes that the writer has no control over the act being requested and that its performance is completely at the whim of the reader of the letter. Threatening, on the other hand, is explicitly connected in *The Principles of Letter Writing* with the writer's social power:

> It is menacing, when we do it with threats; after all, someone's official office is in a sense a threat, as for instance when a bishop sends a message to admonish one of his subordinates under the force of his office, or when some lord addresses a slave under threat of cutting out his eyes or head or his right hand, and the like. (*Principles*, 19)

With explicating, we come the closest to the classical logical argument. Authority is again invoked, but in this case it is the authority of precepts, of the teaching of *authors*, that is used by the writer of a letter to have his audience perform or not perform a certain act. The ninth and last type of petition, the absolute, seems to indicate a directive where no social position or moral precepts are employed to influence the reader. The writer of the letter is merely expressing an attitude toward some prospective action by the recipient.

The distinctions informing the other classes are certainly less straightforward. The semantic differentiation I have made between *exhortatoria* as "inciting" and *hortatoria* as "encouraging" is largely arbitrary. Both terms, however, indicate a strong attachment on the part of the writer toward the action to be performed by the recipient as well as some specific social right to offer the counsel, and in this way they reaffirm the constant presence of both personal and hierarchical relationships between writer and recipient. Somewhat similarly, both *ammonitoria* and *correptoria* imply the privilege of the writer of a letter to judge negatively the actions of the addressee, whatever the exact distinction may be between them.

Thus in addition to signifying a hierarchical dimension, also implicit in these latter categories is the clear indication of a personal bond between the writer and reader. Advising, admonishing, and censuring all display a personal concern on the part of the writer for the actions of the reader that goes far beyond today's official IRS form letter. Similarly, although the discussion of the conclusion in *The Principles of Letter Writing* first points to a referential function — "[the conclusion] is offered to point out the usefulness or disadvantages possessed by the subjects treated in the letter" (*Principles*, 19) — the examples offered soon make it clear that the advantages and disadvantages being discussed will usually refer to the personal attitude of the writer toward the recipient. "If you do this," states one example, "you will have the entirety of our fullest affection," and the other offers, "If you fail to do this you will without doubt lose our friendship" (*Principles*, 19).

The almost exclusive focus of the dictaminal manuals on the relationship between writer and reader and their devaluation of the classical tradition of rhetorical argumentation is in part, of course, due to the medieval feudal notions of hierarchy and personal service. But such an explanation, although certainly relevant, is by itself overly simplistic. The other two major rhetorical genres of the Middle Ages, the *Ars poetriae* (the Art of Poetry), and the *Ars praedicandi* (the Art of Preaching), did not so completely ignore such large parts of Cicero and of classical rhetoric in general.[8] The art of poetry, for example, made ample use of the figures of both diction and thought found in book 4 of the *Ad Herennium*, and the art of preaching adapted many of the invention techniques found in both the *Ad Herennium* and *De Inventione*. One possible explanation is simply the institutional context from which the *ars dictaminis* derived. Unlike the medieval pulpits, the function of both imperial and papal chanceries was not to convince, but to command. Similarly, the communications which these bureaucracies received were more dependent upon the reader's good will than they were upon any expertise in argumentation.

The formulaic rhetoric of personal relations taught by the *ars dictaminis* thrived throughout the Middle Ages and pursued several distinct avenues of development. Around 1300, Lawrence of Aquilegia, a successful traveling teacher of the *ars dictaminis*, wrote a treatise, *The Practice and Exercise of Letter Writing* (*Practica sive usus dictaminis*), which brought to its logical conclusion the tendency in the genre of making the act of writing a letter an automatic procedure. At the same time, however, it was

Les Perelman

still reminiscent of the *formulae* from which the *ars dictaminis* had evolved. Rather than being a formal treatise at all, the *Practica* is a series of seven charts, allowing one to compose a letter simply by making a set of choices from various menus. Thus in composing a letter to a pope, one would select the appropriate salutation, copy the connective phrases and then select an appropriate narration and petition from those offered, copy another connective phrase, and then select an appropriate conclusion from another list.

The techniques of letter writing underwent changes less radical but still as interesting as Lawrence of Aquilegia's mechanistic dead end. Like many other communicative conventions, the medieval letter became a fairly conservative form, maintaining dictaminal characteristics in contexts far removed from the chanceries that had created it. As Wieruszowski notes, the basic structure of the manuals was prominent in Northern Italy in the age of Dante, even though the examples became somewhat modified to reflect the social reality of the Italian city-state. An amusing example of how the forms of the *ars dictaminis* migrated into other areas of medieval life is found in the collections of letters to and from medieval students. Haskins has edited and translated some interesting examples that demonstrate how the Bolognese "Approved Format" even structured communication between parents and children. Since the *ars dictaminis* was part of the curriculum at most schools, students applied what they learned to their own pragmatic concerns. A twelfth-century letter from two brothers at school in Orleans to their parents on the theme, still common today, of asking for additional funds provides an excellent illustration of the use of the basic structure:

> To their very dear and respected parents M. Martre, knight, and M. his wife, M. and N., their sons, send greetings and filial obedience. This is to inform you that, by divine mercy, we are living in good health in the city of Orleans and are devoting ourselves wholly to study, mindful of the words of Cato, "To know anything is praiseworthy," etc. We occupy a good and comely dwelling, next door but one to the schools and market-place, so that we can go to school every day without wetting our feet. We have also good companions in the house with us, well advanced in their studies and of excellent habits — an advantage which we as well appreciate, for as the Psalmist says, "With an upright man thou wilt show thyself upright," etc. Wherefore lest production cease from lack of material, we beg your paternity to send us by the bearer, B., money for buying parchment, ink, a desk, and the other things which we need, in sufficient amount that we may suffer no want on your account (God forbid!) but finish our studies and return home with honor. The bearer will also take

charge of the shoes and stockings which you have to send us, and any news as well. (17–18)

Even though the narration is slightly longer than most and the letter lacks a formal conclusion, the general requirements of the formulaic letter are met. The salutation and securing of good will reaffirm the prescribed relationship between children and their parents. The narration and the use of precepts are also used to put the recipients in a more receptive frame of mind for the petition, the request for additional funds.

Another letter collected by Haskins, this time from a father rebuking his son, provides an example of even more faithful adherence to the structure of the "Approved Format":

> To his son G. residing at Orleans, P. of Besançon sends greetings with paternal zeal. It is written, "He also that is slothful in his work is brother to him that is a great waster." I have recently discovered that you live dissolutely and slothfully, preferring license to restraint and play to work and strumming a guitar while the others are at their studies, whence it happens that you have read but one volume of law while your more industrious companions have read several. Wherefore I have decided to exhort you herewith to repent utterly of your dissolute and careless ways, that you may no longer be called a waster and that your shame may be turned to good repute. (15–16)

Some of the later treatments of the *ars dictaminis* sought to reestablish a connection between the art of letter writing and argumentative tradition of classical rhetoric. This tradition was strongest in France, where, Murphy surmises, "it helped to keep rhetorical interest alive during a period when Cicero's politically oriented rhetoric was simply not acceptable" (*Rhetoric in the Middle Ages*, 267). What appears to be the most comprehensive reinclusion of Ciceronian doctrine is the unedited *Compendium rhetorice*, summarized by Murphy. The *Compendium* seems to add a fairly extensive treatment of invention techniques to the traditional approach of the Bolognese "Approved Format" (*Rhetoric in the Middle Ages*, 236). In fifteenth-century England, though, a more traditional reliance on the legacy of the dictamen provided part of the basis of the rise of business writing in English (Richardson, "Business Writing and the Spread of Literacy in Late Medieval England," and "First Century of English Business Writing").

The *ars dictaminis*, then, stands as an early example of the development of an applied, as opposed to a theoretical, rhetoric. Yet Murphy's claim, in the conclusion to his excellent chapter on the genre in *Rhetoric in the Middle Ages*, that it is a rare example of an applied rhetoric (268)

Les Perelman

ignores the reality that forensic rhetoric in the classical period was itself very much a practical rhetoric, and that much of the hostility and ambivalence over rhetoric found in Greek philosophy from Socrates onwards stem from the hostility over the Sophistic tradition of rhetoric as largely a practical technique for delivering effective speeches in law courts. Still, as a pragmatic rhetorical form, the *ars dictaminis* stands both as the first discernible ancestor of the modern manual of business communication and as a unique rhetorical tradition that transformed the complex rhetorical traditions of the classical period with their emphasis on persuasion into a phatic rhetoric of personal and official relations.

NOTES

I wish to thank the Writing Program of the Massachusetts Institute of Technology for a Research Affiliation, during which this study was completed.

1. For a lengthy example of how the rules of the Roman law court still provided much of the basis of rhetorical training even though these rules were largely irrelevant to actual legal procedures under the Frankish kings, see Alcuin of York's *Disputatio de rhetorica et de virtutibus* in Howell, 66–155.

2. Although I disagree with Murphy's emphasis on how individuals rather than institutions influenced the development of the *ars dictaminis,* throughout this paper, I draw heavily on his chapter on the genre in *Rhetoric in the Middle Ages.*

3. Murphy, *Rhetoric in the Middle Ages,* 250, notes that the *Froman Dictandi* has never been edited.

4. Murphy in "Alberic of Monte Cassino," 139, argues that the latter title is more correct.

5. Compare Alberic's "eius dico quibus capitur benevolentia, docilitas, attentio," with Cicero, *De Inventione,* 40, "quod eveniet si eum benivolum, attentum, docilem confecerit."

6. Rockinger (29–46) edits the first of the three sections under the incorrect title of *De dictamine* (see Murphy, *Rhetoric in the Middle Ages,* 207n). The third section has been edited by Davis.

7. Rather than give the terms in Latin, I have, except for *captatio benevolentiae,* translated them into English. In addition, I have reversed Murphy's order of *Divisio* and *Narratio,* since Narrative precedes Division in both *De Inventione* and in the *Ad Herennium.* For reasons I will give below, I do not equate the Ciceronian *Confirmatio* with the dictaminal *Petitio.*

8. For a much fuller discussion of this topic, especially in terms of the *ars poetriae,* see Gallo.

BIBLIOGRAPHY

Alberic of Monte Cassino. *Breviarium de dictamine*. In Rockinger, 29–46.
Alberic of Monte Cassino. *Flores Rhetorici*. Ed. D. M. Inguanez and E. H. M. Willard. Montecassino: Miscellanea Cassinese, 1938.
Alberic of Monte Cassino. *Flowers of Rhetoric*. Trans. Joseph M. Miller. In *Readings in Medieval Rhetoric*, ed. Joseph M. Miller, Michael H. Prosser, and Thomas W. Benson. Bloomington: Indiana University Press, 1973.
Adalbertus Samaritanus. *Praecepta dictaminum*. Ed. Franz-Josef Schmale. Quellen zur Geistesgeschichte des Mittelalters 3 Weimar: Hermann Bohlaus Nachfolger, 1961.
Bach, Kent, and Robert M. Harnish. *Linguistic Communications and Speech Acts*. Cambridge: MIT Press, 1979.
Cassiodorus Senator. *Institutiones*. Ed. Roger A. B. Mynors. Oxford: Oxford University Press, 1963.
Cicero, Marcus Tullius. *De Inventione*. Ed. and Trans. H. M. Hubbell. Loeb Classical Library 386. Cambridge: Harvard University Press, 1976.
Constable, Giles. "The Structure of Medieval Society According to the *Dictarores* of the Twelfth Century." In *Law, Church, and Society: Essays in Honor of Stephan Kuttner*, ed. Kenneth Pennington and Robert Sommerville, 253–67. Philadelphia: University of Pennsylvania Press, 1977.
Constable, Giles, ed. *The Letters of Peter the Venerable*. 2 vols. Cambridge: Harvard University Press, 1967.
Davis, Hugh H. "The *De rithmis* of Alberic of Monte Cassino: A Critical Edition." *Medieval Studies* 28 (1966): 198–227.
Denholm-Young, N. "The Cursus in England." In *Collected Papers on Medieval Subjects*, 26–45. Oxford: Basil Blackwell, 1946.
Gallo, Ernest. *The* Poetria Nova *and Its Sources in Early Rhetorical Doctrine*. The Hague: Mouton, 1971.
Giry, A. *Manuel de diplomatique*. New ed. Paris: F. Alcan, 1925.
Haskins, Charles Homer. *The Renaissance of the Twelfth Century*. Cambridge: Harvard University Press, 1927.
Haskins, Charles Homer. *Studies in Medieval Culture*. Oxford: Oxford University Press, 1929.
Howell, Wilbur S., ed. and trans. *The Rhetoric of Alcuin and Charlemagne*. Princeton: Princeton University Press, 1941.
Hugh of Bologna. *Rationes dictandi prosaice*. In Rockinger, 52–94.
Isadore of Seville. *Etymologiae*. Ed. Wallace M. Lindsay. 2 vols. Oxford: Oxford University Press, 1911.
Jakobson, Roman. "Closing Statement: Linguistics and Poetics." In *Style in Language*, ed. Thomas A. Sebeok, 330–77. Cambridge: MIT Press, 1960.

Les Perelman

Julius Victor. *Ars rhetorica*. In *Rhetores latini minores*, ed. Karl von Halm, 371–448. Leipzig: Teubner, 1863.

Kennedy, George. *The Art of Persuasion in Greece*. Princeton: Princeton University Press, 1963.

Kennedy, George. *Greek Rhetoric Under Christian Emperors*. Princeton: Princeton University Press, 1983.

Lanham, Carol Dana. Salutatio *Formulas in Latin Letters to 1200: Syntax, Style, and Theory*. Münchener Beitrage zur Mediavistik und Renaissance-Forschung 22. Munich: Arbeo-Gesellschaft, 1975.

Lawrence of Aquilegia. *Practica sive usus dictaminis*. In Rockinger, 956–66.

LeClercq, Jean. "Le Genre épistolaire au moyen âge." *Revue du moyen âge latin* 2 (1946): 63–70.

Murphy, James J. "Alberic of Monte Cassino: Father of the Medieval *Ars Dictaminis*." *American Benedictine Review* 22 (1971): 129–46.

Murphy, James J. *Rhetoric in the Middle Ages*. Berkeley and Los Angeles: University of California Press, 1974.

Murphy, James J., ed. *Three Medieval Rhetorical Arts*. Berkeley and Los Angeles: University of California Press, 1971.

Patt, William D. "The Early 'Ars Dictaminis' as a Response to a Changing Society." *Viator* 9 (1978): 133–55.

Poole, Reginald Lane. *Lectures on the History of the Papal Chancery*. Cambridge: Cambridge University Press, 1915.

The Principles of Letter Writing. Trans. James J. Murphy. In Murphy, *Three Medieval Rhetorical Arts*, 5–25.

Rationes dictandi. In Rockinger, 9–28.

Rhetorica ad Herennium. Ed and trans. Harry Caplan. Loeb Classical Library 403. Cambridge: Harvard University Press, 1981.

Richardson, Malcolm. "Business Writing and the Spread of Literacy in Late Medieval England." In *Studies in the History of Business Writing*, ed. George H. Douglas and Herbert W. Hildebrandt, 1–9. Urbana, Ill.: Association for Business Communication, 1985.

Richardson, Malcolm. "The First Century of English Business Writing, 1417–1525." In *Studies in the History of Business Writing*, ed. George H. Douglas and Herbert W. Hildebrandt, 23–44. Urbana, Ill.: Association for Business Communication, 1985.

Rockinger, Ludwig. *Briefsteller und Formulbücher des eilften bis vierzehnten Jahrhundrets*. 1863. New York: B. Franklin, 1961.

Schmale, Franz-Josef. "Die Bologneser der *Ars dictandi*." *Deutches Archiv* 13 (1957): 16–34.

Searle, John R. "A Taxonomy of Illocutionary Acts." *Expression and Meaning: Studies in the Theory of Speech Acts*, 1–29. Cambridge: Cambridge University Press, 1979.

Southern, R. W. *Western Society and the Church in the Middle Ages*. Harmondsworth, Eng.: Penguin, 1970.

Thatcher, Oliver, and Edgar McNeal. *A Source Book for Medieval History*. New York: Scribner's, 1905.

Wieruszowski, Helene. "*Ars dictaminis* in the Time of Dante." In *Politics and Culture in Medieval Spain and Italy*, 359–78. Rome: Edizioni di Storia e Letteratura (no. 171), 1959.

Zeumer, Karl, ed. *Formulae merowingici et karolini aevi*. Monumenta Germaniae Historica, Legum 5. Hanover: Hahn, 1886.

5

THE ROLE OF

NARRATIVE STRUCTURE

IN THE TRANSFER OF IDEAS

THE CASE STUDY

AND MANAGEMENT THEORY

ANN HARLEMAN STEWART

The case study report — which I will call simply the case study — constitutes a special form of scientific and technical writing. It is widely used but not well understood. Intuitively we know that a case study communicates information and that it is a kind of story. But how does it communicate? And what kind of a story is it?

Discourse analysis offers a methodology that reveals the linguistic and textual strategies employed by the case study and allows us to formulate explicitly the conception of it that we hold intuitively. This essay examines the case study as discourse — as the text involved in an act of communication that takes place within a particular speech community. I have chosen to examine the case study as it is used in teaching management theory. Illustrative texts come from casebooks in the field, selected in consultation with Boston University School of Management faculty, which show a representative range of subject matter, pedagogical principles, and style.

A discourse analytical approach, by its very nature, demands particularization: unless the context is fully specified, it is impossible to view a text as discourse. Hence the analysis here focuses on one particular kind of case study used in one particular kind of activity. It is offered as a model for a discourse analytical approach to the case study in other areas. I will look first at the functions of the management case study within its communicative context; then I will consider its form — its structure as a narrative text — and the ways in which that form serves its functions.

Functions of the Case Study

Harvard Business School is generally credited with the invention of the case study method of teaching; certainly it is identified with that method today (Christensen, 7). In 1910, Harvard instructor Copeland was advised by Dean Gay to augment his lectures with student discussion, which then began to revolve around cases; by 1921, Copeland had published the first collection of cases intended for use in teaching (Leenders and Erskine, 12). These cases and the many that followed tell the story of actual problems met, explored, and resolved. They translate theory into practice. "Instinctively," says Roland Christensen, generally acknowledged as the method's greatest exponent, "the faculty may well have seen the case method as a bridge between the classroom and the realities of business practice" (7).

The management case study teaches theory by fulfilling two functions: (1) illustration (translating from the abstract to the concrete), and (2) socialization (conveying the paradigm that governs the theory's application).

ILLUSTRATION

A case study attempts to show what a problem actually looks like (Reynolds, 53), so as to provide material for a specific application of theoretical principles. Two properties make a case study effective in rendering the abstract concrete. A good case study is, first of all, specific. The more concrete details, the better: names, places, time, objects, events — all these contribute to specificity.

> Paul is 42 years old, married with two teenage daughters, and lives comfortably in Hinsdale, Illinois, comfortably as a classical musician's salary will allow that is. Besides his position as third violinist at the symphony, he gives private lessons in his home and teaches music at a nearby college. (Glueck, 183)

Details accumulate, building up a densely textured picture. The reader begins to see a particular situation — in this case, the violinist Paul Anyon at a particular stage in his career.

Second, an effective case study is realistic. Proponents of the case method of teaching have called the case study "a chunk of reality . . .

brought into the classroom," a "snapshot of reality" (Lawrence, 215), a "slice of life" (Erskine et al., 12). Realism means including facts that don't fit neatly or that turn out to be irrelevant to the solution. The student is asked to deal with what Christensen (9) calls "the 'as is,' not the 'might be'."

> At a recent social event, Paul had become obviously drunk and was getting abusive with one of the ladies on the Women's Symphony Committee. Chuck decided the best way to help was to take Paul home. He had a terrible time getting him in his car. First Paul denied he was drunk and said he wanted to stay. Then he said he could get home himself and didn't want to leave his car there.

Replicating real-world problems means reproducing the messiness — the vagueness, ambiguity, and uncertainty — with which a problem first presents itself. Here the reader, asked to identify with Chuck, the orchestra's personnel manager, must decide which facts to accept and, ultimately, whether any of them are relevant to the problem at hand (the question of Paul's upcoming promotion). The realistic case study incorporates such exigencies as lack of crucial information, conflicting objectives, needs too great for resources. As in life, things do not lay themselves out neatly at the outset. The messiness of the "as is" brings home the central thing the neophyte needs to know about translating from abstract theory to concrete situation: the almost inevitable lack of fit between the two. As Lawrence puts it, "a good case keeps the class discussion grounded upon some of the stubborn facts that must be faced in real life situations. It is the anchor on academic flights of fancy" (215).

Yet specificity and realism result not from a faithful recounting of the facts but from their artful selection and arrangement. Truth does not guarantee realism; nor completeness, specificity. As the later discussion of form will show, both realism and specificity reside in the telling; they are properties of the text.

SOCIALIZATION

The second function of the case study is to help bring the neophyte into the community of the discipline. A case study conveys the theoretical paradigm to new members of the theoretical community by telling a story that shows the paradigm in action. Reading a case study, the neophyte sees not only what problems look like, but also what problem-solvers look like. By setting out the problem in such a way as to suggest how to play the role of problem-solver, the case study is in effect socializing the neophyte. Socialization results from achieving Fayerweather's four objectives for the case method (2):

- orienting to the nature of the business;
- imparting specific knowledge;
- teaching principles useful in guiding business decisions;
- training in the analysis of business problems.

Other exponents of the case method refer to "learning by doing" (Erskine, 17), "relating analysis and action" (Christensen, 9), developing "proficiency in analyzing . . . reaching decisions . . . and formulating programs" (Robert W. Merry, head of the Harvard Business School, quoted in Erskine, 16).

The case study in management, then, gives the reader the discipline's typical vision of a particular problem situation and, at the same time, elicits problem-solving behavior like that of the experienced practitioner. The case study of the violinist Paul Anyon concludes:

> You are Chuck. Do you discuss Paul's problem with the concert-master or the conductor? What, if anything, do you do for Paul?

Another of Glueck's cases (185) ends with the injunction:

> You are Ray Buffa, personnel manager at Columbia. Bob has just described the incident to you at lunch. Bob has asked you to comment on the whole incident from the company's point of view. Ray had just filed the memo on Bob in his personnel file.

It is important to note that the problem-solver's role is modeled not directly but obliquely. In order not to give away the solution, the case study must elicit the desired behavior without actually depicting it. This is achieved through ingenious use of the narrative mode, in two ways. First, the details of the problem are presented within what Kuhn has called the "paradigm" of the particular discipline.[1] The material is viewed through the lens of a particular theory, so that the reader sees it through the eyes of a particular theoretical community. Second, the story is told in such a way that the reader experiences himself or herself imaginatively as a member of that community. Solving the problem then becomes an exercise in role-playing for the reader. As Lawrence (215) puts it, "a good case . . . is the target for the expression of attitudes or ways of thinking."

INVOLVEMENT

Through illustration and socialization, the case study in management conveys knowledge that augments the abstract knowledge of principles. Merton (133) distinguishes between abstract or theoretical knowledge (*wissen*), on the one hand, and two kinds of relatively concrete knowledge, on the other: familiarity or direct acquaintance with phenomena (*kennen*), and practical knowledge or know-how (*können*). These three

Ann Harleman Stewart

kinds of knowledge are related to the functions of illustration and socialization in the following way:

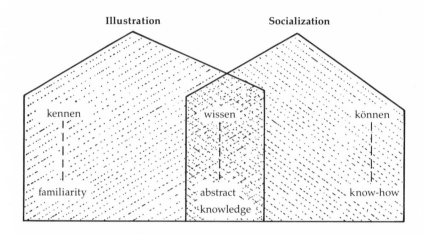

In performing its illustrative function, the case study provides familiarity with specific instances; in performing its socializing function, it provides problem-solving experience.

However, neither illustration nor socialization can occur without the reader's involvement, on a personal as well as an intellectual level, with the material presented. Christensen (3) emphasizes the necessity for the "active intellectual and emotional involvement of the student." Stories engage. They catch, hold, and focus our attention. In a well-told story the facts come alive, and the neophyte finds himself or herself immersed. It is the case study's narrative form — and the particular adaptation made of it — that secures involvement.

Form of the Case Study

Though some case writers and proponents of the case method of teaching have implicitly acknowledged a relation to storytelling (Fayerweather, 8), the case study has never been analyzed as a narrative text. In the following sections, I will look first at the narrative structure of the management case study and then at its use of the elements of narrative. In the process of determining how the form of the case study allows it to fulfill its functions with the communicative situation — by looking at text in context — we shall be able to see in detail the textual characteristics of the case study report. Surprisingly, we shall not only see ways in which the case study makes use of the conventions governing narrative form. We shall also see the ways in which the case study departs from those conventions to create a special kind of narrative text.

NARRATIVE STRUCTURE IN THE CASE STUDY

The narrative structure of a text exists on what van Dijk (153–55) calls the macrolinguistic level — above the level of individual sentences or paragraphs, on the level of discourse.[2] Narrative structure organizes content. By means of what Chafe (11) calls "subchunking," it carves up the total content into smaller, more manageable units presented in a logical and predictable sequence. Subchunking not only makes processing easier for the reader but also holds and directs the reader's attention. Narrative subchunking consists in the ordering of events in time.

The centrality of time distinguishes narrative from other rhetorical modes. Elizabeth Harris (142–43) schematizes the possible rhetorical modes in the following way:

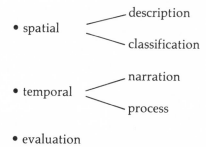

- spatial
  - description
  - classification
- temporal
  - narration
  - process
- evaluation

Narration, like process, is a temporal mode. It contrasts with the spatial modes of description and classification. Because we are speaking of a concept and its linguistic expression, we are already at some remove from reality. It is not real time, but temporality that concerns us. Psycholinguistic research sees temporality — reflected grammatically as tense and lexically as adverbials — as basic to the conceptual framework underlying natural language (Miller and Johnson-Laird, 411). Underlying the expression of temporality in natural language (and therefore in narrative) is a time line, which Miller and Johnson-Laird represent as:

$$A \qquad\qquad\qquad B$$

$$\cdots\cdots\cdot\big|\cdots\cdots\cdots\cdots\big|\cdots\cdots\cdots \longrightarrow$$

Ann Harleman Stewart

Here time is a sequence of discrete points (events), with some reference point (A or B) to which the speaker/hearer is oriented, moving backward (the past) and forward (the future) from that point and locating events with respect to it. A time line runs through all narrative.[3]

The events of the story are sequenced along this time line in such a way as to hold and focus the reader's attention. As Labov (366) puts it, every good narrator is continually warding off the question: "So what?" Labov finds the following sequence in a well-formed narrative (363):

1. Abstract
2. Orientation
3. Complication
4. Evaluation
5. Resolution
6. Coda

Briefly, the abstract presents a quick summary of the story about to be told; the orientation provides background information and setting; the complication constitutes the problem to be solved; the evaluation shows the significance of each action to the story as a whole and to its theme; the resolution solves the problem, resulting in a reversal of the situation; the coda signals that the narrative is finished and returns speaker and hearer to the present moment.[4] In Aristotelian terms, a fully formed narrative has a beginning (abstract and orientation), middle (complication, evaluation, and resolution), and end (coda). The lifelong experience of stories that comes from participating in the traditions of his or her culture, both oral and written, leads a reader to expect these elements and to perceive as incomplete any story that lacks them.

A striking feature of the management case study, in comparison with ordinary narrative, is that its form is truncated. Take the case study "Johnson Control, Inc." (Schwartz, 276–92). It begins with an abstract:

> By late September 1974 time had run out and Project Manager John Riley was faced with a critical decision concerning one of his division's major projects—the Eastern Electric contract.

This is followed immediately by an extensive orientation, which gives John Riley's background, the history of his company, and a description of the internal organization and working procedures of the company. The next section of the narrative, the complication, presents the problem (Eastern Electric's delay in deciding to continue with the project, while the deadline for completion rapidly approaches). There the report stops. There is no evaluation, no resolution, no coda.

The truncated structure of "Johnson Control, Inc." is typical of the case study in general. The last three of the six segments found in ordinary narrative are omitted. Reynolds' recommendations for case writing make this explicit; in his view, a case study should comprise three sections — opening, case body, and closing — defined as follows (95):

Opening: (First few paragraphs)	Name and title of responsible manager Name, location and product line of organization Date Synopsis of decision or problem setting

Case body:	Company history, if relevant
	Environmental facts, if relevant
	Expanded description of the decision or problem situation
	    Organizational relationships
	    Other case characters
	    Products and processes
	    Financial data
	    Marketing information
	    Human interaction facts
	    etc.

Closing: (Last paragraph or two)	Scenario to establish a sense of urgency about the problem or decision

Here the opening constitutes an abstract, the case body presents both the orientation and the complication, and the closing brings the problem into focus, centering the reader's attention on it and making it vivid enough ("sense of urgency") to trigger reader identification. In effect, the case study is the first half of a fully formed narrative:

```
FULLY FORMED NARRATIVE        CASE STUDY REPORT

        Abstract    ◄─────────────── Opening
        Orientation ◄───────────────  Case Body
        Complication ◄══════════════  Closing
        Evaluation
        Resolution
        Coda
```

Within the truncated narrative of the case study report, the orientation section generally shows much greater length and density than in ordinary narrative. An example is the orientation section in "Johnson Control, Inc.,"

Ann Harleman Stewart

which exhibits the "layered" structure typical of the case study orientation. The section proceeds from largest to narrowest context, placing the complication within concentric circles:

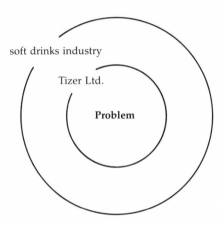

This report presents the concentric contexts out of order: first the inner circle, then the outer one, and finally the middle one. Often, however, the order of presentation moves from the outside in, as in "Tizer Limited (A)" (Stopford et al., 61–78). This case, as the abstract makes clear, deals with the adjustment of a new employee to the company:

> In the spring of 1972 Mr P. Quinn described to the casewriter his move from Polyfoil Ltd, an aluminum foil manufacturer, to Tizer Ltd, the soft drinks manufacturer. Mr Quinn had been the general manager of Polyfoil Ltd, a subsidiary of Alcan Ltd, until February 1970, when he assumed the position of managing director of Tizer Ltd. Mr Quinn was reviewing both his evaluation of Tizer prior to joining the company, and his subsequent approach to the task of returning the company to a position of profitability.

The Role of Narrative Structure in the Transfer of Ideas

The orientation here shows the following structure:

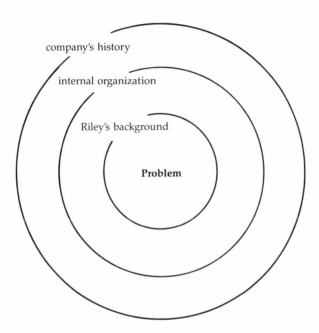

The elaborate orientation characteristic of the case study serves both of the functions discussed in the preceding section. It deepens the reader's involvement by the sheer volume of information it gives: the more one knows about a subject, the more deeply one is engaged by it. An elaborate orientation provides what Schegloff calls "common-sense geography"—the context-within-context that children practice when they give their address as town, state, country, the world, the solar system, the universe (Traugott and Pratt, 273). The degree of detail involved supports the function of illustration by enhancing concreteness and realism, and

Ann Harleman Stewart

the function of socialization by immersing the reader in the problem.

Elaborating the orientation section is one way in which the case study narrative compensates for its truncated structure; another is the use of subheadings. For example, we find the following:

"The Inspection Machine" (Gellerman, 15–26)
- [Abstract]
- Farini Deliberates
- Swanson Is Consulted
- The Decision-Making Process
- The Outcome

"The Colonial Beef Company" (Schwartz, 17–29)
- [Abstract]
- The Meat-Packing Industry
- Portion Control
- Company History
- Marketing
  - Market
  - Product
  - Price
  - Distribution
  - Promotion
- Production, Cost Control, and Labor Relations
- Finance
- The Future

Subheadings, whether colorful (as in the example from Gellerman) or controlled (as in the example from Schwartz), point up the subchunks into which the narrative falls. At the same time, they label or title those subchunks to focus the reader's attention on the core idea of each one. Thus subheadings give the reader toeholds to use in scaling the problem. The lengthened orientation furnishes a wealth of information; the subheads help the reader organize it. Case studies that do not use subheadings tend to have specific, directive titles that focus attention on central issues. DuBrin, for example, uses lively titles that offer a clue to the nature of the problem: "Isolation Blues," "The Maladroit Firing," "Bruce, the Behavior Mod Landlord"; Glueck has titles like "How High the Doc" (about an alcoholic surgeon). Both the longer orientation and the use of subheadings or pointed titles help the reader with the task of solving the problem—which is also the task of completing the narrative.

The most striking difference between the case study and ordinary narrative is that, in the case study, it is not the storyteller but the reader who must answer the question, "So what?" Cutting off the narrative after the

The Role of Narrative Structure in the Transfer of Ideas

complication section propels the reader into solving the problem, because of the momentum created by his or her expectations — the internalized story grammar. As narrative, the case study fails to meet the requirements for a "minimal story" held by most narrative theorists since Aristotle: it does not show a change of state.[5] The essence of plot is reversal (Aristotle's *peripateia*), "the passage from one equilibrium to another" (Todorov, 111) — from complication to resolution. For instance, a much-cited, typical minimal story is Prince's "John was unhappy; then he met a woman; then, as a result, he was happy" (31), in which the protagonist's emotional state undergoes a reversal from the beginning to the end of the story, with an intervening event supplying the causal link between the two states. But causality, because it would constitute interpretation of the problem presented, cannot be indicated in a case study narrative; neither can the reversed state, which would constitute a solution to the problem. Therefore it is the reader who, by deciphering the cause of the problem, supplies the evaluation; it is the reader who, by solving the problem, supplies the resolution. And finally it is the reader's coda that brings the narrative to closure.

Gellerman (xiii–xiv) indicates the kind of interaction between reader and text that results in the reader's completing the story:

> Ben Caldwell, a 42-year-old engineering manager, has been recruited from a larger company to become manager of Media Corporation's printing plant in Harperville. The Harperville plant, Media's largest, is twelve years old and has already had four managers, all of whom came from other Media Divisions. Two of these were fired, one resigned, and one accepted a demotion and transfer to another division. For the past year-and-a-half, the plant was managed by Jim Storch, a 34-year-old plant accountant who had been given the title of acting plant manager.
>
> Storch had accepted the acting plant managership somewhat reluctantly. His main interest was in accounting. But he was a loyal company man, and when the previous plant manager resigned he realized that Media desperately needed someone to manage on a temporary basis, while a fully-qualified plant manager was sought. However, as the "temporary" assignment continued for more than a year, Storch began to like general management and felt that he was growing into the job. About two months before Caldwell was hired, Storch told Adam Siemanski, Media's Vice President for Manufacturing, that he'd like to be considered for the plant manager's job on a permanent basis. Siemanski was careful to make no commitments, but praised Storch for having run the plant in a reasonably efficient manner during his tenure as acting plant manager.
>
> When Caldwell accepted the job, Siemanski told him that Storch had also applied for it. Siemanski said that he didn't know how serious Storch had really been, and was uncertain as to whether Storch would be seriously disappointed to see the job go to an outsider—even a highly qualified outsider like Caldwell. Siemanski told Caldwell to organize his management team at Harperville as he saw fit, and to do his best to keep Storch happy.

[handwritten marginalia: What's wrong? Plant managers' graveyard? Why did it take so long? Doesn't anybody want it? disappointed? demoralized? won't be easy; use S. as and executive, not as an accountant]

Ann Harleman Stewart

From the reader's point of view, the truncated narrative structure of the case study is a powerful motivator. He or she feels the pull toward closure, rooted in human psychology and reinforced by the expectations a lifelong experience of ordinary narrative has set up. Trying to create closure, the reader is drawn into interaction with the text. He or she asks questions concerning the origin and consequences of the facts reported, striving to forge the causal connections that will make the problem yield to interpretation (adding an evaluation section to the narrative structure) and ultimately to solution (adding a resolution). By violating the reader's narrative expectations and leaving the story unfinished, the case study draws the reader into its construction in the role of problem-solver. At this point, the elements of narrative come into play; the case study's adaptation and manipulation of the elements of narrative provides the resources the reader needs to carry the story to completion.

NARRATIVE ELEMENTS IN THE CASE STUDY

Narrative structure is implemented by means of plot, character, and point of view.[6] The first of these elements, plot, is the particular sequence of events that actualizes the narrative structure in a given story. We can think of the structure discussed in the preceding section as a set of ordered slots; the plot of a given story is the sequence of events with which that story fills the slots. Plot unfolds over time. What Scholes and Kellogg (209) call the essential temporality of the narrative act threads events together into a structure with coherence and inevitability.

In the case study, plot becomes the basis for the reader's problem-solving activity. In reading ordinary narrative, readers frequently project from the temporal axis onto the causal axis, interpreting succession in time as causal connection (Warren, Nicholas, and Trabasso). Indeed, tellers of ordinary stories often invite readers to do this, since constantly making the cause-and-effect explicit would be inelegant and tedious. Readers of the case study, generalizing from their experience of ordinary narrative, seek the origins of a problem in events that happened earlier in time.

In projecting from the temporal to the causal, the case study employs a resource not found in ordinary narrative (with a very few idiosyncratic exceptions): the use of schematics. Organizational charts, bar and line graphs, flowcharts, piecharts—all these supplement the information presented verbally. Take the following bar graph (Stopford et al., 306):

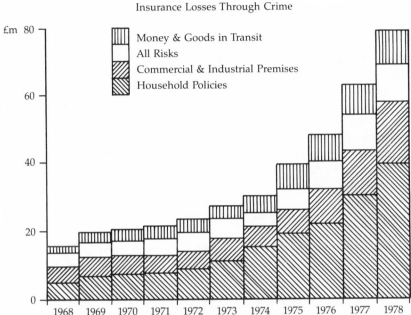

Exhibit 3
Insurance Losses Through Crime

This schematic summarizes events over time and makes a trend clear. It organizes facts that could be (and largely have been) presented verbally and imposes a structure on them. Because they summarize, schematics stand outside the plot. Conceptually, they are juxtaposed with the events of the story, laid side-by-side with the time line. Because they represent analysis of facts — facts arranged in such a way as to lead the reader to certain conclusions — schematics introduce a kind of "back-door" causality into the case study narrative. As we have seen, the goals of the case study demand that interpretation of the facts be left to the reader; but schematics can guide the reader toward interpretation.

In presenting the events of the plot sequence, the case study restricts itself to the past tense, in contrast to ordinary narrative, which often uses the present and sometimes even the future as the main tense in which the action is presented.[7] The reason lies in the choice of realism over immediacy. The past tense gives a sense of definiteness ("It did happen"), the solidity of completed events; whereas the present tense conveys the immediacy of an event in progress. Thus the past tense, though it increases the distance between the reader and the narrative, enhances the reality of the problem situation by conveying it as the culmination of events that have already taken place.

Character, the second element of narrative structure, creates empathy in the reader (DuBrin, 11). He or she identifies with the character who faces the problem: the personnel manager of a symphony orchestra who must deal with an alcoholic violinist (Glueck, 183–84); the vice-president for international operations who must determine whether a new mill is endangered by guerilla activities (Gellerman, 105–18); the committee members who must decide whether or not to admit men to Women's Medical College (Schwartz, 143–53). The character thus beset is the protagonist of the case study.

But identification with the protagonist helps the reader solve the problem only if he or she can dilute it enough to maintain the perspective of an expert called in to solve the problem. Distance is the crucial element. That is why the case study, in contrast to ordinary narrative, offers only "flat" characters — characters who are simple and do not develop in the course of the narrative (Forster, 75). A range of variation exists: compare the following passages.

> Shutting down the machine would have disrupted the agency's work during a peak period. More importantly, it would have raised doubts about the machine's effectiveness only a few weeks after it had been delivered. The government's original decision to purchase the machine had attracted considerable controversy in the newspapers, and even in Congress. A shutdown could easily lead to investigations, adverse publicity, and administrative delays. Farini, having gone through a stressful period when the machine was initially sold, had always been fearful of having, in effect, to "sell it again" by reappearing before various committees, while simultaneously having to fight a public relations "battle." The resulting delays would hamper the agency's efforts to learn to use the machine efficiently. An engineer by training, Farini had a personal distaste for administrative delays. Besides, he had faith in his machine. (Gellerman, 20)

> When asked about growth over the next five years William Baker expressed confidence that a 32 percent growth rate would be achieved. He considered the best growth prospects to be acquisition of a contract cleaning business and expansion into nearby geographic areas. He expected that increasing demand for security services would be a source of rapid expansion for Safeguard. Baker

asserted that the contract cleaning industry was maturing rapidly. It would become increasingly difficult for small, inefficient firms to survive; future volume should be concentrated in a few large companies. The ability of any company to become larger would depend on its ability to manage its people and resources. (Schwartz, 243)

In the first passage, we look into both the mind and the emotions of the character. We know how Farini assesses the problem, what his reasoning is; and we also know how he feels: his dislike of administrative delays, his faith in his machine. He is endowed with an emotional past, including a previous "stressful period," from which these feelings come.

In the second passage, in contrast, we look only into the mind of the character. We hear Baker's reasoning and his predictions; but we know nothing at all of how he feels about his ideas or how his past may have shaped them. The first passage here depicts a character less flat than the one in the second. However, for the case study in general, the range of characterization is considerably narrower than for ordinary narrative. Both passages employ indirect rather than direct presentation (Rimmon-Kenan, 59) — that is, neither passage contains the kind of authorial intrusion that defines or attaches labels to characters. Instead, both passages follow the maxim of "Show, don't tell" (Booth, 8), letting us see and hear the characters rather than merely telling us about their qualities. The difference between the two passages lies in *what* they show — mind and emotions in the first, mind only in the second — rather than in *how* they show it.

The third element of narrative structure, point of view, is the most complex. Point of view involves both the question of who sees and the question of who speaks (Rimmon-Kenan, 72). Is the narrator the person from whose perspective the events of the story are viewed? In ordinary narrative, it frequently is not. (For example, in *Great Expectations* — told in the first person by its protagonist — Pip as a child sees the events of the narrative, but Pip as an adult tells the story.) Degree of identity between viewer and speaker correlates with degree of empathy between narrator and reader. The closer the one who speaks is to the one who sees, the greater will be the empathy between narrator and reader.

The relation between viewer and speaker is reflected in the choice of grammatical person for the narrator's voice. In a first-person case study, viewer and speaker usually coincide. Consider the following passage from "The Boss Is the Boss," about a division manager whose choice for branch manager conflicts with that of his superior (White et al., 79):

I tell you I was stunned there for a minute. Bill had been brought into the organization about 14 months ago specifically to train for a managerial post with us — this arrangement no doubt having something to do with the fact that Bill's father (head of a large equipment company in the city) and Jim were very good friends. Undoubtedly he was management material, and I knew nothing whatever about him that would suggest he wouldn't make a first-rate branch manager some day. In fact I didn't really know very much about him at all, since he had never worked in the Local Division; I knew his connection with Jim (everybody said that he was the "fair-haired boy" of Number One), the plan to push him along as fast as possible, that he had been married and had one child, but that his wife had obtained a divorce, and I had heard that on a couple of occasions since he came with us he had been seen downtown at night heavily under the influence. But I would never in the world have thought of Bill in terms of the job that was opening up now.

Here the narrator and the one through whose eyes we see the situation are identical. The lack of distance between the two creates a high degree of empathy in the reader, which the informal, confiding tone enhances. "I tell you I was stunned there for a minute" and "I would never in the world have thought" carry the tone of someone speaking to a friend.

In contrast to the first-person narrator, the third-person narrator can reflect varying distances between viewer and speaker. Compare these two passages:

Swallowing his resentment, Byrum left the branch office. He greeted Shuford and welcomed him into the section. He described the organization of the section and the responsibilities of the in-service operation unit. Also, since Shuford was new in this job, he was welcome to come to the chief's desk at any time to discuss his problems and to seek advisory assistance. But, when Byrum had completed his orientation remarks, he was almost knocked off his feet [when] Shuford made [a] comment. (Glueck, 179)

In June 1970, the first move into the hotel industry was made with the purchase of Pondust Ltd. involving Lex in the construction of a Hilton Hotel in Stratford-on-Avon. In December of the year, a ten year management agreement was signed between Lex and the Hyatt International Corporation for the construction by Lex of an hotel at Heathrow Airport that would be managed by Hyatt.

October 1971 saw the purchase of the The [sic] Carlton Tower Hotel from the Sonesta Corporation for £4.6 million. This well established luxury grade hotel was operated by Lex. In January 1972, Lex initiated the building of a hotel at London Gatwick

The Role of Narrative Structure in the Transfer of Ideas

Airport for operation by Lex. (Stopford et al., 101–2)

Both passages show a less intimate, less casual tone than the first-person passage above. Nevertheless, they stand at different points on a continuum from relatively close to extremely distant narrator. We can position them relative to the first-person narrator in the following way:

first person	third person = viewer	third person ≠ viewer

*————————— * ————————— *

LESS DISTANCE		MORE DISTANCE

In the third-person passage from Glueck, the narrator positions himself so close to the protagonist, Byrum, that seeing the action and recounting it come from almost the same perspective. Closeness of speaker to viewer engenders a corresponding closeness between reader and protagonist, and we feel with Byrum his resentment and his surprise. In contrast, the third-person passage from Stopford does not even contain a protagonist. We do not know the people behind the actions described. (Who made the purchase of Pondust Ltd.? Who signed the contract between Lex and Hyatt International?) This passage gives the reader no one with whom to identify. The distant narrative voice is that of an anonymous puzzle-giver who simply presents the problem.

Speaker/viewer closeness is enhanced or diminished by the choice of person because of the psycholinguistic phenomenon known as the Empathy Hierarchy (DeLancey, 644), which ranks elements in discourse as follows:

- first person
- second person ⎤ Discourse Participants
- third person ⎦
- human
- animate
- natural forces
- inanimate

We find it easiest to empathize with discourse elements at the top of the hierarchy and progressively more difficult as we move down. As Lyons (638) points out, only speaker and addressee, represented grammatically by the first and second person respectively, actually participate in the communicative act. Therefore, using the third person as a lens through which to view events automatically sets the action at some remove from the discourse participants.

Ann Harleman Stewart

The management case study prefers the third-person narrator; very few use the first person. Here again, as with the elements of plot and character, the case study departs from the tradition of ordinary narrative. In their use of point of view, most case studies go beyond the third-person narrator to what I will call the "zero narrator." The range of options for the case study looks like this:

first person	third person = viewer	third person ≠ viewer	zero narrator

```
* —————————— * —————————— * —————————— *
```

| LESS DISTANCE | | | MORE DISTANCE |

The zero narrator, in which no voice tells the story, is created by two means: pure dialogue and exhibits. Both devices contain no narrative presence. They simply set information down on the page, forming a text by sheer juxtaposition.

Pure dialogue, unmediated by even the slimmest of *he said*'s, occurs in the following passage from "How High the Doc?" (Glueck, 180):

> Barret: Gary, what seems to be the problem?
> Gary: Well, Ms. Barret, I just don't feel very good, and I'd just like to lie down for a while.
> Barret: If you don't feel good, you'd better take the rest of the day off.
> Gary: I don't think I need to do that.
> Barret: Gary, can you tell me what's going on around here?
> Gary: Well, most people just don't like to work for Dr. Collins. He's pretty slow and seems to be out of it most of the time.
> Barret: Have you talked to Ms. Johnston, the circulating R.N., about this?
> Gary: I've talked to her and Dr. Martin. Ms. Johnston gave me a hard time as usual. She says I am getting too big for my britches, and if I don't like the situation, I can ask for a transfer. Dr. Martin says that he's with Dr. Collins most of the time, and he looks fine to him.
> Barret: Thank you Gary, this will be kept confidential.

A brief set of stage directions introduces this exchange, but no narrative voice intrudes. An entire case study report may consist of dialogue, without even an introduction, as in DuBrin's "The Price of Success" (158–63).

Like pure dialogue, exhibits are simply set down side-by-side with the verbal text — more precisely, intercalated with it — without narrative interpretation. They vary: letters written by participants in the case, records of transactions, legal documents, texts (legal and otherwise) which have some bearing on the case or which participants have consulted, newspaper articles, and so on. Schematics could be put into this category. (In fact, they are sometimes labeled "exhibits" by the case writer.) However, to the extent that they provide some interpretation of the data, they are not, strictly speaking, free of narrative intrusion. Exhibits are "eternal" information, valid for the entire narrative, unlinked to any specific part of it. They could in theory occur anywhere, though they are most often gathered at the end.

The zero narrator compensates for diminished reader empathy by pulling the reader into the construction of the text. Pure dialogue and exhibits support the function of illustration by enhancing realism, using what Fayerweather (9) calls "live material" — reports, letters, quotations — the stuff of which real-life cases are made. They support the function of socialization by leaving their connection to events unstated. The reader must discover it. In the process, he or she engages with the material and begins the activity of problem-solving.

Conclusion

In most scientific and technical fields, the transfer of knowledge entails dealing with problems that can only be solved with uncertainty (Bazerman, 160) through an activity in which intuition and inference play a key role and ambiguity abounds. The problem-solving process combines knowledge and inspiration, experience and innovation, in proportions that cannot be predicted. As Fleck (10) puts it:

> Whereas an experiment can be interpreted in terms of a simple question and answer, experience must be understood as a complex state of intellectual training based upon the interaction involving the knower, that which he already knows, and that which he has yet to learn.

How can such a process be communicated to the newcomer unfamiliar with the discipline? How can the problems themselves be conveyed, if they are shot through with uncertainty and ambiguity, and each is in some way unlike any other?

The case study is one way. The analysis here, offered as a model for a discourse analytical approach to the case study as it is used in other areas, gives us insight into the nature of the case study in general. Viewing the management case study from a discourse-analytic perspective, as a text embedded in a communicative situation, has shown precisely how the case study report allows scientific and technical problems and prob-

Ann Harleman Stewart

lem-solving processes to be set forth in all their variety and complexity. Because it tells a story, the case study, like all narrative texts, engages the reader. Its grounding in concrete detail serves the function of illustration and at the same time makes the abundance and complexity of that detail manageable by fitting it into the ordered sequence of components expected in narrative. However, as we have seen, the case study in management does more than merely adopt the conventions of ordinary narrative; it adapts them to suit its particular communicative purpose. By truncating the narrative structure, and by selecting and reshaping the narrative elements of plot, character, and point of view, the case study draws the reader into the story as problem-solver, thereby fulfilling the function of socialization. The resulting text is a special kind of narrative — a story interactively constructed by writer and reader together.

NOTES

I would like to thank the following people for their help: Charles Bazerman, James Paradis, Bruce A. Rosenberg, Jules J. Schwartz, the staff of the Harvard Public Library, and especially Edwin A. Murray, Jr., of Boston University's School of Management.

1. Kuhn (*Essential Tension*, xix) distinguishes two senses in which he uses the word "paradigm": (1) "exemplary problem solutions"; and (2) "the entire global set of commitments shared by the members of a particular scientific community." He notes with regret that the second sense has captured the imagination of scholars, though the first is closer to what he meant. In my opinion, the two senses are inextricably connected; in this essay I use the word in both senses at once.

2. On macrostructures in general, see chapter 5 of van Dijk. Van Dijk and Kintsch treats in detail the relation of the reader to discourse macrostructures, as does Gulich and Raible.

3. According to Rimmon-Kenan (14), recounting events in chronological order is what makes a text a narrative; however, as she points out (17), this temporality is not strict but multilinear. Because stories nearly always involve more than one character, events that are in reality simultaneous must be recounted sequentially. The most complete analysis of time and tense in narrative is that of Genette, who stresses the unreal nature of narrative time: stories transpose from what he calls the "temporal plane" (real time) to the "spatial plane" of the text (86).

4. For another version of Labov's approach, see Rumelhart's discussion of story schemata. For the application of schematic analysis to real-life stories, see Stein and Glenn.

5. Nearly all narrative theorists agree on the necessity for a change of state in narrative, though many would take issue with Prince's precise formulation. See, for instance: Culler; Smith (185); Brémond.

The Role of Narrative Structure in the Transfer of Ideas

6. Here I follow Rimmon-Kenan (43ff); however, she prefers the term "focalization" (after Genette) to "point of view." Scholes and Kellogg list four elements of narrative: meaning (theme), character, plot, and point of view.

7. Prince (149) claims that "narrative prefers tensed statements (or their equivalent) to untensed ones," so that "Every human dies" is less narrative than "Napoleon died in 1821." But this conflates the two ideas of time and specificity; as much contemporary fiction testifies, the present tense is fully as narrative as the past — provided what is narrated is specific (e.g., "Then, in 1821, Napoleon dies").

BIBLIOGRAPHY

Barnes, Barry. *T. S. Kuhn and Social Science*. New York: Columbia University Press, 1982.

Bazerman, Charles. "Scientific Writing as a Social Act: A Review of the Literature of the Sociology of Science." In *New Essays in Technical and Scientific Communication: Research, Theory, Practice*, ed. Paul V. Anderson, R. John Brockman, and Carolyn R. Miller, 156–84. Farmingdale, N.Y.: Baywood, 1983.

Bernhardt, Kenneth L., and Thomas C. Kinnear. *Cases in Marketing Management*. Rev. ed. Plano, Tex.: Business Publications, 1981.

Bock, Edwin A., ed. *Essays on the Case Method*. Syracuse: Inter-University Case Program, 1971.

Booth, Wayne C. *The Rhetoric of Fiction*. Chicago: University of Chicago Press, 1961.

Brémond, Claude. *Logique du récit*. Paris: Seuil, 1973.

British Institute of Management. *Case Study Practice: An Account by Specialists Working in Different Branches of Management Education of Their Experiences in the Use of Case Studies*. London, 1960.

Chafe, Wallace L., ed. *The Pear Stories: Cognitive, Cultural, and Linguistic Aspects of Narrative Production*. Advances in Discourse Processes, 3. Norwood, N.J.: Ablex, 1980.

Christensen, Roland. *Teaching by the Case Method*. Cambridge: Harvard Business School, Division of Research, 1981.

Culler, Jonathan. *Structuralist Poetics*. Ithaca: Cornell University Press, 1975.

DeLancey, Scott. "An Interpretation of Split Ergativity and Related Patterns." *Language* 57 (1981): 626–57.

Dijk, Teun A. van. *Text and Context: Explorations in the Semantics and Pragmatics of Discourse*. London and New York: Longman, 1977.

Dijk, Teun A. van, and Walter Kintsch. *Strategies of Discourse Comprehension*. New York: Academic Press, 1983.

DuBrin, Andrew J. *Casebook of Organizational Behavior*. New York: Pergamon Press, 1977.

Dukes, William F. "N=1." *Psychological Bulletin* 64 (1965): 74–79.

Ann Harleman Stewart

Eckstein, Harry. "Case Study and Theory in Political Science." In *Strategies of Inquiry*, ed. Fred I. Greenstein and Nelson W. Polsky, 79–137. Reading, Mass.: Addison-Wesley, 1975.

Erskine, James A., Michiel R. Leenders, and Louise A. Mariffette-Leenders. *Teaching with Cases*. London, Canada: University of Western Ontario School of Business Administration, 1981.

Fayerweather, John. "The Case Method as a Research Assistant Sees It." Boston: Intercollegiate Case Clearing House, 1949. Offprint.

Fleck, Ludwik. *Genesis and Development of a Scientific Fact*. Trans. Fred Bradley and Thaddeus J. Trenn. Chicago: University of Chicago Press, 1979.

Forster, E. M. *Aspects of the Novel*. 1927. Harmondsworth, Eng.: Penguin, 1963.

Gellerman, Saul W. *Cases and Problems for Decisions in Management*. New York: Random House, 1984.

Genette, Gérard. *Narrative Discourse: An Essay in Method*. Ithaca: Cornell University Press, 1981.

George, Alexander L. "Case Studies and Theory Development: The Method of Structured, Focused Comparison." In *Diplomacy: New Approaches in History, Theory, and Policy*, ed. Paul Gordon Lauren, 43–68. New York: Free Press, 1979.

Glueck, William F. *Cases and Exercises in Personnel*. Dallas: Business Publications, 1978.

Gragg, Charles I. "Because Wisdom Can't Be Told." In *The Case Method at the Harvard Business School*, ed. M. P. McNair, 6–54. New York: McGraw-Hill, 1954.

Gulich, Elisabeth, and Wolfgang Raible. *Linguistische Textmodelle*. Munich: Fink, 1977.

Harris, Elizabeth. "A Theoretical Perspective on 'How To' Discourse." In *New Essays in Technical and Scientific Communication: Research, Theory, Practice*, ed. Paul V. Anderson, R. John Brockman, and Carolyn R. Miller, 139–55. Farmingdale, N.Y.: Baywood, 1983.

Harris, John K. "On the Use of Assumptions in Case Study." Boston: Intercollegiate Case Clearing House, 1975. Offprint.

Hinkle, Charles L. *Cases in Marketing Management: Issues for the 1980's*. Englewood Cliffs, N.J.: Prentice-Hall, 1984.

Hodgetts, Richard M. *Cases and Incidents on the Basic Concepts of Management*. New York: Wiley, 1972.

Hymes, Dell. *Foundations in Sociolinguistics*. Philadelphia: University of Pennsylvania Press, 1974.

Ivens, Michael William, and Frand Broadway, eds. *Case Studies in Management*. London: Business Publications, 1964.

Kaplan, Abraham. *The Conduct of Inquiry: Methodology for Behavioral Science*. Scranton, Pa.: Chandler, 1964.

Katz, Robert Lee. *Cases and Concepts in Corporate Strategy*. Englewood Cliffs, N.J.: Prentice-Hall, 1970.

Kuhn, Thomas. *The Essential Tension: Selected Studies in Scientific Tradition and Change*. Chicago: University of Chicago Press, 1977.

Kuhn, Thomas. *The Structure of Scientific Revolutions*. 2d ed. Chicago: University of Chicago Press, 1970.

Labov, Williaim. "The Transformation of Experience in Narrative Syntax." *Language in the Inner City*, 354–96. Philadelphia: University of Pennsylvania Press, 1972.

Lawrence, Paul R. "The Preparation of Case Material." In *The Case Method of Teaching Human Relations and Administration*, ed. K. P. Andrews, 215–24. Cambridge: Harvard University Press, 1953.

Leenders, Michiel A., and James Erskine. *Case Research: The Case Writing Process*. London, Canada: University of Western Ontario, 1978.

Lyons, John. "Deixis, Space, and Time." *Semantics*, chap. 15. 2 vols. London and New York: Cambridge University Press, 1977.

McHale, Brian. "Free Indirect Discourse: A Survey of Recent Accounts." *PTL* 3 (1978): 249–87.

Mantel, Samuel J. *Cases in Managerial Decisions*. Englewood Cliffs, N.J.: Prentice-Hall, 1964.

Merton, Robert. *Sociology of Science*. Chicago: University of Chicago Press, 1973.

Miller, George A., and Philip N. Johnson-Laird. *Language and Perception*. Cambridge: Harvard University Press, 1976.

Myers, Ann D., and Louis Weeks. "Writing and Teaching Cases." *Casebook on Church and Society*. Nashville: Abingdon, 1974.

Odell, Lee, Dixie Goswami, Anne Herrington, and Doris Quick. "Studying Writing in Non-Academic Settings." In *New Essays in Technical and Scientific Communication: Research, Theory, Practice*, ed. Paul V. Anderson, R. John Brockman, and Carolyn R. Miller, 17–40. Farmingdale, N.Y.: Baywood, 1983.

O'Donnell, Cyril. *Cases in General Management*. Rev. ed. Homewood, Ill.: R. D. Irwin, 1965.

Petersen, Bruce T. "Conceptual Patterns in Industrial and Academic Discourse." *Journal of Technical Writing and Communication* 14 (1984): 95–107.

Pigors, Paul John Williams. *Case Method in Human Relations: The Incident Process*. New York: McGraw-Hill, 1961.

Prince, Gerald. *A Grammar of Stories*. The Hague: Mouton, 1973.

Reynolds, John I. *Case Method in Management Development: A Guide for Effective Use*. Geneva: International Labour Office, 1980.

Rimmon-Kenan, Shlomith. *Narrative Fiction: Contemporary Poetics*. London and New York: Methuen, 1983.

Ronstadt, Robert. *The Art of Case Analysis: A Guide to the Diagnosis of Business Situations*. 2d ed. Dover, Mass.: Lord, 1977.

Rumelhart, David E. "Notes on a Schema for Stories." In *Representation and Understanding: Studies in Cognitive Science*, ed. Daniel Bobrow and A. Collins, 211–36. New York: Academic Press, 1975.

Schegloff, Emmanuel A. "Notes on Conversational Practice." In *Studies in Social Interaction*, ed. David Sudnow, 75–119. New York: Free Press, 1972.

Scholes, Robert, and Robert Kellogg. *The Nature of Narrative*. New York: Oxford University Press, 1966.

Ann Harleman Stewart

Schwartz, Jules J. *Corporate Policy: A Casebook*. Englewood Cliffs, N.J.: Prentice-Hall, 1978.

Smith, Barbara Herrnstein. *On the Margins of Discourse*. Chicago: University of Chicago Press, 1978.

Stein, Nancy L., and Christine G. Glenn. "An Analysis of Story Comprehension in Elementary School Children." In *New Directions in Discourse Processing*, ed. Roy O. Freedle, 53–120. Norwood, N.J.: Ablex, 1979.

Stopford, John M., Derek F. Channon, and John Constable. *Cases in Strategic Management*. Chichester, Eng., and New York: Wiley, 1980.

Todorov, Tzvetan. *The Poetics of Prose*. Trans. Richard Howard. Ithaca: Cornell University Press, 1977.

Traugott, Elizabeth Closs, and Mary Louise Pratt. *Linguistics for Students of Literature*. New York: Harcourt Brace, 1980.

Turban, Efraim, and N. Paul Loomba, eds. *Case Readings in Management Science*. Rev. ed. Plano, Tex.: Business Publications, 1982.

Vaible, Dale L. *Cases in Marketing Management*. Columbus, Ohio: C. E. Merrill, 1976.

Warren, William H., David W. Nicholas, and Tom Trabasso. "Event Chains and Inferences in Understanding Narratives." In *New Directions in Discourse Processing*, ed. Roy O. Freedle, 23–52. Norwood, N.J.: Ablex, 1979.

White, Bernard J., John H. Stamm, and Lawrence W. Foster. *Cases in Organization: Behavior, Structure, Processes*. Dallas: Business Publications, 1976.

White, Hayden. "The Value of Narrativity in the Representation of Reality." *Critical Inquiry* 7 (1980): 5–27.

Yin, Robert K. *The Case Study Strategy: An Annotated Bibliography*. Washington, D.C.: Case Study Institute, 1982.

Zaleznik, Abraham, and David Moment. *Casebook on Interpersonal Behavior in Organizations*. New York: Wiley, 1964.

6

SCIENTIFIC RHETORIC

IN THE NINETEENTH AND

EARLY TWENTIETH CENTURIES

HERBERT SPENCER,

THOMAS H. HUXLEY, AND

JOHN DEWEY

JAMES P. ZAPPEN

The study of rhetoric and communication since ancient Greece and Rome has been concerned with the relationship of rhetoric to modes of inquiry and to the social community, with the relationship of language to thought and action. Aristotle explored the relationship of rhetoric to logic and to politics, for example, and Cicero viewed oratory as the union of wisdom and eloquence in service of the state. This concern reappears in discussions of scientific rhetoric in the nineteenth and early twentieth centuries, which explore the relationship of language to science and to civilization. Some studies of British and American rhetoric in the nineteenth century note the decline of classical rhetoric and the currency of belletristic, elocutionary, practical, and psychological-epistemological rhetoric during this period (Berlin, 13–41, 58–76; Connors, Ede, and Lunsford, 2–5; Ehninger, xxiii–xxx; Halloran; Howell, 695–717; Ried; Stewart, 136–52). Other studies note the persistence of classical rhetoric despite, and sometimes in conscious reaction against, the then more widely current rhetorics (Crowley, "Evolution of Invention"; Crowley, "Invention"; Johnson; Rosner). Most of these studies, including those that note the persistence of classical rhetoric, also note its eventual demise and its replacement by the so-called practical rhetorics. Several of these studies attribute these changes in part to the rise of experimental science and the specialization of the curriculum in general in British and American colleges and universities in the latter part of the nineteenth century (Berlin, 62–64; Connors, Ede, and Lunsford, 3–4; Halloran, 260–62; Ried, 232–33; Rosner, 164–66). Discussions of scientific rhetoric in the nineteenth and early twentieth centuries suggest, however, that neither of these forces in itself necessarily led to the development of practical rhetorics — and, with it, the separation of rhetoric from science and other specialized subjects and from societal concerns. Rather, these discussions suggest that science and scientific rhetoric in the service of organized, professionalized communities may have encouraged the development of practical rhetorics but that science and scientific rhetoric also served broader social communities and that, in this context, scientific rhetoric remained inseparable from its modes of inquiry and from the social communities it sought to serve, and language remained inseparable from science and civilization.

In this chapter, I explain how rhetoric is related to modes of inquiry and to the social community in classical rhetoric and in scientific rhetoric in the nineteenth and early twentieth centuries. I begin with a brief summary. Next, I show how Aristotle's rhetoric is related to logic and to politics and ethics and how late-eighteenth- and early-nineteenth-century versions of it sever this relationship. Finally, I show how several scientific rhetorics from the nineteenth and early twentieth centuries, despite their considerable differences, nonetheless reaffirm the relationship of rhetoric to inquiry and to the social community, to science and civilization.

Summary

Classical rhetorics such as Aristotle's had noted the relationship of rhetoric to logic or dialectic and to politics and ethics, which were identified with the good of the social community (George A. Kennedy, 65–67; Randall, 280–81). Nineteenth-century rhetorics, with some exceptions, did not share these concerns, and even a self-avowed Aristotelian rhetoric such as that of Richard Whately distinguished and separated the role of logic from that of rhetoric and ignored politics almost entirely (Berlin, 28–30; Ehninger, ix–xv, xxvii–xxx; Einhorn, "Consistency," 93–96; Einhorn, "Public Persuasion," 49–51; Howell, 698–703, 707–12; Stewart, 139–40). The scientific rhetorics of Herbert Spencer, Thomas H. Huxley, and John Dewey seldom used the term *rhetoric*, except pejoratively. Nonetheless, these rhetorics reaffirmed the relationship of what they called composition, language, or communication to science, usually some form of Baconian science, and to civilization. In this respect, they were *rhetorical* in the classical sense of the term.[1]

These nineteenth- and early-twentieth-century scientific rhetorics were not, however, all of a kind. They differed, in large measure, because they were based upon different views of science and civilization and of their relationship to both. Spencer's science, which he claimed was inductive but which in practice was largely deductive, provided the basis for both his theory of English composition and his sociology, which held that the development of civilization was an entirely natural evolutionary process (James G. Kennedy, 87–118; Peel, 131–65). His theory of composition was functional in the context of his views of science and civilization, but it did not recognize science as a mode of inquiry or civilization as a process of building a social community. Rather, it engaged the method of science to establish its one and only principle of economy, and it served a narrow reportorial role in the natural evolution of civilization (James G. Kennedy, 101–2).

Both Huxley's view of language and Dewey's theory of communication, in contrast, were inseparable from science, construed as a mode of inquiry, and from civilization, construed as a process of building a social community. Huxley's science was based upon facts rather than deductions (Paradis, 73–113, 165–73). His view of language was a logical corollary to a science based upon facts, and it provided the basis of all language education. His view of civilization was synonymous with politics construed in the classical sense, and as such it was at odds with the natural process of evolution (Paradis, 115–63). However, his view of language and language education was directed toward improvement of the human condition, and it served a broad and constructive role in the development of civilization.

Finally, Dewey's science, his theory of communication, and his view of civilization were all part of a broad philosophical and educational program intended to collapse the dualism between man and nature, theory and practice, the individual and society, and so on (for example, Dykhuizen, 178–79; Frankel, 29–38). Like Huxley's view of language, Dewey's theory of communication was inseparable from science construed as a mode of inquiry and from civilization construed as a process of building a social community. His method of science was identical with his method of communication, and both sought to promote the public good and so to foster the development of civilization. However, by the early twentieth century, science was no longer what it was in the latter half of the nineteenth century, a science based upon facts. It was, increasingly, science organized into professional, academic, and industrial communities (Bernal, 134–78; Mason, 352–63). As a result, Dewey's method of science and communication, which was based upon the model of organ-

James P. Zappen

ized physical science, was less concerned with enabling public discussion about the public good than with promoting organized inquiry and disseminating the results of that inquiry. This method was suited to organizational, especially professional, rather than social communities; indeed, it collapsed the dualism of science and civilization (inquiry and community, thought and action) by identifying the social community with organized science. Dewey's method of science and communication was widely influential in several fields of communication, including scientific and technical communication.

The Relationship of Rhetoric to Logic and to Politics and Ethics: Aristotle

Aristotle's system of sciences places rhetoric in relation to logic or dialectic and to politics and ethics, but not to science. As set forth in the *Prior Analytics* and *Posterior Analytics*, science achieves true knowledge through syllogistic demonstration and observation of facts, deduction and induction (Hill, 24, 28–29; George A. Kennedy, 61–63; Randall, 32–51). Logic or dialectic, in contrast, as set forth in the *Topica*, achieves only probable knowledge since it is based upon generally accepted opinion, not facts (Hill, 24; George A. Kennedy, 64–65; Randall, 37–39). Therefore, as Aristotle explains in The *"Art" of Rhetoric*, a rhetoric that seeks to achieve true or scientific knowledge is no longer rhetoric, but science (1.4.1359b4–7). Because it is concerned with probable knowledge only, Aristotle's rhetoric is related to logic and also to politics and ethics, but not to science.

Through its relationship with logic and with politics and ethics, Aristotle's rhetoric provides a vehicle for doing public business in the legislative assemblies, the lawcourts, and on formal occasions (Hill; George A. Kennedy, 63–76; Randall, 279–87). As Aristotle explains in the *Rhetoric*, rhetoric is the counterpart of dialectic, and it is also an offshoot of politics and ethics (1.1.1354a1–2; 1.2.1356a7). Like dialectic, rhetoric rests its "proofs and arguments" upon "generally accepted principles," probabilities rather than truths. (1.1.1355a11–b13). Rhetoric is synonymous with invention (though it also includes style and arrangement and perhaps delivery); it is "the faculty of discovering the possible means of persuasion" (1.2.1355b1). It derives these means of persuasion from three sources: the character and virtues of the speaker, the emotions of the hearer, and the speech itself, insofar as it proves or seems to prove (1.2.1355b3–56a6). Because it depends upon these sources, rhetoric is related to logic and to politics and ethics, the proofs from the speech presumably being related to logic, those from character and the emotions to politics and ethics (1.2.1356a7). It uses proofs derived from these sources to do public business in three kinds of speeches: deliberative, forensic, and epideictic, the rhetoric of the legislative assemblies, of the lawcourts, and of formal occasions (1.3.1358a1–59a6). Of the three kinds of speeches, rhetoric gives more attention to deliberative and forensic than epideictic, and it privileges deliberative, which deals with questions of policy in the legislative assemblies, as "nobler and more worthy of a statesman" than forensic (1.1.1354b10–55a10).

Through its relationship with politics and ethics, Aristotle's rhetoric serves the public good, the good of the social community, the *polis* or state. As Aristotle explains in the *Politics*, political science is the science concerned with man's political association, with the laws, customs, and institutions of the community, the *polis* (1.1.1252a1–3; Rackham, Introduction, *Politics*, xvi–xvii). Within his system of sciences, which he describes in the *Nicomachean Ethics*, political science is the master science that directs all the others. Political science has as its end happiness, the good of man, not the good of the individual but the good of the state, of the two the greater and more perfect good (1.1–2). For this reason, political science directs the other sciences and faculties, including rhetoric: "for it is this that ordains which of the sciences are to exist in states, and what branches of knowledge the different classes of the citizens are to learn, and up to what point; and we observe that even the most highly esteemed of the faculties, such as strategy, domestic economy, oratory, are subordinate to the political science" (1.2.1094a4–b8). Within the context of Aristotle's system, rhetoric serves the end of political science, the good of the social community.

These statements on the relationship of rhetoric to logic and to politics and ethics are elitist to the extent that they reflect aristocratic ideals based upon gender, class, and wealth and power (Berlin, 18; Rackham, Introduction, *Nicomachean Ethics*, xxvii–xxviii). Nevertheless, they articulate issues of recurring interest in the history of rhetoric and of particular interest in the nineteenth and early twentieth centuries when, the traditional relationship between rhetoric and other sciences having been severed, the scientific rhetorics sought to restore it.

The Separation of Rhetoric from Logic and Politics: Richard Whately

By the early nineteenth century, the new science had discredited the old logic of probabilities, and two logics — one deductive and syllogistic, the other inductive and scientific — vied for credibility (Howell, 698–706; McKerrow). The most widely current rhetorics were those now usually designated belletristic, elocutionary, practical, and psychological-epistemological (Berlin, 19–34; Ehninger, xxiii–xxx; Howell, 707–14; Stewart, 136–52). These rhetorics, having severed their traditional relationship with logic, were left with, at most, a modified and restricted form of invention to go with style, arrangement, and delivery (memory, the traditional fifth part of rhetoric, was usually ignored). The belletristic and elocutionary rhetorics were concerned with style and delivery, respectively, and the practical rhetorics were concerned largely with arrangement, especially paragraph arrangement, and with style. The psychological-epistemological rhetorics — including George Campbell's *Philosophy of Rhetoric* (1776), Joseph Priestley's *Lectures on Oratory and Criticism* (1777), and, in the nineteenth century, Whately's *Elements of Rhetoric* (1828) — were concerned in part with invention, but invention of a sort that was left to rhetoric after logic, whether deductive or inductive, had assumed responsibility for the discovery of proofs.[2] As a self-avowed Aristotelian rhetoric, Whately's *Rhetoric* provides a particularly apt illustration of the change that the psychological-epistemological rhetorics brought to the classical tradition in rhetoric in general and to Aristotle's rhetoric in particular.

Whately's *Rhetoric* distinguishes and separates the role of logic from that of rhetoric and all but ignores politics. In its new role, rhetoric becomes, so Spencer and Huxley observe, virtually synonymous with rule teaching. A churchman, eventually Archbishop of Dublin, Whately wrote both the *Elements of Logic* (1826) and the *Rhetoric* for Oxford divinity students to help them to develop their argumentative powers for use in their defense of the true faith (Ehninger, ix–xii, xv–xvi; McKerrow, 177–78). In the *Logic*, Whately presents both the technical rules (as in Aristotle) and a defense of the utility of syllogistic reasoning (McKerrow, 178–84). In the *Rhetoric*, he separates logic from rhetoric, the discovery of proofs from the presentation of proofs to an audience, on both Aristotle's and Francis Bacon's authority (Ehninger, xii–xv; Einhorn, "Consistency," 93–96; Einhorn, "Public Persuasion," 49–51; Howell, 698–703, 707–12). He proposes "to treat of 'Argumentative Composition,' *generally*, and *exclusively*; considering Rhetoric (in conformity with the very just and philosophical view of Aristotle) as an off-shoot from Logic" (4). However, unlike Aristotle, he does not include the discovery of proofs within the domain of rhetoric. Rather, he distinguishes inquiry from proof, the discovery of proofs from their presentation to an audience. To logic he assigns inquiry, "the *ascertainment* of the truth by investigation"; to rhetoric, proof, "the *establishment* of it to the satisfaction of *another*" (5–6, 35). He justifies this distinction on grounds that Bacon has already established the rules of inquiry and even suggests that Bacon would approve his own emphasis on *"Dialectics"* rather than the "accumulation of facts," deductive rather than inductive logic, as more appropriate to the needs of his time (5–6, 15).

Having assigned the discovery of proofs to logic, Whately leaves to rhetoric only their presentation to the satisfaction of an audience. His *Rhetoric* belongs to the tradition of psychological-epistemological rhetorics, so-called because they were concerned with the adaptation, selection, and expression rather than the discovery of proofs, a "managerial" or supervisory role (Berlin, 28–30; Ehninger, xxviii–xxix; Einhorn, "Consistency," 96; Einhorn, "Public Persuasion," 50–51; Stewart, 139–40). Psychological-epistemological rhetorics such as Campbell's and Priestley's had concerned themselves with the managerial rather than the investigative role of rhetoric, but they had not formulated the principles and methods for such a rhetoric. Whately's *Rhetoric* does so by providing a system for the classification of proofs: a division of the forms of arguments and rules for their use for the purpose of conviction (35–168) and a division of the "Active Principles" of human nature — including both the passions (emotions) of the hearer and the character of the speaker — and rules for their use for the purpose of persuasion (175–230).

Whately passes over almost in silence the separation of rhetoric from politics. Although he provides a role for the emotions of the hearer and the character of the speaker, he notes with approval Aristotle's complaint that previous writers on rhetoric had subsumed "the Science of Legislation and of Politics" as part of their own art (3–4, 10–11). His own rhetoric, in contrast, is ecclesiastical, not political, and it "remains strangely aloof from the world of men and affairs" (Ehninger, xii).

The Science of English Composition and Sociology: Herbert Spencer

Although rhetoric in the late eighteenth and early nineteenth centuries thus severed its relationship with invention, construed in the classical sense, and hence with logic and politics as well, the scientific rhetorics of Spencer, Huxley, and Dewey reaffirmed the relationship of composition or language or communication to modes of inquiry and to social communities, to science and civilization. These scientific rhetorics were based upon Baconian science, in one form or another the prevailing standard in science in the middle and late nineteenth century. Baconian science in the middle of the century was largely the legacy of Scottish Realism, which was itself a reaction against skeptical tendencies in British philosophy that culminated in the writings of David Hume (Bozeman, 3–21; Campbell, 352–58). In its most reductive sense, it was simply the "accumulation of facts" that Whately rejected in favor of deductive logic. It was justified almost wholly on grounds of its industrial applications, but it was only later in the century, for this reason, associated with Bacon.

Spencer's theory of composition is functional in the context of his views of science and civilization, but it does not recognize science as a mode of inquiry or civilization as a process of building a social community. Rather, it engages the method of science to establish its principle of economy and serves a narrow reportorial role in the natural evolution of civilization (James G. Kennedy, 87–118; Peel, 131–65). Once a railway engineer and an occasional participant in radical politics, Spencer became a prolific writer and contributed to such fields as sociology (especially in its relationship to biology), education, and many others (James G. Kennedy; Peel). He is best remembered for his contributions to sociology, including *Social Statics* (1850), *The Study of Sociology* (1873), and *The Principles of Sociology* (1876–1897), which set forth his view of social evolution as a natural process analogous to biological evolution and earned him the title "the arch-Social Darwinist" (James G. Kennedy, 7). He is also remembered for *Education: Intellectual, Moral, and Physical* (1861), which earned him a reputation as the most uncompromising proponent of scientific education in England in the middle of the nineteenth century (Barnard, 136–42; Evans, 215–16; Saffin, 198–200). He has only recently been remembered for his essay "Philosophy of Style" (1852), which influenced E. D. Hirsch's philosophy of composition in the twentieth century (Hirsch, 76–82; Secor, 82–84; Stewart, 142).

Spencer's science provides the basis for both his theory of composition and his sociology. Spencer claims to base his science upon Baconian induction, but in practice he appears to operate upon deduction, to use principles to explain facts rather than to derive principles from facts (Peel, 158–65). In *Education*, he claims to base his science upon the observation of facts and upon experimentation and the derivation of principles from facts, and he justifies his science on grounds of its industrial applications. On Bacon's authority, he claims to begin with the observation of facts, with "an accurate acquaintance with the visible and tangible properties of things" (106–7). And he claims to proceed from rudimentary facts through the experimental discovery of the relationship of facts to the organization of knowledge, which is simply the "union of facts into generalizations," or principles (104–7). He justifies his science on grounds of its industrial applications: for virtually all men are employed in industry, and efficiency in "the production, preparation, and distribution of commodities . . . depends on Science" (44–45). In practice, however, Spencer appears to operate by deduction, to use principles to explain facts. In *The Study of Sociology*, he claims, as a basic principle of his sociology, that the nature of the unit determines the nature of the aggregate, and he explains that by nature he means "essential" rather than "incidental" traits (43–45). He thus permits himself to dismiss as "incidental" any facts that appear to provide evidence counter to his own generalizations or principles about society (Peel, 160–65). For this reason, Huxley was moved to observe that "Spencer's idea of a tragedy is a deduction killed by a fact" (Irvine, 24; Paradis, 4–5).

Spencer's theory of English composition engages his science to establish its principle of economy (Hirsch, 76–82; Secor, 82–84; Stewart, 142). His theory, set forth in "Philosophy of Style," addresses literary texts, for the most part, and in this sense it is belletristic (Stewart, 142). Yet it is also scientific — not in the sense that it embraces science as a mode of inquiry, but in the sense that it engages science to establish its principle of economy (Secor, 82–83). Spencer's theory is apparently functional in the context of his claim to an inductive science. However, Spencer does not explain how the principle of economy might serve inductive science but instead engages his science to establish the principle. In *Education*, he rejects the rote learning and rule teaching that he claims is characteristic of classical education in the middle of the nineteenth century (22–23, 109–10). At the beginning of "Philosophy of Style," he directs these criticisms at the rules of logic, grammar, and rhetoric in general and of the rhetoricians (including Whately) in particular, despite the fact that he borrows extensively from them (9–10; Denton). In place of rules, he offers a principle of composition based upon a "scientific ordination," which he calls the principle of economy or efficiency and by which he means "the least possible mental effort" on the part of the reader (10–11).

Spencer uses this principle to explain facts about both the style and arrangement of an effective composition and in so doing illustrates his deductive approach to science. He applies the principle to style in his comparison of the English and French languages. For example, he refers to the phrase *un cheval noir*, or *a black horse*, which, he asserts, is more economical in English than in French because the picture of black conveys only an abstract quality and so is readily formed by the addition of horse (in English) whereas the picture of horse conveys images of color, kind, and the like and so must be reformed by the addition of black (in French) (16–18). Spencer applies the principle of economy to the overall arrangement of an effective composition as well. He asserts that this principle explains, for example, the need to "progress from the less interesting to the more interesting," to avoid "long continuity of the same kind of thought, or repeated production of like effects," and so on (44–45). He apparently believes that economy of effect exists first of all in the reader, quite apart from concerns with the writer or with the formal properties of a text (Secor, 84).

Spencer's sociology also engages his science to establish his view that the development of civilization is an entirely natural evolutionary process (James G. Kennedy, 87–118; Peel, 131–65). Like his theory of composition, Spencer's sociology illustrates his deductive approach to science. His theory of composition is functional in the context of his view of civilization, which assigns to language a narrow reportorial role (James G. Kennedy, 101–2), rather than an active role in building a social community. In *Social Statics*, Spencer expresses his belief in the natural evolution of the human race toward perfection: "Progress, therefore, is not an accident, but a necessity. Instead of civilization being artificial it is a part of nature; all of a piece with the development of an embryo or the unfolding of a flower" (32). On the principle that the nature of the unit (in this instance, the individual) determines the nature of the aggregate (the society), he affirms the natural rights of the individual and advocates a laissez-faire approach to government, hence his general proposition "that every man may claim the fullest liberty to exercise his faculties compatible with the possession of like liberty by every other man" (36–45, 109–36).

In *The Principles of Sociology*, Spencer includes among his most important principles the two processes of change that bring about the natural evolution of civilization: a tendency toward differentiation and growing complexity and a trend from militancy to industrialism (1:491–587; Peel, 166–223). He explains the process of differentiation in a series of analogies between organisms and societies, both of which, he claims, differentiate or increase in structure as they increase in mass, as cells combine to form complex organisms, for example, and tribes combine to form nations (1:491–548). He explains the trend from militancy to industrialism as a transition from a society characterized by compulsory cooperation to a society characterized by voluntary cooperation, both necessary stages in the natural evolution of civilization (1:549–87). However, he cannot satisfactorily account for either primitive societies that exhibit an industrial character or modern societies that exhibit a militant character (Peel, 198–214). At this point, his sociology illustrates the limitations of his deductive science. His theory of composition is nonetheless functional in the context of his view of the natural evolution of civilization, for such a view does not take into account the use of language to transmit a social way of life, to build a social community, but rather assigns to language a narrow reportorial, or *"inter-nuncial,"* role analogous to, but beyond the scope of, physical stimuli (1:459–60; James G. Kennedy, 101–2).

Science, Language, and Civilization: Thomas H. Huxley

Huxley's theory of language, in contrast to Spencer's theory of composition, is inseparable from science construed as a mode of inquiry and from civilization construed as a process of building a social community. His view of language is a logical corollary to his science, and it provides the basis of all language education and serves a broad and constructive role in the development of civilization. Huxley was an accomplished scientist who before the age of thirty had been elected to the Royal Society and had won the Society's Gold Medal. He became known popularly for his defense of Charles Darwin's theory of evolution, for his support of scientific education, and for his defense of science and its role in civilization (Ashforth; Irvine; Paradis). Huxley defended Darwin's theory at scientific and public meetings and so earned a reputation as "Darwin's Bulldog," and he extended the theory to include man in his most important essay, "Man's Place in Nature" (1863) (Ashforth, 23). On a famous occasion, he revealed the low esteem accorded to rhetoric when, in reply to Bishop Wilberforce, he remarked that he would rather have an ape for a grandfather than a man who obscured the truth by "aimless rhetoric" and "eloquent digressions" (Ashforth, 36; Irvine, 4–6). Huxley supported scientific education in "Science and Culture" (1880), "On Science and Art in Relation to Education" (1882), and other essays, but, unlike Spencer, he held a balanced view of the role of science in education (Barnard, 142–43; Evans, 215–16; Saffin, 198, 257–60). Finally, he defended science itself and its role in civilization in "The Progress of Science 1837–1887" (1887), "Evolution and Ethics" (1893) and its "Prolegomena" (1894), and other essays.

Huxley's science is based upon facts rather than deductions and so is Baconian in the sense in which Bacon was understood in the middle of the nineteenth century (Paradis, 73–113, 165–73). Huxley claims to admit hypotheses in science, and he eschews applications. But he most often refers to facts to justify his conclusions, and he often justifies science on grounds of its industrial applications. In "The Progress of Science," Huxley argues that Bacon's science was "hopelessly impracticable" because it rejected hypotheses and misguided because it sought "practical advantages" (1:46–56). He claims that, in fact, "the invention of hypotheses based on incomplete inductions . . . has proved itself to be a most efficient, indeed an indispensable, instrument of scientific progress" and that "the joy of the discovery" rather than "practical utility" accounts for the growth of science in the late eighteenth and early nineteenth centuries (1:46–47, 51–54).

James P. Zappen

Yet Huxley often has recourse to facts. In "The Progress of Science," he alludes to the recent growth of science and proclaims "this new Nature begotten by science upon fact" (1:51–52). In "Man's Place in Nature," he introduces his discussion on the origin of man with reference to "the chief facts upon which all conclusions respecting the nature and the extent of the bonds which connect man with the brute world must be based" and other references to the factual basis of his discussion (7:81). Moreover, Huxley, like Spencer, emphasizes the industrial applications of science. In "The Progress of Science," he argues that science and industry are identical, "that science cannot make a step forward without . . . opening up new channels for industry; and . . . that every advance of industry facilitates those experimental investigations, upon which the growth of science depends" (1:54–56).

Huxley's view of language as proper signification is a logical corollary to a science based upon facts, and it provides the basis of all language education. In "On Science and Art," Huxley complains about the classical education he experienced in his youth and cites the same emphasis on rule teaching that Spencer complains about in *Education* (3:180–81). But he most frequently decries the kind of teaching that misuses words: "The difference between good and bad teaching mainly consists in this, whether the words used are really clothed with a meaning or not" (3:168–70). To ensure the correct use of words, proper signification, he relies upon facts. In "On Science and Art," he turns to the seventeenth century and cites Harvey, Bacon, and Locke to confirm his insistence upon the correspondence between words and things, or facts (3:168–70, 173–74, 186–88). He is particularly fond of Bacon's remark that truth comes more readily from error than from confusion because error can more readily be corrected by "knocking your head against a fact" (3:173–74).

This view of language as proper signification provides the basis of all language education, directed either toward personal pleasure or toward social and practical pursuits. In "Science and Culture," Huxley argues that the industrial applications of science are a necessary but not a sufficient condition for industrial prosperity because industry is a means, not an end, the end being human wants, the wants being determined by innate and acquired desires (3:156). He claims that language education provides a means of directing the acquired desires away from base wants toward "pleasures, which are neither withered by age, nor staled by custom, nor embittered in the recollection by the pangs of self-reproach" (3:156–57). He also engages language education to address social and practical pursuits. In "Science and Culture," he argues that language education in English, French, and German can provide access to the "three greatest literatures of the modern world" and to "full knowledge in any department of science" (3:154). In "On Science and Art," he maintains that English provides models for imitation and practice in composition, which is generally neglected by Englishmen, and that it provides an essential part of the preparation for an Englishman "to go anywhere, to occupy the highest positions, to fill the highest offices of the State, and to become distinguished in practical pursuits, in science, or in art" (3:184–86).

Huxley's view of civilization is synonymous with politics construed in its classical sense, and as such it is at odds with the natural process of evolution (Paradis, 115–63). However, his view of language and language education is directed toward improvement of the human condition, and it serves a broad and constructive role in the development of civilization. In later works, Huxley explains what he has come to believe is a conflict between civilization and evolution, art and nature, good and evil. In "Evolution and Ethics," he explains that civilization is synonymous with politics, that the "civilized state, or polity," is "political" in the sense in which the Greek Stoics used the term, to denote "the sacrifice of self to the common good," a meaning so remote as to "now sound almost grotesque" (9:74–75). In the "Prolegomena," he claims that this view of civilization is at odds with evolution, and he explains the conflict in a lengthy analogy between a garden and a human society (9:1–17). He argues that the analogy breaks down because, on the one hand, an administrator in a human society neither would nor could adopt horticultural principles, neither would nor could, for example, discriminate between the fit and the unfit and select for survival only the most fit (9:17–23). Nor, on the other hand, would even the most basic rules of conduct acceptable in human society, for example, the "golden rule," be useful to the horticulturist: "What would become of the garden if the gardener treated all the weeds and slugs and birds and trespassers as he would like to be treated, if he were in their place?" (9:31–33).

Despite his pessimistic view of natural evolution, Huxley believes that improvement of the human condition is possible through the exercise of human purpose. At the end of the "Prolegomena," he argues that "man, as a 'political animal,' is susceptible of a vast amount of improvement, by education, by instruction, and by the application of his intelligence to the adaptation of the conditions of life to his higher needs" (9:44). Huxley had not forgotten that between "Man's Place in Nature" and "Evolution and Ethics" he wrote "Science and Culture" and other essays in support of education, in both science and language. His view of language and language education contributes to the human effort to develop a "worthy civilization" (9:44–45), for it helps to ensure the correct use of words, to turn human wants toward worthy pleasures, and to provide preparation for social and practical pursuits.

James P. Zappen

Scientific Facts and Organized Science:
Karl Pearson, Arthur James Balfour,
and Henry Adams

Science had changed in at least two important respects by the late nineteenth and early twentieth centuries, and both proponents and critics of science observed these changes. First, science no longer seemed to be firmly based upon facts. As late as the third edition of *The Grammar of Science* (1911), Karl Pearson still cites Charles Darwin's account of his painstaking collection of facts as a model of Baconian science (32–33). But other observers of science such as Arthur James Balfour and Henry Adams assert that this model is fundamentally wrong. In "Reflections Suggested by the New Theory of Matter" (1904), Balfour notes that the discovery of the atom calls into question "those 'plain matters of fact' among which common-sense daily moves with its most confident step and most self-satisfied smile" and asserts that the human race, before this discovery, had "lived and died in a world of illusions" (207–8). In *The Education of Henry Adams* (1918), Adams alludes to the "metaphysical bomb" called radium and accuses Pearson of shutting out of science "everything which the nineteenth century had brought into it" (450–52).

Second, science had reaped the rewards of its industrial applications and had, in the process, taken on increasingly intricate forms of organization — professional, academic, and industrial (Bernal, 134–78; Mason, 352–63). As a result, it was still Baconian science, but Baconian science in an entirely different sense, for both proponents and critics of science acknowledged Bacon as the visionary who foresaw the possible applications of pure science. In his essay "Bacon" (1912), Balfour calls Bacon a seer because he foresaw the need for pure science as a basis for "industrial invention" (35–36). In *Education*, Adams supposes that witnesses to the Great Exposition of 1900 knew nothing of science that Bacon did not know three hundred years earlier (379). Dewey recognizes both of these changes in Baconian science and brings them to bear upon his views of science, communication, and civilization.

Scientific Method, Communication, and
Professional Communities: John Dewey

Dewey's science, his theory of communication, and his view of civilization are all part of a broad philosophical and educational program intended to collapse various dualisms (for example, Dykhuizen, 178–79; Frankel, 29–38). Like Huxley's view of language, Dewey's theory of communication is inseparable from science construed as a mode of inquiry and from civilization construed as a process of building a social community. Dewey's method of science and communication, however, is based upon the model of organized physical science, in particular as applied to professional communities of social scientists, and so is suited to organizational, especially professional, rather than social communities. His method collapses the dualism of science and civilization by identifying the social community with organized science. Probably America's most influential philosopher and educator, Dewey made significant contributions to philosophy, social science, education, and numerous other fields (Boydston; Dykhuizen; Frankel). To philosophy, in works such as *Experience and Nature* (1925), *The Quest for Certainty* (1929), and *Logic: The Theory of Inquiry* (1938), Dewey brought "antifoundationalism," the belief that philosophy ought to abandon its quest for certainty, a belief that has influenced contemporary philosophy, though in several directions, principally through the work of Richard Rorty (Sleeper, 1–9).[3] Through his social science, set forth in *The Public and Its Problems* (1927), *Liberalism and Social Action* (1935), and other works, Dewey and his students influenced not only the universities but the practice of law, economics, social psychology, and political science (Frankel, 3–4). Finally, by his approach to education, described in *How We Think* (1910 and 1933), *Democracy and Education* (1916), and other works, Dewey established the foundation of the "experimentalist-oriented progressive school," widely popularized by William Heard Kilpatrick (Gutek, 191–201; Peters, 106–9).

Dewey's science is Baconian in the sense in which Bacon was understood in the late nineteenth and early twentieth centuries. That is, it looks for its method not in the accumulation of facts but in organized physical science. It is based upon facts, but it does not regard those facts as intuitively obvious. At the beginning of *The Public and Its Problems*, Dewey disputes the contention that facts have meaning in and of themselves: "Many persons seem to suppose that facts carry their meaning along with themselves on their face. Accumulate enough of them, and their interpretation stares out at you" (*LW* 2:238). He explains that the meaning of facts derives not from the facts themselves but from the method of the physical sciences: "Take away from physical science its laboratory apparatus and its mathematical technique, and the human imagination might run wild in its theories of interpretation even if we suppose the brute facts to remain the same" (*LW* 2:238). As a model for this method, Dewey's science looks to organized physical science and to Bacon, the visionary. In *Liberalism and Social Action*, Dewey applauds the achievements of physical science and credits Bacon with the vision to foresee that those achievements were possible: "The prophetic vision of Francis Bacon of subjugation of the energies of nature through change in methods of inquiry has well-nigh been realized" (*LW* 11:51–52). He argues, however, that these achievements were made possible only by organized science, "organized intelligence," the "combined effect of science and technology," and that they were purchased at great cost, as "industrial entrepreneurs have reaped out of all proportion to what they sowed" (*LW* 11:51–54). For this reason, Dewey believes that Bacon's vision was only partially realized, for "the conquest of natural energies has not accrued to the betterment of the common human estate in anything like the degree he anticipated" (*LW* 11:53). Nonetheless, Dewey admires the power and achievement of the physical sciences, and he looks to organized physical science as the model for his method of science and communication.

Dewey's method of communication, set forth in his analysis of reflective thinking, is identical with his method of science. Dewey developed this method as a part of his educational practice for the purpose of involving students in cooperative problem-solving experiences as opposed to inert subject matter, and the method became the foundation of the progressive movement in education (Gutek, 193–94; Peters, 107–8). This method, as set forth in *Democracy and Education* and *How We Think*, is a generalization of the method of the physical sciences. It includes five steps, as a response to a confused situation: examining suggestions, or possible solutions; locating and defining the problem; using the suggestions to develop a hypothesis; reasoning, or elaboration of the hypothesis; and testing the hypothesis (*MW* 9:159–70; *LW* 8:199–209). This method is a method of both science and communication. As such, it is concerned with the relationship of words to facts and of the process of reflective thinking to its product. In *How We Think*, Dewey, like Huxley, turns to the seventeenth century, to Bacon and Locke, for cautions about the relationship of words to things, or facts (*LW* 8:131–34). He provides advice on how to organize words into meaningful sentences and units of consecutive discourse (*LW* 8:301–14). He distinguishes the process from the product of reflective thinking, logical method from logical form, actual thinking from the setting forth of the results of thinking (*LW* 8:171–76). But he also insists upon the necessary connection between the two, "the internal and necessary connection between the actual process of thinking and its intellectual product," and he observes that for a mature learner the psychological process of reflective thinking terminates in the logical product of "scientifically organized material" (*LW* 8:176–82). As the logical form of the psychological process, Dewey's method of communication is identical with his method of science.

Dewey's view of civilization, like Huxley's, is synonymous with politics in the classical sense. His method of science and communication, however, is based upon the model of organized physical science and so is suited to organizational and especially to professional rather than social communities. In his essay "Philosophy and Civilization," Dewey revives the classical Greek view that regards all philosophy as a civic enterprise (Frankel, 5–6). He insists upon the intrinsic connection between philosophy and civilization, by which he means "that complex of institutions which forms culture," politics in the classical sense (*LW* 3:3–4). Elsewhere, he identifies politics with pursuit of the public good, and he proposes to use his method of science and communication, based upon the model of organized physical science, to identify and achieve that good. In *Liberalism and Social Action*, Dewey identifies the public good as the greatest good of the greatest number but rejects public discussion in favor of organized science as a means of achieving that good. He claims that public discussion, as "a kind of political watered-down version of the Hegelian dialectic, . . . has nothing in common with the procedure of organized cooperative inquiry which has won the triumphs of science in the field of physical nature" (*LW* 11:50–51, 54).

Inspired by the success of organized physical science, Dewey proposes to use its method to enhance inquiry in the social sciences. In *The Public and Its Problems*, he defines the problem of modern political life as the "eclipse" of the public due to the survival of archaic political and legal forms and arrangements in a machine age (*LW* 2:313–15). He seeks to make "the interest of the public" the guide and criterion of governmental activity, and to that end he proposes to search for means "by which a scattered, mobile and manifold public may so recognize itself as to define and express its interests" (*LW* 2:327). However, he does not seek to enhance the methods of public discussion about the public interest. Rather, he proposes to use the method of organized physical science to enhance inquiry in the social sciences and the dissemination of the results of that inquiry for the purpose of public discussion and the formation of public opinion (*LW* 2:339). Again, he proposes to address "the improvement of the methods and conditions of debate, discussion and persuasion," but he seeks to do so by perfecting the processes of inquiry and the dissemination of conclusions (*LW* 2:365). He does not propose to involve the public in the process of inquiry, which in his analysis of reflective thinking might include defining a problem, developing a hypothesis, and suggesting and testing solutions. He tacitly presumes that the organizational (professional) communities responsible for inquiry can represent the public interest and the public good on these issues.

Dewey's attempt to bring the method of science and communication to bear upon civilization has been criticized on grounds that it presupposes the existence of a community but does not identify the source of the community's shared ideas, views, and values (Bitzer, 77–81). It has also been criticized because it seeks to identify a "shared substantive interest" rather than to develop competent participants in public discussion

(Hauser and Blair, 161–63). Nonetheless, his method was widely influential in textbooks in speech communication, where it was designated "the motivated sequence" (Ehninger, Monroe, and Gronbeck, 143–61; Simons, 165), and in organizational communication, where it was "for many years the only organizational pattern taught in group discussion classes" (Bradley and Baird, 235). It provides theoretical support for the traditional identification of scientific and technical communication with organizational communities (for example, Bazerman; Farrell and Goodnight, 292–300; Miller and Selzer; Paradis, Dobrin, and Miller). And it reflects widespread practice in the methods of inquiry and organization of scientific articles, test reports, and design and feasibility reports; in these forms, it appears in virtually every textbook on research report writing and scientific and technical communication.

Dewey's method of science and communication collapsed the dualism of science and civilization. Insofar as this method was successful, it restored the traditional relationship of rhetoric to inquiry and to community. It brought together the method of science and the method of communication in the interest of building a social community. However, in so doing, it identified the social community with organized science. The utility of this method is that it enlists the power of the method of science as a method of communication in the service of a particular organizational community, its limitation that (if only implicitly) it forecloses participation in that community by those outside it.

The scientific rhetorics of Spencer, Huxley, and Dewey are not all of the same kind. Insofar as they are similar, these rhetorics reaffirm the relationship of rhetoric to inquiry and to the social community and so provide some (perhaps indirect) support for the supposition that the ideals (at least) of classical rhetoric persisted well into the nineteenth century (Crowley, "Evolution of Invention"; Crowley, "Invention"; Johnson; Rosner).[4] Insofar as they differ, these rhetorics suggest a range of possible relationships of rhetoric to inquiry and to the social community. Spencer's rhetoric, however narrow and reductive, is functional in the context of his claim to an inductive science and his belief in the natural evolution of civilization. Huxley's rhetoric, at its worst similarly reductive, nonetheless shows how rhetoric might aid scientific inquiry by ensuring the proper use of words and might help to improve the human condition and promote the development of civilization by serving personal, social, and practical goals. Dewey's rhetoric is more problematic. On the one hand, this rhetoric identifies social with organizational, especially professional, communities and aids science in the service of those communities. In this respect, it illustrates how science and scientific rhetoric in the service of organized, professionalized communities, rather than science or the specialization of the curriculum in itself, may have encouraged the development of practical rhetorics and the separation of rhetoric from science and from societal concerns. In just this way, it has been the most influential of these rhetorics in several fields of communication, including scientific and technical communication. On the other hand, Dewey's rhetoric enlists the method of organized physical science as a method of communication to promote the public good and so to foster the development of civilization. In this respect, it too reaffirms its relationship to inquiry and to the social community, to science and civilization.

NOTES

I am indebted to S. Michael Halloran and Merrill D. Whitburn for their comments on various drafts of this paper.

1. The terminology is not yet settled. Spencer uses the term *composition* fairly consistently. Huxley uses the terms *language* and *literary education* almost interchangeably. Dewey uses the term *communication* to subsume several other meanings, including *discussion, dissemination,* and *persuasion.*

2. Titles and dates for Campbell, Priestley, and Whately are from Ehninger; for Spencer, from Peel; for Huxley, from Paradis and *Huxley's Works*; and for Dewey, from Dykhuizen.

3. Rorty argues that philosophy ought to abandon its quest for the foundations of knowledge and ought rather to promote "conversation" between and among disciplines (313–94). Although he acknowledges that science is Dewey's favorite mode of communication, Sleeper nonetheless emphasizes the broader social purposes of Dewey's theory of communication, especially as set forth in *Experience and Nature,* and so provides a counterbalance to Rorty's (and my own) reading of Dewey (116–23).

4. John Stuart Mill's use of Plato in *A System of Logic Ratiocinative and Inductive* (1843) and *On Liberty* (1859) provides more direct evidence of the persistence of classical rhetoric in the scientific rhetorics of this period. Turner includes a brief introduction to Mill's use of Plato in *On Liberty* (386–87, 401–3).

BIBLIOGRAPHY

Adams, Henry. *The Education of Henry Adams: An Autobiography.* 1918. Boston: Houghton, 1927.

Aristotle. *The "Art" of Rhetoric.* Trans. John Henry Freese. Loeb Classical Library 193. London: Heinemann, 1926.

Aristotle. *The Nicomachean Ethics.* Trans. H. Rackham. Rev. ed. Loeb Classical Library 73. Cambridge: Harvard University Press, 1934.

Aristotle. *Politics.* Trans. H. Rackham. Corrected ed. Loeb Classical Library 264. Cambridge: Harvard University Press, 1944.

James P. Zappen

Ashforth, Albert. *Thomas Henry Huxley*. Twayne's English Authors Series 84. New York: Twayne, 1969.

Balfour, Arthur James. *The Mind of Arthur James Balfour: Selections from His Non-Political Writings, Speeches, and Addresses, 1879–1917*. Selected and arranged by Wilfrid M. Short. New York: Doran, 1918.

Barnard, H. C. *A History of English Education from 1760*. 2d ed. London: University of London Press, 1961.

Bazerman, Charles. *Shaping Written Knowledge: The Genre and Activity of the Experimental Article in Science*. Rhetoric of the Human Sciences. Madison: University of Wisconsin Press, 1988.

Berlin, James A. *Writing Instruction in Nineteenth-Century American Colleges*. Studies in Writing and Rhetoric. Carbondale: Southern Illinois University Press, 1984.

Bernal, J. D. *Science and Industry in the Nineteenth Century*. 1953. Bloomington: Midland Book–Indiana University Press, 1970.

Bitzer, Lloyd F. "Rhetoric and Public Knowledge." In *Rhetoric, Philosophy, and Literature: An Exploration*, ed. Don M. Burks, 67–93. West Lafayette: Purdue University Press, 1978.

Boydston, Jo Ann. *Guide to the Works of John Dewey*. 1970. Carbondale: Arcturus Books–Southern Illinois University Press, 1972.

Bozeman, Theodore Dwight. *Protestants in an Age of Science: The Baconian Ideal and Antebellum American Religious Thought*. Chapel Hill: University of North Carolina Press, 1977.

Bradley, Patricia Hayes, and John E. Baird, Jr. *Communication for Business and the Professions*. 2d ed. Dubuque: Brown, 1983.

Campbell, George. *The Philosophy of Rhetoric*. Ed. Lloyd F. Bitzer. New ed. Landmarks of Rhetoric and Public Address. 1850. Carbondale: Southern Illinois University Press, 1963.

Campbell, John Angus. "Scientific Revolution and the Grammar of Culture: The Case of Darwin's *Origin*." *Quarterly Journal of Speech* 72 (1986): 351–76.

Connors, Robert J., Lisa S. Ede, and Andrea A. Lunsford. "The Revival of Rhetoric in America." In *Essays on Classical Rhetoric and Modern Discourse*, ed. Robert J. Connors, Lisa S. Ede, and Andrea A. Lunsford, 1–15, 259–61. Carbondale: Southern Illinois University Press, 1984.

Crowley, Sharon. "The Evolution of Invention in Current-Traditional Rhetoric: 1850–1970." *Rhetoric Review* 3 (1985): 145–62.

Crowley, Sharon. "Invention in Nineteenth-Century Rhetoric." *College Composition and Communication* 36 (1985): 51–60.

Denton, George B. "Herbert Spencer and the Rhetoricians." *Publications of the Modern Language Association of America* 34 (1919): 89–111.

Dewey, John. *The Later Works, 1925–1953*. Ed. Jo Ann Boydston. 16 vols. Carbondale: Southern Illinois University Press, 1981–1989.

Dewey, John. *The Middle Works, 1899–1924*. Ed. Jo Ann Boydston. 15 vols. Carbondale: Southern Illinois University Press, 1976–83.

Dykhuizen, George. *The Life and Mind of John Dewey*. Ed. Jo Ann Boydston. Carbondale: Southern Illinois University Press, 1973.

Ehninger, Douglas. Editor's Introduction. *Elements of Rhetoric*, by Richard Whately, ix–xxx.

Ehninger, Douglas, Alan H. Monroe, and Bruce E. Gronbeck. *Principles and Types of Speech Communication*. 8th ed. Glenview, Ill.: Scott, 1978.

Einhorn, Lois J. "Consistency in Richard Whately: The Scope of His Rhetoric." *Philosophy and Rhetoric* 14 (1981): 89–99.

Einhorn, Lois J. "Richard Whately's Public Persuasion: The Relationship between His Rhetorical Theory and His Rhetorical Practice." *Rhetorica: A Journal of the History of Rhetoric* 4 (1986): 47–65.

Evans, Keith. *The Development and Structure of the English Educational System*. London: University of London Press, 1975.

Farrell, Thomas B., and G. Thomas Goodnight. "Accidental Rhetoric: The Root Metaphors of Three Mile Island." *Communication Monographs* 48 (1981): 271–300.

Frankel, Charles. "John Dewey's Social Philosophy." In *New Studies in the Philosophy of John Dewey*, ed. Steven M. Cahn, 3–44. Hanover: University of Vermont by the University Press of New England, 1977.

Gutek, Gerald Lee. *An Historical Introduction to American Education*. Crowell Series in American Education. New York: Crowell, 1970.

Halloran, S. Michael. "Rhetoric in the American College Curriculum: The Decline of Public Discourse." *Pre/Text: An Inter-Disciplinary Journal of Rhetoric* 3 (1982): 245–69.

Hauser, Gerard A., and Carole Blair. "Rhetorical Antecedents to the Public." *Pre/Text: An Inter-Disciplinary Journal of Rhetoric* 3 (1982): 139–67.

Hill, Forbes I. "The Rhetoric of Aristotle." In *A Synoptic History of Classical Rhetoric*, ed. James J. Murphy, 19–76. Studies in Speech. New York: Random, 1972.

Hirsch, E. D., Jr. *The Philosophy of Composition*. Chicago: University of Chicago Press, 1977.

Howell, Wilbur Samuel. *Eighteenth-Century British Logic and Rhetoric*. Princeton: Princeton University Press, 1971.

Huxley, Thomas H. *Huxley's Works*. 9 vols. New York: Appleton, n.d.

Irvine, William. *Apes, Angels, and Victorians: A Joint Biography of Darwin and Huxley*. 1955. London: Readers Union, 1956.

Johnson, Nan. "Three Nineteenth-Century Rhetoricians: The Humanist Alternative to Rhetoric as Skills Management." In *The Rhetorical Tradition and Modern Writing*, ed. James J. Murphy, 105–17. New York: Modern Language Association of America, 1982.

Kennedy, George A. *Classical Rhetoric and Its Christian and Secular Tradition from Ancient to Modern Times*. Chapel Hill: University of North Carolina Press, 1980.

Kennedy, James G. *Herbert Spencer*. Twayne's English Authors Series 219. Boston: Twayne, 1978.

McKerrow, Raymie E. "Richard Whately and the Revival of Logic in Nineteenth-Century England." *Rhetorica: A Journal of the History of Rhetoric* 5 (1987): 163–85.

Mason, S. F. *Main Currents of Scientific Thought: A History of the Sciences.* Life of Science Library 32. New York: Shuman, 1953.

Mill, John Stuart. *Collected Works of John Stuart Mill.* Ed. John M. Robson and others. Toronto: University of Toronto Press, 1963– .

Miller, Carolyn R., and Jack Selzer. "Special Topics of Argument in Engineering Reports." In *Writing in Nonacademic Settings,* ed. Lee Odell and Dixie Goswami, 309–41. Perspectives in Writing Research. New York: Guilford, 1985.

Paradis, James G. *T. H. Huxley: Man's Place in Nature.* Lincoln: University of Nebraska Press, 1978.

Paradis, James, David Dobrin, and Richard Miller. "Writing at Exxon ITD: Notes on the Writing Environment of an R&D Organization." In *Writing in Nonacademic Settings,* ed. Lee Odell and Dixie Goswami, 281–307. Perspectives in Writing Research. New York: Guilford, 1985.

Pearson, Karl. *The Grammar of Science.* 3d ed. Meridian Library. 1911. New York: Meridian, 1957.

Peel, J. D. Y. *Herbert Spencer: The Evolution of a Sociologist.* New York: Basic, 1971.

Peters, R. S. "John Dewey's Philosophy of Education." In *John Dewey Reconsidered,* ed. R. S. Peters, 102–23. International Library of the Philosophy of Education. London: Routledge, 1977.

Priestley, Joseph. *A Course of Lectures on Oratory and Cricitism.* Ed. Vincent M. Bevilacqua and Richard Murphy. Landmarks of Rhetoric and Public Address. 1777. Carbondale: Southern Illinois University Press, 1965.

Rackham, H. Introduction. *The Nicomachean Ethics,* by Aristotle, xiii–xxxiii.

Rackham, H. Introduction. *Politics,* by Aristotle, xi–xxvii.

Randall, John Herman, Jr. *Aristotle.* New York: Columbia University Press, 1960.

Ried, Paul E. "The First and Fifth Boylston Professors: A View of Two Worlds." *Quarterly Journal of Speech* 74 (1988): 229–40.

Rorty, Richard. *Philosophy and the Mirror of Nature.* Princeton: Princeton University Press, 1979.

Rosner, Mary. "Reflections on Cicero in Nineteenth-Century England and America." *Rhetorica: A Journal of the History of Rhetoric* 4 (1986): 153–82.

Saffin, N. W. *Science, Religion and Education in Britain, 1804–1904.* Kilmore, Austral.: Lowden, 1973.

Secor, Marie J. "The Legacy of Nineteenth Century Style Theory." *Rhetoric Society Quarterly* 12 (1982): 76–94.

Simons, Herbert W. *Persuasion: Understanding, Practice, and Analysis.* 2d ed. New York: Random, 1986.

Sleeper, R. W. *The Necessity of Pragmatism: John Dewey's Conception of Philosophy.* New Haven: Yale University Press, 1986.

Spencer, Herbert. *Education: Intellectual, Moral, and Physical.* 1860. New York: Appleton, 1897.

Spencer, Herbert. "The Philosophy of Style." In *Essays: Moral, Political and Aesthetic,* 9–47. New and enlarged ed. New York: Appleton, 1889.

Spencer, Herbert. *The Principles of Sociology*. 3 vols. New York: Appleton, 1897.

Spencer, Herbert. *Social Statics, Abridged and Revised; together with The Man versus the State*. 1892. New York: Appleton, 1897.

Spencer, Herbert. *The Study of Sociology*. Ann Arbor: Ann Arbor Paperbacks — University of Michigan Press, 1961.

Stewart, Donald C. "The Nineteenth Century." In *The Present State of Scholarship in Historical and Contemporary Rhetoric*, ed. Winifred Bryan Horner, 134–66. Columbia: University of Missouri Press, 1983.

Turner, Frank M. *The Greek Heritage in Victorian Britain*. New Haven: Yale University Press, 1981.

Whately, Richard. *Elements of Rhetoric: Comprising an Analysis of the Laws of Moral Evidence and of Persuasion, with Rules for Argumentative Composition and Elocution*. Ed. Douglas Ehninger. 7th ed., rev. Landmarks in Rhetoric and Public Address. 1846. Carbondale: Southern Illinois University Press, 1963.

PART TWO

THE DYNAMICS OF

DISCOURSE COMMUNITIES

7 TOWARD A SOCIOCOGNITIVE

MODEL OF LITERACY

CONSTRUCTING MENTAL MODELS

IN A PHILOSOPHICAL

CONVERSATION

CHERYL GEISLER

A writer writes. A reader reads. The effort to understand these apparently simple acts and the relationship between them has motivated numerous research agenda in recent years. Reading research, writing research, composition studies, rhetorical theory, anthropology, critical theory, sociolinguistics, cognitive science, literary studies — each of these terms invokes an affiliation, a national conference, and a set of epistemic beliefs that have all been pressed into the service of explaining these peculiarly human acts.

Against this backdrop, the goal of synthesizing a sociocognitive model of literacy has received increasing attention (Langer, "Musings . . ."). If achieved, such a model would allow researchers to consider human acts such as reading and writing along two dimensions that have often been seen at odds: the axis of individual cognition and the axis of social interaction. Although such a goal is clearly beyond the scope of any individual study, the results presented here move in that direction. In particular, they suggest that experts at advanced philosophical argument use acts of reading and writing to construct and act upon *socially configured mental models*. The presence of such mental models, I will argue, indicates that a purely conversational model of literacy may be missing the point of why individuals propose and maintain written interaction in the first place.

Cheryl Geisler

Design: Reading and Writing about Philosophy

The study reported here examined the practices of four individuals asked to read and write about the ethical issue of paternalism. Two were disciplinary insiders: professional philosophers familiar with ethical philosophy, both men. Expert 1 had recently completed his Ph.D. and had accepted a position at a prestigious university. Expert 2 was still working on his degree. Two were disciplinary outsiders: second-semester freshmen at a private university who had not yet taken an introductory freshman philosophy course, both women. Novice 1 was an engineering student who had received an A in her humanities course the previous semester. Novice 2 was a design student who had received a B in her writing course the previous semester.[1]

All four participants were asked to complete the same reading/writing task: they were asked to read eight articles on the ethical issue of paternalism and to write an original essay defining paternalistic interference and describing the conditions, if any, under which it could be justified. They were told that the intended readers were to be "well-educated people who may at some time in their lives have to deal with the issue of paternalism." The philosophers were solicited through contacts with the philosophic community and worked on the project as consultants. The freshmen were solicited through advertising on campus and completed the work as regular student employment.

Paternalistic interference is an issue for ethical philosophers because it appears to violate widespread assumptions about individual rights and yet occasionally to be justified. John Stuart Mill claimed that the individual had exclusive rights to make decisions regarding his or her own welfare. This "harm principle" has become the starting point for many ethicists' discussions on the nature of rights. Paternalism is a problem in these discussions because it involves the interference by one person in the affairs of another for his or her own good; it thus appears to violate the harm principle. Nevertheless few would argue that it cannot be justified in some cases: parents' paternalism toward children; teachers' paternalism toward students; government paternalism toward the mentally incompetent. In an effort to define the boundaries between justified and unjustified action, ethical philosophers have offered conflicting definitions of paternalistic interference and conflicting specifications of the conditions under which it can be justified.

The two expert philosophers described here were both familiar with Mill's harm principle and with the general discussion of individual rights. Neither, however, was familiar with the issue of paternalism or the particular literature they were given at the start of the project. The two novice freshmen were unfamiliar with the technical issues of ethics, but both readily recognized that they had been subject to the paternalism of parents and school.

All participants worked on the task at their own rate for between 30 and 60 hours spread over 10 to 15 weeks during the spring of 1985. Data were collected during this time in three ways: First, participants were asked to verbalize their thoughts into a tape recorder whenever they worked on the project, producing "think-aloud" protocols (Newell and Simon; Ericsson and Simon). Second, participants were asked to keep all of the writing they produced. And third, participants were interviewed between working sessions concerning what they had accomplished and what they were hoping to accomplish on the task. The resulting transcripts and texts amounted to over 750,000 words.

Framework for Analysis:
A Hybrid Model of Literacy

The departure point for the data analysis was a hybrid sociocognitive model of literacy combining aspects of Scribner and Cole's model of literacy practice and Heritage's model of conversational turn-taking. These two models take complementary sociocognitive perspectives on human action. By combining them, we achieve a hybrid model of some theoretical power.

Along the cognitive axis of the hybrid model, we locate the cognitive components suggested by Scribner and Cole's model of literacy practice. Scribner and Cole proposed this model to account for their observations of the Vai, a West African tribe with literacy in three different scripts. Their research indicated that individuals literate in each of these scripts showed different patterns of cognition. The model they put forward emphasized the effects of social context on the three cognitive components examined in this study: activities, knowledge representations, and goals.[2]

While the first and last of these cognitive components are familiar to researchers on reading and writing, the middle component of knowledge representation merits some introduction. Researchers in cognitive science now generally believe that knowledge representations in the form of mental models play a central role in defining expertise (Glaser; Johnson-Laird). A mental model is an abstraction from everyday, often spatial or visual, perception that allows people to think about a situation without the clutter of unnecessary details or the cumbersome (and sometimes impossible) requirement of actually manipulating physical objects. An example of a mental model that nearly everyone uses are the "mental maps" with which we plan shopping trips and give visitors directions.

Cheryl Geisler

Researchers investigating particular domains of expertise have found that individuals who are good at something—baseball (Chiesi, Spilich, and Voss), radiology (Lesgold), chess (Chase and Simon), social science (Voss, Greene, Post, and Penner), physics (Larkin), geometry (Anderson, Greeno, Kline, and Neves)—make use of mental models that are even more abstracted from everyday experience than mental maps. Where most of us would see blurs and blobs in an X-ray, for example, a student of radiology sees isolated organs, muscles, and bones; a skilled radiologist sees even more abstract "systems."

As of yet, we have little understanding of the special mental models that may be used by those expert at advanced literacy practices in academic fields such as philosophy. Some suggestive remarks have been made, however, by researchers centered at the Ontario Institute for Studies in Education (OISE). In a much-cited article on the relationship between speech and writing, Olson has claimed that literacy depends on decontextualized features of language. In speaking, he argues, we attend to the intentions of the speaker, to what is meant; in writing, on the other hand, our attention must shift to the meaning of the language itself, to what is actually said. In a similar vein, Bereiter and Scardamalia have argued that learning to write means learning to move away from dependence on conversational input from an interlocutor. Although these claims have implications for the kinds of knowledge representations that experts in fields such as philosophy might be expected to construct, these implications have not yet been investigated.

Along the second, social axis of literacy, the hybrid model locates the turn-taking sequence described by conversation analyst John Heritage (*Garfinkel and Ethnomethodology*). According to Heritage, conversational participants build, maintain, and shift contexts through the mechanism of three-turn sequences. In the first turn, a speaker proposes a given context by using the first part of an adjacency pair such as a greeting, question, or invitation. In the next turn, a second speaker responds with one of the following: the preferred response (an acknowledgement, acceptance, or answer); a dispreferred response plus some account for it ("Oh, that would be nice, but I've already made plans"); a completely unexpected response (staring the first speaker in the eye and not returning the greeting). Finally, in an optional third turn, the first speaker can repair any contextual misunderstandings indicated by the second speaker's response.

Applied to the uses of reading and writing in philosophy, this conversational sequence suggests a mechanism by which social context can be created and sustained through written language. A written text can be seen as one philosopher's proposal. The writing of a new text can be seen as the other philosopher's response. Through a series of such written interactions, the context of a philosophical conversation can be built, maintained, or shifted. Applied in this way, Heritage's conversational model refines the many suggestions that have been made concerning the conversational nature of literacy (Bartholomae; Bazerman, "A Relationship between Reading and Writing"; Bizzell; Bruffee; Latour and Woolgar; McCloskey).

The analysis in this study used the hybrid model of literacy in a two-stage procedure. At the first level, the text, protocol, and interview data were analyzed to provide information concerning the three cognitive components suggested by Scribner and Cole. Here my questions concerned the way the *readers*, reading texts that represent previous conversational turns, became *writers*, taking a turn of their own. What activities did they engage in? What knowledge representations did they construct and manipulate? What goals did they have?

At the second level of analysis, the descriptive data were examined for evidence of the ways in which the individuals made use of their reflexive awareness of the social dimension. If we assume that written interactions can be appropriately described as conversational, we can then ask how the philosophers' cognitions exhibited characteristics that are peculiarly conversational. The undeveloped state of sociocognitive theory prevents us from being definitive about what would constitute an answer to this question; nevertheless, the implications seem to be at variance with the OISE position. As we have already noted, Olson seems to argue that advanced literacy involves *moving away* from conversation. The sociocognitive model we have constructed following Heritage leads us to expect some movement *toward* it. Untangling these expectations was one of the major goals for this second level of analysis.

The design of this study as a comparison of expert and novice cognitions plays a crucial role in working toward answers to questions at both levels of analysis. Using the hybrid model, we can view expert/novice studies as comparisons of organizations along the cognitive axis at what we assume are qualitatively different places along the social axes. That is, we assume the experts are effective participants in the conversation of the disciplines of philosophy whereas the novices are not. We can use the data from novices, then, to highlight the significant cognitive characteristics that accompany effective conversational participation. In this way, the novice practices serve a heuristic function in helping us to pick out significant features of expert practice.[3]

Cheryl Geisler

First-Level Results: Descriptions of Literacy Practice

ACTIVITIES

We begin our description of the cognitive literacy practices of the four participants with an examination of their activity structures. To determine how the participants sequenced their activities, I coded the think-aloud protocols using a set of categories developed inductively from the data. These five-categories — reading, reflecting, organizing, drafting, and revising — were defined as particular constellations of (a) the materials consulted, (b) the materials produced, and (c) the sequencing principle guiding attention. Specific definitions are given in figure 7.1.

	Materials Consulted	Materials Produced	Sequencing Principle
READING	articles	notes	order of words in articles
REFLECTING	articles notes	notes	on-the-fly
ORGANIZING	notes	linear order of topics	on-the-fly
DRAFTING	notes articles outline	continuous draft intended for product	outline
REVISING	draft	annotations to draft	order of words in draft

Figure 7.1. Definitions of categories used to segment the activities of each participant

Once the protocols were coded, I examined the way participants distributed these activities over 100 percent of their working time. The results of this analysis indicate that all four participants used the same activity structure to complete the task. All began by reading, followed with a period of reflecting, moved to organizing, and then finally to drafting interspersed with revising. The only major departure from this sequence occurred with Novice 1 who divided her working time into two halves, the first concerned with the definition of paternalism and the second with its justification. Within each half, however, the sequencing from reading to drafting/revising occurred, albeit in a more abbreviated form the second time round.[4]

KNOWLEDGE REPRESENTATIONS

The knowledge representations used by the participants were examined using a construct developed from the interview data, the construct of authorship. Like many professionals, we began this study with the assumption that authorship was an important attribute of the texts on paternalism. We had even taken care to choose articles by authors who cross-referenced each other. The interview data caused us to reexamine this assumption. In particular, the two novices did not talk about the articles as having authors. In fact, one of them regularly referred to the collection of articles as "the book" and, on occasion, described herself as checking what "the book said" about an issue. On the other hand, the experts both regularly spoke in terms of the authors they were reading.

To analyze participants' use of the construct of authorship, I examined the protocol data for the presence of *author mentions*, which were defined to include:

- names of specific authors (e.g., "Childress")
- nominals standing for an aggregate of authors (e.g., "these guys");
- nominals standing for roles of authors (e.g., "a moral philosopher");
- pronouns standing in for any of the above ("she"; "they").

The results of this examination showed that the novices attended to authorship an average of 3.5 times in each 1000 words of think-aloud protocol. The experts, on the other hand, attended to authorship at least twice as often in the case of Expert 1 and almost four times as often in the case of Expert 2.

FINAL TEXTS

To examine what participants saw as the desired goal of their task, I analyzed the final texts they produced using a modified version of Langer's system for the analysis of structure (*Children Reading and Writing*; see Appendix). The product of this analysis is a complex tree diagram in which each T-unit of a text forms a node that can either be subordinated or coordinated to other nodes in the tree.[5] In addition to this structural analysis, a cross-check was made of the texts for the presence of author mentions.

On a global level, several generalizations can be made concerning the differences between the expert and novice texts. To begin with, experts' texts are longer (1280, 1680, 2930, and 6010 words[6]). In addition, they show an advantage in both the number of T-units (70, 93, 121, and 271) and the average length of the T-units (18, 18, 24, and 22 words/T-unit).

Cheryl Geisler

Finally, they show greater subordination (11, 11, 19, and 16 levels) and contain a greater number of author mentions (0, 12, 44, and 74 author mentions).

A review of the individual texts makes clear the source of these global differences. The expert texts follow a similar pattern. Major sections present the terms of definition and justification given by the task. Subordinate to them, secondary units present cases of paternalism and approaches to these cases. Further, in both expert texts, author mentions are almost exclusively associated with the secondary units presenting approaches. That is, both experts used authorship attribution to define what we call an "approach" which, in turn, is the major structure of their final texts.

In addition, the experts organized their presentation of approaches similarly. Each began with an approach he considered faulty. Then, through a critique, he eliminated that approach. The order in which the approaches were characterized and eliminated was determined by how faulty the approach was. Very wrong approaches were dealt with early; more complex and harder to refute approaches were dealt with later. Then, after all the elimination was done, the resulting approach, the main path taken by the expert himself, was left as the only remaining alternative. This organization can be visualized in terms of a set of faulty and main paths through an issue as shown in diagram A of figure 7.2.[7]

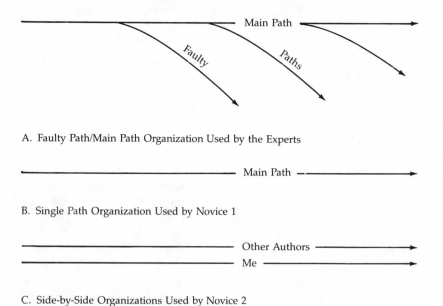

A. Faulty Path/Main Path Organization Used by the Experts

B. Single Path Organization Used by Novice 1

C. Side-by-Side Organizations Used by Novice 2

Fig. 7.2. Organizing structures in participant's texts

Units 5 through 8 of Expert 2's text can serve as an example of this faulty path/main path organization. Unit 5, dealing with the approach taken by Dworkin, is a typical faulty path, containing both a characterization of Dworkin's approach (52–53) and a critique that eliminates that approach (54–60):

> (52) The prominence of such examples as these in the discussion of the moral status of paternalism suggests to Dworkin (source one above) the following "rough" definition of paternalism (pg. 7):
> > (53) D1: "Paternalism is the interference with a person's liberty of action justified by reasons referring exclusively to the welfare, good, happiness, needs, interests, or values of the person being coerced."
>
> (54) The definition D1 is faulty in several respects, and is not made any better by Dworkin's admission that it is "rough". (55) First, as it stands, if the definition is right, there can be no unjustified (i.e. wrong) paternalistic action for D1 says paternalism is justified. (56) Doubtless this is part of the "roughness". (57) Perhaps what Dworkin intends is something more like the following:
> > (58) D1: "Paternalism is interference with a person's liberty of action of such a sort that if justified at all it is justified exclusively by its positive bearing on the welfare, good, happiness, needs, interests or values of the person's being coerced."
>
> (59) But this will still not work, as can be seen from Example 3 above. (60) In the case of the drug laws, potential buyers who can't buy because the product is not on the market are not coerced at all though they are the ones whose benefit is intended.

The units following this one deal similarly with the approaches taken by Buchannon and Carter, by Gert and Culver, and by Childress. The ordering is keyed to how faulty Expert 2 considered the approach. With Dworkin, whom he dealt with first, the approach is highly flawed and the critique is intended to be devastating. With Childress, whose approach he dealt with last, the approach is plausible and his critique is more pro forma:

> (94) I will have more to say of this shortly. (95) For now it is enough to point out that plausible definitions satisfying this requirement are in the field. Here, for instance, is Childress' definition (pg. 17, source 3):
> > (97) D5: "Paternalism is nonacquiescence in a person's wishes, choices and actions for that person's own benefit."
>
> (98) The definition is not without flaw ([99] surely he means "or"

and not "and", [100] and "nonacquiescence" is even fuzzier than "paternalism") (101) but it illustrates the point.

Although the novices used similar terms of definition and justification to structure the major units of their texts, their secondary units point to significant differences. In her secondary units, Novice 1 used a typological organization. In the first major section she enumerated the factors important to defining paternalism (7 units); in the second, she enumerated the conditions for justification (7 units). Although her protocols suggest she was aware of disagreements between authors, her final text neither includes specific authors' names nor indicates any difference in approach among them. Thus, in contrast to the faulty path/main path structure used by the experts, her text seems to represent the issue of paternalism as a single main path with everybody on it (see diagram B in figure 7.2).

Novice 2 organized the secondary units of her text with greater awareness of disagreements. Unlike Novice 1, she had an abiding and continuing personal disagreement with all of the authors she read. From her protocols and interviews, we know that she had seen her own family disregard her grandfather's wishes not to be placed on a respirator and she was convinced that this had been wrong. Thus, based on a family experience, she was fundamentally opposed to paternalistic interference. In her text, she was careful to state her position by giving her own definition of paternalism and her own approach to justification.

What is interesting to note, however, is that her claims stand in ambiguous relationships to the claims of the authors she is opposing. She does not, for example, make clear how her own definition of paternalism relates to other definitions she reviews earlier. Is it in agreement? Is it in disagreement? Is it a qualified agreement? She is not clear.

Further, even when she is more careful to specify that her claim about justification is in disagreement, she still fails to articulate the grounds for her differences. Instead, she simply characterizes the opinion of others and then gives her own as a contrast:

> (68) If we accept the following descriptions of Rosemary Carter, Bill is considered incompetent. (69) There is a group of people who we as a society label as being incompetent, therefore justifying paternalistic acts toward them. (70) These people are described and labelled as the following: those who are unable to understand or practice satisfactorily the basic requirements of survival, and so whose lives would be at worst in constant peril, and at best grossly unhappy, if not for the intervention of others. (71) Those suffering from mental retardation, below a certain level,

and those suffering from certain kinds of insanity are included in this class.

(72) Rosemary Carter's description of competence as a means for justification also speaks for both James Childress and Gerald Dworkin, with the following exceptions: . . .

(77) Altogether, these people tend to describe the same conditions for justification, but in a different manner with different examples. (78) While these conditions for justification are accepted by some of today's society, I feel that paternalism can be justified under only one condition, that of prior consent. (79) The conditions of mental retardation, and insanity do not give justification for paternalistic actions. (80) These persons should have the right to incorporate their views and feelings into medical decisions. (81) After all these people do have the ability to communicate to certain extents. (82) Why should the views of these people be carelessly disposed of.

Structurally, what is lacking here is the critique used so extensively by both experts. Instead of an argument structure that eliminates other authors' approaches on the way to validating her own, Novice 2 simply presents the two approaches side by side, and distinguishes between them on the basis, not of truth, but of authorship: Here is what others believe: here is what I believe (figure 7.2, diagram C).

SUMMARY

Before proceeding to the results of the second-level analysis, we can summarize the first-level descriptions as follows:

1. The literacy practices of the two experts in this study appear to be aimed at producing positions on the issue of paternalism by characterizing and critiquing approaches taken by other authors. To achieve this goal, both experts read, reflected on what they read, organized their thoughts, and wrote and revised a draft. Throughout their working time, they attended to the authorship of claims and, in their final texts, they used authorship as the defining attribute of the approaches they characterized and critiqued.

2. Like the experts, the two novices in this study appeared to use literacy practices to create positions on the issue of paternalism. To do so, they read the articles, reflected on what they had read, organized their thoughts, and wrote and revised a draft.

3. Unlike the experts, however, the novices did not seem to represent

Cheryl Geisler

their knowledge as a series of approaches distinguished by authorship. What they did instead, however, varied.

4. Novice 1 developed a knowledge representation consisting of positions on each of a number of subissues. We know from the protocols that the majority of her reflecting time was spent identifying these subissues and figuring out her position on them. Her final text presents these positions, but it does not explicitly identify them as her own. Nor does it distinguish her positions from positions taken by other authors. Consonant with her goal, she did not attend to the authorship of claims with anywhere near the frequency of either of the experts.

5. Perhaps driven by her personal experience, Novice 2, on the other hand, developed a knowledge representation in which authorship played some role. Her final text carefully distinguishes between her own position and the position taken by the authors she disagreed with. This structure remains different from that employed by the experts, however, because it does not indicate the relationship between the position she takes and the position she's opposing. Indeed, during most of her reflecting time, Novice 2 tried to construct her own position with little attention given to the positions of the authors she had read. Thus, despite the presence of some author mentions in her final text, she did not attend to authorship in her working time at any greater rate than did Novice 1.

Second-Level Results: Socially Configured Mental Models

Turning to the second-level analysis, we can now ask how the expert cognitions described above were shaped by their participation in a philosophical conversation. Although the descriptive data of this study cannot support a definitive answer to this important question, they do suggest a possible hypothesis for future research. Specifically, I will argue that the expert cognitions seemed to involve the construction and manipulation of socially configured mental models — knowledge representations shaped by attributes of the social axis, but which depart in systematic ways from standard conversation.[8]

To begin the case for socially configured mental models, we return to evidence from the knowledge representation data. There we found that, indeed, experts' practices were configured by at least one attribute of the social axis: the authorship of claims. Further, insofar as attention to authorship indicates an awareness of other interlocutors, these practices appear to be somewhat conversational. Here we have evidence, then, that advanced literary practices in philosophy *are* configured by social context, just as the model of written conversation would suggest.

Toward a Sociocognitive Model of Literacy

Other evidence warns us, however, against assuming these practices are isomorphic with those of standard conversation. The first evidence comes from the data on activity structure. As shown in figure 7.3, the participants in this study structured their activities in four-part sequences of reading, reflecting, organizing, and drafting/revising. Standard conversation, by contrast, is structured as two-part interchanges with an optional third turn for repairs. Assuming that reading is the equivalent of the first speaker's conversational turn and drafting/revising is the equivalent of the second speaker's response, we see that these participants' literacy practices involved two activities that are not found in standard conversation: reflecting and organizing. Their literacy practices, then, appear to have opened up a reflective space for cognition that simply would be unavailable to oral interlocutors.

	Conversational Practice	Literacy Practice
Turn 1:	Proposes context	Writes
Turn 2:	Responds	Reads Reflects Organizes Drafts/Revises
Turn 3:	Repairs misunderstandings	

Figure 7.3. Comparison of the activity structures of conversational practice and literacy practice

The kind of mental work that the experts may have been accomplishing in this additional reflective space is further suggested by the final texts they produced. In several respects, these texts reflect mental models of written interaction that are not isomorphic with those of standard conversation. To begin with, they are made up of "approaches" that are only indirectly related to other authors' actual claims. For example, Expert 1 did not assume a one-to-one isomorphism between the set of claims made by Dworkin and the approaches he discussed in his own argument. Instead, once he had characterized and dismissed the definition Dworkin actually gave, he went on to consider what Dworkin might have meant:

> Perhaps what Dworkin intends is something more like the following: . . . (59) But this will still not work. . . .

If Expert 1's goal were simply to respond to previous interlocutors, then discussing what Dworkin might have said makes little sense. But if his

Cheryl Geisler

intention were to construct a mental model made up of a wide range of approaches, then this abstraction is a sensible inventional strategy.

The abstract nature of the experts' mental models is also suggested by the way they organized their texts. As noted earlier, both experts arranged their discussions of approaches in descending order of faultiness: more faulty approaches were discussed first; less faulty approaches discussed later. This written practice differs from standard conversation in two ways. First, conversational interlocutors rarely take on the burden of creating a spontaneous single response to multiple previous speakers' first turns. Instead, they respond to claims locally as they arise, one at a time. Second, on those few occasions when they do address multiple prior claims, the linear ordering is ad hoc — indeed, if meaningful, we assume that it arises from cognitions outside of the current conversation ("I see you've been giving this some thought"). Thus, the experts' mental models appear to be consolidated and linearized in ways that are unpredicted and almost inconceivable accomplishments within the constraints of standard face-to-face interaction.

The final evidence concerning the abstract nature of the experts' mental models concerns the conventions by which they treat previous authors. Basically, the authors in these written interactions were treated differently than interlocutors in standard conversations: personal attributes and social affiliations are off-limits; actual intentions are irrelevant.[9] For example, Expert 1 did not argue against Dworkin's approach on the grounds that he was a "Reaganite conservative" — even though his protocol shows that he thought so. Nor did Expert 2, when attributing an approach to Buchannon and Carter, consider whether these two authors liked each other or, indeed, whether they had ever met. These personal considerations, important in everyday conversation, were inappropriate according to the conventions of written interaction these experts followed.

Furthermore, authors' rights to the third-turn repairs, so common in standard conversation, were restricted in these written interactions. As mentioned earlier, Heritage suggests that third-turn repairs are always an option for first-turn speakers who feel they have been misinterpreted. Thus, in oral conversations, we routinely expect to be able to say, "No, that is not what I meant to say. What I really meant was . . ." Authors, however, are not routinely extended this right. Thus, for example, Dworkin could not reply to Expert 1's critique by saying that he didn't *really* mean what he wrote. Miswritings, unlike misspeakings, are not good grounds for repairing intersubjective knowledge. Of course, authors have many other ways they can repudiate misinterpretations of their work or repudiate previous positions, but, as Olson points out, these rely on conventions for what words mean rather than on independent evidence of what the author actually intended. In fact, these conventions of interpretation are so widely available that third-turn repairs may be made by someone other than the original author—a freedom less often assumed by third parties in oral interactions.

Taken together, this evidence suggests that our philosophers were creating special mental models that, like those used in so many other domains, departed in characteristic ways from everyday practice—in this case, the practice of standard conversation. Although they were configured by some of the attributes of everyday conversation and might even be taken as identical by those less than expert, the mental models of advanced literacy in philosophy appear to be different. By expanding their activity structure, abstracting approaches, consolidating and linearizing their responses, and accepting restrictions on their right of repair, the philosophers in these literacy interactions were able to produce knowledge beyond that which is ordinarily possible in everyday conversation.

Concluding Remarks:
Toward a Sociocognitive Model

Thus far, I have argued that the expertise of advanced literacy practices exhibited by the philosophers studied here can best be characterized as the construction and manipulation of special socially configured mental models. In closing, I would now like to consider some of the implications this claim has for a sociocognitive model of literacy.

According to the hybrid model with which this study began, social and cognitive practices are arrayed along two intersecting dimensions of human action. As it now stands, this two-dimensional model cannot account for mental representations that depart from standard conversational practice: The individual cognitions suggested by Scribner and Cole were assumed to be directly embedded in the social practices of everyday conversation outlined by Heritage. To accommodate the existence of abstract mental constructs, we must amend this model in at least one of two ways.

First, we might say that advanced literacy practices are embedded in *different* social contexts than those of standard conversation. That is, we might assume that those who make use of advanced reading and writing propose and maintain specialized contexts for their interpretation. Learning to read and write, then, would mean learning to function in these specialized contexts, learning the rules of new discourse communities such as the community of philosophers.

Some precedents already exist for arguing that departures from standard conversation define specialized contexts. In schools, for example, teachers ask questions for which they already have the answers; thus they reserve for themselves the unusual right to bring a turn-taking sequence to a close or extend it until the correct answer is reached (Mehan). In news interviews and interrogations, questioners systematically withhold acknowledgements of the truth or newsworthiness of respondents' answers; they thus simultaneously maintain the required institutional indifference and acknowledge the role of the overhearing audience (Heritage, "Analyzing News Interviews"). Whenever such unusual practices are invoked, according to Heritage (*Garfinkel and Ethnomethodology*), participants know they are operating in specialized contexts.

The trouble with amending our model to allow for alternative social contexts is that the novices in this study showed less, not more, evidence of being in everyday conversation. If learning to read and write in philosophy required moving toward more specialized contexts, then we would expect novices to show greater, not fewer, signs of conversational practice. In this study, however, we saw evidence of the reverse: it was the novices, not the experts, who were operating in a world without interlocutors.

A second way of amending the hybrid model of literacy is suggested by my use of the concept of "mental models." Mental models in all domains characteristically exhibit a specific duality of reference: they *both* move away from everyday practice and remain rooted there. In radiology, for example, mental models of the body both surpass what we can do with ordinary understanding and have implications for everyday treatment. In effect, they create a new plane of understanding by projecting and abstracting from everyday entities while, at the same time, remaining connected to those entities. Indeed, it is this ability to go beyond mundane reasoning while speaking to it which justifies the social expense of developing expertise.

In professions like philosophy, we see a similar duality: written interactions are both rooted in the everyday practices of conversation and go beyond them. In this study, for example, both philosophers felt impelled to discuss their ideas with colleagues as well as work on them in the privacy of their office. Like most academics and researchers, they accompany their writing with conversation — in the hallways, on the phone, and at conferences. Mental models like those described above may be the mechanism by which they are able to overlay abstract cognitions on everyday conversational practices.

We can amend our hybrid model, then, by projecting outward from the social and cognitive axes to hypothesize a new kind of practice that both extends and refers back to standard conversational practices. The suggestion is that by opening up the activity structure of oral conversation, literacy in philosophy provides experts with the reflective space necessary to construct socially configured mental models. These mental models create, in effect, a new plane of intersubjective knowledge, a third dimension of culturally shared abstractions. Such a three-dimensional model of literacy would help us explain not only how ways of thinking inconceivable in oral conversation are interwoven with and supported by distinctive social practices, but also why — throughout history — people have considered reading and writing to be their link with a more timeless wisdom of the ages.

APPENDIX: ANALYSIS OF STRUCTURE

The analysis of text structure was carried out in four phases. In the first phase, texts were divided into T-units.

In the second phase, this list of T-units was divided into rhetorical units linked by: (a) explicit connecting phrases such as conjunctions, comparatives, demonstratives, enumeratives, and various linking phrases; (b) anaphoric links or any transition from the indefinite to the definite article; (c) intended parallel structures; (d) some connecting punctuation; and (e) narrative schemata.

In the third phase, the structure of each rhetorical unit was diagrammed as a series of subordinations and coordinations in which each T-unit was attached to one of the rightmost nodes of the developing tree. T-units were coordinated if they served the same function, were in some standard relationship to one another, concerned the same superordinate T-unit, or elaborated upon a multi-T-unit entity rather than a single T-unit. They were subordinated if one was an elaboration of the other.

In the fourth phase, rhetorical units were joined together into an integrated tree.

NOTES

Research presented here was supported by a grant from the Fund for the Improvement of Post-Secondary Education to the author and David S. Kaufer, Christine Neuwirth, and Preston Covey at Carnegie Mellon University. Some of the material in this paper was originally presented at the 1987 annual convention of the American Educational Research Association in Washington, D.C.,and has further benefitted from discussions with S. Michael Halloran, Nancy Nelson Spivey, Charles Bazerman, Sister Barbara Sitko, and Mark Stein.

1. Gender and expertise were inextricably mixed in these case studies. Both experts were men; both novices were women. Although we will focus on expertise rather than gender in our interpretations, it is important to realize that academic expertise may be more comfortable to men than to women. Belenky, Clinchy, Goldberger, and Tarule, for instance, have suggested that women may prefer a style of "connected knowing" that prizes identification rather than the distance of "separate knowing" commonly prized in philosophical argument.

Cheryl Geisler

2. The fourth component, technology, actually combines cognitive and social concerns and was not included in the initial hybrid model.

3. The status of the novice data, considered independently of the experts, is beyond the scope of this article. See, however, North for one treatment.

4. A comparison of the percentage of working time given by the participants to each of the five activities indicates the following: All four participants gave the greatest percentage of their time to reading (37% average) through the articles on paternalism. All gave the smallest percentage of time to organizing topics into a linear structure (5% average). The participants varied in the percentage of time given to revising and reflecting. Novice 2 and Expert 1 revised extensively; Novice 1 and Expert 2 revised for proportionately less time. Novice 1, Novice 2, and Expert 1 spent about the same percentage of time reflecting; Expert 2 spent proportionately more time.

Interesting differences between the experts and novices occurred with respect to drafting. Even though all participants spent about the same percentage of their time in reading and organizing, both philosophers took a smaller percentage of their time to draft (29% and 32% for the novices vs. 17% and 13% for the experts). Since both experts completed the task in less time than both novices, the difference in the actual time spent drafting was even greater. The experts also delayed drafting longer than the novices. The two novices began drafting about 35% of the way through their work. The two experts, by contrast, began drafting at 61% and 76% of the way through their work.

5. Reliability checks on sample texts revealed 100% agreement among six raters (who apply a coding scheme to data) on T-unit segmentation, 89% agreement between two raters on the location of a T-unit attachment, and 87% agreement between two raters on the type of attachment.

6. Statistics are ordered: Novice 1, Novice 2, Expert 1, Expert 2.

7. An example of what is involved in teaching students to construct the faulty path/main path organization is found in Kaufer, Geisler, and Neuwirth.

8. The argument made here extends an observation by Bazerman ("Physicists Reading Physics") on the existence of special-purpose reading schemata among professional physicists.

9. The difference between authors and everyday people has also been commented on by Foucault (121–22).

BIBLIOGRAPHY

Anderson, John R., J. G. Greeno, P. J. Kline, and D. M. Neves. "Acquisition of Problem Solving Skills." In *Cognitive Skills and Their Acquisition*, ed. J. R. Anderson, 191–230. Hillsdale, N.J.: Erlbaum, 1981.

Bartholomae, David. "Inventing the University." In *When a Writer Can't Write: Studies in Writer's Block and Other Composing Process Problems*, ed. Mike Rose, 134–65. New York: Guilford Press, 1985.

Bazerman, Charles. "Physicists Reading Physics: Schema-Laden Purposes and Purpose-Laden Schema." *Written Communication* 2 (January 1985): 3–23.

Bazerman, Charles. "A Relationship between Reading and Writing: The Conversational Model." *College English* 41 (February 1980): 656–61.

Belenky, Mary Field, Blythe McVicker Clinchy, Nancy Rule Goldberger, and Jill Mattuck Tarule. *Women's Ways of Knowing: The Development of Self, Voice, and Mind.* New York: Basic Books, 1986.

Bereiter, Carl, and Marlene Scardamalia. "From Conversation to Composition: The Role of Instruction in Developmental Processes." In *Advances in Instructional Psychology, Vol. 2*, ed. R. Glaser, 1–64. Hillsdale, N.J.: Erlbaum, 1982.

Bizzell, Patricia. "College Composition: Initiation into the Academic Discourse Community." *Curriculum Inquiry* 12 (1982): 191–207.

Bruffee, Kenneth A. "Collaborative Learning and the 'Conversation of Mankind.' " *College English* 46 (November 1984): 635–52.

Chase, William G., and Herbert A. Simon. "The Mind's Eye in Chess." In *Visual Information Processing*, ed. W. G. Chase, 215–81. New York: Academic Press, 1973.

Chiesi, H. L., G. J. Spilich, and J. F. Voss. "Acquisition of Domain Related Knowledge in Relation to High and Low Domain Knowledge." *Journal of Verbal Learning and Verbal Behavior* 18 (1979): 257–74.

Ericsson, K. Anders, and Herbert A. Simon. *Protocol Analysis*. Cambridge: MIT Press, 1984.

Foucault, Michel. "What is an Author?" *Language, Counter-memory and Practice.* Ed. Donald Bouchard. Trans. Donald Bouchard and Sherry Simon. Ithaca: Cornell University Press, 1977.

Glaser, Robert. "Education and Thinking: The Role of Knowledge." *American Psychologist* 39 (1984): 93–104.

Heritage, John. "Analyzing News Interviews: Aspects of the Production of Talk for an Overhearing Audience." In *Handbook of Discourse Analysis, Vol. 3: Genres of Discourse*, ed. T. A. van Dijk, 95–117. New York: Academic Press, 1984.

Heritage, John. *Garfinkel and Ethnomethodology*. Cambridge: Polity Press, 1984.

Johnson-Laird, P. N. "Mental Models in Cognitive Science." *Cognitive Science* 4 (1980): 71–115.

Kaufer, David, Cheryl Geisler, and Christine Neuwirth. *Arguing from Sources: Exploring Issues through Reading and Writing.* San Diego, Calif.: Harcourt Brace Jovanovich, 1989.

Langer, Judith A. *Children Reading and Writing: Structures and Strategies.* Norwood, N.J.: Ablex Press, 1986.

Langer, Judith A. "Musings . . . A Sociocognitive View of Language Learning." *Research in the Teaching of English* 19 (1985): 325–27.

Larkin, Jill. "Understanding, Problem Representations, and Skill in Physics." In *Thinking and Learning Skills, Vol. 2: Research and Open Questions*, ed. S. F. Chipman, J. Segal, and R. Glaser, 141–59. Hillsdale, N.J.: Erlbaum, 1985.

Latour, Bruno, and Steve Woolgar. *Laboratory Life: The Social Construction of Scientific Facts.* Beverly Hills: Sage, 1979.

Lesgold, Alan. "Human Skill in a Computerized Society: Complex Skills and Their Acquisition." *Behavior Research Methods, Instruments, and Computers* 16 (1984): 79–87.

Cheryl Geisler

McCloskey, Donald N. *The Rhetoric of Economics*. Madison: University of Wisconsin Press, 1985.

Mehan, Hugh. *Learning Lessons: Social Organization in the Classroom*. Cambridge: Harvard University Press, 1979.

Newell, Allen, and Herbert A. Simon. *Human Problem Solving*. Englewood Cliffs, N.J.: Prentice-Hall, 1972.

North, Stephen M. "Writing in Philosophy Class: Three Case Studies." *Research in the Teaching of English* 20 (1986): 225–62.

Olson, David. "From Utterance to Text: The Bias of Language in Speech and Writing." *Harvard Educational Review* 47 (1977): 257–81.

Scribner, Sylvia, and Michael Cole. *The Psychology of Literacy*. Cambridge: Harvard University Press, 1981.

Voss, J. F., T. R. Greene, T. A. Post, and B. C. Penner. "Problem Solving Skill in the Social Sciences." In *The Psychology of Learning and Motivation: Advances in Research Theory, Vol. 17*, ed. G. H. Bower, 165–213. New York: Academic Press, 1983.

8

SOCIAL CONTEXT AND

SOCIALLY CONSTRUCTED TEXTS

THE INITIATION OF A GRADUATE

STUDENT INTO A WRITING

RESEARCH COMMUNITY

CAROL BERKENKOTTER,

THOMAS N. HUCKIN, AND

JOHN ACKERMAN

In the last few years researchers using various empirical and hermeneutic techniques have studied the difficulties that young adult writers confront as they enter the university culture (North; McCarthy) and more specifically their major fields (Herrington; Faigley and Hansen). These studies suggest that students entering academic disciplines need a specialized literacy that consists of the ability to use discipline-specific rhetorical and linguistic conventions to serve their purposes as writers. Academic disciplines have been characterized as *discourse communities* (Bizzell "Cognition"; Herrington; Porter); however, these communities are not nearly as tangible as the *speech communities* that Shirley Brice Heath described in her study of the children of Trackton and Roadville. Academic or professional discourse communities are not necessarily located in specific physical settings, but rather their existence can be inferred from the discourse that members of a disciplinary subspecialty use to communicate with each other. In this sense, the discourse that one group of

Carol Berkenkotter, Thomas N. Huckin, and John Ackerman

like-minded people use *defines* the community and is its product as well.

In this essay we follow a skilled adult writer, Nate, entering a research community (and by implication, a discourse community) by examining the introductions he wrote to research papers over the first year and a half of his tenure in a doctoral program. We view these introductions as evidence of the writer's socialization into this particular community, and suggest that they provide valuable information regarding the writer's ability to instantiate into text the "institutionalized norms" (Fahnestock and Secor) of his audience. Elsewhere we have discussed the story of this student's initiation into the rhetoric program at Carnegie Mellon University (1988). In this essay we foreground microlevel evidence of his socialization: his increasing mastery of the community's linguistic, rhetorical, and topical conventions, as seen in the introductions to three papers.

The data that we report on here are part of a study that was conducted at Carnegie Mellon during the 1984–85 academic year. One of the authors (CB) was a participant observer in the rhetoric program, attending classes with students, interviewing faculty and students, and collecting case study data from two first-year doctoral students. (One of these students dropped out of the study at the beginning of 1985.) This data, which consisted of Nate's written self reports chronicling his experiences in the program, weekly taped interviews, copies of papers the students wrote, as well as CB's field notes, were reduced and translated into a narrative of Nate's progress as a writer during his first year. This part of the data analysis was carried out by CB and JA. The remaining author (TH), using a series of linguistic measures, independently analyzed the papers Nate wrote between September 1984 and November 1985.[1]

Background of the Study

The theoretical and methodological assumptions on which the study was based are derived from sociolinguistics and from research in the sociology of science. Recent research on scientific publication views texts as socially mediated products and revision as a process of social negotiation (Bazerman, "The Writing"; Gilbert and Mulkay; Knorr-Cetina; Latour and Woolgar; Myers; Yearly). In different ways these studies demonstrate how researchers advance knowledge claims within the linguistic conventions of scientific discourse — conventions which codify audience expectations.

The ways in which linguistic behaviors are derived from community context has also been documented by another group of researchers studying the development of school literacy in young children (Dyson; Heath; Schultz, Florio, and Erickson). These studies suggest that the cognitive components of language acquisition are developed within and therefore are intimately connected to the language user's home (i.e., cultural community) environment. As language users travel from one community context to another — from home to public (or private) school, from high school to college, from college to graduate or professional training, from graduate school to the work force — they must master new ways of speaking, reading, and writing, ways that are appropriate within each community. The application of this knowledge constitutes what Dell Hymes has called "communicative competence."

Through a synthesis of the above research perspectives with the findings from our data, we developed four assumptions that inform the discussion of these findings:

1. Members of a research community share a "model of knowing" (Miles and Huberman, 20).   This model of knowing is embedded in the research methodology that incoming students in graduate programs learn and is encoded in the language that community members use.

2. A research community extends beyond a student's graduate school to include researchers at other institutions. The vanguard of these researchers constitutes an "invisible college" (Crane, 34–40, 49–56), wherein they share their work with one another through publications in professional journals and through papers delivered at professional meetings.

3. Papers and publications are among a research community's *communicative forums*; significant issues are raised, defined, and debated within these forums. In this sense, to publish and to be cited is to enter the community's discourse.

4. Graduate students are initiated into the research community through the reading and writing they do, through instruction in research methodology, and through interaction with faculty and with their peers. A major part of this initiation process is learning how to use appropriate written linguistic conventions for communicating through disciplinary forums.

The Rhetoric Program at Carnegie Mellon

Carnegie Mellon is a private technical university known for its strength as a research institution. Several departments, including cognitive psychology and computer science, are ranked among the foremost in the country. The research reported here was conducted in the English Department, specifically the rhetoric program, which has been in existence as a doctoral program since 1980. Carnegie Mellon's Ph.D. in Rhetoric is one of a number of doctoral programs in rhetoric and composition that have been developed within English departments in the last several years. David W. Chapman and Gary Tate, in a 1986 survey of 123 doctoral programs in English, identified 53 institutions claiming to offer a specialization of composition/rhetoric. They point out that of these institutions, only sixteen have more than ten doctoral students enrolled, and only three universities actually offer a doctorate in rhetoric: Louisville, Carnegie Mellon, and Texas Woman's (129).

The Ph.D. in Rhetoric at Carnegie Mellon was developed under the aegis of Richard Young, who did a good deal of innovative hiring during his tenure as department head between 1978 and 1983. The current program enables students to enter a field that draws on the expertise of researchers and scholars in a number of disciplines. Rhetoric program faculty include cognitive psychologists, classical and contemporary rhetoricians, a linguist, a speech communication specialist, and a computer scientist. The rhetoric program also has strong ties with the Psychology Department, and it is quite common for English Department students to engage in directed research with psychology faculty. As students proceed through their graduate work, they take several courses in historical rhetoric and contemporary rhetorical theory. But the spine of the program is the training that graduates receive in empirical research methodology.

This training is quite rigorous. Students take an introductory course, "The Process of Research" (team taught in 1984–85 by a rhetorician and a cognitive psychologist), in which they are introduced to the principles of what faculty members call "rhetorical research." They read an introductory textbook on research in the social sciences, learn how to formulate research questions, learn the principles of experimental research design, and receive basic instruction in statistics. As a next step, students often choose to take advanced quantitative research courses in which they learn more about experimental research design and statistical procedures. Students also learn the technique of protocol analysis (gathering and analyzing data from subjects who "think aloud" while performing writing and reading tasks). Second-year students are encouraged to take courses on information processing theory in order to learn the intellectual model and theoretical assumptions that underlie protocol analysis methodology.

The rhetoric program's interdisciplinary curriculum appears to be aimed at producing an intellectual hybrid: a scholar familiar with historical and contemporary rhetorical theory, who can communicate through such forums as *College English* and *College Composition and Communication*, yet also a competent researcher, who can write social science expository prose for educational research publications such as *Research in the Teaching of English* and *Written Communication*. Students therefore need to become knowledgeable about invention theory as well as ANOVA tables, Aristotle and Ong as well as Campbell and Stanley, experimental design confounds and the Pearson product-moment r as well as contemporary writing pedagogy. Course work often includes carrying out research projects, giving oral presentations, and writing "publishable" or "national conference"–quality papers. With these assignments many faculty members in the rhetoric program attempt to introduce graduate students to the major communicative forums for research and scholarship.

Since students' assignments frequently require them to write using a knowledge of the conventions of empirical research reporting, we wondered to what extent students whose background was, as Nate's, in English studies would be hindered by writing in an unfamiliar genre. Because writers in different disciplines use different rhetorical and linguistic conventions, we would expect to see a student such as Nate experiencing considerable difficulty without direct instruction in writing about research. Indeed, there is considerable research that suggests that mastering the conventions of the research report is a formidable task (Faigley and Hansen; Hill, Soppelsa, and West; Selinker, Todd Trimble, and Trimble).

Research on the Structure of Article and Thesis Introductions

In this study we were concerned with the subject's ability to write introductions, the composing of which creates a special set of problems for the student who is learning the conventions of expository prose in the natural and social sciences. John Swales and Hazem Najjar suggest that:

> Introductions to research articles or papers have become in the last few years an important proving ground for our current capacity to understand the process and product of specialized academic writing. The extensive case studies of Latour & Woolgar (1979), Knorr-Cetina (1981) and Gilbert & Mulkay (1984) provide solid evidence for the complexity of the compositional process at the Introduction stage. All three studies show that writing an introduction to a research article is not simply a wrestling with words to fit the facts, but is also strongly modulated by perceptions of the anticipated reactions of peer-colleagues. Knorr-Cetina's analysis of the evolving drafts of a single paper . . . show(s) how the first draft's bold announcement of a new method ultimately becomes the reporting of a comparative analysis; how the early exuberance of the primary researchers turns into the careful understatement of a wider group; and how dangerous knowledge-claims are made safe as insurance against potential damage to the research laboratory's reputation if difficulties subsequently emerge. (175–76)

Swales, Graham Crookes, and Tony Dudley-Evans, analyzing introductions in scientific and social science publications and graduate student theses, found introductions to exhibit a structural schema which can be broken down into a series of rhetorical "moves." The number and the complexity of these moves depends on such variables as space constraints (in professional journals), the nature of the research and the research field (Dudley-Evans, 132), and whether the writer composes in a professional or a training (university) context.

Swales examined the introductions to forty-eight articles in the natural and social sciences, and found that most of them contained a sequence of four rhetorical moves through which a scientist creates a *research space* for his work. Using these moves, the writer: (1) establishes the field in which he or she is working, (2) summarizes related research in the area of concern, (3) creates a research space for the present study by indicating a gap in current knowledge or by raising questions, and (4) introduces the study by indicating what the investigation being reported will accomplish for the field ("Structure of Introductions," 80–92; *Article Introductions*, 178–80). An article by Cynthia L. Selfe in *Research in the Teaching of English* includes an illustration of this four-move schema (figure 8.1).

As Swales's model predicts, this writer immediately identifies the research context in which she will later place her own study by defining the terms that constitute the general research area and naming the researchers who coined the term "writing apprehension." She then establishes a historical context by enumerating previous studies. In three sentences, through highly condensed summarizing, she presents an overview of the field. Having established this overview, she is ready to make the next rhetorical move by raising issues and questions that have not been addressed in the literature. Swales points out that the onset of this third move is often marked by a contrastive connector like "however" and/or some negative element that will be found in the thematic sentence-initial position. In this instance, the writer uses both features, combining "however" with the negative construction "no substantial research" in the thematic position of the first sentence of that move. A second negative, "It is not even certain," appears in the thematic position in the following sentence, linking new information to that in the previous sentence. By identifying two issues that have not yet been addressed — "defining the relationship between writing apprehension and the processes students employ as they compose," and "whether there are definable differences between the composing process[es] of high and low apprehensives" — the writer creates a niche or "research space" for her own study. This she introduces in the next sentence, "The current study was designed to address this particular

1. Establishing the Field:
The term "writing apprehension," originally coined in 1975 by Daly and Miller (1975b), refers to a generalized tendency to experience "some form of anxiety when faced with the task of encoding messages."

2. Summarizing Previous Research:
Much of the early research in writing apprehension was concerned with defining the theoretical construct of writing apprehension and establishing the validity of the Writing Apprehension Test (WAT), an instrument designed to measure that construct (Daly & Miller, 1975b, 1975c). Later research has explored the correlative and predictive functions of the WAT. Specific studies have connected scores on WAT with choice of academic majors and careers (Daly & Shamo, 1976, 1978), scores on self-concept and self-confidence measures (Daly, 1979), and performance on various assessments of writing skill and writing quality (Daly, 1978a, 1978b; Daly & Miller, 1975a, 1975d).

3. Creating a Research Space by Indicating a Gap:
To date, however, no substantive research has been done to define the relationship between writing apprehension and the processes students employ as they compose. It is not even certain, for example, how or to what extent the theoretical construct of writing apprehension is evidenced during the act of composing, whether, in other words, there are definable differences between the composing process [sic] of high and low apprehensives.

4. Introducing Present Research:
The current study was designed to address this particular question.
The research project reported in this paper had three main goals:
    1. To record the predrafting processes of several high and several low writing apprehensives engaged in academic writing.
    2. To analyze the predrafting processes of both groups.
    3. To examine the results of this analysis for evidence of differences related to writing apprehension.

Figure 8.1. Illustration of four rhetorical moves in article introductions (after Swales 1981)

question," and presents her purpose by enumerating the three goals of the research project she is to report.

The regularity with which these four moves appear in scientific journal article introductions suggests that they constitute the basic schema. However, as Swales himself has noted, many variations can and do occur. In separate studies, Bazerman and Huckin have shown that scientific journal conventions change over time. And Crookes, in a follow-up study of Swales 1981 using the same three categories but half as many articles, found that there were only five cases (out of 24) which had a clear 1-2-3-4 sequence of moves. Four cases had only a Move 2 and Move 4. And seven

Carol Berkenkotter, Thomas N. Huckin, and John Ackerman

of the eight social science articles had five or more moves. It seems that in the "softer" sciences the writer is often compelled to address not a single problem but multiple problems. These problems emerge from the summary of previous research (Move 2). Each is addressed, in turn, by a separate Move 3. Thus there is a characteristic reiteration of Moves 2 and 3, resulting in an overall 1-2-3-2-3-2-3-4 sequence or something similar.

In a study of master's theses, Dudley-Evans found this longer reiterative pattern to be so common as to constitute a virtual schema unto itself. He examined the introductions of seven theses in plant biology, ranging in length from 320 words to 4,640 words, and found that Swales's four-move schema was not adequate to describe their rhetorical complexity. In all of these theses, which were rated "satisfactory" to "good" by a plant biology professor, the writers went to far greater lengths to establish and justify the research topic than was done in Swales's journal articles. Dudley-Evans proposed a six-move schema to describe these introductions:

Move 1: Introducing the Field
Move 2: Introducing the General Topic (within the Field)
Move 3: Introducing the Particular Topic (within the General Topic)
Move 4: Defining the Scope of the Particular Topic by:
    (i) introducing research parameters
    (ii) summarizing previous research
Move 5: Preparing for Present Research by:
    (i) indicating a gap in previous research
    (ii) indicating a possible extension of previous research
Move 6: Introducing Present Research by:
    (i) stating the aim of the research
       or
    (ii) describing briefly the work carried out
    (iii) justifying the research.

Figure 8.2. A Six-move schema of rhetorical moves for master's theses in scientific fields
(Dudley-Evans, 1986)

Although Dudley-Evans does not venture an explanation for the differences between journal article introductions and thesis introductions, we suppose that the latter are more elaborate because students are expected to display their knowledge in a more comprehensive way, and to presuppose less knowledge on the part of the reader, than are writers of specialized journal articles.

We found the Dudley-Evans' student-oriented schema more appropriate than Swales's professional-oriented one for the study at hand, since the subject was a graduate student learning the conventions of research report writing. It should be noted that neither Swales's nor Dudley-Evans' models should be taken as prescriptive. They do, however, provide us with an analytical framework for gauging Nate's development of formal, text-based schemata which enabled him to communicate with others in his field through professional forums.

Entering the Conversation of a Writing Research Community by Acquiring Genre Knowledge

The research described above suggests that writing the introduction to a research report involves bringing into play a considerable amount of procedural as well as content knowledge. Because such introductions contain a great deal of information (sometimes as many as thirty summaries of related research presented as brief "gists") in a relatively small space, writers must master both the technique of summarizing and the procedures that will enable them to summarize according to their rhetorical purposes. Learning to use the conventions of the article introduction may well constitute the most difficult part of research writing, especially for novice researchers.

The first-year student we chose to study entered the Carnegie Mellon program with substantial experience as a writing teacher, as an expressive writer, and as a creative writer. Nate had received a B.A. and an M.Ed. in English and in Curriculum and Instruction and had taught freshman composition for six years prior to entering the program, so he brought considerable experience and linguistic expertise to graduate school. His background, however, like that of many students who entered the Ph.D. program from English departments, had not included training in the genres of social science expository writing that were the preferred form of academic discourse in many of his courses. Nate had not written experimental research papers or literature reviews and therefore was not familiar with the conventional structure of the research report in the sciences and social sciences, i.e., introduction, methods, results, discussion. He therefore could not have been expected to know, for example, where in such a report, writers place their key findings (Swales and Najjar); nor could he have been expected to possess or to utilize the procedural knowledge described above. On the other hand, Nate could be observed over a period of several months becoming familiar with his professors' research agendas and with the disciplinary issues being discussed in the classrooms, hallways, and offices, at department colloquia, conferences, and other gatherings. At the same time he was also learning social science research methodology and immersing himself in the professional journals and technical reports which essentially constituted the textual counterpart of his new field of study. Thus, not only was he learning how to converse within

Carol Berkenkotter, Thomas N. Huckin, and John Ackerman

the immediate context of a graduate program, but he was also learning the conventions appropriate to a larger research network.

We hypothesized that the attendant changes appearing in Nate's writing can best be understood from the sociolinguistic perspective of language operating in a "multidimensional space." Richard A. Hudson, paraphrasing Robert B. LePage, argues that writers can and do belong and respond to more than one community at once, and that a writer "chooses" to address a community with corresponding linguistic and topical conventions (13–14). For a writer entering a new community, as was the case with Nate, this choice was hardly clearcut or final. The texts chosen for analysis were introductions to end-of-term project reports written in Nate's first three semesters. These reports served as mileposts in that they represented the culmination of a semester's thinking on the given research topic and the writer's compiled linguistic and substantive knowledge in his new discipline. Since these texts are introductions to papers that Nate wrote for course assignments rather than articles submitted for professional journals or theses, we cannot expect him to exhibit a command of the conventions that Swales or Dudley-Evans describe. Yet, in spite of the obvious differences in school and professional contexts, constraints, and purposes for composing, this writing increasingly shows signs of the adoption of the conventions of his newly adopted community.

Thus the introductions to Nate's research reports can be viewed not only for presence of the rhetorical features that mark acceptance in a national community of researchers but for facility with and dependence on topics and language from both his past and from his immediate social context. In these introductions we shall see Nate integrating new topical and rhetorical information with old, the latter derived from his teaching background and familiarity with literary forms of discourse.

The first introduction is from a report on a survey that Nate conducted three months after he entered the program. This survey was completed in his first research methods course, which all students entering the rhetoric program were required to take. His professors told the class that the research questions from which they developed their surveys should grow from a "felt difficulty," that is, an intensely felt issue, question, or problem. (The sentences have been numbered for later reference.)

TEXT 1

How and Why Voice is Taught: A Pilot Survey

Problem

The English profession does not agree on what a "writer's voice" means or how the concept should be used to teach writing, equating it to personal style, literary persona, authority, orality, or even grammar.

(1) When teachers, writers, and researchers comment on the phenomen

of voice, they usually stay on a metaphorical level. (2) Voice is "juice" or "cadence." (3) The concept appears to be too illusive and too closely tied to personal rhetorical philosophy, disallowing a generally accepted definition for common usage. (4) A novice writing teacher, then, might say "You don't know what it is. (5) I don't understand it. (6) How or why should I teach it?" (7)

It should be taught. (8) Most experienced teachers and accomplished writers recognize that in spite of the wide range of definitions the concept of voice is somehow central to the composing process. (9) Some believe that without voice, true writing is impossible. (10) Until the profession understands the phenomenon or in some way addresses what these experts are saying, a paradox exists, and the novice writing teacher confronts a mixed message. (11) Voice should not remain just another eccentricity in an already idiosyncratic profession. (12)

Background
Who are these "accomplished" teachers, writers and thinkers who uniquely honor a writer's voice? (13) Aristotle, Coleridge and Moffet [sic] have acknowledged the impact of the "self" on an audience. (14) Donald Murray and other contemporary rhetoricians state without reserve that this *self*, the writer's voice, is "at the heart of the act of writing." (15) From my experience writing and teaching writing I know that a writer's voice can spirit a composition and, if the voice is misplaced or confused, can drive a teacher or writer batty. (16) If I say to my class "No, No the voice is all wrong here," or "Yes, I can hear you now," I might induce the kind of *authority* I seek, but I am probably sending one of those strange undeciferable teacher-messages that students rightfully ignore or misinterpret. (17) I am liable to get talk-writing or emotions unbound. (18) Like the accomplished experts and theorists, I tacitly know that voice is important, but I am not necessarily equipped to translate this importance for my students. (19)

Are there other teachers who face or at least perceive the same dilemma? (20) I sense that there are, but a hunch is not good enough. (21) Since I have invested time and energy searching the question of voice, I worry that my observations and suspicions are egocentric. (22) Before I tire myself and my colleagues with a series of inquiries and experiments, I must decide if a problem actually exists. (23) Therefore I composed a pilot survey to tell me if I should continue my study of voice and in what direction. (24) The survey, a questionnaire, was aimed at other writing teachers in the Pittsburgh area. (25) By asking if, how, and why voice is taught I hoped to understand the boundaries of my questions and my universe. (26)

This text is a good example of a writer working in a "multidimensional linguistic space" in the sense that in it we can identify traces of the writer's past experience and interests merging with new research methods, problems, and rhetorical forms. Nate had entered the rhetoric program in part because he wanted to learn research methods to help him answer questions growing out of his experience as a freshman writing teacher. He chose to survey ways that college-level writing teachers used the concept of voice. Nate's view that writers have a "personal voice" was central to his teaching philosophy and guided his participation in a National Endowment for the Humanities seminar the summer before he entered the Ph.D. program. Thus, the introduction to his survey reveals the pedagogical values he brought to the rhetoric program, implicit in his claim that an understanding of "voice" is essential to an understanding of the writing process. At the same time the introduction was his first presentation of research to social science–oriented readers who would expect to see a term like "voice" defined operationally.

That Nate seems to be addressing more than one audience in this paper is suggested by the vocabulary and genre features he uses. He mixes terminology suitable for social science expository writing ("phenomenon," "paradox," "acknowledged," "pilot survey") with colloquialisms like "batty," "liable to," and "hunch." He talks in neutral language about "a series of inquiries and experiments" and then changes register and talks in a more personal vein about "the boundaries of my questions and my universe."[2] Although he appears to be following a social science text schema by labeling segments of the introduction "Problem" and "Background," his use of these subheadings seems imitative rather than based on true genre knowledge. His problem statement consists of a series of assertions about the importance of teaching and researching voice.

Nate's aim here appears to be persuasive; he wishes to convince his readers that it is important to begin to isolate the phenomenon of voice in order to characterize and thus define it. In sentences 13–19 he attempts to elaborate on the problem, first by referring to such diverse authorities as Aristotle, Coleridge, Moffett, and Murray. Instead of including citations to specific works, however, he mentions these four names only in passing; most of the support he marshals for his claims comes from personal testimony. By not placing his research within a larger disciplinary frame of reference, he cannot offer his audience a warrant in the form of citations which designate an established field to which his present study will contribute (Toulmin, 97–107). From the perspective of his immediate audience, Nate's persuasive strategies would likely be ineffective, since he neither bases his claims on shared knowledge nor uses conventions that will enable him to establish warrants for his claims. From the perspective of his NEH or freshman compositon writing communities, on the other hand, his strategies would probably be quite effective.

A comment in one of Nate's self reports shows he was aware of his new role in a research community and a change in his writing:

I always intended to be sensitized to the scientific canon, something I accept like my father's lectures on handshakes, something I just need to do if for no other reason than you have to know something from the inside before you can fairly criticize it.

Yet the warrants behind the claims in his report rest in his shared experience with fellow teachers and writers and not in explicit connections with previous research or scholarship. Although this writing does not create a "research space" in the way Swales describes, we can still say the text is socially constructed. It reflects Nate's recent participation in a linguistic community where the rhetorical moves of social science are less attractive and personal appeals and experience are more common. Readers from Nate's previous community would (and did) find his claims accurate and without need of further substantiation. What interests us here is that this writing, though originating with a personal "felt difficulty," was a first attempt at social science prose. Nate responded (predictably) by relying mostly on the wealth of substantive and linguistic knowledge that he brought to the program.

Writing for a Local Audience in the Rhetoric Program

Six months later in the program, Nate wrote an introduction to a research report for his "Process of Composing" course. This report detailed a pilot study he conducted using protocol research methodology. Nate began this introduction as he had Text 1, by introducing a problem that his research was to address. However, Text 2 reflects a new area of personal inquiry and research. Here we see him drawing on newly acquired theoretical knowledge of cognitive psychology as well as on issues that he was being exposed to in his coursework.

TEXT 2

Reframing: The Role of Prior Knowledge in the Process of Reading to Write

Introduction

The Problem

It is nearly impossible to ignore the remarkable efforts by researchers and theorists over the last 15 years to understand the composing processes of writers. (1) It is equally remarkable to consider how little is known about the reading process, especially as a companion process to writing. (2) Many of the academic exercises our students encounter or the competencies we aspire for them embrace both domains. (3)   Only recently have researchers begun to study relationships between reading and writing processes, focusing primarily on how reading affects the development of a writer (Smith, 1982; Scardamalia and Bereiter, 1984). (4)

One reason for this seeming oversight may rest in our short-sighted image of the writer. (5)   Romantic philosophies and practices urge self-determinism; and writing is seen as a lonely struggle, the writer armed only with a blank legal pad, introspection, and the admittedly noble cause of writing to discover a universe. (6)   Though I do not argue the place or nature of expressive writing, I do argue that another image of the writer is equally viable. (7)   Writers collaborate, for one thing, with other writers (Ede and Lunsford, 1984) and with other language communities. (8)   Among others, Patricia Bizzell (1984) draws our attention to the price paid for ignoring the conventions and genres of an academic community. (9)   Working from that image, the writing in college is social, and assignments include the artful manipulation of texts and task, of plans and intentions, of community and self. (10)

If composing is multi-dimensional, what processes must a writer manage in order to move gracefully from the act of critical reading into the act of critical writing? (11)   And if "grace" is not possible, what constraints interrupt and alter the process for a writer who must first read to write? (12)   In this report and proposal I describe what I am calling reframing, one cognitive component in the process of reading to write. (13)   To reframe means to map semantic schemas from prior knowledge onto key propositions in freshly encountered material. (14) Readers reframe to create manageable "gists" dependent on experience related to the subject domain and their representation of the task. (15)   Reframing is best understood as a constructive act of reading: a lessening of informational loads, a creating of plans and a shaping of content—all of which drive the draft that soon follows. (16)

Text 2 differs in many ways from Text 1. Although Nate and his classmates were asked to begin with an "interesting feature" in the protocol data that they had collected, an assignment that appears to invite a personal perspective, Nate writes with much less a sense of a "felt difficulty" and without personal testimony. Here, his writing is "collaborative" in that this text refers to issues he and his peers had discussed in the immediate context of the graduate course. For example, in the second paragraph Nate alludes to an alternative "image of the writer" and cites examples (lines 7 and 8) from scholarship on "collaboration" and "academic communities." Comments from Nate's self reports and his professor's positive reception of this argument suggest that Nate had successfully entered into a local conversation. This conversation would, however, exclude many readers. Sentences 14–16, for example, are written in language that would have been understood by Nate's professor, but is jargon ("semantic schemas," "key propositions," "informational loads," etc.) to readers unfamiliar with psycholinguistics. Nate also appears to be using a more situationally appropriate register in Text 2 than he had in Text 1. Instead of colloquialisms like "hunch" and "batty," we find him employing more formal lexical choices, which include "encounter," "aspire," "viable," and "admittedly." Finally, the I-centered focus of Text 1 seems to be giving way to a broader, more communal perspective: whereas the first-person singular pronoun was used heavily in Text 1 (19 times), here there is a 4-4 split between the first-person singular and the first-person plural.

Genre features also point to Nate's growing identification with a disciplinary community. Indeed, this text exhibits the sequence of rhetorical moves Dudley-Evans observed in the introductions to graduate plant biologists' theses (although not in the detail that appeared in those texts). In sentence 1 Nate introduces the general field, "the composing processes of writers" (Move 1). In sentences 2 and 3 he introduces the general topic within the field, "the reading process, especially as a companion process to writing" (Move 2). Sentence 4 introduces the particular topic, "relationships between reading and writing processes" (Move 3). In sentences 4–10 he defines the scope of the particular topic by introducing research parameters and summarizing previous research (Move 4). Sentences 11–12 prepare for present research by raising questions (Move 5). And in sentences 13–16 he introduces the present research (Move 6) by describing briefly the work carried out (but see discussion below).

Text 2 occupies a transitional position between Texts 1 and 3. On the one hand, Nate can be said to be constructing an argument in this introduction that will enable him to create a "research space" for his study. Not having received formal instruction in the rhetorical moves of introductions, he has apparently picked them up, at least superficially, from his reading: he displays all four of Swales's moves and all six of Dudley-Evans', in the right order. On the other hand, he does not situate the field and the topic in the kind of detail that would be called for in a thesis (Moves 1–3). Further, his attempt to summarize previous research (Move 4), though more focused than in Text 1, is still somewhat vague and discursive. Move 5 is clear enough, yet coming on the heels of weak Moves 1–4, it might not be fully expected. Move 6 is also quite clear, but it does not adequately describe the work actually carried out in this study (case studies using protocol analysis).

Although Nate's assignment was actually to write a proposal for more research based on his pilot study, as if he were seeking funding, his argument would not succeed in the eyes of a reviewer outside his research seminar. First, he does not provide readers outside of the seminar with enough explicit detail. Second, and more important, he does not establish his authority by citing previous publications and acknowledging

Carol Berkenkotter, Thomas N. Huckin, and John Ackerman

established arguments within an existing research forum. If Nate's report were submitted to a journal referee or grant reviewer, we could expect the reader to puzzle over what is assumed to be shared knowledge. For example, he does not establish a connection between his comments on collaboration and social contexts (sentences 8–10) and the material which follows in the last paragraph. It would not immediately be clear how the questions posed in sentences 11–12 relate to the discussion in the preceding paragraph. However, for Nate's *immediate* audience, his professor and even other members of his research seminar, this argument is much less elliptical. The antecedents to the propositions on collaborative writing, social contexts, and critical reading and writing are traceable to earlier drafts, comments by his professor and classmates, and class discussion as evidenced by Nate's self reports during the semester. We suggest that Text 2 is transitional because it exhibits the outward signs of the rhetorical devices of a social science subspeciality, with a system of warrants, claims, and rhetorical structures, while at the same time is clearly a collaborative, local construct, dependent upon the shared knowledge of a limited set of readers.

Writing to Join a Conversation among Composition Researchers

Text 3 is the introduction to a research report Nate wrote in December 1985, after having been in the rhetoric program for a year and a half. The immediate occasion of the report was a term project for a "Computers and Rhetorical Studies" course. Nate also used this introduction for a shorter paper that he wrote for a psychology course on human problem-solving. Thus the paper was written for two immediate readers – his rhetoric professor, whose background was in computer science, and a senior psychology professor. As we shall see, however, Text 3 reflects not only Nate's immediate rhetorical situation, but also his intellectual identification with the research agenda of the professor of his "Process of Composing" course, for whom he wrote Text 2. Through that professor he became familiar with studies by researchers beyond his local university setting who were asking questions about the interactions between reading and writing processes (as seen in his references to Smith, Langer, and other researchers). In this sense, Nate was not only fulfilling course assignments with this project, he was also writing to participate in a local dialogue and enter into the professional conversation of a research subspeciality.

This text deals with the same topic as Text 2: how writers use background knowledge when writing from source materials. It is the first time in his graduate career that Nate has been able to run a follow-up study and write a second paper on the same topic; hence it is interesting to compare these two texts. Like Text 2, this introduction displays the sequence of six rhetorical moves described by Dudley-Evans. Sentences 1 and 2 introduce the general field, "relationships between writing and reading processes" (Move 1). Sentences 3 and 4 narrow the topic to "how reading and writing facilitate each other" (Move 2). Sentences 5–8 narrow the topic further to "the role of experiential knowledge" (Move 3). Overlapping with Move 3 is Move 4, in which Nate defines the scope of his topic by summarizing previous research (sentences 6–8). He then prepares for present research (Move 5) by indicating how previous research by Judith Langer can be extended (sentences 9–12). Finally, he introduces the present research (Move 6) with a lengthy discussion of aims and justification (sentences 13–27).

However, Text 3 differs from Text 2 in significant ways. It elaborates more on every one of the six rhetorical moves and is more than twice as long. Where Text 2 devotes four sentences to introducing the topic (Moves 1–3), Text 3 devotes eight. Where Text 2 discusses four previous studies (Moves 4–5), Text 3 discusses twelve. Most important, where Text 2 introduces present research (Move 6) by simply stating a thesis, Text 3 introduces present research via an elaborate, hierarchically organized series of hypotheses. Clearly, Nate has not only become aware of the standard rhetorical moves of this genre, he has also learned how to use them to better effect. Text 3 draws more on information reported in antecedent texts by other researchers than does Text 2. It is also more sensitive to the possibility that, without the necessary evidence and warrants, some readers may not accept the claims the writer is about to make. Although there remain a few "off-register" metaphorical expressions such as "dead center," (5) and "nourished" (6) most of the prose in this text is cast in the neutral, "objective" style that characterizes the research writring that Nate had been reading in the fields of psycholinguistics, cognitive psychology, and educational research. Readers may want to flip back a few pages and compare the style of this text to the more informal, "oral" style in Text 1. Here Nate is projecting a more "scientific" *persona*. In fact, one of the most striking differences between Text 1 and Text 3 is the transformation of the relationship between persona and subject matter. In Text 3 the writer directs the reader's attention toward the issues under discussion, rather than to his own sensibility as he had done in Text 1. Even in Text 2, the writer had occasionally adopted the first-person pronoun. For example, in sentence 7 of that text he had asserted, "Though I do not argue the place or nature of expressive writing, I do argue that another image

Carol Berkenkotter, Thomas N. Huckin, and John Ackerman

TEXT 3
Toward a Generative Computer Environment:
A Protocol Study

The Problem

Although reading and writing have received national attention with the advent of the literacy crisis, only recently have researchers begun to study relationships between reading and writing processes. (1)   That research has focused primarily on how reading affects the development of young writers (Smith, 1982; Scardamalia and Bereiter, 1984). (2) There is little research at all that looks specifically at how reading and writing facilitate each other (for a speculative study see Petrosky, 1982). (3)   This dearth is especially curious in the light of the amount of academic learning that depends on simultaneous expertise in both modes of expression.* (4)

*It is increasingly accepted that reading, along with writing, is a constructive act where the reader, like the writer, uses goals, knowledge, and strategies to make meaning. (This note belongs to Nate's text.)

   Dead center in the reading-to-write question is the role of experiential knowledge. (5)   Accomplished writers (who are surely accomplished readers) admonish novice writers for straying too far from topics nourished by experience or substantial study (Murray, 1981 & McPhee, 1984). (6)   Similarly, research overwhelmingly supports our intuitions that background knowledge significantly affects the construction of meaning in a text (Anderson, 1977; Goodman and Goodman, 1978; Harste, Burke and Woodward, 1982; and Langer, 1984). (7)   What advice, then, do we give our students—when they continually face reading and writing assignments demanding facility with both text-based and experience-based knowledge? (8)

   The Study

Judith Langer (1985) partially answered that question by analzying the effects of text-based topic knowledge on 10th grade writing. (9)   She found, via a free-association test, a direct and positive relationship between her subjects' ability to hierarchically display the meaning of a passage and the ability to compose later a "coherent" draft. (10)   Following Langer's lead, this study explores how topic knowledge affects academic writing and, more specifically, how experiential knowledge becomes the major variable in a reading and writing scenario. (11) Although Langer's study begins with much the same question for research, important distinctions must be noted. . . . (12)   (Here Nate elaborates on differences between his project and Langer's. We have omitted this passage for the sake of brevity.)

   The primary goal of this study is to describe how experts use experiential knowledge to invent original, effective organizational patterns in their plans and drafts. (13)   Bonnie Meyer (1984) has documented a reader's affinity for hierarchical text plans, or what might be called the traditional mental representations that guide comprehension in print. (14)   Since Aristotle we know that rhetorical discourse follows common logical patterns. (15)   From years of exposure to these basic plans—antecedent/consequent, comparison, description/response, time-order—a writer who is first a reader might naturally turn such a plan into a traditional albeit unoriginal plan for writing. (16)   However, a writer becomes "noteable" when he or she strategically deviates from these norms (Elbow, 1984), creating what is essentially an organic, experience-based plan that improves upon time-worn organizational patterns. (17)   Stephen White (1985), through extensive product analyses of personal narrative assignments, has begun to document how students successfully create autonomous, experience-based text structures. (18)   This study seeks to explore this phenomenon as well, tracing the decisions and variables that speed the process. (19)

An exploratory study need not be run blind. (20)   Findings from previous research and protocol analyses suggest the following list of predictable behaviors in the reading-to-write scenario. (21)   A subject might:

Balance text-based and experiential knowledge successfully to complete the task—
> using both to form a coherent, organized, and original design for the draft.
> choosing a personal organizing principle inherent in the recollection to structure the paper and otherwise structure the key issues in the texts.
> choosing one of Meyer's text-specific organizational patterns to structure a draft, adding substance with experience-based elaborations. (22)

Lean on experiential knowledge and lose sight of the task—
> selecting only those issues in the reading that comfortably match experience, ignoring other germane issues.
> ignoring the texts altogether, digressing into a narrative or personal elaboration which distorts the task.
> misrepresenting key points in the texts by illogically attaching personal background knowledge. (23)

Rely on text-based knowledge exclusively, ignoring any and all related experience. (24)

These predictions in effect create a working hypothesis on the range of behaviors possible in a reading-to-write assignment. (25)   Coupled with the findings here they will form a data base on which a model of expert behavior can be built. (26)   That model and a computer tutorial based on that model are the long range goals of this research and should offer substantive answers to the educational question of how can facility with experiential and text-based knowledge be taught. (27)

Carol Berkenkotter, Thomas N. Huckin, and John Ackerman

of the writer is equally viable." In contrast to the twenty-three first-person singular pronouns in Text 1 and the four first-person singular pronouns in Text 2, here Nate avoids the first-person singular pronoun altogether. The frequent use of first person, the informal oral style, and the metaphorical constructions in Text 1 created the sense of the writer's personal involvement with the object of study. In Text 3 the writer's expression of a personally "felt difficulty" has been replaced by a "neutral" description of a "significant" research issue. The writer documents the significance of this issue by using citations. For example, the string of citations that appear in sentence 7 refers anaphorically to subject and verb of the sentence ("research . . . supports") and serves to instantiate the writer's claim that "research supports our intuitions that background knowledge significantly affects the construction of meaning in a text." Nate's use of this technique as well as his "socially appropriate" persona and style are signs of his increasing command over the conventions of writing about research.

Text 3 would probably be the most difficult of the three introductions to decipher for readers outside of the community of specialists to whom Nate was writing. To many readers Nate's meaning would appear to be obfuscated by a thicket of jargon. One encounters throughout a technical terminology familiar primarily to a specialized readership of cognitive psychologists and psycholinguists. Some examples of this terminology are: "experiential knowledge" (5, 11, 13), "experience-based knowledge" (8), "experienced-based plan" (17), "autonomous experience-based text structures" (18), "text-based knowledge" (8), "text-based topic knowledge" (9), "topic knowledge" (11), "hierarchically display(ed) meaning" (11), "reading and writing scenario" (11), "hierarchical text plans" (14), and "mental representations" (14). Nate's use of this terminology suggests that he is able to speak in the discourse of a specialized readership. His use of this lexicon also indicates that he is building a conceptual framework that will allow him to interact with other members of this specialist community, to identify important research issues and problems, and in a general sense, to share (although perhaps not to be cognizant of) the community's epistemological assumptions.

The differences between these three texts written over three consecutive semesters suggest some summary inferences regarding the manner in which Nate appears to have migrated toward the specialist's perspective. Text 3 is "intertextual" in a way that Texts 1 and 2 are not. It is heavily indebted to concepts and terminology in the literature that Nate cites (de Beaugrande and Dressler, 10–11; Porter, 35). While Text 3 gains strength through this intertextuality, it remains collaborative as well, since it is staged within a local conversation and is directed at an immediate readership. In Text 1 the writer had been an isolated newcomer inquiring whether anyone shared his "dilemma." In Text 2, we see the embryonic researcher learning a theoretical model and research methodology reflected in the terminology he is beginning (albeit somewhat awkwardly) to use. By Text 3 Nate has assimilated a literature and a lexicon and therefore is more comfortably able to speak in the discourse of his subspecialty.

Conclusion

In his case study of two biologists revising to accommodate their referees' criticisms, Myers raises the questions, "How does a researcher learn all [the] complex conventions of the scientific article? What part do such negotiations play in the education of a doctoral student, or in the choice of problem or shifts of specialty?" ("Texts as Knowledge Claims," 628). From the changes appearing in the three texts above, we can infer some of the complex social negotiations that writers engage in as they prepare to enter an academic field. Although we are reluctant to generalize from our findings to other students entering academic discourse communities as graduates, we would like to offer the following observations and speculations.

First, it appears that, for students with backgrounds similar to Nate's, making the transition from *composition teacher* to *composition researcher* (i.e., from practitioner to specialist) involves a difficult passage from one academic culture to another. Developing communicative competence requires that they master the ways of speaking, reading, and writing which are indigenous to the new culture.

Second, although many students entering interdisciplinary doctoral programs with an emphasis on empirical research like the one at Carnegie Mellon will be reading in new and unfamiliar fields, students with prior training in the sciences or social sciences may be more likely to bring previously developed procedural schemata for writing about research than those with backgrounds in literary studies or composition pedagogy. We base this observation partly on Nate's predictable difficulty mastering the conventions and language of social science reporting and partly on observational data from the earlier study (1988) which indicated that most entering graduate students struggled to gain competence with either key issues or the locally preferred conventions for reading and writing. Though far from conclusive, the earlier study and our analysis here raise the question of what type of training or teaching experience best prepares a graduate student to enter a community of writing researchers.

Finally, we suggest that the development of *academic* communicative competence (or academic literacy) involves the ability to adapt one's discourse as the situation requires. In this study we saw a writer struggling in his first assignments to use a comfortable voice and style to address

Carol Berkenkotter, Thomas N. Huckin, and John Ackerman

an uncomfortable and unfamiliar writing assignment. As his training progressed, he learned through exposure, practice and reinforcement to use a different voice and style. Some theorists have proposed that similar struggles characterize undergraduates' writing instruction and experiences (Bartholomae). How much information regarding the discoursal expectations of those who teach, write, and read in the sciences, the social sciences, and the various humanities needs to be made explicit to students in their undergraduate and graduate curricula? At what level of sophistication should such information be presented? In what instructional contexts should it be provided?

Like many sophisticated language users, Nate was able to adapt his discourse over time to achieve various intellectual social and professional ends. We do not mean to imply that he was a linguistic chameleon, as is a professional journalist who may infiltrate a wide range of discourse communities (Swales, *Article Introductions*, 7). Nor did Nate, in the process of becoming a composition researcher, abandon his previous writing community of friends and teachers. Rather, he brought bits and pieces of his experience as writing teacher to his new role as an apprentice researcher.

This is not to say that his passage does not raise some interesting questions for scholars interested in the growth of knowledge in composition studies. How, for example, do the sociopolitical constraints that govern the "manufacture of knowledge" (Knorr-Cetina) in this emerging field affect a graduate student's choice of research program? To what extent are the issues that concern composition teachers subsumed by the agendas of mentors as they join powerful research or scholarly enterprises, such as the one that we studied? How will the increasing graduate specialization in rhetorical studies and educational research affect the development of the canon within composition studies? We raise these questions because composition studies is a young field bound to be affected by the above factors.

Socialization studies such as the one we have reported above may also raise pedagogical questions that will concern composition teachers and scholars: What does learning the multiple registers and codes of various academic communities entail both cognitively and socially for undergraduate students? How does acquiring specialized literacy affect the graduate writer's world view, or his or her ethnic and gender identity? Finally, to quote Nate, what does it mean to the undergraduate or graduate student to become "sensitized to the scientific canon," or the literary canon, or the canons of the many subspecialties within these broad fields of inquiry?

It is to Nate that we turn to provide, if not an answer, an insight:

> I just need to do it if for no other reason than you have to know
> something from the inside before you can fairly criticize it.

NOTES

1. Our goal in analyzing Nate's enculturation and growth as a writer was to bring multiple perspectives and methodologies into play. Our analysis is based on close familiarity and participation in the CMU discourse community, on the relative detachment and objectivity afforded by the linguistic methods, and on the triangulation of our observations and interpretations. The assumptions and procedures of this eclectic methodology are elaborated in our 1988 article.

2. A more detailed account of Nate's register shifts can be found in Berkenkotter, Huckin, and Ackerman (1988).

BIBLIOGRAPHY

Bartholomae, David. "Inventing the University." In *When a Writer Can't Write,* ed. M. Rose, 134–65. New York: Guilford, 1985.

Bazerman, Charles. "Modern Evolution of the Experimental Report in Physics: Spectroscopic Articles in *Physical Review,* 1893–1980." *Social Studies of Science* 14 (1984): 163–95.

Bazerman, Charles. "Scientific Writing as a Social Act: A Review of the Literature of the Sociology of Science." In *New Essays in Technical and Scientific Communication: Research, Theory, Practice,* ed. P. V. Anderson, R. J. Brockmann, and C. R. Miller, 156–84. Farmingdale, N.Y.: Baywood, 1983.

Bazerman, Charles, "What Written Knowledge Does: Three Examples of Academic Discourse." *Philosophy of the Social Sciences* 11 (1981): 361–82.

Bazerman, Charles. "The Writing of Scientific Non-fiction: Contexts, Choices, Constraints." *Pre/Text* 5 (1984): 39–74.

Berkenkotter, Carol, Thomas Huckin, and John Ackerman. "Conversations, Conventions and the Writer: Case Study of a Student in a Rhetoric Ph.D. Program." *Research in the Teaching of English* 22 (1988): 9–44.

Bizzell, Patricia. "Cognition, Convention, and Certainty: What We Need to Know about Writing." *Pre/Text* 3 (1982): 213–43.

Bizzell, Patricia. "College Composition: Initiation into the Academic Discourse Community" [Review of *Four Worlds of Writing* and *Writing in the Arts and Sciences*]. *Curriculum Inquiry* 12 (1982): 191–207.

Chapman, David W., and Gary Tate. "A Survey of Doctoral Programs in Rhetoric and Composition." *Rhetoric Review* 5 (1987): 124–86.

Crane, Diana. *Invisible Colleges.* Chicago: University of Chicago Press, 1972.

Crookes, Graham. "Towards a Validated Analysis of Scientific Text Structure." *Applied Linguistics* 7 (1986): 57–70.

de Beaugrande, Robert, and Wolfgang Dressler. *Introduction to Text Linguistics.* London: Longman, 1981.

Dudley-Evans, Tony. "Genre Analysis: An Investigation of the Introduction and Discussion Sections of MSc Dissertations." In *Talking about Text,* ed. M. Coulthard, 128–45. Birmingham, Eng.: English Language Research, 1986.

Dyson, Anne H. "Emerging Alphabetic Literacy in School Contexts: Toward Defining the Gap Between School Curriculum and Child Mind." *Written Communication* 1 (1984): 5–55.

Fahnestock, Jeanne. "Accommodating Science: The Rhetorical Life of Scientific Facts." *Written Communication* 3 (1986): 275–96.

Fahnestock, Jeanne, and Marie Secor. "The Rhetoric of Literacy Criticism." Paper delivered at the Penn State Conference on Rhetoric and Composition, July 1982.

Faigley, Lester, and Karen Hansen. "Learning to Write in the Social Sciences." *College Composition and Communication* 34 (1985): 140–49.

Gilbert, Nigel G., and Michael Mulkay. *Opening Pandora's Box: A Sociological Analysis of Scientists' Discourse.* Cambridge: Cambridge University Press, 1984.

Heath, Shirley Brice. *Ways with Words: Language, Life, and Work in Communities and Classrooms.* New York: Cambridge University Press, 1983.

Heath, Shirley Brice. "What No Bedtime Story Means: Narrative Skills at Home and at School." *Language in Society* 11 (1982): 49–76.

Herrington, Anne. "Writing in Academic Settings: A Study of the Contexts for Writing in Two College Chemical Engineering Courses." *Research in the Teaching of English* 19 (1985): 331–61.

Hill, S., B. F. Soppelsa, and G. K. West. "Teaching ESL Students to Read and Write Experimental-Research Papers." *TESOL Quarterly* 16, 3 (1982): 333–48.

Huckin, Thomas. "Surprise Value in Scientific Discourse." Paper presented at the Conference on College Composition and Communication, Atlanta, Ga., 1987.

Hudson, Richard A. *Sociolinguistics.* Cambridge: Cambridge University Press, 1980o.

Knorr-Cetina, Karen D. *The Manufacture of Knowledge: An Essay on the Constructivist and Contextual Nature of Science,* Oxford: Pergamon, 1981.

Latour, Bruno and Steve Woolgar. *Laboratory Life: The Social Construction of Scientific Facts.* Beverly Hills: Sage, 1979.

McCarthy, Lucille P. "A Stranger in Strange Lands: A College Student Writing Across the Curriculum." *Research in the Teaching of English* 21 (1987): 233–65.

Miles, Matthew B., and A. Michael Huberman. "Drawing Valid Meaning from Qualitative Data: Toward a Shared Craft." *Educational Researcher* 13 (1984): 20–30.

Myers, Greg. "The Social Construction of Two Biologists' Proposals." *Written Communication* 2 (1985): 219–45.

Myers, Greg. "Texts as Knowledge Claims: The Social Construction of Two Biology Articles. *Social Studies of Science* 15 (1985): 593–630.

North, Stephen M. "Writing in a Philosophy Class: Three Case Studies." *Research in the Teaching of English* 20 (1986): 225–62.

Porter, J. E. "Intertextuality and the Discourse Community." *Rhetoric Review* 5 (1986): 34–47.

Selfe, Cynthia L. "The Predrafting Processes of Four High- and Four Low-Apprehensive Writers." *Research in the Teaching of English* 18 (1984): 45–64.

Selinker, Larry, R. Mary Todd Trimble, and Louis Trimble. "Presuppositional Rhetorical Information in EST Discourse." *TESOL Quarterly* 10, 3 (1976): 281–90.

Shultz, Jeffrey J., Susan Florio, and Frederick Erickson. "Where's the Floor? Aspects of the Cultural Organization of Social Relationships in Communication at Home and in School." In *Children in and out of School: Ethnography and Education*, ed. P. Gilmore and A. A. Glatthorn, 88–123. Washington, D.C.: Center for Applied Linguistics, 1982.

Swales, John. *Aspects of Article Introductions*. Aston Reearch Reports No. 1. Aston, Eng.: University of Birmingham, 1981.

Swales, John. "Research into the Structure of Introductions to Journal Articles and its Application to the Teaching of Academic Writing." In *Common Ground: Shared Interests in ESP and Communication Studies*, ed. R. Williams, J. Swales, and J. Kirkman, 77–86. Oxford: Pergamon, 1984.

Swales, John, and Hazem Najjar. "The Writing of Research Articles: Where to Put the Bottom Line?" *Written Communication* 4 (1987): 175–91.

Toulmin, Stephen. *The Uses of Argument*. Cambridge: Cambridge University Press, 1958.

Yearly, Steven. "Textual Persuasion: The Role of Social Accounting in the Construction of Scientific Arguments." *Philosophy of the Social Sciences* 11 (1981): 409–35.

9 MEANING ATTRIBUTION IN

AMBIGUOUS TEXTS

IN SOCIOLOGY

ROBERT A. SCHWEGLER AND

LINDA K. SHAMOON

The recognition that academic writing is a social activity — shaped by and in turn reshaping a discourse community — has led to a shift in the focus of study away from the text formats and styles employed in various disciplines to broader interest in the conventions and shared knowledge that bind together acts of reading, writing, and thinking in an interpretive community (Moore and Peterson). As James Porter convincingly argues, the study of academic discourse needs to pay attention not only to texts but to "the social framework regulating textual production," to the shared "assumptions about what objects are appropriate for examination and discussion, what operating functions are performed on those objects, what constitutes 'evidence' and 'validity,' and what formal conventions are followed" (39).

Surprisingly, though the analysis of academic and professional texts has recently shifted in focus "from the formal features of an isolated text toward the whole text as an instance of language functioning in a context of human activity" (Brandt, 93; Miller and Selzer; Swales and Najjar; Peters), and though survey research and case studies have helped identify some general discourse conventions and audience expectations for academic and professional writing (Herrington; Odell and Goswami; Eblen; Myers; Brown and Herndl), little attention has been paid to the interaction of specific readers and texts. The present study, therefore, examines the responses of readers in a particular interpretive community (academic sociology) to one common form of discourse in the field (undergraduate writing) in order to identify the conventions guiding reader response and interpretation of texts. In so doing, the study demonstrates a method of inquiry into text-reader relationships that may be of use in understanding the conventions shaping discourse in other interpretive communities.

Prior studies of academic writing have often focused primarily on texts (Swales and Najjar) and have not taken into account the incompleteness of the evidence provided by the texts. Because they are addressed to specialized readers, even well-formed academic texts (both professional and student) often contain omissions in information, method, or form which are to be supplied through inference by skilled readers belonging to the disciplinary community (Popken). Moreover, because they are sharply focused in topic and method, individual academic texts, no matter how exemplary, make available for examination only a small portion of the discourse conventions of a discipline.

Cognitive psychology and reading theory have demonstrated the likelihood, however, that the social, cultural, and methodological constraints of a discourse community as well as its semantic and formal conventions are represented in detail in the memory of expert readers from the community, where the representations constitute an important part of the prior knowledge necessary to comprehend a text. Such knowledge is manifested in the sets of expectations (schema or frames) employed in comprehension and in the processes of inference and interaction between textual cues and prior knowledge that readers employ in building a mental representation of a text's meaning (van Dijk and Kintsch; Kucer).

Since text and context come together in the act of reading, many of the assumptions and constraints shaping discourse in an academic discipline should be observable in the expectations of expert readers, in the interpretive strategies they employ, and in the way specific elements of texts satisfy or fail to satisfy the readers' expectations. Bazerman's study of the professional reading of physicists makes use of this kind of evidence to show how "structured background knowledge (or schemata)" guides the ways physicists comprehend and evaluate texts and to examine the role of reading in creating the shared understandings that are key elements in the social construction of disciplinary knowledge (20–21). Yet Bazerman does not examine in detail the interaction of textual features and reader expectations, nor does he provide ways of identifying the formal and semantic conventions governing discourse within a disciplinary community.

The study reported in this paper examines reader-text interaction to identify discourse conventions guiding student writing and instructor response in sociology. Admittedly, the conventions regulating different kinds of written discourse in a discipline — including research articles, popular reports, and student papers — can be expected to differ. Yet the papers produced by students — novice members of an academic discourse community — share many features with texts produced by professional sociolo-

Robert A. Schwegler and Linda K. Shamoon

gists, features generally representative of sociological discourse. Moreover, student writing is itself a legitimate and important subject for study, both because of the central role it plays in the process of initiation into a discipline (Bizzell) and because pedagogy can perhaps be improved through an accurate understanding of its features. Moreover, the relative brevity and straightforwardness of student papers make them more amenable to the techniques of inquiry employed in this study than are the complex and often idiosyncratic writings of professional sociologists.

Discourse conventions can regulate both global and local features of texts. Global features include: (1) superstructures (types of discourse, broad generic patterns), (2) macrostructures (gist or line of reasoning), and (3) macropropositions (summarizing statements, categories of information). Local features include: (1) the choice and sequencing of individual statements and pieces of information (micropropositions), and (2) the style of sentences. In both reading and writing activities, decisions at the global level tend to dictate choices at the local level. The present study, therefore, tries to identify disciplinary constraints and conventions governing the higher-level features of undergraduate writing in sociology.

We have not chosen, however, to focus on the most obvious feature of the texts, their formal superstructure. In examining some four hundred student research papers gathered from twelve sociology classes, we concluded that on the level of superstructure, undergraduate research papers in sociology appear to employ a two-part expository structure that they share with student writing in many academic fields. This superstructure consists of a statement of task or problem followed by investigation and proof. Textbooks for undergraduate academic writing also view this structure as basic to research papers in most disciplines, including sociology (Maimon; Sociology Writing Group). Since the superstructure appears to reflect the conventions of academic discourse in general rather than those of sociological discourse, we chose to exclude from the study questions of textual superstructure.

Instead, the study focuses on semantic macrostructures and macropropositions and on the formal features often associated with them. Drawing on evidence from highly rated papers among those gathered for the study and on current research in discourse comprehension, we examine four areas in which student texts in sociology seem likely to be shaped by disciplinary conventions:

> the kinds of information provided in the openings of papers;
> the kinds of information provided in the bodies;
> the semantic macrostructures or lines of reasoning;
> and the macrostructural cues in the bodies of papers.

Meaning Attribution in Ambiguous Texts in Sociology

In addition, the study is guided by two questions:

1. To what extent do university sociology instructors expect student writing to adhere to disciplinary constraints and conventions in each of the areas being examined?

2. What specific semantic or formal conventions can be identified on the basis of responses and evaluative comments the instructors make during the reading of student texts?

Readers

Readers chosen for the study were eight university sociologists, all experienced researchers, whose work represents each of the major approaches in the discipline: survey research and large-scale data analysis; participant observation; and social theory. All were familiar with common approaches to undergraduate instruction in the field and with student writing typically submitted in lower-level sociology courses.

Texts

The texts used in the study were research papers submitted at the end of an introductory sociology course whose aim was to introduce students to the subject matter, assumptions, and methods that characterize sociology as a discipline and separate it from other, related fields, such as psychology or anthropology. This is a typical goal for introductory courses in sociology, one that is reflected as well in widely adopted texts such as Light and Keller's *Sociology* and Eshleman and Cashion's *Sociology: An Introduction*. The paper assignment asked students to choose a subject and an approach characteristic of sociology and to make sure their analysis incorporated key elements of sociological thought. Such an assignment is likewise typical of undergraduate courses in sociology (Sociology Writing Group, 7–29).

The papers employed in the study were generally satisfactory (graded as *A* and *B* by the course instructors and the course supervisor) with no major structural flaws. To discourage overly rigorous fault-finding, we told the participants that the papers were originally graded in the *B* to *A* range, and we corrected any particularly irritating errors in grammar, mechanics, and spelling. Though some readers noted the surface errors that remained, none found them distracting; moreover, with the exception of papers altered in substantial ways (see below), most readers found the papers effective and competently written, though clearly student productions.

Robert A. Schwegler and Linda K. Shamoon

The topics of the four papers used in the study represented important areas of contemporary research as well as subjects often covered in introductory courses: mate selection, sex roles, child abuse, and subcultures. The number of papers was limited in order to make possible the comparison of various responses to a text.

Procedures

In individual meetings the participants were given copies of each of the papers and told about aims of the paper assignment and the instructional context. They were asked to verbalize, while reading a paper, both their understanding of what the writer was trying to do or say and their evaluation of the text as a paper for a sociology class.

It took the participants between thirty-five and fifty minutes to read the papers and comment on the reading/evaluation process. Their responses were recorded on audio tape and transcribed for analysis. One of the researchers was present throughout each session in order to take note of overt reading behaviors (scanning the text or rereading a section, for example), to observe body language, and to provide a more accurate estimate of the tone of comments than might be possible from audio tape alone.

Alteration of Texts

In designing this study, we reasoned that omitting or making ambiguous various features of a text would prompt readers to comment on those features they had expected to encounter, thus providing evidence of discourse conventions. We also reasoned that a comparison of readers' comments on altered and unaltered versions of texts might aid in the identification of discourse conventions and their functions. These assumptions were based in part on the recognized tendency of readers to supply canonical interpretations for ambiguous portions of texts (van Dijk and Kintsch) and in part on the observation that skilled readers are able to restore omitted portions of texts with considerable accuracy by drawing on their expectations for the discourse as a whole. The latter pattern of behavior also forms the basis for sentence- and discourse-level cloze tests (Taylor; Kirby; Pollard-Gott and Frase).

Some of the features we chose to alter were those that an examination of student papers gathered for the study identified as likely to be shaped by the conventions and constraints of discourse in sociology. Drawing on an assumption that the generalized schema for academic research papers in the social sciences and in many other fields specifies paper openings containing slots for four kinds of information — topic, method, disciplinary context, conclusions (Schwegler and Shamoon; Shamoon and Schwegler) — we

Meaning Attribution in Ambiguous Texts in Sociology

identified statements providing these kinds of information in each of the four papers chosen for the study.

In order to determine whether the sociology instructors expected to encounter these four categories of information and in order to determine if they expected the slots to be filled or delimited in a manner unique to sociological discourse, we created altered openings for each of the sample papers. The altered openings eliminated some categories of information and "neutralized" others so that the information presented was unlikely to be regarded as specific to sociology and could easily be viewed as general knowledge about human culture and society. The first version of the paragraph below provides domain-specific information which is omitted or "neutralized" (made more general or ambiguous) in the altered version that follows it (altered sections underlined).

Original Version

In our (society) it is assumed that a man and a woman marry because they are in love. Love is seen as a blind, violent, irrational emotion that strikes whomever and wherever it pleases. But when one looks closely, however, he discovers that (who a person marries) is [strongly guided and restricted] to {similar income, class, education, racial and the religious background} of the two people involved (Berger 35). The purpose of my paper, therefore, is to [show that (mate selection in America) is for the most part (homogeneous)]

Key:

⬭ = topic
[ ] = conclusions
{ } = method
〰 = disciplinary context

Altered Version

Most people assume that a man and a woman marry because they are in love. Love is seen as a blind, violent, irrational emotion that strikes whomever and wherever it pleases. But when one looks closely, he discovers that people generally marry someone whose background is similar to theirs. The purpose of my paper, therefore, is to show that this is often the case in America.

Robert A. Schwegler and Linda K. Shamoon

Drawing again on assumptions about the generalized schema for academic discourse (Schwegler and Shamoon; Shamoon and Schwegler), we identified in the sample papers statements representing five categories of information likely to occur in major segments in the bodies of texts, all but the last of which are related to the categories in the opening: data (topic), method, disciplinary context, conclusions, and analysis. Elimination or "neutralization" of information in these categories would have created essays seriously deficient in content, probably unrepresentative of even marginally acceptable student writing. Thus we did not alter statements providing such information and relied instead on responses to the unaltered versions for evidence of whether these slots were filled or delimited in a manner specific to discourse in sociology. The following paragraph from the body of the paper on sex roles illustrates the different categories of information:

In the reading material of school children, the male and female gender roles are observable. Some publishing companies have been issuing identical reading texts with only minor adjustments for over fifty years. Within these specific reading materials from the first to the fifth grades, men are exhibited in masculine roles usually resembling the achiever. The libraries used by children offer few examples of the female heroines or achievers (Andreas 31). By the time a girl reaches junior high school she is already inculcated with certain feminine qualities which she should possess. Picturebooks that a girl reads as a child define the specified sex roles. The literature at her disposal during pre-adolescence, such as Seventeen magazine which includes forty-three advertisements for engagement rings in each issue, does not radically alter her view. Therefore, the roles that children learn through literature are perpetuated and consistently defined by the society as children grow older.

Key: ————— =data
       [ ] =analysis
       ═════ =method
       ∿∿∿ =disciplinary context

Other features we chose to alter were those that cognitive theories of discourse processing identify as essential both to the process of reading comprehension and to the semantic structure of a text. We reasoned that if disciplinary constraints and conventions play any significant role in shaping student writing, then their effects are likely to be evident in such features.

According to current theory, a reader draws on information in the opening of a text and on prior knowledge to construct a tentative schema to account for a text's anticipated macrostructure (its gist or line of reasoning). This schema also guides subsequent efforts to create a mental image of the text's meaning and to place the details it contains within a meaningful framework (Kucer).

We reasoned that the conventions governing discourse in the field might require a macrostructure (line of reasoning) that was recognizably sociological. Thus the willingness or unwillingness of readers to accept as sociological a text whose projected macrostructure embodies a general rather than domain-specific line of reasoning would be a measure of the constraints upon this aspect of writing. We also noted that the effect of altered and unaltered openings on readers' ability to identify a domain-specific macrostructure would help indicate the role played by features of the openings.

In creating a mental image of a text's meaning, readers rely on macro-structural cues and macropropositions in the body of the discourse to confirm the tentative schema identified or constructed earlier in the comprehension process. The sample papers used in this study are all characterized by strong macrostructural cues, generally containing discipline-specific concepts and technical terms. These appear most often in the form of boundary statements at the beginning or ending of paragraphs. Typically, these statements signal the evolving line of reasoning and also contain macropropositions in the form of statements summarizing the propositional content of the paragraph:

> Language is another powerful characteristic of subculture. As with most other subcultures, the Amish have their own language and are uniquely influenced by it.

> The Amish maintain their subculture through strict, comprehensive regulations called the Regal and Ordnung. (Hostetler, 52)

Moreover, the texts sometimes provide additional macrostructural cues in the middle of paragraphs in the form of technical terms or of brief statements that reinforce the boundary statements:

> Their homogeneousness leads to another form of isolation and another method of maintaining their subculture. . . . Psychologi-

Robert A. Schwegler and Linda K. Shamoon

cally, homogeneousness has instilled in the Amish a preference for tradition rather than science. . . .

To explore the extent to which sociology instructors expected to encounter strong, discipline-specific macrostructural cues in the bodies of student papers and to identify as well the role of the cues in helping readers tentatively identify and confirm domain-specific macrostructures, we omitted or "neutralized" these features in some versions of the sample papers. Even with boundary statements and other strong cues removed or modified, however, most paragraphs in the altered texts remained unified, coherent segments of discourse. Most also retained a statement that could function as a topic sentence in a general informative report, as is the case with the following paragraphs (omitted elements underlined and new topic sentence bracketed):

The Amish have learned that music is an excellent medium to arouse emotion and enthusiasm for their way of life. Group singing is a source of community activity; it is both socially and psychologically rewarding. The Old Order Amish hymns stir up emotional support and identification with the traditional way of life. Also, the method of transmitting hymns from generation to generation reflects the Amish belief in practice rather than theory and book learning. Their music is passed on, not through written notes, but by oral communication. [Like everything else in the Amish life, music shows the strength of the Amish religion and serves to strengthen it further.]

Most importantly, to preserve their subculture, the Amish must have a means of enforcing their rules and order. ("Neutralized" version = [Finally, the Amish have a means of enforcing their rules and orders]). Major violations are leaving the church and marrying an outsider. These practices, contradictory and threatening to the Amish way of life, are dealt with by excommunication and shunning, until the offender repents. Excommunication is the method of spiritually separating the offender from the community; shunning is the practice of physically disassociating with the offender.

Once cut off in this manner, the offender must leave the community or repent

in order to have some kind of human interaction. Fearful of being totally

on his own, the sinner often repents. In this way, the community places

tremendous pressure on its members to conform, reduces deviation, and

avoids attrition.

The sample papers used in the study thus appeared in three versions:

O (opening altered; body intact)
B (body altered; opening intact)
OB (opening and body altered)

Each version was read by at least two participants, and no reader encountered two versions of the same paper.

Results and Discussion

There is considerable evidence in the readers' responses to altered and unaltered openings that the sociology instructors expected to encounter the four general categories (slots) of information and that they also expected these slots to be filled with specifically sociological information, configured in ways that also mark the text as specifically sociological.

In responding to unaltered openings, readers frequently commented on the presence of information in the four categories and on its sociological nature:

Good definition of functionalist theory [disciplinary context] and its relation to the topic of the paper [method].

Students often look at child abuse from a psychological perspective, but this student seems to be dealing with it sociologically [topic and method].

At the same time, the instructors did not complain about any category of information missing from the openings or about any rhetorical operations they failed to perform, such as stating a thesis. Nor did they comment on the stylistic qualities. This pattern of response suggests that their expectations for the openings were focused primarily on the kind and quality of the information presented.

Robert A. Schwegler and Linda K. Shamoon

In commenting on altered openings, the instructors did not isolate individual categories of missing information. Instead they remarked about the lack of specific detail and the failure to provide a sociological focus. Readers also isolated statements they considered too general and frequently rephrased them, even constructing missing elements through inference:

> "Many people with similar backgrounds" is vague. What the student really wanted to say here is "propinquity" or "heterogamous marriage." This would make the purpose of the paper a lot clearer.

In restating a phrase like "opposites attract" as "a romantic theory of heterosexual attraction" or "fifty-year-old children's best sellers" as "intergenerational literature," the instructors revealed an expectation that the informational slots in the openings of the papers are to be filled with concepts and details belonging specifically and obviously to the domain of sociology.

Some of the comments suggest even more precise limitations on the information filling the slots. References to disciplinary context, for example, must be to reasonably current research. Methods must be drawn from the set of analytic methods and tools generally considered appropriate to the discipline. And topics must be drawn from the set of topics and problems defined by the discipline as worthy of discussion and as amenable to the methods of the field — as sociological problems, for example, rather than subjects appropriate for psychological or anthropological analysis. Or they must be drawn from an even more restricted set of topics, those recognized as appropriate for student research papers: "Aha, sex roles, I was waiting for this one . . ."; "Yes, child beating, I knew we'd get to it."

Readers' responses also point to the importance of the five categories (slots) of information in the bodies of texts. The instructors noted with approval the presence of information in each of the five slots — data, method, disciplinary context, conclusions, and analysis — and they evaluated the information's appropriateness to the line of reasoning employed in the text. The comments do not indicate if readers expected all five kinds of information to appear in each paragraph or similar developmental segment of a text. They do indicate, however, that the instructors expected the information to perform two main functions, each related to the line of reasoning displayed in the text.

Statements of data, method, and disciplinary context were expected to perform *evidentiary* functions, providing support, expansion, and qualification for the argument and assertions structuring an essay. Readers' comments suggested further that they expected the information in each slot to be governed by criteria of appropriateness, currency, consistency, and sufficiency based on disciplinary standards and appropriate to the line of reasoning followed in the text. The following are typical comments:

> The research that is being cited here is pretty controversial. In fact, all the data in this field is tainted by issues of sampling techniques. A student ought to know that.

> Now this student is looking at evidence from the *New York Times* society page. Actually that is class bound; there is lots of other evidence around that goes across class boundaries. This stuff is all over the place.

> This information on child abusers having been abused is from psychology. It is not sociological information. It doesn't belong in this paper.

> This material sounds like it's from psychology. Ah yes, Bettelheim. It's really not appropriate here.

Conclusions and statements of analysis (statements applying the method to data) were expected to perform *analytical* or *interpretive* functions such as exploring the evidence and drawing conclusions about it. Readers often moved from identifying kinds of evidence to commenting on the presence (or absence) of statements of analysis and interpretation: "Now look at this passage with the quotes from children's books. That's good data. Now let's see what is done with it. There ought to be more than just listing it."

The instructors' remarks also illustrated the extent to which both disciplinary conventions and the semantic strategies of an essay require statements of analysis and interpretation and also constrain them in form and content:

> This paper is describing the features of subculture. It should include some analysis. A paper like this has to do more than describe. It would have been interesting if the paper had taken the indicators of subculture and applied them; instead it just described.

In addition, readers generally looked for commentary on the data in an essay or for manipulation of it: "Ah, finally, it looks like we're finally getting an analysis of certain texts." At the same time, they expected recognition of the scholarly context, especially acknowledgment of conflicting interpretations, of questions that have been raised about the reliability of the data or about the soundness of the method: "Now this is pretty controversial stuff. But the student is writing it as if moving from note card to note card which is a summary of a source. But there is plenty to focus on in this area. I want to see some awareness of the complexity in this subject."

Finally, the sociologists made it clear that they expected statements of analysis and interpretation to conform with the assumptions and perspectives of the discipline. Statements reflecting value systems other than those of sociology were dismissed, often with considerable force, as unsociological and unscientific:

> This is a personal comment. I teach objectivity. They are beginners and they don't know how to make an objective analysis, so I don't let them make personal comments.

> What I see here is "female-headed households" and "single parents." Now this is value-laden language. It's close to personal preconceptions which I don't allow in the paper. In fact, this whole issue is tied to low income status. That's the real issue. It would have been correct to see it from that perspective.

The willingness of readers to forgive the student writers for slips and false starts so evident during the reading of the openings seemed to disappear in the middle of the texts. Instead of restoring missing or ambiguous elements from their own knowledge, the instructors applied stringent disciplinary standards to the categories of information presented in the bodies and were quite willing to reject writing they felt did not meet the standards for student discourse in sociology.

On the basis of what appeared to be initial, general schema activated by information about the classroom context and the paper assignment, the sociology instructors approached the student texts looking for categories of information appropriate to sociological discourse. Their comments reveal, however, that as soon as possible they attempted to identify or construct a schema to account for the text's probable macrostructure. There is considerable evidence in both the readers' remarks and their evaluations of individual essays that they expected the probable (and actual) macrostructures to be discipline-specific and that they considered any paper lacking a discipline-specific macrostructure to be unacceptable as sociological discourse.

At the end of unaltered openings and of altered openings for which they were able to infer sociological content, readers paused. Appearing to draw on information from the text, from their knowledge of the discipline, and from prior experience with student writing, they attempted to predict the gist of the upcoming text:

> Okay, here is a structuralist-functionalist perspective on sexual identity. Now I expect a paper like this to continue to . . .

Yes, okay, this is correct. What this student is saying is that people think that romantic love accounts for why they choose the person they want to marry, but that factors such as common heritage and background are more important. That is absolutely right.

Though the predicted macrostructures probably function as hypotheses to guide the process of comprehension, most of the instructors' comments seem to present them instead as constraints upon the writer: "Now the student is saying that the Amish as a subculture differ in clothing, in farming techniques, in language and so on. Okay, if they want to say that, I expect this paper to say also that there are similarities with the main culture."

In short, the instructors seem to expect that student writing in sociology will follow a line of reasoning characteristic of sociological thought. They appear to project on an essay a macrostructural pattern that is characteristic of sociological discourse and to view this as a standard for measuring the student's achievement and for determining whether or not the remainder of the text is acceptable as student writing in the discipline:

So what they're saying here is "Let's have a look at intergenerational literature." Now I expect this paper to go on to tell me just how important literature is as a variable in development.

The conventional character of these patterns to which the student writers were expected to adhere was made plain in many of the instructor's comments. The patterns appeared to have two sources. One source was the approaches commonly employed in the professional literature of the field:

This is a definition applied to understand certain social phenomena, something Spradley does very well in his book on alcoholics as a subculture.

The other source was the patterns generally considered to be appropriate for student writing in sociology courses:

This is a common kind of paper, one in which the student looks at a lot of different perspectives on a puzzling phenomenon and it's particularly common with topics like child abuse which this student is talking about.

One sign of the strength of the readers' expectations for a discipline-specific macrostructure is their apparent willingness to suspend judgment about a text's probable direction throughout the reading of an altered opening until the body of the text indicates that the line of reasoning will be sociological: "I now see what is going on in this paper. Perhaps the first full page is not what the writer wanted to speak about."

Robert A. Schwegler and Linda K. Shamoon

Readers may well be able to adopt a tentative schema for a general interest informative report on the basis of the kind of information provided in the altered openings, but the comments of participants did not reveal any willingness to do this even as a way of rejecting an essay as unsociological. Moreover, despite the specific expectations readers held for information in the openings of essays, they considered texts with altered openings and intact bodies generally satisfactory and were willing to forgive the writers for failing initially to provide the appropriate kinds of information. Thus although there appear to be clear conventions governing the openings of student papers in sociology, they probably can be followed with some flexibility. In contrast, strong, discipline-specific macrostructural cues in the bodies of papers would appear to be necessary elements of acceptable student texts in sociology, at least according the responses of the readers in the study. Those papers with altered openings but intact macrostructural cues were considered acceptable by the readers because the information in the bodies of the essays enabled them to arrive at and confirm sociological macrostructures for the texts. Yet those papers with intact openings but altered bodies were considered unacceptable even if readers were able to arrive at an initial prediction of the macrostructure:

> The opening promised one thing, and the body did not live up to it. It promised to look at the role of children's lit. in sex role formation, but it was purely descriptive. It only used a few sources. It was not well organized either.

And papers with both altered openings and altered bodies were deemed entirely unacceptable, of course.

It is important to remember that papers lacking strong macrostructural cues retained considerable information, enough, one might conjecture, to allow readers to infer missing elements, much as they did in response to the altered openings. None of the readers chose to do this, however. The altered bodies also retained topic sentences that might be construed as signalling a general-interest informative report. While some readers appeared to recognize this possibility, they rejected it as inappropriate, regarding it as the kind of paper assembled from textbooks and encyclopedias:

> You know, I don't know what the specific assignment was, but it looks as if the class was using a few textbooks, something like Light and Keller or Hoestetter. I have that one on my shelf right here, and it looks as if the student is putting a paper together from that.

The presence or absence of discipline-specific macrostructural cues also seemed to affect readers' perceptions of categories of information presented in the discussions. In reading unaltered bodies, readers commented on the quality of the evidence and analysis. In reading the altered bodies, however, they not only failed to take note of the evidence, they also complained about the lack of statements of analysis and interpretation — even though such statements were generally retained in the texts.

Disciplinary macrostructural cues may have encouraged readers to accept a text as sociological discourse, but they did not guarantee approval of the quality of the reasoning:

> So, now the paper is presenting material from children's books as a means of supporting the idea of sex role reinforcement, but what they are not saying is let's look at how that factor interacts with other family and social factors. This line of argument would be more effective if it considered literature as one of many determining factors in psycho-social development.

Nonetheless, the ability of readers to perceive the macrostructure of a text as appropriate to sociological reasoning and the presence of strong, discipline-specific macrostructural cues guiding the process of comprehension both appear to be essential conventions of student discourse in sociology.

Conclusions

Based on the richness and suggestiveness of responses to the texts used in the study, the practice of altering texts to elicit comments revealing readers' expectations would seem to be a useful method for investigating the conventions and constraints governing discourse in an interpretive community. Much of what goes on in the mind of readers remains unsaid, of course, but the process does offer revealing insights into the reader-text transaction.

The responses of the participants indicate clearly, moreover, that in terms of semantic structures, sociology instructors expect student writing to adhere to disciplinary constraints and conventions. This is particularly true in the case of the textual macrostructure, the gist or line of reasoning. And it is true also of semantic elements on a slightly lower level, macrostructural cues and macropropositions, particularly in the bodies of texts. Macropropositions designating categories of information in the openings of texts are more variable elements, however. This is perhaps a reflection of their role as a bridge between the general schema readers

Robert A. Schwegler and Linda K. Shamoon

bring with them from the contexts of the task and the specific schema they adopt in the act of reading.

Though the discourse conventions identified in this study include slots for information, it would be a mistake to conceive of the texts discussed here as general frames filled with sociological content. At their highest level, that of the semantic macrostructure, student texts that met with the approval of the instructors were shaped almost completely by the assumptions and constraints of the discipline. The same is true of other high-level elements including many of the macropropositions. Yet it is also true that at this level the categories or slots filled with sociological information bear general resemblance to those in other texts. This should not be surprising given the broad similarities on such general patterns as statement and support that exist among even such clearly different disciplines as literary criticism, business management, physical anthropology, and sociology. Nonetheless, the internal configurations or delimitations of the categories of information in the sociology texts and their relationships to each other and to the semantic macrostructure are so constrained by disciplinary conventions and assumptions that they, too, can be regarded as shaped to a great extent by the discourse patterns of the discipline.

BIBLIOGRAPHY

Bazerman, Charles. "Physicists Reading Physics: Schema-Laden Purposes and Purpose-Laden Schema." *Written Communication* 2 (January 1985): 3–23.
Bizzell, Patricia. "Cognition, Convention, and Certainty: What We Need to Know about Writing." *Pre/Text* 3 (Fall 1982): 213–43.
Brandt, Deborah. "Text and Context: How Writers Come to Mean." In *Functional Approaches to Writing: Research Perspectives*, ed. Barbara Couture, 93–107. Norwood, N.J.: Ablex, 1986.
Brown, Robert L., Jr., and Carl G. Herndl. "An Ethnographic Study of Corporate Writing: Job Status as Reflected in Written Text." In *Functional Approaches to Writing: Research Perspectives*, ed. Barbara Couture, 11–28. Norwood, N.J.: Ablex, 1986.
Dijk, Teun A. van ed. *Handbook of Discourse Analysis.* 4 vols. London: Academic, 1983.
Dijk, Teun A. van and Walter Kintsch. *Strategies of Discourse Comprehension.* New York: Academic, 1983.
Eblen, Charlene. "Writing Across-the-Curriculum: A Survey of a University Faculty's Views and Classroom Practices." *Research in the Teaching of English* 17 (December 1983): 343–48.
Eshleman, J. Ross, and Barbara G. Cashion. *Sociology: An Introduction.* 2d ed. Boston: Little, Brown, 1985.
Frederiksen, Carl H. "Cognitive Models and Discourse Analysis." In *Studying*

Meaning Attribution in Ambiguous Texts in Sociology

Writing: Linguistic Approaches, ed. Charles R. Cooper and Sidney Greenbaum, 227–67. Written Communication Annual, vol. 1. Beverly Hills: Sage, 1986.

Herrington, Anne J. "Writing in Academic Settings: A Study of the Contexts for Writing in Two College Chemical Engineering Courses." *Research in the Teaching of English* 19 (December 1985): 331–61.

Kirby, Clara L. "Using the Cloze Procedure as a Testing Technique." *Reading Diagnosis and Evaluation*, ed. Dorothy L. De Boer, 68–77. Newark, Del.: International Reading Association, 1970.

Kucer, Stephen L. "The Making of Meaning: Reading and Writing as Parallel Processes." *Written Communication* 2 (1985): 317–36.

Light, Donald, Jr., and Suzanne Keller. *Sociology*. 4th ed. New York: Random.

Maimon, Elaine P., et al. *Writing in the Arts and Sciences*. Cambridge: Winthrop, 1981.

Miller, Carolyn R., and Jack Selzer. "Special Topics of Argument in Engineering Reports." *Writing in Nonacademic Settings*, ed. Lee Odell and Dixie Goswami, 309–41. New York: Guilford, 1985.

Moore, Leslie E., and Linda H. Peterson. "Convention as Connection: Linking the Composition Course to the English and College Curriculum." *College Composition and Communication* 37 (December 1986): 466–77, 488, 506.

Myers, Greg. "The Social Construction of Two Biologists' Proposals." *Written Communication* 2 (July 1985): 219–45.

Odell, Lee, and Dixie Goswami, eds. *Writing in Nonacademic Settings*. New York: Guilford, 1985.

Peters, Pamela. "Getting the Theme Across: A Study of Dominant Function in the Academic Writing of University Students." In *Functional Approaches to Writing: Research Perspectives*, ed. Barbara Couture, 169–85. Norwood, N.J.: Ablex, 1986.

Pollard-Gott, Lucy, and Lawrence T. Frase. "Flexibility in Writing Style: A New Discourse-Level Cloze Test." *Written Communication* 2 (April 1985): 107–27.

Popken, Randall L. "A Study of Topic Sentence Use in Academic Writing." *Written Communication* 4 (1987): 209–28.

Porter, James E. "Intertextuality and the Discourse Community." *Rhetoric Review* 5 (Fall 1986): 34–47.

Schwegler, Robert A., and Linda K. Shamoon. "The Aims and Process of the Research Paper." *College English* 44 (December 1982): 85–93.

Shamoon, Linda K., and Robert A. Schwegler. "Teaching the Research Paper: A New Approach to an Old Problem." *Freshman English News* 11 (1982): 14–17.

Sociology Writing Group, The. *A Guide to Writing Sociology Papers*. New York: St. Martin's Press, 1986.

Swales, John, and Hazem Najjar. "The Writing of Research Article Introductions." *Written Communication* 4 (April 1987): 175–91.

Taylor, Wilson. "Cloze Procedure: A New Tool for Measuring Readability." *Journalism Quarterly* 30 (1953): 415–33.

Tomlinson, Barbara. "Talking about the Composing Process: The Limits of Retrospective Accounts." *Written Communication* 1 (1984): 429–45.

10 TEXTS IN ORAL CONTEXT

THE "TRANSMISSION" OF

JURY INSTRUCTIONS

IN AN INDIANA TRIAL

GAIL STYGALL

Modern rheorical scholars exhibit a curious reluctance to examine legal texts. Although in the historical context, rhetoric and law have long been intertwined, current rhetorical studies have ignored the social dynamics of legal texts. Perhaps it is because we understand legal texts to be the quintessential "bad" text—wordy, unreadable, and incomprehensible—hardly models for a discipline that seeks, in its pedagogy, to improve students' writing. Yet there are clear lessons for rhetoricians in legal texts. With a centuries-old literate tradition, the legal community should be of clear interest to those who study written communication. Moreover, those who write legal texts are members of a well-defined social context, bound by their membership and participation in a discourse community. This community presents what we might call a prototypical case for our scrutiny of the influence of discourse community membership on texts.

Though the literate tradition and well-defined social context of the law present inviting opportunities for the study of written communication, two a priori assumptions about texts in professional communities cloud our analysis. First, our stance toward the incomprehensible legal texts is often pedagogical: we can correct or improve these texts. Second, we assume that the purpose of these texts is a straightforward information transfer between writer and reader. In this article, I want to complicate both of these assumptions. In the case of the first assumption, we risk ignoring the importance of professionals communicating primarily within their discourse community. Legal texts, for example, cannot be "improved" without understanding why lawyers continue to write what ordinary readers consider unreadable texts. In complicating the first assumption, then, I am suggesting that the demands of the legal community's discourse conventions always take precedence over the needs of ordinary readers. In the case of the second assumption, we assume that the text has failed if a propositionally based information transfer has not occurred. That is, if an audience of a professional text cannot accurately report the "gist" of the text in propositional form, then we assume that the communication itself has failed. Here, I want to suggest that legal texts that fail in information transfer can still be successful in educating and socializing a nonprofessional audience. These complications of our assumptions provide a better explanation of why these so-called unreadable texts demonstrate a tenacious stability in the face of unrelenting criticism from readers outside the community.

I have chosen jury instructions as an appropriate example of a legal text that demonstrates the linguistic and rhetorical features thought to mark these legal texts as incomprehensible. Jury instructions usually contain nearly every impediment to comprehension known to language scholars. Words that have broad, ordinary uses constrict to narrow, specific meanings within the law. Highly convoluted, densely embedded sentences require jurors' careful attention (Charrow and Charrow, 1334–50). The word count of sentences grows astronomically. Rare or archaic constructions abound, odd prepositions connect difficult concepts, and subordinate clauses lose their relative pronoun heads. Sentence-to-sentence cohesion ties disappear, and all pretense toward global cohesion is abandoned (Elwork, Sales, and Alfini, 184–86). If jurors were examining the text of these instructions in a college classroom, they could easily spend weeks disassembling and examining the propositions, searching other legal texts for the right interpretive rules. But jurors don't have weeks: they must deliberate immediately after instructions are given.

It should be no surprise that the rhetorician's first impulse is to try to "improve" these texts. But it is also problematic to attempt to improve a text that serves powerful purposes within a community. In the case of jury instructions, the legal community demands that instructions be, first and foremost, an accurate statement of the law. Consequently, the form of instructions that advocates choose is the form that best serves this intracommunity audience, the trial, and appellate court judges, who may rule on what comprises an accurate statement of the law. Most appropriate for the appellate audience is a written document. The advocates submit, or tender, written instructions to the trial court judge. The judge, in turn, reads these instructions aloud to the jury, who may see the judge turn the pages of the written text while reading it to them. If the outcome of the trial is appealed, the appellate court judges read the entire trial

Gail Stygall

record, including the instructions, as a text, not as an oral presentation. Even in those jurisdictions in which the judge allows the jurors to have a copy of the written instructions, the jurors will first hear the instructions read. Thus, jurors hear the reading of a written text within a wholly oral context of a trial. Ultimately, to the legal community, improving the text of these instructions can only mean writing a better or more accurate statement of the law. Improvement does not mean writing a more comprehensible text for an ordinary audience.

The purpose of jury instructions is to tell the jurors what law is relevant to the case they have heard, a relatively simple transfer of information from one community to another. Most analyses of instructions suggest that they fail in this primary purpose. Yet instructions succeed in a parallel purpose: socializing the jurors into the legal community. This parallel purpose replaces a proposition-based information transfer as purpose. Instructions to the jury are, of necessity, the bridge between the legal and lay communities. When analysis of the entire trial is included in attempting to understand how jurors process the language of jury instructions, we see that earlier sections of the trial both block and support different kinds of concept construction necessary to apply the instructions. These blocks and supports mirror the processes valued by the legal community and thus the trial becomes a kind of minimal legal education for the jurors through their socialization as temporary members of the legal discourse community. This socialization process does not require that jurors understand the law in the same way as attorneys, only that they adopt the legal perspective in their deliberations. Jury instructions actually provide some assistance for jurors in this socialization, notwithstanding the difficulty of the language. Jury instructions reconstruct roles by strictly delineating what each trial participant is allowed to do and provide common metaphors to bridge the law and the jurors' experiences. When the text of the instructions is considered as a part of the entire trial, the text becomes the formalization of the legal socialization process the jurors have undergone during the trial.

Methodology and the Case at Trial

In order to examine the complications of our assumptions about these legal texts, I chose to examine jury instructions in context, in an actual trial. The Honorable Betty Barteau, Judge of the Marion County Superior Court, Civil Division, Room 3, agreed to participate. Though my data collection was primarily ethnographic, I included formal discourse theories in my analysis of the data I gathered. The form of my presentation here is what John Van Maanen calls a "formal tale," a construction of the events I witnessed within a preexisting theoretical framework (130–131). Thus, not only did I reconstruct the events of the trial from my own vantage point, but I also recognize that my decision to use formal discourse theories is a rhetorical choice, one made in order to challenge conventional assumptions about these texts (cf. Clifford and Marcus for a thorough discussion of the issue of textual representations of ethnographic fieldwork). In collecting the data, I attended jury pool procedures, watched trial proceedings, interviewed attorneys, the judge, the court employees, and jurors. Informal conversations were also a part of the field data, talking to attorneys and court employes while the jury was on a break or "out" for deliberations.

The case I selected for analysis in this study was one of four tried during the first four months of 1987 during which I collected data. There was nothing unusual about the case of Edith Masheck versus Capitol Drilling Supplies. The legal issues were not complex. All the attorneys were trial veterans, their skills well-matched. Most of the instructions read to the jury were from Indiana's book of standardized civil instructions to juries. All in all, the Masheck case represents a baseline from which to examine the assumptions about the comprehension and purposes of these texts from a professional community.

The case of Edith Masheck, Plaintiff, versus Capitol Drilling Supplies, Incorporated, Defendant, was tried on April 1 and 2, 1987. A personal injury suit, a case of "slip and fall" in the talk of civil trial attorneys, Edith Masheck sued a contractor, Capitol Drilling Supplies, for the injuries she received when she fell on a water-covered landing, breaking her ankle. Capitol Drilling Supplies' employees were supervising an area of minor construction, at St. Francis Hospital, Ms. Mascheck's place of employment as a registered nurse. The jury returned a verdict of $8,000 for the plaintiff.

Edith Masheck was a very credible plaintiff. She had been employed as a nurse at St. Francis Hospital since 1968. At the time of her fall, she was the Diabetes Coordinator for the hospital, an administrative nursing position. Married to a minister, she is the mother of four grown children. On November 2, 1984, on her way to lunch about 11:45 A.M., Ms. Masheck took her usual route down the stairs from the fourth floor of the Tower Building of the hospital. Encouraged by the "wellness" practices of the medical community, Ms. Masheck always used the stairs for exercise. Fifty-seven years old and in good general health, Ms. Masheck also walked one to three miles after work, several days each week. Wearing standard nurse's shoes, Ms. Masheck nonetheless fell at the water-covered third-floor landing, breaking her right fibula, injuring several ligaments and leg muscles. She was unable to work for the next two and one half months, her leg and ankle encased in a cast.

Capitol Drilling Supplies had been hired by St. Francis Hospital to drill through several concrete walls and landings to provide another contractor access for new heating and cooling ducts. The employees of Capitol Drilling were using a diamond blade, water-cooled saw to drill through the concrete. Normal operation of such a saw always meant water would be in the adjacent area. Capitol's employees had made arrangements for a water vacuum to be used in the area, but on this day, had apparently left for lunch without completing the cleaning of the area. No Capitol employees were in the stairwell when Ms. Masheck fell. Nor were there any warning signs to caution her.

The trial presented a number of issues to the jury. They had to decide if Capitol Drilling Supplies was negligent in not cleaning up their construction area. They also had to decide if Ms. Masheck contributed in any way to her own fall. The jurors also had to find a direct link between Capitol's construction practices and Ms. Masheck's injuries. Having made these decisions in favor of Ms. Masheck, the jury would next assess damages to Ms. Masheck and award an amount of money to her.

Legal Discourse Conventions: Blocks to Ordinary Comprehension

For advocates, and even for trial court judges, the audience that finally matters is the appellate court. And appellate courts do not make jurors' understanding of instructions a priority for reviewing the instructions given by trial courts. As I have already suggested, the primary function of jury instructions is to provide an accurate statement of the law. One Indiana case, *Board of Commissioners v. Briggs* (1975) Ind. App. 337 N.E. 2d 852, illustrates the problem. The Court remarked:

> While the instructions could possibly be confusing to the average juror, it is not any more confusing than many of the other Pattern Jury Instructions, and on the whole is certainly not misleading as to the issues of this case. We find no basis for this objection. *Board of Commissioners v. Briggs, supra* at 868.

The court here asserts that making an accurate statement of the law takes priority over juror comprehension, even as the court acknowledges that a disputed instruction may have caused difficulties in juror understanding. Thus if jurors are to understand at all, it must be through the frame of the law's priorities. Attorneys consequently "protect the appellate record" by offering jury instructions that are at once an accurate statement of the law and a favorable view of their client's case. Judges "protect the appellate record" by accepting instructions for the trial that are both accurate statements of the law and balanced representations of the parties' views, so as not to be reversed at the appellate level. Juror comprehension is a tertiary concern for the judge and the attorneys.

In this section, I want to detail how lawyers' use of discourse conventions for "good" legal communication results in blocking jurors' ordinary strategies for text comprehension. Legal discourse rules impose their own sense of order and coherence on jurors. Two conventions of legal discourse function to block these ordinary means of comprehending legal texts. First, instructions are coherent only by reference to extratextual information contained in legal reference works, such as case law reporters. What organizes and structures the jurors' instructions is found in legal texts and not in any particular utterance during the trial. A second discourse rule prevents attorneys from directly linking the names of legal concepts mentioned in the instructions with the testimony of witnesses. To improve the comprehensibility of these instructions, then, would mean violating two important discourse rules, rules that are clearly privileged within the legal community.

EXTRATEXTUAL COHERENCE

Beyond the level of the individual case, all attorneys inhabit a textual domain, created by legal training, maintained by participation in the legal community. Attorneys learn the law by reading cases, thousands of them while in law school. Attorneys maintain their knowledge by continuing to read cases, as appellate and supreme courts write new decisions. They are awash in a constant sea of new texts. Thus, even while participating in a particular case, attorneys remain aware of a set or superstructure of cases generally relevant to a class of cases or to a segment of the trial. Jury instructions represent a segment of trial for which a set of cases exist that frame and constrain how jurors are given their instructions. Even though the interests of advocates and judges may differ, each is aware of a coherence-generating algorithm from the governing set or superstructure of cases relevant to this trial segment. This superstructure of cases represents the second block.

None of this textual domain is revealed to the jury. As James Boyd White suggests,

> . . . the most serious obstacles to comprehensibility are not the
> vocabulary and sentence structure employed in the law but the
> unstated conventions by which the law operates — what I call the
> "invisible discourse" of the law. Behind the words, that is, are

> expectations that do not find expression anywhere but are part
> of the legal culture that the surface language simply assumes. (139)

In order to examine this unexpressed set of conventions, I surveyed the
case law relevant to giving jury instructions. In doing so, I found that
the instructions become coherent by virtue of an algorithm that may be
applied to any set of instructions. Using the entries provided in *Indiana
Digest*, under "Trial, Instructions to the Jury (VII), Subsection 242,
Confusing and Misleading Instructions," I constructed a set of macrorules
that apply to instructions from the information contained in each case
listed in the category. I examined each of the cases listed for particular
instances of the court's discussion of rationales for accepting or rejecting
instructions. No single decision articulates all the rules for interpreting
jury instructions. However, when the category is taken as a whole, these
decisions represent four major rules, macrorules, and particular application rules, or microrules. These rules are displayed in figure 10.1.

Macroproposition 1: The trial court verdict is presumed to be supported by
the evidence.

Macrorule 1: An instruction not supported by the evidence must be refused.

Macroproposition 2: Jurors apply the law as given by the instructions to
the facts at hand.

Macrorule 2: The instructions must be a correct statement of the law.
　　Microprocessing Rules for #2
　　1. Jurors must be given a single path of law.
　　2. Instructions must include all relevant law.
　　3. A correct instruction does not override the giving of an incorrect
　　　　instruction on the law.

Macrorule 3: The instructions must not be confusing or misleading to jurors.
　　Microprocessing Rules for #3
　　1. An instruction is misleading if one-sided.
　　2. An instruction must not be ambiguous.
　　3. The charge should contain definitions for all legal terms.

Macrorule 4: The instructions are a unified, single piece of text.
　　Microprocessing Rules for #4
　　1. All nonmandatory instructions have equal weight.
　　2. No single instruction needs to contain all applicable law.
　　3. Jurors will match definitions with applications and judgment standard
　　　　instructions, even if separated by other instructions.

Fig. 10.1. Algorithm for instructional coherence

The two macropropositions in figure 10.1 are higher level generalizations of the legal discourse. First, appellate judges assume that the trial

court's decision was supported by the evidence; and, second, appellate judges assume the jury tried the case on the facts, after receiving instructions on the law. The four macrorules following apply to any giving of instructions and are hierarchically arranged, applying in order.

I confirmed the algorithm in the context of the instructions given in the Masheck trial. A veteran of thirteen years on the bench, the judge rejected several submitted instructions on the basis of macrorules one and three. The plaintiff's attorney submitted a more elaborate damage instruction than the one the judge actually gave. She rejected two elements of this damage instruction for lack of evidence in the trial to support giving the instruction. These elements were impairment of earning capacity and disfigurement and deformity; she could deduce neither element from the testimony given. She refused a second plaintiff's instruction because it was a reemphasis of the concept that the acts of a corporation's employees are one and the same as the acts of the corporation. Her giving of this instruction would have contradicted the third macrorule, by giving undue prominence to the issue of the corporation's possible negligence.

The judge also refused instructions offered by the defendant's advocate. One instruction reiterated the necessity for jurors to remove sympathy for parties from their deliberations. Just as reemphasizing the possibility of corporate negligence was rejected when the plaintiff tendered that instruction, so, too, was this defendant's attempt at repetition, on the basis of the third macrorule. The judge also rejected a second cautioning instruction on damages, also on the basis of the third macrorule. The problem of comprehensibility of instructions, then, becomes more focused. The legal community can make sense out of the instructions. They have an extensive text world which provides coherence for the instructions. Jurors, however, have no such reference and are thus blocked from using it to make sense of the instructions. Catherine Pettinari notes a similar problem in surgical reports. New surgeons had considerable difficulty in separating what constituted shared surgical knowledge from what was not shared, a separation necessary to prepare the standard surgical report. What the new surgeons did not yet know was that the shared information could be moved to the background and deemphasized. Shared and nonshared information took different grammatical forms, but knowledge of the uses of those forms was at least partially a product of being a full member of the surgical community. Likewise, the lawyers in this case, being full members of the legal discourse community, have access to the shared knowledge necessary to make the text coherent, even when the text may be incomprehensible for jurors. Professional communities, with large bodies of knowledge, follow the conventions necessary for understanding inside the community. Generic standards of clarity and coherence may thus be difficult to formulate once a discourse participant achieves full professional status. And as Lester Faigley suggests in his text analysis

Gail Stygall

of a letter selling real estate masquerading as a "prize" announcement, the extratextual topic may be "more typical than exceptional" (140).

THE BAR ON ELABORATIVE INFERENCES

Though jurors have no access to the attorneys' text world, they do have access to the language of the text of the instructions throughout a jury trial. My tracking of instructional language throughout the course of the trial suggests that the actual words and phrases of the jury instructions are present at every step in the trial. (See the Appendix for a partial text of the jurors' final instructions.) However, because of a legal text convention barring elaborative inferences, the jurors do not hear the name of the legal concept directly linked with an exemplification of that concept. In this section, I will first briefly describe the points at which the jurors hear parts of the text of the instructions, and then illustrate how the bar on elaborative inferences functions. The effect of this second legal discourse convention is to prevent jurors from comprehending the text through any ordinary strategy.

As diagrammed in figure 10.2, jurors will hear fragments of the language of final instructions even before the trial actually begins, in their introductory session with the entire jury pool. Instructional language is indeed woven into the text of the trial. The evidence portion of the trial is bracketed by instructions, specific to the case. Additionally, in opening statement, both attorneys made reference to particular instructions, attempting to link certain testimony with certain instructions. Each attorney concentrated, of course, on interpretations of instructions most helpful to his case. The plaintiff's attorney stressed negligence and preponderance of the evidence linked to certain witnesses; the defendant's attorney stressed conflicts in the evidence and contributory negligence. But the linkage was subtle, as attorneys may not directly argue or interpret during opening statement. In closing argument, references to instructions were even more explicit. Both sides made reference to instructions by saying, "the judge will tell you that . . ." and "that means . . ." Thus, though rarely does the most abstract form of instructions surface in other parts of the trial, instructional language is present throughout the trial, primarily in embedded clauses. Though I would not argue that the references to key terms and language of instructions were extensive in other segments of the trial, I would suggest that repetition and association do create a broader base for juror comprehension than they would have if instructions were assumed to stand alone. From jury pool meeting to final argument, the language of instructions is present.

Trial Sequence	What Jurors Hear
Jury pool slide presentation	Burden of proof language
Voir dire in particular court	Instructional language embedded in question form
Preliminary instructions	Issues instruction General instructions on burden, credibility, preponderance of evidence court's rulings on admissibility of evidence, negligence, resolving conflicts in evidence proximate cause
Opening statement	Instructional language linked to events of case
Plaintiff's case	Events
Defendant's case	Events
Closing argument	Instructional language linked to events of case
Final instructions	Repetition of general instructions, how to deliberate instructions, instructions on the law pertinent to the actual evidence of the plaintiff's and defendant's cases; no repetition of issues instruction
Verdict	Three hours of deliberation

Fig. 10.2. Opportunities for jurors to hear language of instructions

If jurors indeed hear the language of the instructions throughout the trial, why don't they become more easily socialized to it by the end of the trial? I would like to suggest that the reason can be found in the bar on elaborative inference. Because of this bar, disallowing simultaneous naming and exemplifying, jurors have no opportunity to hear the language of instructions directly linked with what they are told to "count" as evidence, the direct testimony of witnesses. This bar is maintained because to directly link the terms found in the instructions with the evidence given would be to allow witnesses to draw legal conclusions, an act forbidden to nonlawyers. The attorneys function as advocates in the trial, not as witnesses, and thus are not available to offer legal definitions as a part of the evidence. Unfortunately, this lack of explicit connection between the evidence and what the evidence means in the terms of the instructions leaves jurors without the rules for elaborative inferences necessary for a more complete understanding of their instructions.

Let me offer an example from this trial of an implicit attempt to exemplify one of the terms of art, specifically contributory negligence. Questioning the plaintiff, Mr. B probes for illustrations of Ms. Masheck failing to act reasonably cautious. He inquires if she had noticed any construction, if she had hurried, if she normally took the elevator, if she was wearing wedge heels, all of which might indicate that she was less than cautious. The following interchange is a continuation of Mr. B's exploration of Ms. Masheck's possible contributory negligence:

> Mr. B: Were the materials and the wheelbarrow and other items there on the landing as you were coming down there blocking your intended route of travel or was there a way to get around them?
>
> Ms. M: Oh, you could get around them. You could get around them. . . . it was not blocking, no.
>
> (several questions later)
>
> Mr. B: Did you slow down in any manner or become more cautious? What did you do?
>
> Ms. M: I just saw and walked, I mean, the normal. I was aware there was a hose and that stuff was there, yes I slowed down.

Though with little assistance from Ms. Masheck, Mr. B is attempting to illustrate a number of possible ways in which Ms. Masheck may have been less than reasonably cautious. By his questioning, Mr. B suggests that a reasonably cautious person would have stopped walking down the stairs when she saw hoses and a wheelbarrow on the landing. But Mr. B cannot directly ask Ms. Masheck if her actions were negligent. Ms. Masheck asserts that the passage was not blocked. Though Mr. B tries several strategies, he is unable to move Ms. Masheck toward admitting her own negligence.

The significance of this passage of testimony lies in the difficulty of jurors' connecting the testimony to the final instructions. Mr. B's case required that he demonstrate that Ms. Masheck contributed to the cause of her injury, by an act or omission on her part. The most effective way to do this would be to announce "I will now present evidence that Ms. Masheck contributed to the cause of her injury" and then proceed to question her. However, he is not allowed to do this and so he is forced to hope that he can jog the jurors' memories in final argument that Ms. Masheck was not particularly cautious for the circumstances. Because Mr. B is barred from explicitly making the connection during the presentation of evidence, Mr. B can only plan to make the link explicit in final argument.

These elaborative inferences are necessary for jurors' full comprehension of the text of the final instructions in relation to the evidence presented in the trial. Elaborative inferences occur "when the reader uses his or her knowledge about the topic under discussion to fill in additional detail not mentioned in the text, or to establish connections between what is being read and related items of knowledge" (van Dijk and Kintsch, 51). Without the advocates' explicit use of elaboration during the presentation of evidence or in final argument, jurors may not be able to make the appropriate matches. In this case, advocates were only partially successful in creating elaborative inferences, leaving the jurors to make their own constructions.

Without elaborative inferences and without reference to the lawyers' text world, jurors must relinquish their ordinary means of processing new texts and information. We should expect that these types of professional discourse and text conventions operate in a number of professional communities. The legal texts here only stand as a representative of the situation in which the nonprofessional audience is most fully disassociated from the ordinary strategies. A layperson reading an engineer's report, a doctor's diagnosis to another doctor, or an advertising executive's marketing plan might experience the text in similar ways. In the case of jurors, however, a decision must be reached. If lawyers replace ordinary text strategies with community-specific strategies, then what can jurors, who have no access to the legal conventions, use in their place?

Initiating the Novice into the Process of the Law

If the possibility of jurors' ordinary comprehension remains elusive by virtue of the legal conventions, the literal transfer of propositions from the final instructions may not be the goal, either of the jury or of the legal system. In this section, I would like to suggest that the blocks to ordinary comprehension are replaced with three supports, definitively shaping the jurors into the rational perspective demanded by the law. The first support is found in the distinct delineation of duties presented in the final instructions. The second is the metaphoric relations of law and people underlying the instructions. Finally, the trial process mimics and accelerates the actual type of education would-be attorneys undergo. Each of the three guides of the jurors into new channels of organizing and understanding legal information. In short, socialization replaces information transfer.

One of the necessary elements of initiation would seem to be knowledge of the duties and permissible activities of participants in the trial. Figure 10.3 displays the analysis of the actors and permissible acts taken from the Masheck final jury instructions. These categories and the permitted acts are consistent throughout the jury charge. Moreover, the categories are mutually exclusive. Jurors do not instruct; witnesses do not compensate. Each category of actor has a particular set with which to act and no others. Though it is tempting to analyze the much-remarked occurrence of performative verbs evident in this classification scheme, these verbs and their actors have more importance in how they divide ordinary activities into new structures of reality.

One markedly different division demonstrated here is the complete deletion of the advocates from the actors' categories. A fiction of the law, the advocate becomes the party for the duration of the trial, not just the representative of the party. The parties speak only if they are called as witnesses. Although ordinarily one might think of the advocate as the person doing the suing, defending, introducing, and complaining, the jurors are presented with a strict conflation of advocates into the parties bringing and defending the case being tried. This strict division of acts in the instructions provides confirmation to the jurors that the legal view must dictate the new reality. By providing no acts for advocates, the instructions also emphasize that opening statement and closing argument are not evidence. Those two segments of the trial are presented by virtual nonentities. Thus, a first aspect of the litany of acts and actors is to delete the advocates.

A second important aspect of initiation through the recognition of roles is the focus on rationality of the jurors' activities. According to these final instructions, jurors must work hard at thinking activities: finding, crediting, weighing, determining, basing, holding, and construing. Other than believing, which can result in yielding after listening, jurors do not harass, cry, feel, guess, sympathize, speculate, or any other set of more emotionally marked, intangible mental acts. Instead, many of these mental acts have physical aspects connotated. "Credit" and "reconcile" have their associations with accounting and mathematics, as does "compensate." "Weigh" and "find" have possible associations with real mass, physical objects, as do "hold" and "base."

The judge and the witnesses have limited roles, both in the instructions and in the trial. Jurors hear the judge ruling on motions, reading instruc-

Actor	Permitted Actions		
The Law	contains contemplates embodies bars requires		
The Judge	instructs means rules controls sustains says		
Witnesses	testify state give evidence have interests, biases, prejudices		
Jurors	find credit consider reconcile believe agree listen hold	weigh determine compensate have duties base construe yield	
Parties	sue defend introduce perform support recover attack rely injure damage	complain convince contract recognize escape act ask produce omit exercise	intend prove assume wrong interpose have burdens fail offer cause

Fig. 10.3. Actors and permissable acts:
Masheck final jury instructions

tions, and controlling the introduction of exhibits, but not taking a direct part in the presentation of evidence, the heart of the trial. Thus by paralleling the limited activities of the judge, the instructions confirm, one last time, that the jurors' focus should be primarily on the acts of the parties. Witnesses, as I suggested in the analysis of the bar on elaborative inferences, also have limited roles. The acts permitted witnesses in the instructions reflect this limit. This limit, restricting witnesses to the "facts," those items to which they testify, focuses attention on the limited set of items the jury can consider. These two actor categories, then, also provide further and final confirmation of the boundaries of the trial process jurors have just experienced.

Moreover, by requiring that jurors rely on rational perspectives in their acts, the instructions point the jurors toward relying on their own sense of narrative sequence. Jurors, by this analysis, have been given license to construct, albeit rationally, a story of the trial. Civil trials reconstruct and narrate the ordinary events of life. Coherence for ordinary events of life is already present in jurors' discourse processing. No new professional discourse must be thoroughly studied and internalized. Instead, jurors may use narrative episodes from their own experience, into which the evidence of the trial flows. By measuring the acts of the parties against their own experience, jurors indeed use rational means for making their decision. But, in no way is this discourse strategy the same as the text world algorithm of the professional legal community.

Concurrent with the development of roles and narratives assigned to those roles, the instructions also contain "the law" as a separate actor. Research in both linguistics and psychology in the past ten years has linked metaphor with dynamic cognitive structuring of thought and comprehension (Dirven and Paprotte, ix). Consequently, the appearance of an abstract concept in full human personification, as the law is presented in these instructions, should elicit further examination. These metaphors are, by my analysis, the second support socializing jurors into the process of the law. Consider the following representations of the law in the instructions.

> In deciding this case you must determine the facts from a consideration of all the evidence in *light of the law* as it is contained in these instructions.

> *All the law* in the case is not *embodied* in any single instruction.

> You are instructed that *the law contemplates* that all six of your minds shall agree in your verdict.

Lakoff and Johnson suggest that when we wish to highlight particular aspects of a concept that we will use consistent metaphors for that concept (92). Two metaphoric concepts of law are presented within these instructions. First, jurors have a structuring metaphor of law as an entity. The law has a bodily presence and it produces light. Second, as these examples from the instructions suggest, the law is not just an entity, but a rational entity. In discussing this process of metaphoric personification, Lakoff and Johnson also suggest that particular aspects of the personification will be emphasized (33). The law contemplates, controls, and requires. In short, it thinks. This conceptualization of the law provides the jurors with further emphatic demonstration of the primacy of reason in the trial setting. The "law is a rational entity" metaphor structures the jurors' perceptions of the law.

A further elaboration of the hierarchical relations present in the roles of participants in the trial is provided by the combined metaphors of "the law is up" and "the law is light." "The law is up" metaphor provides a key to the hierarchy operating within the trial setting. Through its ability to require and bar, the "law is up" metaphor combines with the "law is a rational entity" to become the governor of the trial. Further, "the law is light" metaphor puts reason once again at the top of the list of human abilities. The associations with light are potentially endless, but this particular use is clearly associated with reason and insight.

Certainly the recent research in metaphor has continued to explore specifications of the relations between metaphor and cognition. Elizabeth Closs Traugott suggests use of parameters to categorize the aspects of metaphor contributing to understanding. Two of those parameters are relevant here, reference and conceptualization. By Traugott's proposed analysis (22–23), "the law is a rational entity" metaphor is low in reference; that is, its use is fairly common and we typically have little trouble connecting the reference with the literal sense. The consequence is that this metaphor is probably perceived as a convention. On the conceptualization parameter, however, perceiving the law, a nonanimate abstract concept, as an animate entity, specifically a rational entity, probably requires a somewhat higher degree of reconceptualization. As contact with the legal community is somewhat more limited to the average person than, for example, a religious group, to imagine the law as animate necessitates more distance than imagining the church as a living body. With low reference value and a higher conceptualization value, these parameters suggest the continuing usefulness of the metaphor in the instructions. If initiation does demand some limited reconceptualization, then these metaphors, appearing in the instructions, function to move the jurors closer to an unconscious understanding of the trial proceedings from a legal perspective.

With both the strict division of roles and the metaphoric conceptualization of the law, jurors move toward a legal perspective. A final support for this movement toward the legal perspective is found in the similarities between the abbreviated legal education that jurors receive during a trial and the actual legal education of an attorney.

Lawrence Friedman, in *A History of American Law*, devotes a chapter

Gail Stygall

to history of legal education in the United States. He pinpoints a change from teaching by lecture and hornbook to teaching by case law in the late nineteenth century, originating from Harvard. Friedman notes:

> This method cast out the textbooks, and used casebooks as teaching materials; these were collections of reports of actual cases, carefully selected and arranged to illustrate the meaning and development of principles of law. The classroom tone was profoundly altered. There was no more lecturer, expounding "the law" from received texts. The teacher now was a Socratic guide, leading the student to an understanding of concepts and principles hidden as essences among the cases. (531).

In concluding this section, Friedman observes that every accredited law school eventually used the casebook approach.

The importance of this teaching method to procedures observed by the jurors in trial rests in the inductive nature of such a teaching approach. Friedman defines the casebook method as scientific and inductive in nature (531–32), and insofar as jurors are triers of fact, the process of the trial mirrors the inductive method of the law classroom. Socratic method in the law classroom prompts students to elaborate the holding in each case studied toward an inductively reasoned conclusion. Law students in their first year often find the process disconcerting, after years of college courses such as "Principles of Accounting" or "Principles of Economics." Searching for the general principle in a casebook is fruitless; the general principle emerges from skilled questioning in the classroom. Similarly, the lack of explicit elaborative inferences in the trial itself may be considered a sign of the typical legal education's forced attention to "scientific" or inductive reasoning. Moreover, jurors are clearly not to question matters of law; hence, instructions on the law may not necessarily evoke understanding of the legal concepts so much as they focus attention on the most highly valued process of legal thinking: rationality.

Conclusion

To ignore the intracommunity demands of a professional discourse is, in some ways, to trivialize the nature of language and text in a professional community. In the case of jury instructions, a written text surfacing within an oral speech event, two legal discourse conventions require the legal participants to produce a "good" legal text at the same time they produce a "bad" generic text. Knowledge about the importance of certain topics remains hidden to ordinary readers, masked by implicit references to professional texts beyond the view of the outsiders. Knowledge about the relationship between naming and exemplification also remains within the professional community. The two legal discourse conventions function to block jurors' access to normal strategies of discourse processing. Is this situation unusual? I think not. Membership in a professional community inevitably means learning a new semantic system — not just words or technical terms — but new connections and new relationships. What this suggests is that pedagogy alone cannot diagnose or correct faulty communication between professional and nonprofessional or between professional communities.

Moreover, instead of looking for a simple information transfer, we may have to examine what does take place, even when information transfer has failed. No one expects jurors to become members of the legal community as a result of a single turn serving on a jury. But that is precisely what we are saying if we expect the information transfer to occur. In the case of *Masheck v. Capitol Drilling*, we do have communication that is successful in its own way: privileging rationality and socializing the jurors into "thinking like lawyers."

Few discourse communities provide the kind of written record of decisions found in the legal community. By examining a community in which these discourse conventions are recorded, we may be able to further describe the discourse practices of other less formal professional communities. In short, we need to explore professional discourse communities, outside the experimental setting and into the normal arena of their practice. With the legal community providing so rich a resource of the intersection of text and orality, a cultural artifact so deeply embedded in this society, we have only just opened the door to understanding the functions of text in this discourse community.

APPENDIX

Partial Text
Final Jury Instructions
Edith Masheck v. Capitol Drilling Supplies, Inc.

When I say that a party has the 'burden of proof' on any issue or use the expression, 'if you find from a preponderance of the evidence,' I mean that you must be convinced from a consideration of all the evidence in the case that he issue which a party has the burden of proving is more probably true than not. You are the sole judges of the weight of the evidence and of the credibility of witnesses. In giving weight and credit to the testimony of any witness, you may take into consideration any interest a witness may have in the result of the trial, any bias or prejudice of the witness disclosed by the evidence. You may consider the oppor-

Gail Stygall

tunity or lack of opportunity of the witness observing or knowing the things about which he has testified and the reasonableness of the testimony considered in the light of all the evidence in the case. The term 'preponderance of the evidence' means the weight of evidence. The number of witnesses testifying to a fact on one side or the other is not necessarily of the greater weight. The evidence given upon any fact in issue which convinces you must strongly of its truthfulness is of the greater weight. If there are conflicts in the evidence, it is your duty to reconcile the conflicts, if you can, on the theory that each witness has testified to the truth. If you cannot so reconcile the testimony, then it is within your province to determine whom you will believe and whom you will disbelieve.

NOTES

The Judge of the Marion Superior Court, Civil Division, Room 3, the Honorable Betty Barteau deserves my special acknowledgement, as do her court reporters, Jane Barnard and Marty Condos, and her bailiff, Mary Williams. Their patience and willingness to devote time and expertise to this study went far beyond mere tolerance of my presence in the courtroom and court offices.

BIBLIOGRAPHY

Board of Commissioners of Delaware County v. Briggs, 337 N.E. 2d 852 (Ind. App. 1975).
Charrow, Robert P., and Veda R. Charrow. "Making Legal Language Understandable: A Psycholinguistic Study of Jury Instructions." *Columbia Law Review* 79 (1979): 1306–74.
Clifford, James, and George E. Marcus, eds. *Writing Culture: The Poetics and Politics of Ethnography*. Berkeley, Calif.: University of California Press, 1986.
Dijk, Teun A. van, and Walter Kintsch. *Strategies of Discourse Comprehension*. New York: Academic Press, 1983.
Dirven, Rene, and Wolf Paprotte. Introduction. *The Ubiquity of Metaphor: Metaphor in Language and Thought*, ed. Wolf Paprotte and Rene Dirven, vii–xix. Amsterdam Studies in the Theory and History of Linguistic Science 29. Amsterdam: John Benjamins Publishing, 1985.
Elwork, Amiram, Bruce D. Sales, and James J. Alfini. "Juridic Decisions: In Ignorance of the Law or in Light of It?" *Law and Human Behavior* 1 (1977): 163–90.
Faigley, Lester. "The Problem of Topic in Text." In *The Territory of Language: Linguistics, Stylistics, and the Teaching of Composition*, ed. Donald McQuade, 123–41. Carbondale, Il.: Southern Illinois University Press, 1986.
Indiana Digest, 26, *Cumulative Annual Pocket, (1986)* "Trial."
Indiana Pattern Jury Instructions. Indianapolis: Bobbs-Merrill, 1968.
Indiana Rules of Court 1986. St. Paul: West Publishing, 1986.

Lakoff, George, and Mark Johnson. *Metaphors We Live By*. Chicago: University of Chicago Press, 1980.

Pettinari, Catherine. "The Function of a Grammatical Alternation in 14 Surgical Reports." In *Linguistics and Literacy*, ed. William Frawley, 145–85. New York: Plenum, 1982.

Traugott, Elizabeth Closs. " 'Conventional' and 'Dead' Metaphors Revisited." In *The Ubiquity of Metaphor: Metahpor in Language and Thought*, ed. Wolf Paprotte and Rene Dirven, 17–56. Amsterdam Studies in the Theory and History of Linguistic Science 29. Amsterdam: John Benjamins Publishing, 1985.

Van Maanen, John. *Tales of the Field: On Writing Ethnography*. Chicago: University of Chicago Press, 1988.

White, James Boyd. "The Invisible Discourse of the Law: Reflections on Legal Literacy and General Education." In *Literacy for Life*, ed. Richard W. Bailey and Robin Melanie Fosheim, 137–50. New York: Modern Language Association, 1984.

PART THREE

THE OPERATIONAL FORCE

OF TEXTS

TEXT AND ACTION

THE OPERATOR'S MANUAL

IN CONTEXT AND IN COURT

JAMES PARADIS

Modern professional knowledge, it has been widely noted, is formally embodied and disseminated in literary networks (Price; Garvey et al.). Studies by Gilbert and Mulkay, Latour, and Bazerman have shown that the socio-rhetorical strategies of publication help to formalize a specialized field, not only by defining its territory and identifying the members of the network, but also by furnishing the means for constructing and maintaining consensus — or, at least, the impression thereof. The rhetorical practices of disciplines have broader social consequences, as well, since expert knowledge is routinely exported to society in innumerable manifestations of modern instrumental control — the codes, procedures, and industrial products that shape, amplify, and direct our daily behavior. Nearly all of these products are transferred from institutional settings of expertise by means of written operational discourse, which helps frame them in terms of relevant actions carried out in social contexts. These texts, which form the basis of most informal and formal training and certification processes, are exegetical, serving to interpret for the lay public the meanings, applications, and procedures by which expert products, whether VCRs, tax codes, or angina medicines, are integrated into the behavioral flow of society itself. The rhetorical process by which this immense body of expert knowledge is transformed into the basis of subsequent human action is a question of considerable importance.[1]

The semantic complexity of everyday life, Alvin Weinberg has argued, is a social problem of Malthusian character. Any individual's "semantic apparatus" is increasingly taxed as he or she attempts to keep abreast of what Weinberg has called the "proliferation of the semantic environment" that attends unrelenting population and technological growth (2–3, 26). That is, we are physiologically fixed, despite numerous technological aids and props, in an environment of rapid population growth and technological innovation that vastly increase the amounts and complexities of available information.[4] Innovation, with its ever-evolving intellectual sophistication, is increasingly accomplished within the specialized research networks referred to above, as well as in the expert domains of professional schools and in the design clusters of engineering houses. The technological complexity that governs everyday life is thus supported in environments sequestered within their own networks of expertise, out of which products are then "released," so to speak, to the public at large. The lay person is largely isolated from the professional origins of technologies, whose procedurally sensitive behaviors are crucial to transacting the business of everyday life — for example, filing complex tax forms, negotiating computer protocols, using new tools with expanded capabilities. Procedurally sensitive processes often require that the operator adhere to specific protocols or operational sequences, which can be counterintuitive. Millions of operations manuals, protocol books, instructions sheets, guide books, and codes cycle throughout society to steer individuals and their experts through the complexity of our increasingly artificial social environments (Simon 4–5). This vast body of task-oriented literature thus helps to adjust machinery to human norms, or, human norms to machinery, depending upon one's philosophy of technics.[3]

The rhetorical export of expertise and its products has some major implications that I would like to examine in the light of two recent liability cases concerning injury by specialized construction tools. In both cases, a major issue was made of the role of operator's manuals in enabling a user to develop an adequate working knowledge of an unfamiliar power tool. The tool, a direct-acting studgun used to fire nails and other fasteners into various construction materials, was the product of a relatively old firearms technology that had recently been adapted to a new social environment — the construction workplace. Operator's manuals outlining the principles of use accompanied the studguns, and the question arose of just what role such manuals should play in the user's mental construction of the tool and how effectively the operator's manuals in question elaborated the procedurally sensitive processes of safely applying the studguns to various tasks. The formalities of courtroom discovery forced a comparison of the images and norms of the public mind with those of the expert. In effect, the inquiry sought to determine, in the context of tort law and legal liability, the rhetorical role of operator's manuals in the social construction of a technology. This question ultimately touched on the role of written discourse in constructing a world of "reasonable"

James Paradis

actions that could resolve the polarities inherent in almost any technology between mechanical function and social purpose.

Operator's manuals, I will argue in this study, typically employ four textual elements that attempt to bind, by means of representative human actions, the worlds of external objects with those of human behavior. First, they construct a written analogue of the tool or process itself. This analogue reduces the tool or process to a series of verbal and visual terms that are, in effect, idealizations substituting for the thing itself. Second, the manual introduces a fictional operator who represents an average or suitably qualified individual. This everyman is the agent, the initiating and guiding force, capable of making a range of commonsense decisions about how to apply the tool. The third textual element of operator's manuals is environment, the material context of conditions and situations requisite for effective and safe use of the instrument. A fourth textual element of the manual is the action itself. This procedural element can be a loose narrative of representative steps the operator takes to apply the tool. Or, it can be a narrative sequence of precisely defined actions that furnish a behavioral template on which the operator must model his or her actions. Together, these elements help to construct a *teleological* view of reality, by which I mean a reality subordinated to human purpose. The operator's manual is a conceptual framework that infuses human purpose into mechanical devices or their equivalents, thus aligning the neutral products of technology with the value-laden ends of society. Not all operator's manuals are effective in constructing this mechanical world dominated by human purpose; yet, even in poorly executed operator's manuals, these textual elements of object, agent, conditions, and action are all implied. If they are either poorly treated or absent, the operator must invent his or her own version of them in order to pursue a course of action.

As a technology becomes more complex, the rhetorical effort required to sort and reduce its expertise to some course of activity comprehensible to the operator-everyman becomes greater. As the differential between expertise and common sense becomes greater, or as the audience itself becomes more diverse, the demands made upon the operator's manual increase. We have enough information in our daily environment to operate simple tools like hammers or to carry out basic procedures like mailing letters. But with processes associated with more complex technologies and social institutions — whether computers or the filing of taxes — we require additional support. Expert advisors who can personally direct us are extremely effective but costly means, because the ratio of human time expenditure to productive activity is so unfavorable. Group training and certification improve this ratio but require substantial institutional support, as well as dislocations and time commitments of the learning operators. Texts improve the ratio still further, because they can circulate the same expertise to the masses. But the inherent linearity and rigidity of written discourse, coupled with the necessary reduction of complex situations to sequential units of simple action, increase the possibility of omission, ambiguity, and misunderstanding. We now need specialists, technical writers and editors, who can anticipate these problems and who can apply rhetorical strategies to achieving operational coherence and simplicity.

In what follows, I begin with a manufactured product — a studgun — and examine the rhetorical frame two operator's manuals attempt to build around it. I explore how instructions for a publicly marketed tool serve to mediate between the expert world of technologists and manufacturers and the lay operator world where the tools are employed. I conclude with a consideration of the same manuals in light of recent legal liability proceedings in order to illustrate how these texts are socially burdened by tort law and the concept of liability, the larger object of which I argue is to impose purpose on the basically neutral world of technology. In this light, the operator's manual can be seen to play a profound role in the effort — sometimes specious — to adapt technology to human ends.

The Studgun as Mechanism

The studgun is a versatile tool that dramatically improves the effectiveness with which construction workers can drive nails and other fasteners into a multitude of construction materials. The distinctive aspect of the studgun design is its blend of hammer function and firearm technology.[4] The resulting device, euphemistically known as a "powder-actuated fastening tool," exploits the mechanisms and dynamics of a gun, with a chamber that receives a projectile and powder charge, which in turn is discharged with a trigger (see figure 11.1). Studguns fire a variety of fasteners, including pins (nails) and studs (threaded bolts), into materials as different as wood, hard concrete, and structural steel. The tools range in cost from less than a hundred to several hundred dollars and are marketed by several companies that have developed a variety of studgun models with different capacities, as well as a range of accompanying fasteners, powder charges, and accessories.

There are two types of powder-actuated studguns, the more powerful being the direct-acting or high-velocity tool, which can drive fasteners into thick structural steel or hard concrete. In the high-velocity tool, a powder charge directs expanding gases against a fastener-projectile. Fasteners in these direct-acting studguns are capable of attaining speeds of high-powered rifles. In contrast, the piston-driven studgun, a low-velocity tool, drives the fastener with a piston that absorbs much of the energy of the powder charge. Piston-driven tools are therefore less likely to force fasteners through construction materials into free flight and are generally safer than direct-acting tools. However, piston-driven studguns do not have the penetrating capabilities of the direct-acting tools and are not as effective for applications in thick steel or very hard concrete.

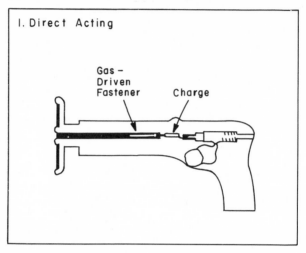

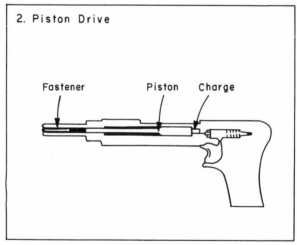

Fig. 11.1. Diagram of a studgun: 1. direct-acting, 2. piston-driven

Both the great virtue and risks of the technology inhere in the range of driving forces studguns can impart to their nail-like and bolt-like fasteners. The variations in fastener design and intensity of powder charge make it possible to apply the technology to such soft materials as construction-grade framing wood and to such dense materials as 3/4" structural steel (see figure 11.2). Fastener thrust ranges across as many as twelve strengths of powder charge. Fasteners vary in materials, length, shaft diameter, tip design, and shaft design, each variation having a different effect on the net penetrating capability of the discharged fastener. In addition, there are ramrod devices for positioning fasteners at various depths in the gun barrel to achieve still different intensities of thrust, and doughnut-like metal disks are available for collaring fasteners, so that they are not driven too far into soft materials.

This great variety of choice, however, brings an enormously complex firearm technology into the social environment of the construction workplace. The numerous options complicate the decision-making process required of the user, for there are thousands of conceivable combinations of studs, powder charges, and base materials. Compared to conventional firearms, which are used in restricted corridors, studgun technology, used in socially active construction areas, is orders of magnitude greater in complexity.[5] The tremendous force that enables the construction worker to fire nails into concrete or steel is also potentially lethal when used incorrectly or in unknown materials or circumstances. Thus, the adapted firearms technology of the studgun, effectively displacing the common hammer for many applications, has also introduced a difficult to regulate technology into largely unregulated social environments.

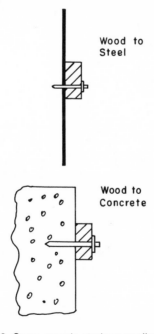

Wood to
Steel

Wood to
Concrete

Fig. 11.2. Some generic studgun applications

James Paradis

This combined studgun effectiveness and danger is nowhere more dramatically illustrated than in the two accidents that formed the subject of this analysis. Both concerned direct-action studguns, in which improper operation on construction sites led to the partial paralysis of one worker and the death of another. Both operators thought they were using the tool correctly, but neither was experienced in the use of studguns. Moreover, the studguns they were using had no safety warnings attached to them, and their respective operator's manuals failed to warn of the specific mechanisms that led to the accidents. Subsequent legal proceedings questioned the adequacy of the rhetorical framework established around the studgun. Questions were raised about the kinds and levels of discourse one would reasonably expect to accompany potentially lethal devices such as the studgun.

In the first case, *Roger Gagne v. Power Anchor Corporation et al.*, a Maine construction worker was trying to frame a window opening in a concrete basement foundation. Other workers had drilled and sledge-hammered a 3′×4′ opening, around which Gagne and his coworker were now using a studgun to attach a preassembled wooden window frame. A fastener fired from a direct-action studgun passed through the wood, rebounded off some object embedded in the concrete, fish-hooked back out, and struck Gagne, lodging in the back of his neck and causing him injury. Although Gagne possessed an operator's card for the studgun in use, his companion who fired the studgun did not. As the result of the injury, Gagne was unable to return to work.

In the second case, *DuCharme v. Star Expansion Corporation*, an employee of an aircraft company in Colorado, who was helping to construct some shelving on a plant wall, was killed by a stud in free flight after it had passed through three layers of materials. The employee, who had gone around a partition wall to clear the area behind, was struck with a $1\frac{7}{8}$″ stud that had passed through a $\frac{1}{32}$″ piece of corrugated steel, a $\frac{1}{16}$″ steel beam, and the plywood partition wall. The fastener passed through these various layers with such force that it went directly through the body of the victim and was never recovered. In this instance, the stud was being fired with the lowest powder charge available as a test firing, in order to determine the suitability of the application. Neither the operator nor the victim had an operator's license.

These two accidents were full of ambiguity. In each accident, the operator applied the technology in questionable ways. The operator in Case 1 fired the direct-action studgun closer than three inches from the edge of the two-by-four inch *wood* frame into the concrete substrate. The operator's manual had cautioned against firing "closer than 3 in. from the edge in *concrete*." In Case 2, the operator fired a low-powder charge into very thin steel, a practice that, although not rejected in the manual as unsafe, was questionable, given the potential force of a high-velocity direct-action studgun. Moreover, neither operator had been licensed to operate his respective studgun. On the other hand, there were no danger warnings on the two studguns in question. No effort had been made by manufacturers to incorporate a semiotics of hazard on the tools, their accessories, or indeed in the manuals. Explicit warnings are one of the most widely followed conventions used in industry to establish an operating context of extreme danger. Neither operations manual mentioned that incorrect or casual use could lead to serious bodily injury or death. Nor had either manual instructed users in any systematic way on the methods of selecting the proper combination of stud and powder charge for an application. Thus, the possible arguments concerning the cause of the accidents were diverse.

In the narratives of accidents, causality is always a central issue. As the philosopher Norwood Hanson once observed, the attempt to determine the cause of an accident is a request for an explanation of the event, and a surprising variety of plausible narratives will be established in terms of each explainer's point of view.[6] An accident involving a studgun might readily be explained in terms of the operator, the environmental conditions, the tool itself, or its procedural guidelines. Were the accidents caused by operator error or by faulty tool design? Was the error a matter of the operator's negligence or of the manufacturer's negligence? Powerful social forces were at work on behalf of each theory. Defenders of the tool would be expected to base their arguments on the industrial integrity of its production and the adequacy of the expertise embedded in the tool's design. Their opponents would be expected to base their arguments on the tool's flawed design, the failure of the manufacturer to warn of operating hazards, and on the unreasonable expectations placed on the operator-everyman in the proper operation of the tool. Such opposing views, established by legal proceedings, would pit the mechanical domain of design expertise against the social domain of human purpose. The territory between these poles becomes the field of argument upon which the various theories of error play.

The Rhetoric of Action: Constructing a Working Image of the Direct-Acting Studgun

In the process of exporting a technology to society, expertise has many possible options, since users can construct working images of a technology in many ways. The casual user can be relaxed about simple consumer technologies in which there is little personal or financial stake other than a few lost hours or dollars. Despite obvious hazards, lawnmowers, familiar objects to the suburbanite or the avid television watcher, require little assistance to learn how to operate. User strategies can be built upon the stock of generic images that, as Boulding has argued, is shared by society (54–55). Everyone "operates" a screwdriver or flashlight without having to be instructed. In a thriving consumer society, this kind of intuitive operational knowhow based on socially shared imagery must be widely available. Many lawnmower purchasers can by mere inspection decode the fraction of the technology necessary to operate the instrument satisfactorily. Hence, the sport of dispensing with the manual: "When all else fails," the saying goes, "consult the manual." The highly accessible technologies common in a consumer society are thus based on a social substrate of shared generic imagery, a kind of Platonic world of idealized forms and processes that is presumably the product of elementary and secondary school education, supplemented by television culture. Commercial designs are built up on these familiar images as part of the so-called idiot-proofing process well-known in the engineering sectors of product design, where the ideal is an intuitive design that needs no manual.

Access to more complex technologies, many of which have great institutional impact, usually requires a formal framework of explanation. The public stock of imagery no longer suffices to guide the operator successfully or safely through the necessary operating procedures. These technologies cannot be exploited without a carefully constructed framework of explanation that illustrates the contexts and conditions of effective action. Many technologies of health, explosives, and computers with complex protocols would be unfathomable without the systematic learning made possible by manuals. Frequently, as in health or computer technologies, operators require formal education, training, or on-site apprenticeships. One is licensed to apply the technology, authorized to convert the knowledge of expertise to operations in the public sector.

Written discourse plays a necessary role in the exportations of expertise, whether of simple casual consumer technologies or of complex instruments of institutional proportions. Texts can break down and sort the complex phenomenological reality of events and objects. As a signifying system, language precipitates versions of experience from the complex contents of "reality." These reductions are necessary distortions. They help to establish perspective in simplified points of view that clarify the structure and purpose of artifacts, yet also hide their deeper complexities. Language, as Berger and Luckman have noted, "objectivates [our] shared experiences and makes them available to all within the linguistic community" (68); written discourse renders that experience into a true *object*, independent of time and space (Boulding, 55; Joos, 41–42). Moreover, texts have permanence. Written discourse reduces and fixes human experience so that it may be reprocessed – read, studied, and manipulated as object. "By creating a text 'out there', a material object detached from man (who created and interprets it)," Goody observes, "the written word can become the subject of a new kind of critical attention" (129). Operator's manuals thus recreate the artifact or tool itself in a context of critical analysis, giving us control – or, at least the impression of control – over the imagery for the object or process. In text, we can resolve the technological object into its parts in such a way that it remains dissected, as an organism remains dissected in an anatomy manual. We bring into the textual field and associate as equivalent elements the implement, the operator, the environment, and the operation. This reductionism, in ignoring the vast phenomenological differences in these elements, enables the user to see them as a system and to manipulate them logically. One learns how to operate on the artifact by operating on the text.[7]

If we examine the public rhetoric of studgun technology, we find a number of documents treating the various objects and processes associated with the end action of firing a stud into construction material. These documents fall roughly into two basic groups. The technology has a commercial status and is marketed in a variety of catalogs, price lists, and advertisements. It also has a functional status as outlined in the operator's manuals, treating the assembly, operation, and maintenance of the tools. Studguns, in addition, are typically labelled with a variety of safety warnings and symbols, which reinforce the conditions of operation outlined in the operator's manual. These documents, which define the tool operationally, commercially, and socially, can be at odds when the commercial object of maximum sales volume is allowed to conflict with the social object of effective and safe operation. Sales literature and operator's manuals can exaggerate function and downplay hazard.

Operating procedures for the direct-acting studgun in the Star operator's manual illustrate several rhetorical conventions of operational discourse. We find, for example, a procedural outline for selecting a power load for the studgun titled "To Determine Correct Power Load." As already noted, not every operator will use this textual formulation to learn how to select a power load, since it is possible to figure out the procedure through training, observation, or, for that matter, guessing. Still, *this textual version governs all studgun usages*, as official rules always govern practice. An operator's manual is company-formulated – an operationally explicit version of how the stewards of the expertise recommend that the public apply the technology. In reducing the power selection process to a protocol, the manual, we assume, invests us with expert behavior. Hence, willy-nilly, it has the status of authority, a status of contract. Each specified iteration must be treated by the lay user as an expert formula-

266

James Paradis

tion of how one should apply the technology.

Three rhetorical conventions found in operational discourse rather stringently shape the user's action: taxonomies or terminological standards, conditional generalizations, and segmented action sequences. We find all three of these conventions in the prose sample taken from the operations manual of the Star Power Tool Model 100:

> To Determine Correct Power Load.
> 1. The fastener and the power load that should be used for a given installation depends on the thickness of the object being fastened and the nature of the material into which the fastening is to be made.
> 2. The harder the material the stronger the power load, and the shorter the fastener.
> 3. Caution: In making an initial test fastening always start with the Green color load, Power level 3. If fastener does not penetrate to required depth, then try the next strength power load until desired penetration is obtained.
> 4. High Velocity special .22 caliber power loads are available for driving fasteners as follows:
>   .22 CALIBER STANDARD (WADDED — BRASS CASE)
>   #6022-036 Green Power Load — Power Level 3
>   #6022-056 Yellow Power Load — Power Level 4
>   #6022-076 Red Power Load — Power Level 5
>   #6022-096 Purple Power Load — Power Level 6
>   .22 CALIBER LONG (WADDED — NICKEL CASE)
>   #6022-156 Gray Power Load — Power Level 7
>   #6022-176 Brown Power Load — Power Level 8
> 5. To vary the amount of penetration: (a) Fasteners can be positioned in the barrel by using the ramrod provided with the tool kit. (b) By using .22 caliber crimped loads Power levels 1 or 2.

These conventions reflect a rhetorical preoccupation with accuracy and clarity. Terminological standards establish a morphology of the tool or process that helps us relate form to function. Such a referential language that thousands of individuals can hold in common enables us to share common iterative behavioral priorities of operational discourse. This attempt to create a unity of action among diverse users is based on terminological standards that reduce the possibilities of ambiguity. Taxonomies, typically established within the professional design community, impose conventions that identify components and functions of the implement in question.

For the studgun, these naming conventions extend to parts, accessories, and the various fasteners and powder charges. In the sample given above, for example, we find a taxonomical table that identifies several kinds of .22 caliber power loads, or shells, organized in increasing order of strength. This schemata ranks the levels of function in powder loads. But such specialized terminology can also be misleading, since its meaning often depends on the user's prior conceptual depth or experience. These conventions usually develop first within a larger framework of expertise that uses them to summarize its own experience. The color distinctions of the green, yellow, red, purple, gray, and brown powder loads can have only limited meaning to the general user. The scheme ranks in a rudimentary sense the increasing powers of charges. But no specific kinds of application are specified for these distinctions. We are not shown a specific instance of how an operator might use the chart to select a powder charge for a given kind of application. No description predicts what will happen if we use a green powder charge with a 1" stud in ¾" structural steel. Indeed, for the outsider, the occasional user, such a hierarchy may give a false impression of precision in a selection process that, as noted in Rule 3, is conducted by trial and error.

Procedural discourse always faces this formidable problem of constraining the operator's action within set physical limits. Like the Sorcerer's Apprentice, the operator may initiate actions according to some known procedure that subsequently gets out of hand, because some terminological detail has been forgotten or some conditional detail has been neglected. This problem of control, as Wiener observed in his classic *God and Golem, Inc.*, is inherent in all human artifice, whose effects are difficult to anticipate in totality (63). The operator's manual attempts to establish barriers to undesirable forms of behavior by restricting the terms and conditions of use, but this process requires both insight and considerable rhetorical skill.

Conditional generalizations, for example, attempt to limit an operator's activity on the tool by establishing circumstantial limits within which the tool is effectively and safely operated. In Rule 2 of the prose sample above, harder materials are said to require stronger power loads and shorter fasteners. This rule of thumb, which establishes a relationship between materials, power charges, and fasteners, seeks to channel behavior in certain directions. The assertions of Rule 2, however, are based on assumptions that exist outside the text. That is, the full information upon which the generalization has been made is not available in the text. For example, the outsider can only speculate on the meaning of an unqualified distinction such as *hardness*, when no fastener dimension and no specific base material are mentioned. The generalization of Rule 2, in fact, is nearly devoid of content for an outsider, once we recall that the possible combinations of materials, fasteners, and powder charges range in the thousands:

> *Permutations of Studgun Applications*
> = *Shell Charges* (6 levels)
> × *Fastener Designs* (type, length, diameter)
> × *Base Materials* (type, thickness, hardness, condition, combinations)
> × *Accessories* (disks, barrel types, ramrod positions)

Such mechanical complexity, which vastly exceeds that of any firearm, cannot be reduced to commonsensical proportions in textual generalizations of the kind given in the paragraph cited above. In the heading of the manual section — "To Determine Correct Power Load" — "correct" is a misleading ideal. For the designated procedure leads to no predictable result, given the myriad possible combinations.

This discrepancy between mechanical complexity and discursive reduction is a problem common to all operational discourse. The reductive text's utility is achieved through a simplification that does not admit the complexity of the phenomenological reality. This differential becomes serious when it burdens the user with guesswork that can result in serious error. In the instance I am discussing the authors fail to make explicit the variety of assumptions insider operators — whether designers or experienced users — routinely apply when selecting fasteners and charges. The language of reduction in the instance of the direct-action studgun does not encompass the detail that the expert operator must master in order to determine an appropriate power load.

Further efforts in operator's manuals to reduce ambiguity and constrain behavior are typically made by specifying action. In this distinctive rhetorical convention of operational discourse, the user is given behavioral templates on which to model his or her actions. These templates usually have a narrative, dramatic quality that unfolds a series of actions in steps through time. The operator's manual becomes a kind of script for the human-machine interface, in which human physiology is unified with machine action to achieve a utilitarian objective — for example, fastening studs to a sheet of steel. Rule 3 of the cited instructional sample directs the operator to begin with the weakest possible charge and to work upward in charge strength until the "desired" penetration is achieved. Such action statements attempt to resolve the technology into a series of discrete operations that direct the human-machine interaction so as to deliver the technology to the user's purpose. Once again in the sample we are examining, the selection process is underspecified. The shortage of action statements forces the operator to formulate his or her own actions on the extratextual basis of individual judgment. The operator must invent a procedure in the process of applying the tool.

The Legal Framework and Conflicting Interests

That every operator's manual has a legal significance should come as no surprise. Written discourse is inherently accountable. Evidence that a given technology is a reasonable solution to a problem is a matter of demonstration, in which texts — quite frequently the operator's manuals — will inevitably play a powerful testimonial and illustrative role. The document is a *testament* that the technology can be explained, which is to say made understandable and controllable for the lay user. Language plays a crucial role in this rendering of technology into human terms (Miller). Indeed, rendering public technologies into written procedures is a decisive step in the socialization of a technology. The operator's manual not only assumes a contractual importance in its capacity as written claim, but it also becomes evidence that the expert, who usually has an exclusive hold on the expertise, has sufficiently reasoned out and articulated how it is to be made fit for public use. Hence, manufacturers who neglect to frame their technology in text are open to the charge of negligence.

The legal process has an ancient preoccupation with texts. As Goody has argued, the alliance between the law and the written artifact, which has been nearly universal among cultures, serves to reaffirm the uniformity and stability of the law (153–54, 170). Texts are viewed as more stable than oral discourse; they can be collated and preserved from artibrary rewording. In modern practice, there is a steady effort to convert experience to text. Depositions are taken, documents are amassed, transcripts of testimony are made, and all these are sorted and arranged in casebooks, drawing important elements out from a background reality. This reconstructed reality can now be processed and opened to collaborative exegesis. Narratives are fashioned from these materials as a way of probing causality. This process of objectification is important in analyzing potentially conflicting accounts of experience, for the material record allows one individual to collate his or her own version of reality with that of others.

In sorting through the merits of the two studgun cases mentioned above, the legal process converged on the respective operator's manuals. One of the main strategies for reconstructing the accidents was to assess the way in which the tool, its operator, the conditions of operation, and the recommended procedures were elaborated in the operator's manuals. Each manual, issuing from an authoritative source, whether manufacturer or distributor, was treated as a reference tool with procedural authority over the studgun. Legal analysis naturally focused on these procedural elaborations as a way of assessing the intentions of the manufacturer and the nature and limits of the knowledge made available to the user.

In both the Power Anchor and Star studgun cases, an important part of the legal inquiry concentrated on aligning the material facts of each accident with a "theory" of tool use, as provided in the operator's manual. The events of each accident were compared with the written procedures concerning the relevant action and conditions, in order to determine the degree to which the text anticipated the event. For example, in the Power Anchor accident, where a stud appeared to have fish-hooked off of spalled concrete behind the $2'' \times 4''$ frame, all elements of the operator's manual dealing with use of the studgun in such a situation and for such purposes were scrutinized, including the warnings related to such uses. In the Star studgun accident, where a stud had passed through three layers of construction materials, parts of the manual governing studgun charge selection and use on walls and in steel materials were examined for the degree to which they anticipated that kind of event. Hence, a sustained line of inquiry sought to reconstruct the circumstances and events of the accidents by reference to relationships worked out in the manual — the tool, action, conditions, and operator. The operator's manual was thus interpreted within a theory of verisimilitude, in which it was expected to caution against, and thus anticipate, the actual events.

In the legal domain, a variety of specialized concepts composing tort law have institutionalized the expectation that the relations between operational texts and human actions should be governed by verisimilitude. Of special significance to operator's manuals is the notion that the manual is a *warranty* — both a promise that the fact is as represented and a promise that the information in an instructional publication used for a specific purpose is suitable for that purpose (Walter and Marsteller 165). In the legal context, operational discourse takes on the social and material consequences of liability, outlined as follows in Section 311 of the Restatement (second) of Torts:

> (1) One who negligently gives false information to another is subject to liability for physical harm caused by action taken by the other in reasonable reliance upon such information, when such harm results (a) to the other, or (b) to such third persons as the actor should expect to be put in peril by the action taken. (2) Such negligence may consist of failure to exercise reasonable care (a) in ascertaining the accuracy of the information, or (b) in the manner in which it is communicated.

This formulation of Section 311 legalizes our social expectations that the reality constructed in the discourse of operations is both reasonable and expert (Walter and Marsteller). Operational discourse, tort law insists, should attempt to resolve mechanical complexity into commonsense terms that channel human action into benign and useful effects. An injury becomes a material — and operational — emblem of an incongruency between text and action.

Claims made on behalf of the plaintiffs in both the Power Anchor and Star cases were substantially based on theories of verisimilitude determined by textual analysis. The charge in each case developed a commonsense argument that the technology of the direct-action studgun was "unreasonably" dangerous, entailing risks that were unannounced to potential users. For example, the claim against Power Anchor, Inc. was as follows:

> Our action on behalf of Mr. Gagne and his wife is based on our contentions that the stud gun is unreasonably dangerous and that its warnings are inadequate for a number of reasons. Notably, we believe that there was a failure to adequately warn users of the hazards associated with the use of the tool.
>
> In particular, the content, format, and presentation of warnings set forth in the owner's manual are such that they do not call attention to the general hazards associated with the use of the gun in proximity to the edge of concrete surfaces. Further, the warnings attached to the gun itself and contained on the gun's tool box do not begin to bring home to potential users the gravity of the risks engendered by the gun's use.

In this claim, *reason* is normative, a state of conditions that is assumed to govern the individual's encounter with the mechanical complexity of material culture. Reason, taken as a self-evident human faculty, is the norm to which technical complexity must subordinate itself. *Risk* becomes a term used to identify the existence of contingencies that are not subject to operational control or foreseen by commonsense inspection. *Safety*, a matter of the human body, is the condition in which the technological and human — that is, the mechanical and the social — regimes interact without harm to the operator. Reason and safety are thus bound together in the notion of verisimilitude, the notion that things are as they seem in the manual.

In both cases the plaintiffs based their claims largely on an analysis of the studgun as it was represented in the operator's manual. The manual must, as a rational system, be accessible to common sense. Its world therefore must to some degree be *complete* or self-sufficient, understandable on its own terms. However, if the tool is presented algorithmically as a matter of operating protocol, common sense may get in the way. For the point of constructing protocol is to dispense with the complex but often inessential principles behind the procedure. If we had to comprehend fully the rationale of every technology we availed ourselves of, even electric power would be removed from common social use. On the other hand, as procedures become elaborated in detailed protocols, they increasingly leave the realm of commonsense behind. They demand strict compliance and assume a highly problematic responsibility to be accurate and exhaustive. This is a paradox of all procedural discourse as it is exported to lay social settings.

In the legal context, our rhetorical analysis of the studgun manuals assumes a new significance. For example, the failure of the Star operator's manual to reason out a stud selection procedure is a problem for the user, who has no way of knowing what the implications of his or her uses are. The erratic coverage of the power load selection process, characteristic of the manual as a whole, fails to meet the expectation that the rhetorical system is reasonably self-explanatory. Many of the statements have meaning only when supplemented with "insider" knowledge not contained in the text. Consider Item 5, for example:

> To vary the amount of penetration: (a) Fasteners can be positioned in the barrel by using the ramrod provided with the tool kit. (b) By using .22 caliber crimped loads Power Levels 1 or 2.

Nowhere in the manual is it explained how the ramrod works, what "crimped" loads are, or where Power Levels 1 and 2 fit into the scheme of ammunition used to propel the studs. It is not at all clear in what way these factors "vary the amount of penetration." The loose terminology and incoherent syntax, here as throughout the manual, underscore the inconsistency of the taxonomical, conditional, and action statements, which introduce ambiguity rather than reduce it. The result is that the operator is burdened with guesswork as he or she tries to determine a course of action.

The lack of safety warnings was a central issue in both the Star and Power Anchor studgun cases. Neither the Star manual nor the Power Anchor manual warned of the serious hazards attending the use of high-velocity studguns. This omission of prominent, explicit warnings made it easy to assume that the direct-action studgun is just another construction tool, blurring the fact that a gun-like implement, normally regulated with the strictest care, was being introduced into a social environment. Neither manual used the words *hazard, dangerous, warning, death, caution,* or *injury.* Nor did they invoke any of the conventions of hazard warnings, used in most competitors' manuals, such as red or amber colors, redundant warnings, highlighting, typography, placement, or illustration — all of which are well established techniques of safety warning (Clement). The rhetorical effect of this bland treatment of hazard was to normalize the technology in such a way as to assert its fundamentally benign character, whereas operator's manuals of many other direct-action studguns used explicit death warnings to reinforce the impression of social emergency.

In the Power Anchor operator's manual, the entire issue of safety was relegated to small print on the next-to-last page in a hodgepodge list of "Safety Rules". The "do not" mentality revealed in this language is authoritarian and nonrational, with none of the saving graces of operationalism's explicit detail and careful sequential logic:

> Observe These Safety Rules
> Do not load tool until you are ready to fasten.
> Never fasten closer than ¾" from the edge in steel.
> Never fasten closer than 3" from the edge in concrete.
> Do not attempt to fasten into brittle material or hollow material such as tile, hardened steel, solid rock, cast iron, face brick, marble or sheet rock.
> Always keep head and body back of the tool when firing.
> Operators should always wear safety goggles.
> When working on ladders and scaffolds, do not lean out too far thereby putting yourself out of balance. Make sure you brace yourself solidly.
> Clean the tool daily.
> Always know the material into which you are fastening.
> Never guess. Check constantly to avoid firing into unsuitable material. Always try the lightest charge first.
> Do not use the tool in explosive atmosphere.

There is no effort to provide any explanatory rationale for the rules. They are simply grouped together and dispatched at the end of the manual. This neglect to place any priority on human consequence reduces the user to a nonentity.

How can we explain these lapses in procedural specification, hazard warnings, and safety recommendations? One cannot ignore the fact that the operator's manual is a rhetorical field on which different, often inconsistent interests vie for accommodation. The tool is a different object to the various constituencies whose professional ends are in some way or other bound up with it. To the engineer or designer, the studgun is an expression of functions that have been tested within the quantitative context of such specialized fields as mechanical design, materials behavior, and ballistics. This insider invokes his or her vast mental library of images and processes to supplement any fragmentary discourse in the manual. The capitalist, on the other hand, thinks of the same tool in terms of production, marketing, and finance — questions that have far-reaching monetary consequences. The tool in the operator's manual has a commercial significance. The operator sees the studgun as a utilitarian object whose purpose is to drive studs with speed, force, and accuracy. We must expect that these different groups will conceptualize the studgun within the different frameworks of their professional interests (Hanson, 32–33). Hence, the objective that an operator's manual render a consistent, self-contained public version of a given technology may well be defeated by the larger reality that powerful institutional interests are vying for definition of the technology.

Certainly rhetorical ineptitude helps to account for the failure of safety warnings in the Star and Power Anchor manuals. In neither case had experienced manual writers overseen the manual writing process, and the engineers and marketing personnel who wrote the manuals were inept at rationalizing and operationalizing the technology for inexpert users.[8] Design and marketing interests appear to have dominated composition and production of the manuals, since there was little evidence of a systematic manual writing effort from the user's point of view. In the context of legal inquiry, the kinds of rhetorical failures seen in the samples we have examined proved to be decisive arguments that direct-action studgun technology, framed as it was in inconsistent and often incoherent language, was misrepresented. Failure to place priority on language and clarity is also a failure to give special emphasis to the social function of operator's manuals. These lapses are consistent with a rigid positivist model of knowledge, in which the written discourse is considered an unwieldly approximation of a deeper material truth that is better understood in physical or mathematical terms. The relation between text and action is treated as unreliable. Language devalued leads to such half-truths as "No one reads manuals, anyway," or "Any tool can be dangerous if improperly used," or "You can't warn of every possible improper use."

Conclusion: The Metaphysics of Operator's Manuals

The operator's manual, we can conclude from the Power Anchor and Star cases, is a critical part of the machine-human interface by which technologists may help to accommodate humans and technology. But this accommodation remains problematic. As Norbert Wiener once noted, "A goal-seeking mechanism will not necessarily seek *our* goals unless we design it for that purpose and in that designing we must foresee all steps of the process for which it is designed, instead of exercising a tentative foresight which goes up to a certain point . . ." (63). The rhetorical process of preparing the operator's manual obliges the expert to imagine the consequences of operation and to lay these out for the user. It is a crucial step in the socialization of expertise. We can only maintain that individuals are responsible for their actions if we enable the rational individual to take charge of the growing presence of technology. We can only insist that operators retain legal responsibility for their actions if we provide them the means to understand the human consequences of their behavior.

As individuals avail themselves of the specialized knowledge modern society has spawned, the "semantic environment" (Weinberg, 2–3) becomes an information marketplace in which expertise is constantly reconstructed in behavioral terms of action for the nonexpert. This procedural discourse, however, is not without its social problems. As a given technology becomes more complex, it becomes harder to understand and to manipulate according to the dictates of common sense. The exportation of complex technologies is increasingly achieved by the detailed operationalizing of human behavior in the immense body of procedural literature that accompanies industrial products. But, as we have seen, there is a conflict between obligatory procedures of operationalism and the exercise of independent human reason.

Procedures without any accompanying rationale become imperative and defeat our social (and legal) expectations that human activity be governed by reason, human judgment, and initiative. In all strictly procedural discourse, a tension will arise between the instrumental need to be algorithmic and the legal obligation to be reasonable. On the one hand, we ask the operator to relinquish his or her individual inclination so as to conform to some algorithmic activity; on the other hand, we expect these principles governing our behavior to be reasonable, not arbitrary. As higher-level experts set the conditions of instrument assembly, operation, and maintenance and serialize them in repeatable unit human actions, the lay user may increasingly be faced with a situation in which he or she no longer understands the potential consequences of specific actions. And if, as was the case in the two manuals we have considered, the procedures are incomplete, the operator may well be obliged to use guesswork and to operate unknowingly on the margins of safe use.

In many instances, this problem of complexity can only be mastered by the training of individuals who can then comprehend the reasoning behind the procedures. Training programs were pronounced as obligatory in the two manuals we have examined, but, in fact, the programs were

James Paradis

not readily available and there was considerable doubt as to their quality.[9] Moreover, the manuals we have examined remained the central instruments of the training.

As Simon has argued, the technical object must be rescued from the control of the specialist and related to the broad social environment (176). This question is a significant one for all individuals involved in the processes of production — the designers, the producers, and the writers. In the operator's manual, we shift from the initial design and manufacturing orientation toward objects to a new orientation toward human thought and behavior. The operator's manual constructs this anthropocentric ethos in which material things are subordinated to human purpose. Simon speaks of the tool and its environment as object and mold. "An artifact," he argues, "can be thought of as a meeting point — an 'interface' in today's terms — between an 'inner" environment, the substance and organization of the artifact itself, and an 'outer' environment, the surroundings in which it operates" (9). But *environment*, as we have seen, must also be seen in terms of social circumstances and *artifact* must also be considered to include the rhetorical instruments. The neglect of these instruments can have terrible human consequences, not to mention serious legal implications, as we have seen in the Power Anchor and Star instances.

NOTES

1. A discussion of operationalism is found in Percy W. Bridgman's *The Logic of Modern Physics*, which made successful completion of specified tasks the criterion of positive knowledge. Studies in popularization such as those in Shinn and Whitley have examined the dynamic of publicizing science. See also Dobrin, who analyses instructional literature from the standpoint of speech-act theory.

2. The problem is not solely one of increasing quantities of information per population increase, for, as Boulding notes (55), technological innovations in print, broadcast, and communications media have vastly increased the potential information disseminated per unit individual. One newscaster, salesperson, or partisan can communicate with millions.

3. The literature on the engineered life is considerable. See Florman and Ellul for opposing views on the direction of the machine-human accommodation.

4. Although studguns came on the market in the United States in the late 1940s as construction tools, they were originally developed and patented in England during World War I by Robert Temple, who was attempting to adopt firearms technology to constructing devices for attaching lines with lighted floats to the hulls of submerged enemy submarines, which could theoretically then be spotted on the surface (Schillings). Temple patented a modification of the device in the United States in 1921 as an "explosively actuated penetrating means." Later, Temple proposed using his explosively actuated device as a

means of fastening sheets of steel to damaged ship hulls at sea. In the United States, after the war, Temple developed a variety of studgun applications for the construction industry. A piston-driven version of the studgun was also developed as the cattle stunner for the assembly-line slaughter of livestock. These tools have undergone a steady evolution from the late 1940s to the present.

5. This complexity can be glimpsed by simply multiplying the variations: *types of stud design × varieties of powder charge × kinds of materials of application.* This can easily come to $20 \times 8 \times 20 = 3,200$.

6. Hanson recounts how an aircraft downed in a storm will find plausible causal explanations in disciplines as diverse as those of the mechanic and the psychologist.

7. Popular lore sometimes holds that no one reads manuals, but we must recall that manuals do not have to be read by everyone or even by the majority. A manual's content can be drawn into the operating community by individual readers who instruct others on how the tool should be used. Such local experts, the so-called gatekeepers (Allen), propagate the information in the operating environment.

8. The authors of the two manuals even failed to incorporate all the recommendations of the *American National Standard Safety Requirements for Powder Actuated Fastening Systems* (ANSI), a standard reference document that suggests important rhetorical and semiotical usages to be taken into account by individuals preparing manuals on studgun technology.

9. In one instance, training consisted of a brief orientation and a true-false test given by the renting agent, which no one had ever failed.

BIBLIOGRAPHY

Allen, Thomas. *Managing the Flow of Technology.* Cambridge, MIT Press, 1977.
American National Standards Institute. "Safety Requirements for Powder Actuated Fastening Systems." ANSI A10.3-1977.
Barnes, Barry. *Scientific Knowledge and Sociological Theory.* London: Routledge and Kegan Paul, 1974.
Bazerman, Charles. *Shaping Written Knowledge: The Genre and Activity of the Experimental Article in Science.* Madison: University of Wisconsin Press, 1988.
Berger, Peter L., and Thomas Luckman. *The Social Construction of Reality: A Treatise in the Sociology of Knowledge.* New York: Doubleday, 1986.
Boulding, Kenneth E. *The Image: Knowledge in Life and Society.* Ann Arbor: University of Michigan Press, 1956.
Bridgman, Percy W. *The Logic of Modern Physics.* New York: Macmillan, 1927.
Clement, David E. "Human Factors, Instructions and Warnings, and Products Liability." *IEEE Transactions on Professional Communication* 30 (1987): 149–56.
Cloitre, Michael, and Terry Shinn. "Expository Practice: Social, Cognitive, and Epistemological Linkage." In *Expository Science: Forms and Functions of Popularisation,* ed. T. Shinn and R. Whitley, 31–60. Dordrecht: Reidel, 1985.

James Paradis

Dobrin, David N. *Writing and Technique.* Urbana, Ill.: National Council of Teachers of English, 1989.

Ellul, Jacques. *The Technological Society.* New York: Alfred A. Knopf, 1964.

Florman, Samuel C. *Blaming Technology: The Irrational Search for Scapegoats.* New York: St. Martin's: 1981.

Garvey, William D., Nan Lin, and Carnot E. Nelson. "Communication in the Physical and the Social Sciences." *Science* (11 Dec. 1970): 1166–73.

Gilbert, G. Nigel, and Michael Mulkay. *Opening Pandora's Box: A Sociological Analysis of Scientist's Discourse.* Cambridge: Cambridge University Press, 1984.

Goody, Jack. *The Logic of Writing and the Organization of Society.* Cambridge: Cambridge University Press, 1986.

Hanson, Norwood. *Observation and Explanation: A Guide to the Philosophy of Science.* New York: Harper, 1971.

Joos, Martin. *The Five Clocks: A Linguistic Excursion into the Five Styles of English Usage.* New York: Harper, 1971.

Latour, Bruno. *Science in Action: How to Follow Scientists and Engineers Through Society.* Cambridge: Harvard University Press, 1987.

Miller, Carolyn R. "A Humanistic Rationale for Technical Writing." *College English* 40 (1980): 610–17.

National Institute for Occupational Safety and Health. "Powder Actuated Fastening Tools: Employer's Safety Training Guide." U.S. Dept. of Health, Education and Welfare Pub. No. 78198B, 1977.

National Safety Council. "Powder-Actuated Hand Tools." Data Sheet No. 1-236-79. Chicago, 1979.

Paradis, James. "Bacon, Linnaeus, and Lavoisier: Early Language Reform in the Sciences." In *New Essays in Technical and Scientific Communication: Research, Theory, Practice,* ed. Paul Anderson, John Brockman, and Carolyn Miller, 200–204. Farmingdale, N.Y.: Baywood, 1983.

Powder Actuated Tool Manufacturer's Institute. *Powder Actuated Fastening Systems: Basic Training Manual.* Chicago, 1971.

Power Anchor Corporation. *Maintenance and Operating Instructions for Bauer Model Piccomat.* New York, n.d.

Price, Derek J. de Solla. "Networks of Scientific Papers." *Science* (30 July 1965): 510–15.

Schillings, H. J. "Mr. Temple's Submarine Locator." *Electrical Contractor* (February 1970): 30–31.

Shinn, Terry, and Richard Whitley, eds. *Expository Science: Forms and Functions of Popularisation.* Dordrecht: Reidel, 1985.

Simon, Herbert A. *The Sciences of the Artificial.* 2d ed. Cambridge: MIT Press, 1981.

Star Expansion Industries. *Manual for Star Power Tool Model 100.* New York, 1974.

Walter, Charles, and Thomas Marsteller. "Liability for the Dissemination of Defective Information." *IEEE Transactions on Professional Communication* (September 1987): 164–72.

Weinberg, Alvin M. *Reflections on Big Science.* Cambridge: MIT Press, 1967.

Wiener, Norbert. *God and Golem, Inc: A Comment on Certain Points Where Cybernetics Impinges on Religion.* Cambridge: MIT Press, 1964.

12 UNDERSTANDING FAILURES IN

ORGANIZATIONAL DISCOURSE

THE ACCIDENT AT

THREE MILE ISLAND AND THE

SHUTTLE CHALLENGER DISASTER

CARL G. HERNDL, BARBARA A. FENNELL,

AND CAROLYN R. MILLER

Introduction

The Rogers Commission's report on the space shuttle Challenger accident concluded that there was a "serious flaw in the decision making process" that led to the disastrous launch of the shuttle on January 28, 1986; it also found management practices "at odds with" the need for NASA's Marshall Space Flight Center "to function as part of a system . . . communicating with the other parts of the system" (Presidential Commission 1:104). Misunderstanding and miscommunication, in other words, were found to be contributing causes of the accident.

Earlier, the Nuclear Regulatory Commission's report on the accident at Three Mile Island found that a "breakdown of communications" and "crucial misunderstanding" within Babcock & Wilcox, the manufacturer of the nuclear reactor involved, were precursor events to that disaster (Rogovin and Frampton, 161). One of the documents under examination by the commission was later called a $2.5 billion memorandum (*ADE Bulletin*).

Both these technological disasters involved failures of communication among ordinary professional people, mistakes committed in the course

Carl G. Herndl, Barbara A. Fennell, and Carolyn R. Miller

of routine work on the job, small mishaps with grotesque consequences. Enormous amounts of routine communication are done unthinkingly every day by large numbers of professional people; most of it disappears into the files and remains unremarked and unexamined by scholars interested in professional communication. But disaster makes otherwise routine and invisible communication accessible, and disaster makes the study of it compelling. We propose here, not to account for these communication failures in any comprehensive way, but to use them to investigate the relationship between communication and social structures.

This focus derives from earlier work by one of us suggesting that the linguistic behavior of professionals in large organizations is in part shaped by their group affiliation, specifically, that technical people tend to distinguish themselves from managers linguistically by preferring certain structures in their writing (superfluous nominalizations and narratives), even after demonstrating themselves capable of recognizing and using other structures preferred by managers (Brown and Herndl). The notion that subgroups within an organization may be differentiated not only by their work relationships but also by the way they use language suggests a possible reason for miscommunication within such an organization. Communication failures may be caused, at least in part, by the differentiation of discourse along the lines of social structure.

Bureaucratic organizations are richly differentiated social structures, subdivided into functional, geographical, and hierarchical subgroups. Members of organizations talk in ways that suggest that the divisions are real to them, not just fictions of the organization chart; they designate other groups as "the people across the street," or "those folks on the other side of the building"; they personify functional names and hierarchical relationships: "accounting won't like this"; "better send this one up to the big shots." However, little previous research examines whether patterns of language use in organizations reflect the social structure. The work that has been done focuses on the ways language within such an organization differs from the language of the general environment: Agar, for example, reviews the different patterns of discourse used by representatives of an institution (such as a court or health clinic) and clients seeking the institution's services; Redish has studied the way government agencies communicate with their publics; White discusses how legal discourse affects nonlawyers.

In order to develop methods for studying discourse *within* large organizations, we wanted to cast as wide a net as possible. In fact, we were motivated to conduct a multidisciplinary study when we realized that several disciplines have developed similar ways of conceptualizing the relationship between social structure and discourse: sociolinguistics posits the "speech community," literary theory the "interpretive community," organizational communication the "clique," argument theory the "argument field." Our study, therefore, uses several types of analysis to explore whether the discourse behind the disasters might be differentiated along the lines of social (organizational) structure and whether various discourse features will show differences corresponding to the organizational sources of the discourse. We focus particularly on formal linguistic analysis, pragmatic analysis, and argument analysis.

Communication Failure and the Three Mile Island Accident

In November 1977, roughly eighteen months before the March 1979 accident at Three Mile Island (TMI), an engineer and a manager at Babcock & Wilcox, the builder of the reactor at TMI, proposed changes in the reactor operating instructions that might well have prevented the accident. But the changes were not adopted and disseminated to reactor operators until after the accident. In testimony before the President's Commission on the Accident at Three Mile Island, the manager said, "Had my instructions been followed at TMI-II, we would not have had core damage; we would have had a minor incident" (Mathes, 1).

J. C. Mathes has written extensively on the communication problems at Babcock & Wilcox that delayed action on the proposed changes in the instructions, and our work is greatly indebted to the information he has made available. The problems we analyze here involve five memos exchanged between the Engineering branch and the Nuclear Services branch at Babcock & Wilcox. The memos are reproduced within this chapter, as figures 12.1–12.5. The sequence was as follows:

November 1, 1977: Kelly, Engineering, to "distribution," requesting discussion of new operating instructions he proposed on the basis of his investigation of an "event" at the Babcock & Wilcox reactor in Toledo, Ohio;

November 10, 1977: Walters, Nuclear Services, to Kelly, denying the need to change the instructions;

February 9, 1978: Dunn, Engineering, to Taylor, Engineering, recommending new operating procedures slightly different from those of Kelly;

February 16, 1978: Dunn, Engineering, to Taylor, Engineering, revising the recommendations of the previous memo on the basis of discussion with a person in Nuclear Services;

Carl G. Herndl, Barbara A. Fennell, and Carolyn R. Miller

August 3, 1978: Hallman, Nuclear Services (actually written by
   Walters and signed by Hallman) to Karrasch, Engineering,
   requesting that Karrasch's department resolve the disagreement
   between Hallman's group in Nuclear Services and Dunn in
   Engineering about the proposed instructions.

Dunn testified that he thought the issue had been resolved after his
February 16 memo and that the new operating instructions had been issued
(Mathes, 83). He did not recall receiving Hallman's memo, although he
is on the distribution list. Karrasch testified that he thought the Hallman
memo raised "rather routine questions" and delegated someone in his unit
to "follow up and take any appropriate action" (quoted in Mathes, 125,
128). Thus, no action had been taken by March 28, 1979, when a reactor
"event" similar to the one at Toledo occurred at Three Mile Island; the
major difference was that the Toledo reactor had been operating at low
power and the TMI unit was at 97 percent power. In trying to understand
this communication failure, we will first review the organizational communication analysis Mathes offers and then examine the formal linguistic
features of the memos themselves, analyze the pragmatics of two of the
memos, and finally compare the arguments used by the Engineering branch
with those used by the Nuclear Services branch.

MATHES' ORGANIZATIONAL ANALYSIS

Mathes' analysis of the communication failure at Babcock & Wilcox blames
"the system rather than the individual" (14) and makes a strong causal
attribution: "Ineffective management communication procedures and practices caused the communication failure that culminated in the accident at
Three Mile Island" (23). He identifies several such procedures concerning
the organization as a communication environment. First, the communication networks did not correspond to the lines of authority for decision
making. This problem shows up concretely in the distribution of several
of the memos: Kelly sent his to a distribution list, failing to identify a
primary decision maker (Mathes, 65–66); Dunn distributed "almost exclusively" in Engineering a memo requesting action that would have to
be taken within Nuclear Services (25). Mathes also questions Kelly's decision to sign the memo he sent; as a low-ranking engineer, Kelly may not
have had sufficient status to gain the attention of managers in other departments (62). A second inefficient procedure is the treatment of the
communication process as informational rather than decision making; thus,
both Kelly and Walters present "thoughts" but do not overtly recommend
or reject anything (27–28). A third inefficiency that Mathes identifies is
the lack of adequate feedback. Walters addressed only Kelly in his re-

sponse, but the others on Kelly's distribution list received nothing; Dunn received no feedback on his second memo and therefore assumed his recommendations had been accepted (28). A fourth problem is the mixture of formal and informal, written and oral modes of communication: Walters' memo is handwritten; Karrasch responded to Hallman's memo seven months later in a conversation at the office water cooler, a conversation that puzzled Hallman, who was unable to reach Karrasch for clarification before the TMI accident (29).

This analysis identifies important ways in which communication patterns do not correspond to the organizational structure at Babcock & Wilcox. Its focus on procedures and practices, however, on issues of communication structure (such as media and dissemination) at the expense of linguistic and rhetorical ones, takes us only part way toward understanding the relationship between social structure and discourse and, we believe, only part way toward understanding the nature of this particular failure. Mathes' "rational" ideal of management communication (54), with efficiency as the central criterion, in effect ignores the social influences on language use. Our movement in what follows is analogous to the general movement now going on in organizational communication studies, from structural and quantitative to interpretive and qualitative work (Putnam). Although both types of research assume that communication and social order are related, and further that communication helps create that order, the traditional quantitative approach sees communication as defining a pattern, or constituting a mechanism for social order, but has little to say about the qualities of social order in any given case. Such quantitative studies generally assume that a text is a static message independent of its readers; miscommunication, then, is largely a problem of transmission. The interpretive approach, on the other hand, understands communication as "the *expression* of social order" (Agar, 161; emphasis ours) — that is, communication emerges from the particular qualities of a given social group and at the same time marks its existence. Interpretive research focuses on the social production of discourse. This approach assumes that discourse is not static, that meaning is constructed by readers as well as by writers, and that both activities depend on a collective set of standards for using language that is established and maintained by a self-conscious community. In this approach, miscommunication is understood to arise from differences in the discourse practices of socially distinct groups and might better be termed misunderstanding.

FORMAL LINGUISTIC ANALYSIS

A formal, sentence-level linguistic analysis of the Babcock & Wilcox memos reveals few problems in execution that might provide a basis for misunderstanding. Each writer generally used standard lexical and syntactic forms in his memos, and may, on this basis, be considered a competent user of English.

On the lexical level, the memos contain standard forms, supplemented, not surprisingly, by a number of abbreviated forms (HPI, RCS, PSIG, ESFAS) understood by the members of both the Nuclear Services and Engineering branches. There are only two marked examples of vocabulary use worthy of mention. The first is from the Walters memo and involves the use of *relief* as a verb, not a noun:

> Also will the code and electromagnetic valves relief water (via steam) at significant flow rate to keep the RCS from being hydroed.

The second is from the last sentence of the first Dunn memo, which uses the nominal derivative *core uncovery* from the verb phrase "to uncover the core":

> Had this event occurred in a reactor at full power with other than insignificant burnup it is quite possible, perhaps probable, that core uncovery and possible fuel damage would have resulted.

Syntactically there are few remarkable differences from standard forms in any of the memos. One exception to this general observation is in the following sentence from the first Dunn memo, which is syntactically faulty, since the *that*-clause either contains no overt subject or has a superfluous *during*:

> Such conditions guarantee full system capacity and thus assure that during any follow on transient would be no worse than the initial accident.

There is no evidence elsewhere in Dunn's writing to suggest that this is anything other than a fleeting error, however, and on the whole this memo, like all the others, demonstrates sufficient parallelism, textual cohesion, and syntactic complexity to suggest that the writer is fully competent on the formal linguistic level.

The Walters memo represents an exception to a number of the preceding observations in that it contains several errors of linguistic form. For example:

> *redundancy:* My assumption and the training assumes . . .
> *imperfect parallelism:* In talking with training personnel and in the opinion of the writer the operators at Toledo responded in the correct manner . . .
> *absence of essential punctuation:* If you intended to go solid

what about problems with vessel mechanics. Also will the
code and electromagnetic valves relief water (via steam) at a
significant flow rate to keep the RCS from being hydroed.
faulty logical progression in a conditional: If this is the intent of
your letter and the thoughts behind it, then the operators
are not taught to hydro the RCS everytime the HPI pump is
initiated.

Unlike the other four memos, the Walters memo was handwritten, rather
than typed, and the errors in linguistic form are indicative of a style of
communication closer to spontaneous speech. While they are undeniably
nonstandard features, they do not point to any systemic differences corresponding to social structure, and they do not seem sufficient to cause
misunderstanding. At most, they indicate that Walters was writing in a
different register. This brief analysis of surface linguistic form indicates
that the source of the communication failure does not lie in formal linguistic features and suggests that within this organization, at least, such
features do not distinguish social groups.

PRAGMATIC ANALYSIS

Pragmatic analysis considers more directly than formal linguistic analysis
the ways in which social differentiation shapes discourse. Like the linguistic analysis, it suggests that the writers at Babcock & Wilcox understood
one another, but it further suggests that their concern for social issues
(questions of authority and public status) interfered with the recognition
of the technical problem that was ostensibly at issue. As socially situated discourse, the exchange of memos ceases to be a purely technical
debate.

Although current definitions of pragmatics and the scope of pragmatic
analysis vary widely, the various branches of pragmatics all attempt to
account for the ways in which the meaning of a speaker's utterance depends on the context in which it is used (Levinson). Such knowledge allows speakers to determine what speech acts are appropriate to their
position or status and to exploit communicative conventions to "say"
things which are not directly recoverable from their sentences taken out
of context, as in sentence-level linguistic analysis. This knowledge allows
speakers to match the self-representation implied in their speech to their
understanding of the situation and to predict what inferences listeners or
readers will draw from their utterance. The notion of "context" in such
descriptions is always troublingly vague, but it is generally used to refer
to the "social and psychological world in which the language user operates at any given time" (Ochs and Schieffelin, 1). The essential elements

Carl G. Herndl, Barbara A. Fennell, and Carolyn R. Miller

of this context would include the social role and status of both speaker and listener, the temporal and physical location of both parties, the formality and style conventionally associated with a written or spoken text, and a knowledge of the subject matter (Lyons).

The interchange between Kelly and Walters (figures 12.1 and 12.2) is the clearest example of pragmatic negotiations in this situation. Kelly's memo is addressed to a distribution list of seven Babcock & Wilcox managers, five in the Engineering branch in which he works, and two in the Nuclear Services branch. The memo identifies an incident at the Toledo reactor that could have been disastrous and suggests revisions in the operating instructions to prevent any recurrence. Given the normal assumption that operating instructions should provide safe procedures rather than cause an accident, Kelly's memo constitutes an implied criticism of the Nuclear Services branch, which is responsible for training operators and writing operating instructions. As a result, Kelly couches his memo as a request for response, sacrificing propositional clarity for political expediency.

Kelly's memo shows a sharp distinction between the opening material addressed to his Babcock & Wilcox readers and the indented passage intended as an instruction to reactor operators. In the opening section, he hedges his criticism in several ways. He assigns agency not to any employee but to the two events in Toledo: "Two recent events at the Toledo site have pointed out . . ." He hedges the implicit accusation that the company is not instructing clients properly by inserting "perhaps" and by referring to "guidance" rather than instruction (one who guides bears less responsibility than one who instructs or orders). Furthermore, he includes himself in the group he accuses of failure; "perhaps *we* are not giving enough guidance . . ." (emphasis added). When he addresses the company's responsibility again in the next paragraph, his hedges are even more elaborate. He does not adopt an assertive voice but merely "wonders" what "guidance, if any" the company should provide. Rather than assert that they should make corrections, he couches his comment as an indirect question. The "if any" here denies the urgency he has just established in the preceding paragraph. His closing is equally mitigated. He disowns the indirect assertion that something must be done by characterizing his memo as a request merely for his readers' "thoughts," and refers to this as a "subject" rather than asserting the more threatening possibility that it is a "problem."

But Kelly's description of the event and the proposed instructions to the reactor operator demonstrate that he is also capable of very direct speech acts. When he describes the event, he is not directing anyone or challenging anyone's competence. The description is direct, agency is clearly marked, and lexical cues such as "as a result" and "even though"

Understanding Failures in Organizational Discourse

```
THE BABCOCK & WILCOX COMPANY
POWER GENERATION GROUP

To      Distribution

From    J.J. Kelly, Plant Integration

Cust.   Generic                 Date  November 1, 1977

Subj.   Customer Guidance on High Pressure Injection Operation
```

```
                        DISTRIBUTION

        B.A. Karrasch              D.W. LaBelle
        E.W. Swanson               N.S. Elliott
        R.J. Finnin                D.F. Hallman
        B.M. Dunn
```

Two recent events at the Toledo site have pointed out that perhaps we are not giving our customers enough guidance on the operation of the high pressure injection system. On September 24, 1977, after depressurizing due to a stuck open electromatic relief valve, high pressure injection was automatically initiated. The operator stopped HPI when pressurizer level began to recover, without regard to primary pressure. As a result, the transient continued on with boiling in the RCS, etc. In a similar occurrence on October 23, 1977, the operator bypassed high pressure injection to prevent initiation, even though reactor coolant system pressure went below the actuation point.

Since there are accidents which require the continuous operation of the high pressure injection system, I wonder what guidance, if any, we should be giving to our customers on when they can safely shut the system down following an accident? I recommend the following guidelines be sent:

    a) Do not bypass or otherwise prevent the actuation of high/low pressure injection under <u>any</u> conditions except a normal, controlled plant shutdown.

    b) Once high/low pressure injection is initiated, do not stop it unless: T_{ave} is stable or decreasing <u>and</u> pressurizer level is increasing <u>and</u> primary pressure is at least 1600 PSIG and increasing.

I would appreciate your thoughts on this subject.
JJK: jl

Fig. 12.1. The Kelly memorandum (retyped)

reinforce the description. The indented instructions are even more forceful. The first opens with "Do not," a prohibition, which is one of the strongest possible speech acts. Even the indentation decontextualizes the items and emphasizes their authority. The contrasting styles here are evidence that the pattern of indirection and mitigation in the memo is deter-

Carl G. Herndl, Barbara A. Fennell, and Carolyn R. Miller

```
MEMORANDUM           THE BABCOCK & WILCOX COMPANY

To    J.J. Kelly, Plant Integration

From  J.F. Walters, Nuclear Service

Cust. TOLEDO                    Date   November 10, 1977

Subj. High Pressure Injection during transient

Ref.  Your letter to DISTRIBUTION; Same Subject
      Dated NOV 1, 1977.
```

In talking with training personnel and in the opinion of this writer the operators at Toledo responded in the correct manner considering how they have been trained and the reasons behind this training.

My assumption and the training assumes first that RC Pressure and Pressurizer Level will trend in the same direction under a LOCA. For a small leak they keep the HP system on up to a certain flow to maintain Pressure Level.

In the particular case at Toledo, there was no LOCA of magnitude and with the small leak the inventory in the system came back as expected but due to the recovery of the RCS the RCS pressure cannot respond any quicker than the pressurizer heaters can heat the cold water now pushed back into the pressurizer. Leaving the H.P.I. system on after Pressurizer Level indicator is listed high, will result in the RCS pressure increasing and essentially hydroing the RCS when it becomes solid. If this is the intent of your letter and the thoughts behind it, then the operators are not taught to hydro the RCS everytime the HPI pump is initiated.

If you intend to go solid what about problems with vessel mechanics. Also will the code and electromagnetic valves relief water (via steam) at significant flow rate to keep the RCS from being hydroed.

```
cc. R.J. FINNIN
```

Fig. 12.2. The Walters memorandum (retyped; original handwritten)

mined by the difference in power or community affiliation between speaker and hearer. When Kelly addresses other members of the company he exercises considerable tact. When he adopts the authority of the company instructing a client he drops all mitigation and indirection.

If we look at Walters' response, it is clear that he recognizes the criticism implicit in Kelly's memo. Walters, a supervisor in Nuclear Services, openly defends the operators' actions and Nuclear Services' instructions. In the second paragraph, Walters asserts his personal support for the policy by identifying his position with the policy: "my assumption and the training assumes." At the end of the third paragraph his response ridicules Kelly. In this paragraph, Walters describes a hypothetical chain of events that could follow from Kelly's instructions and argues that Kelly's procedure would lead to "hydroing the RCS when it becomes solid," that is, it would pump dangerously excessive amounts of water into the reactor coolant system (RCS). Even the form of his response is an implied criticism: he says, "If this is the intent of your letter and the thought behind it, then the operators are not taught to hydro the RCS [reactor coolant system] every time the HPI [High Pressure Injection] pump is initiated." This response is doubly critical. By breaking the semantic continuity of the if-then conditional and asserting the obvious—that the operators are not told to overload the system—Walters implies that Kelly's recommendation is not just wrong but absurd. Walters' explicit reference to the "intent and the thoughts behind" the memo announces that he recognizes the criticism implicit in the memo despite Kelly's indirection. In doing so, he not only questions Kelly's knowledge of the training procedures and his right to criticize Nuclear Services' policy, he also underscores the sarcasm in his own response.

This analysis suggests that Walters and Kelly have engaged in a clearly understood, albeit indirect, exchange over their respective responsibilities and competence. Both writers recognize the importance of the technical problem, but it has become part of a negotiation of their social status and their relative institutional positions. One reason why Kelly's memo did not make Nuclear Services rethink its instructions, one reason it "failed," is that Walters may have been too concerned with the public criticism implicit in Kelly's memo, mitigated though it was. He responds to the political threat rather than to the technical problem. The technical disagreement about the safety of the operating instructions is superseded by the concern for public status between members of two different organizational groups.

Although Mathes says that Kelly failed to define his purpose clearly, that he wasn't direct enough, our analysis suggests that Walters thought Kelly was too direct. Because he is an outsider, Kelly presents his memo as an exchange of information rather than as an attempt to influence Nuclear Services' decision making. This social reality limits Kelly's rhetorical options. Mathes' "rational" ideal of management communication would seem to deny that public status and face are negotiated through communication (54). It assumes writers who already know who the decision makers really are (which is not always apparent, even to the decision makers themselves, as Mathes' analysis itself shows), and it assumes recipients who are immune to criticism and threats to their competence and

Carl G. Herndl, Barbara A. Fennell, and Carolyn R. Miller

status. Our pragmatic analysis suggests that this exchange reflects a conflict between social groups rather than flaws in a communication structure. We thus find evidence that discourse reflects not only the existence of social structure but something of the quality of the social relationships it creates. We cannot claim, however, that this causes the participants to misunderstand each other, since they are clearly using the same pragmatic strategies to negotiate their differences. The discourse acknowledges social differentiation but is not itself differentiated.

ARGUMENT ANALYSIS

The argumentative shape of the five Babcock & Wilcox memos provides further information about the nature of their "failure." The analysis below is based on Stephen Toulmin's approach to argument, both on his model for the structure of arguments and on his notion that arguments may be said to belong to a variety of *fields*. According to Toulmin, an argument may be described not so much as a logical or syllogistic structure but as a movement from data (or grounds) to a claim (or conclusion) by means of a warrant, that is, a conceptual connection that is acceptable to those who find the argument sound or convincing. Since the universal standards of logic are not applicable to practical argumentation, according to Toulmin, successful arguments may exhibit considerable variety in the kinds of data, warrants, and claims they use. He accounts for this variety by postulating that arguments belong to "fields." As he develops the notion of field, it includes both cognitive (or semantic) and social dimensions. In *An Introduction to Reasoning*, Toulmin and his coauthors characterize arguments in the fields of law, science, management, arts, and ethics on the basis of what kinds of issues are argued, what kinds of claims are typically made, what kinds of data are offered, and what kinds of reasons (or warrants) are offered as authorizing the connection between data and claim. For example, warrants in science include "mathematical formulas, computer programs, diagrams, graphs, physical models, laws of nature, historical regularities" (250), and those in management primarily focus on profit and survival of the company, although they also include authority, practicality, efficiency, and analogy (301–2). The argument field, therefore, combining as it does sociological and cognitive aspects of argument, serves to connect social structure and language use. It leads us to expect that arguments originating in and used by different social groups will differ and that the differences will be significant, not superficial — that they will indicate different beliefs, commitments, and frameworks of knowledge, which are manifested in differing sorts of data, warrants, and claims.

Understanding Failures in Organizational Discourse

If we divide the five memos into two groups, three from the Engineering branch (Kelly's memo and the two Dunn memos, figures 12.1, 12.3, and 12.4) and two from the Nuclear Services branch (the Walters and Hallman memos, figures 12.2 and 12.5), we can examine the memos within each branch to see what kinds of claims, data, and warrants are used and whether they are distinct from those of the other branch. Our reading of the five memos suggests that in fact the argumentative structures of the memos from Engineering are more similar to each other than they are to those from Nuclear Services, and vice versa: Engineering seems more willing to consider changes based on analysis of recent events, while Nuclear Services relies on established procedures to minimize changes. The data upon which the Engineering memos rely are the details of the incidents at the Toledo plant, what the operators did and what the consequences were (Kelly, paragraph 1; Dunn 1, paragraph 2). The data in the Nuclear Services memos are circumstances within Babcock & Wilcox itself — the nature of the training provided to operators and the internal difference of opinion about what instructions should be given to operators (Walters, paragraph 2; Hallman, paragraphs 2 and 3). All three of the Engineering memos make essentially the same claim — that the instructions should be changed. The Nuclear Services claims are less univocal, but they are all concerned with organizational procedures within Babcock & Wilcox (the operators responded correctly [Walters, paragraph 1], we're holding up the changes because of our concerns [Hallman, paragraph 4], Plant Integration should resolve the disagreement [Hallman, paragraph 5]). Most interestingly, the warrants, or reasons offered for the claims, indicate different ways of thinking about problems. In the Engineering memos, the warrants are based on generalizations from past facts — that if something has happened in the past it may happen again, and that under changed circumstances it may result in worse consequences. The warrants in the Nuclear Services memos have to do with the dangers of "going solid" (as opposed to the dangers of uncovering the reactor core) and with an unstated understanding about how disagreements within the organization should get resolved.

In general, the arguments from the Engineering branch seem to rely on analysis of new events — the unexpected incidents at the Toledo plant, the actions of the operators during those incidents, and extrapolation to circumstances in which the actions of the operators might have much more serious consequences (it is the fulfillment of this extrapolation in the Three Mile Island accident that makes this series of memos of more than routine interest). In contrast, the arguments from the Nuclear Services branch seem to rely on prior organizational commitments — to the training already given the operators, to the assumption behind the training that "going solid" is

Carl G. Herndl, Barbara A. Fennell, and Carolyn R. Miller

THE BABCOCK & WILCOX COMPANY
POWER GENERATION GROUP

To   Jim Taylor, Manager, Licensing

From   Bert M. Dunn, Manager, ECCS Analysis (2138)

Cust.   Date   February 9, 1978

Subj.   Operator Interruption of High Pressure Injection

This memo addresses a serious concern with in ECCS Analysis about the potential for operator action to terminate high pressure injection following the initial stage of a LOCA. Successful ECCS operation during small breaks depends on the accumulated reactor coolant system inventory as well as the ECCS injection rate. As such, it is mandatory that full injection flow be maintained from the point of emergency safety features actuation system (ESFAS) actuation until the high pressure injection rate can fully compensate for the reactor heat load. As the injection rate depends on the reactor coolant system pressure, the time at which a compensating match-up occurs is variable and cannot be specified as a fixed number. It is quite possible, for example, that the high pressure injection may successfully match up with all heat sources at time t and that due to system pressurization be inadequate at some later time t2.

The direct concern here rose out of the recent incident at Toledo. During the accident the operator terminated high pressure injection due to an apparent system recovery indicated by high level within the pressurizer. This action would be acceptable only after the primary system had been in a subcooled state. Analysis of the data from the transient currently indicates that the system was in a two-phase state and as such did not contain sufficient capacity to allow high pressure injection termination. This became evident at some 20 to 30 minutes following termination of injection when the pressurizer level again collapsed and injection had to be reinitiated. During the 20 to 30 minutes of noninjection flow they were continuously losing important fluid inventory even though the pressurizer was at an extremely low power and extremely low burnup. Had this event occurred in a reactor at full power with other than insignificant burnup it is quite possible, perhaps probable, that core uncovery and possible fuel damage would have resulted.

The incident points out that we have not supplied sufficient information to reactor operators in the area of recovery from LOCA. The following rule is based on an attempt to allow termination of high pressure injection only at a time when the reactor coolant system is in a subcooled state and the pressurizer is indicating at least a normal level for small breaks. Such conditions guarantee full system capacity and thus assure that during any follow on transient would be no worse than the initial accident. I, therefore, recommend that operating procedures be written to allow for termination of high pressure injection under the following two conditions only:

1. Low pressure injection has been actuated and is flowing at a rate in excess of the high pressure injection capability and that situation has been stable for a period of time (10 minutes).

2. System pressure has recovered to normal operating pressure (2200 or 2250 psig) and system temperature within the hot leg is less than or equal to the normal operating condition (605 F or 630 F).

I believe this is a very serious matter and deserves our prompt attention and correction.

BMD/lc

cc: E.W. Swanson
      D.H. Roy
      B.A. Karrasch
      H.A. Bailey
      J. Kelly
      E.R. Kane
      J.D. Agar
      R.L. Pittman
      J.D. Phinny
      T. Scott

Fig. 12.3. The first Dunn memorandum (retyped 2 pages)

the most serious potential effect of the types of reactor incidents under discussion, to existing organizational procedures for resolving disputes. Nuclear Services, in a word, is committed to the *maintenance* of an interpretive framework, a framework that it is responsible for disseminating to customers and operators. Engineering is committed to the *explanation* of new data that do not fit the existing interpretive framework.

The difference between these two sets of commitments reflects the difference between the two social groups involved: not only does the formal structure of the organization correspond to the different argumentative commitments, but the differences in argument are consistent with the different organizational functions of the two groups. The differentiated social relations and tasks of the two branches may in fact lead to differentiated conceptual frameworks — sets of shared beliefs, concepts, and purposes that reflect and enhance the social differences. Such differences do not, of course, make the discourse of the two branches mutually incomprehensible, but they do make arguments difficult to resolve. Such differences seem to us likely to have contributed to the failure of communication at Babcock & Wilcox.

Our three analyses of the substance of this communication supplement the procedural perspective of traditional organizational communication studies. Linguistic analysis shows that the failure is not a matter of the basic competence of the writers. Pragmatic analysis demonstrates that Kelly's indirection is not a failure but a consequence of the social context within which he functions. And argument analysis suggests that there are important differences in the ways social groups define problems and construct arguments. Even with ideal communication environment and pro-

Carl G. Herndl, Barbara A. Fennell, and Carolyn R. Miller

THE BABCOCK & WILCOX COMPANY
POWER GENERATION GROUP

To   Jim Taylor, Manager, Licensing

From   Bert M. Dunn, Manager, ECCS Analysis (2138)

Cust.   Date   February 16, 1978

Subj. Operator Interruption of High Pressure Injection

In review of my earlier memo on this subject, dated February 9, 1978,
Field Service has recommended the following procedure for terminating
high pressure injection following a LOCA.

1. Low pressure injection has been actuated and is flowing at a rate in
    excess of the high pressure injection capability and that situation
    has been stable for a period of time (10 minutes). Same as
    previously stated.

2. At X minutes following the initiation of high pressure injection,
    termination is allowed provided the hot leg temperature indication
    plus appropriate instrument error is more than 50 F below the
    saturation temperature corresponding to the reactor coolant system
    pressure less instrument error. X is a time lag to prevent the
    termination of the high pressure injection immediately following its
    initiation. It requires further work to define its specific value,
    but it is probable that 10 minutes will be adequate. The need for
    the delay is that normal operating conditions are within the above
    criteria and thus it is conceivable that the high pressure injection
    would be terminated during the initial phase of a small LOCA.

I find that this scheme is acceptable from the standpoint of preventing
adverse long range problems and is easier to implement. Therefore, I
wish to modify the procedure requested in my first memo to the one
identified here.

cc: E.W. Swanson
       D.H. Roy
       B.A. Karrasch
       H.A. Bailey
       J. Kelly
       E.R. Kane
       J.D. Agar
       R.L. Pittman
       J.D. Phinny
       T. Scott

Fig. 12.4. The second Dunn memorandum (retyped)

cedures, these substantive differences can make it difficult for members
of one group to persuade members of another. However, we do not want
to press the significance of this single case too far. We recognize that
thorough ethnographic data might expand this analysis and elaborate our
sketch of the differentiation of discourse among social groups, but this

Understanding Failures in Organizational Discourse

```
BABCOCK & WILCOX COMPANY              cc:   E.R. Kane
POWER GENERATION GROUP                      J.D. Phinney
                                            B.W. Street
                                            B.M. Dunn
                                            J.F. Walters

To       B.A. Karrasch, Manager, Plant Integration

From     D.F. Hallman, Manager, Plant Performance Services

Cust.                           Date     August 3, 1978

Subj.    Operator Interruption of High Pressure Injection (HPI)
```

References: (1) B.M. Dunn to J. Taylor, same subject,
                  Feb. 9, 1978
             (2) B.M. Dunn to J. Taylor, same subject,
                  Feb. 16, 1978

References 1 and 2 (attached) recommend a change in B&W's philosophy for HPI system use during low-pressure transients. Basically, they recommend leaving the HPI pumps on, once HPI has been initiated, until it can be determined that the hot leg temperature is more than 50 F below T_{sat} for the RCS pressure.

Nuclear Service believes this mode can cause the RCS (including the pressurizer) to go solid. The pressurizer reliefs will lift, with a water surge through the discharge piping into the quench tank.

We believe the following incidents should be evaluated:

1. If the pressurizer goes solid with one or more HPI pumps continuing to operate, would there be a pressure spike before the reliefs open which could cause damage to the RCS?

2. What damage would the water surge through the relief valve discharge piping and quench tanks cause?

To date, Nuclear Service has not notified our operating plants to change HPI policy consistent with References 1 and 2 because of our above-stated questions. Yet, the references suggest the possibility of uncovering the core if present HPI policy is continued.

We request that Integration resolve the issue of how the HPI system should be used. We are available to help as needed.

                                 D.F. Hallman

DFH/feh
Attachments

Fig. 12.5. The Hallman memorandum (retyped)

material is not available. Thus, our conclusions here must be taken as suggestive. In the next section we attempt to reinforce them by adapting our methods to the analysis of another communication failure.

Carl G. Herndl, Barbara A. Fennell, and Carolyn R. Miller

Communication Failure and
the Challenger Accident

The Presidential Commission that investigated the explosion of the space shuttle Challenger in January 1986 published a five-volume report that includes transcripts of the hearings it conducted and copies of many documents from NASA and Morton Thiokol. While this is a rich body of data, it has two weaknesses for our purposes: first, among the written texts made available there are no continued, focused interactions between groups or organizations about a single issue (like the Babcock & Wilcox memos); and second, all the oral interactions are recollected under questioning, sometimes many months after the fact. Nonetheless, this material does benefit from an analysis that builds on our conclusions from the Three Mile Island material. In both of the incidents we discuss below, argument analysis of the substantive elements of discourse — warrants and evidence — describes one way in which discourse reflects social differentiation within organizations and explains how such differences limit the ability of writers and speakers to communicate and direct decision making.

The first incident we take up involves a pair of memos written at NASA headquarters; they were prepared independently, in two different offices, but at roughly the same time, the July before the accident. Both reacted to the growing awareness at NASA that the "O-ring" seals in the solid rocket motors manufactured by Morton Thiokol in Utah were occasionally eroding during flight. (These memos are reproduced in figures 12.6 and 12.7.) The first memo was written by Richard Cook, a budget analyst at NASA's Washington headquarters, who had been at NASA only a few weeks. The second was written by Irving Davids, an engineer with the Shuttle Propulsion Division at NASA headquarters, who had been at NASA for 35 years. A formal linguistic analysis of the Cook and Davids memos reveals little evidence of deviation from standard written language. There are minor differences on the lexical, morphological, orthographic, and syntactic levels, but they do not interfere with readers' comprehension of the memos.

An analysis of the argument structure of these memos at first shows no clear differences between the writers. Both claim that the O-rings are a major problem, both locate their grounds in the writer's discussion with engineers, and both rely on the warrant that engineers are qualified to speak on this topic. But despite their similar argument structures, these memos appear to have been received quite differently, judging by the way NASA managers described Cook and Davids at the Rogers Commission hearings. Cook is described by a Deputy Associate Administrator at NASA

MEMORANDUM   7/23/85

TO: BRC/M. Mann

FROM: BRC/R. Cook

SUBJECT: Problem with SRB Seals

Earlier this week you asked me to investigate reported problems with the charring
of seals between SRB motor segments during flight operations. Discussions with
program engineers show this to be a potentially major problem affecting both
flight safety and program costs.

Presently three seals between SRB segments use double O-rings sealed with putty.
In recent Shuttle flights, charring of these rings has occurred. The O-rings are
designed so that if one fails, the other will hold against the pressure of
firing. However, at least in the joint between the nozzle and the aft segment,
not only has the first O-ring been destroyed, but the second has been partially
eaten away.

Engineers have not yet determined the cause of the problem. Candidates include
the use of a new type of putty (the putty formerly in use was removed from the
market by EPA because it contained asbestos), failure of the second ring to slip
into the groove which must engage it for it to work properly, or new, and as yet
unidentified, assembly procedures at Thiokol. MSC is trying to identify the
cause of the problem, including on-site investigation at Thiokol, and OSF hopes
to have some results from their analysis within 30 days. There is little
question, however, that flight safety has been and is still being compromised by
potential failure of the seals, and it is acknowledged that failure during launch
would certainly be catastrophic. There is also indication that staff personnel
knew of this problem sometime in advance of management's becoming apprised of
what was going on.

The potential impact of the problem depends on the as yet undiscovered cause. If
the cause is minor, there would be little or no impact on budget or flight rate.
A worse case scenario, however, would lead to the suspension of Shuttle flights,
redesign of the SRB, and scrapping of existing stockpiled hardware. The impact
on the FY 1987-8 budget could be immense.

It should be pointed out that Code M management is viewing the situation with the
utmost seriousness. From a budgetary standpoint, I would think that any NASA
budget submitted this year for FY 1987 and beyond should certainly be based on a
reliable judgment as to the cause of the SRB seal problem and a corresponding
decision as to budgetary action needed to provide for its solution.

                         Richard C. Cook
                         Program Analyst

                         Michael B. Mann
                         Chief, STS Resources Analysis Branch

                         Gary B. Allison
                         Director, Resources Analysis Division

                         Tom Newman
                         Comptroller

Fig. 12.6. The Cook memorandum. Reproduced from Presidential Commission 4: 391–92

Carl G. Herndl, Barbara A. Fennell, and Carolyn R. Miller

NASA
National Aeronautics and
Space Administration

Washington, D.C.
20646

Jul 17 1985

MPS.

TO: M/Associate Administrator for Space Flight

FROM: MPS/Irv Davids

SUBJECT: Case to Case and Nozzle to Case "O" Ring Seal Erosion
          Problems

As a result of the problems being incurred during flight on both case to
case and nozzle to case "O" ring erosion, Mr. Hamby and I visited MSFC
on July 11, 1985, to discuss this issue with both project and S&E personnel.
Following are some important factors concerning these problems:

A. <u>Nozzle to Case "O" ring erosion</u>
There have been twelve (12) instances during flight where there have been
some primary "O" ring erosion. In one specific case there was also erosion
of the secondary "O" ring seal. There were two (2) primary "O" ring seals that
were heat affected (no erosion) and two (2) cases in which soot blew by the
primary seals.

The prime suspect as the cause for the erosion on the primary "O" ring seals
is the type of putty used. It is Thiokol's position that during assembly,
leak check, or ignition, a hole can be formed through the putty which
initiates "O" ring erosion due to a jetting effect. It is important to note
that after STS-10, the manufacturer of the putty went out of business and a
new putty manufacturer was contracted. The new putty is believed to be
more susceptible to environmental effects such as moisture which makes the
putty more tacky.

There are various options being considered such as removal of putty, varying
the putty configuration to prevent the jetting effect, use of a putty made by
a Canadian Manufacturer which includes asbestos, and various combinations of
putty and grease. Thermal analysis and/or tests are underway to assess
these options.

Thiokol is seriously considering the deletion of putty on the QM-5 nozzle/case
joint since they believe the putty is the prime cause of the erosion. A
decision on this change is planned to be made this week. I have reservations
about doing it, considering the significance of the QM-5 firing in qualifying the
FWC for flight.

It is important to note that the cause and effect of the putty varies. There
are some MSFC personnel who are not convinced that the holes in the putty
are the source of the problem but feel that it may be a reverse effect in
that the hot gases may be leaking through the seal and causing the hole track in
the putty.

Considering the fact that there doesn't appear to be a validated resolution
as to the effect of the putty, I would certainly question the wisdom of
removing it on QM-5.

B.   Case to Case "O" Ring Erosion

There have been five (5) occurrences during flight where there was primary field joint "O" ring erosion. There was one case where the secondary "O" ring was heat affected with no erosion. The erosion with the field joint primary "O" rings is considered by some to be more critical than the nozzle joint due to the fact that during the pressure build up on the primary "O" ring the unpressurized field joint secondary seal unseats due to joint rotation.

The problem with the unseating of the secondary "O" ring during the joint rotation has been known for quite some time. In order to eliminate this problem on the FWC field joints a capture feature was designed which prevents the secondary seal from lifting off. During our discussions on this issue with MSFC, an action was assigned for them to identify the timing associated with the unseating of the secondary "O" ring and the seating of the primary "O" ring during rotation. How long it takes the secondary "O" ring to lift off during rotation and when in the pressure cycle it lifts are key factors in the determination of its criticality.

The present consensus is that if the primary "O" ring seats during ignition, and subsequently fails, the unseated secondary "O" ring will not serve its intended purpose as a redundant seal. However, redundancy does exist during the ignition cycle, which is the most critical time.

It is recommended that we arrange for MSFC to provide an overall briefing to you on the SRM "O" rings, including failure history, current status, and options for correcting the problems.

    Irving Davids

    cc:
    M/Mr. Weeks
    M/Mr. Hamby
    ML/Mr. Harrington
    MP/Mr. Winterhalter

Fig. 12.7. The Davids memorandum.
Reproduced from the Presidential Commission 1: 248

as "not too knowledgeable," a "young chap," "picking up things in the hallway," a "financial type person" (4:250); his memo is characterized as a "training letter" (4:398). Davids is described as "very senior and very careful," someone "who I guess we gave him his 35-year pin some time ago" (4:250). The warrant that makes the difference here is supplied by the relationship between the readers and the writer; it is the warrant of the writer's standing within the community (related to the rhetorical concept of *ethos*). In this respect, argument and pragmatic analyses are related, since both can attend to the interaction of writers and readers and specifically to questions of relative status. Cook's memo itself betrays his status as a newcomer in several ways: the lack of detailed data and quantified budget estimates, the use of nontechnical language ("eaten away" for *eroded*, "if one fails the other will hold" for *redundancy*), the lack of subheads, the mention of safety concerns in a budget memo (this last

Carl G. Herndl, Barbara A. Fennell, and Carolyn R. Miller

transgression was the subject of intense questioning by Commission Chairman Rogers and others). Cook's status as something of an outsider, a "discourse-learner," is confirmed by the fact that his memo is far more comprehensible to other outsiders (such as we are) than is Davids' memo.

Our belief that there is a warrant generated by Cook's standing within the community is similar to Mathes' claim that Kelly's position within Babcock & Wilcox contributed to the miscommunication at Three Mile Island. Mathes had questioned Kelly's decision to sign his memo on the grounds of his status within the organization. Our discussion of the Cook memo goes beyond this analysis, however, in that it isolates the textual expression of his position in the social order at NASA. Cook's position as a discourse learner leads him to construct a text which seemed to communicate to NASA management his status as a newcomer more forcefully than it communicated his concern over the O-ring issue itself. As before, argument analysis articulates the relation between the discourse and the quality of social relations.

The second incident from the Challenger material is the teleconference at which the decision to approve the launch was made the evening before the accident. It was convened at the request of the Morton Thiokol representative at NASA's Marshall Space Flight Center, who was worried that the weather was too cold to launch the shuttle safely. The teleconference participants included personnel from Morton Thiokol in Utah, NASA's Marshall Center in Alabama, and Kennedy Space Center in Florida. Some were high-level managers concerned with scheduling and making launch decisions, and some were line engineers directly responsible for designing and testing the O-ring seals. The conference lasted over two hours; after the first hour and a half, when Morton Thiokol managers were recommending a delay of the launch, NASA officials requested that Morton Thiokol reconsider their recommendation. The Morton Thiokol group then requested an off-line "caucus," which was intended to last about five minutes but which went on for about thirty. During the caucus, the engineers and managers at MTI debated whether the low temperatures in Florida would interfere with the operation of the O-ring seals. Finally, the vice-president for the booster program telefaxed to NASA a summary of the discussion with a recommendation to proceed with the launch. The debate at MTI, between engineering and management, resulted in a changed decision by management and the telefax stating and explaining that decision (figure 12.8).

The differences between management and engineering were apparent and significant to participants in the caucus as their testimony before the Rogers Commission shows. The engineers argued from extensive experience in handling the failed parts, while management argued from experi-

Understanding Failures in Organizational Discourse

MTI ASSESSMENT OF TEMPERATURE CONCERN ON SRM-25 (51L) LAUNCH

0 CALCULATIONS SHOW THAT SRM-25 O-RINGS WILL BE 20° COLDER THAN SRM-15 O-RINGS
0 TEMPERATURE DATA NOT CONCLUSIVE ON PREDICTING PRIMARY O-RING BLOW-BY
0 ENGINEERING ASSESSMENT IS THAT:

    0 COLDER O-RINGS WILL HAVE INCREASED EFFECTIVE DUROMETER ("HARDER")

    0 "HARDER" O-RINGS WILL TAKE LONGER TO "SEAT"

        0 MORE GAS MAY PASS PRIMARY O-RING BEFORE THE PRIMARY SEAL SEATS (RELATIVE TO SRM-15)

            0 DEMONSTRATED SEALING THRESHOLD IS 3 TIMES GREATER THAN 0.038" EROSION EXPERIENCED ON SRM-15

    0 IF THE PRIMARY SEAL DOES NOT SEAT, THE SECONDARY SEAL WILL SEAT

        0 PRESSURE WILL GET TO SECONDARY SEAL BEFORE THE METAL PARTS ROTATE

            0 O-RING PRESSURE LEAK CHECK PLACES SECONDARY SEAL IN OUTBOARD POSITION WHICH MINIMIZES SEALING TIME

0 MTI RECOMMENDS STS-51L LAUNCH PROCEED ON 28 JANUARY 1986

    0 SRM-25 WILL NOT BE SIGNIFICANTLY DIFFERENT FROM SRM-15

JOE C. KILMINSTER, VICE PRESIDENT
SPACE BOOSTER PROGRAMS

MORTON THIOKOL INC.
Wasatch Division

INFORMATION ON THIS PAGE WAS PREPARED TO SUPPORT AN ORAL PRESENTATION AND CANNOT BE CONSIDERED COMPLETE WITHOUT THE ORAL DISCUSSION

Fig. 12.8. The Morton Thiokol telefax.
Reproduced from Presidential Commission 4: 753

ence with flight records and program needs. During the caucus, the senior manager on the MTI end of the teleconference, Mason, told Lund, the vice-president of Engineering, to "take off his engineering hat and put on his management hat" (4:772). After much discussion, Mason conducted a poll to decide whether to change the recommendation, but he polled only management people because he knew what the opinions of the engineers were (4:765). Under commission questioning, it became apparent that the two top engineering experts disagreed with the management decision. But Mason's belief was that in the absence of conclusive engineering data, a judgment was needed and that managers were the people who make judgments (4:773).

Roger Boisjoly, the top engineering expert on the seals, argued strenuously against the management decision throughout the thirty-minute

Carl G. Herndl, Barbara A. Fennell, and Carolyn R. Miller

caucus and noted in a log made after the caucus but before the launch that "the data does exist to lead us to our engineering recommendation." He also wrote, "our management [made] the decision that it was a low risk based upon *their* assumption that temperature was not a discriminator." (He also wrote, "I sincerely hope that this launch does not result in a catastrophy [sic]" [4:684]). At one point late in the caucus, Boisjoly made a final attempt to change the minds of his managers: as he told the commission, "I tried one more time. . . . I went up and discussed the photos once again and tried to make the point that it was my opinion from actual observations that temperature was a discriminator. . . . I also stopped when it was apparent that I couldn't get anybody to listen" (4:793). He seems then to have realized that what he considered to be argumentatively compelling was quite different from what the managers would believe.

The telefax claims that the launch should proceed and warrants this claim with the statement that the launch will not be significantly different from a previous launch that had both the coldest temperature and the most charring and erosion of O-rings. The discussion had centered on just this point, what the effect would be of the expected temperature, twenty degrees colder than any previous flight. The grounds of the telefax include the statement that the temperature data are "not conclusive." Although Boisjoly couldn't "conclusively demonstrate the tie-in between temperature and blow-by [charring]" (4:675–76), he argued from his own first-hand knowledge gained in examining the physical evidence recovered from previous flights. But in the absence of what they considered to be "hard" engineering data about the future, the managers reasoned on the basis of "the only conclusive data" they had, "flight data," that is, data about past experience with shuttle launches (4:616). As Richard Feynman, one of the commission members, put it, the assumption grew that "we can lower our standards a little bit because we got away with it last time. . . . an argument is always given that the last time it worked" (5:1446). Both engineers and management were using warrants from past experience, but the nature of the experience that convinced them was different. Boisjoly reasoned from *causes* at the level of physical detail— charring and erosion of O-rings. The managers reasoned from *results* at the level of contracts and programs—successful flights. The warrants of each set of interests, or social group, were insufficient to the other. Again, as at Babcock & Wilcox, the differences between them reflect the professional experiences and commitments of the two groups.

As Gouran et al. have concluded, the structural factors involved in NASA's decision procedures appear impeccable; they attribute the erroneous decision to the "social, psychological, and communicative environment" (133), including "perceived pressure" from NASA and "unwillingness . . . to violate perceived role boundaries" (121). Our analysis suggests that the common view that managers at Morton Thiokol were just acquiescing to pressure from NASA is too simple. Rather, it may be that engineers and managers were unable, more than unwilling, to recognize data which deviated from that characteristic of their organizational roles. Different experiences and commitments provided the engineers and managers with different understandings of the problem and with different argumentative resources. These differences manifest themselves in the different warrants and evidence offered by members of each group.

Conclusion

Our analyses of the communication failures associated with the Three Mile Island and Challenger accidents suggest three conclusions for the study of organizational discourse. First, in confirming the theoretical notion that social differentiation often creates differentiated discourse we are led to distinguish two kinds of communication failure, which we have called *miscommunication* and *misunderstanding*. Miscommunication is detected through structural analysis and is due to the lack of a common language or to faulty communication procedures within an organization. Misunderstanding is detected through substantive analysis of what people say or write and what they must share to interpret discourse as it was intended. Put simply, miscommunication revolves around the *how* of communication, while misunderstanding revolves around the *what*. In linguistics this distinction is analogous to the distinction between the formal and social dimensions of language, in organizational communication to quantitative and interpretive research, in argument to logical and substantive analysis. Work in all these disciplines has moved away from formal toward substantive analysis, creating, for one thing, a closer connection between linguistics and rhetoric. We found here that substantive analysis provided richer explication of the communication problems we were exploring.

Second, the conjunction of multiple analyses here raises another question of method. Beyond the critical commonplace that research generally discovers the kind of data suited to the research methodology, we would point out that analytic models describe groups at characteristic levels of generality or specificity. The three methods we have employed describe three levels of groups. Formal linguistic analysis seems to identify groups at the general level of all potentially competent speakers of the language. It might, for example, distinguish very large groups by noting semantic and syntactic differences between different languages or dialects. This suggests that its utility in exploring organizational discourse is largely restricted to discounting explanations based on speakers' fluency or grammatical

Carl G. Herndl, Barbara A. Fennell, and Carolyn R. Miller

competence. Pragmatic analysis operates on a somewhat smaller scale, since pragmatic awareness comes late in language acquisition and is closely tied to social context. We suspect that it will distinguish the discourse of social groups at the level of large cultural institutions (as in Agar's work on institutional discourse). In more localized studies such as ours, it seems most useful in reflecting writers' perceptions of social context and group affiliation. It provides a way of determining the boundaries between social groups as they are actually perceived by the group members rather than as they appear on an organizational chart. It does so, however, only because writers like Kelly and Walters employ the same pragmatic standards to negotiate their social agendas. It doesn't differentiate the discourse of these groups at this level.

Argument analysis seems the best suited to identify groups within large organizations such as Morton Thiokol and Babcock & Wilcox and to describe the way the discourse of such groups differs. Its power comes from the fact that it reveals the substantive differences in discourse. It shows how discourse reflects the knowledge possessed by groups and how this knowledge is constructed and deployed. We suspect that research in organizational discourse will progress by employing similar analytic methods that focus on questions of social knowledge and describe the substance rather than the structure or process of communication.

Finally, we believe that our work illustrates the complexity of the current term "discourse community." Since the relationships between language use and social structure are various and are describable with different analytic methods, the term discourse community becomes either misleadingly vague or intriguingly rich. It is also subject to a troublesome circularity, in which the community is defined by the discourse and vice versa. This theoretical difficulty may best be handled by careful attention to the limitations and capacities of research methods. The term discourse community may then be most useful as an umbrella term that incorporates speech community, interpretive community, argument field, and the like. Our work here begins to suggest how all these terms might be related, how they can inform each other, and how empirical studies can help clarify theory.

BIBLIOGRAPHY

Agar, Michael. Institutional Discourse." *Text* 5 (1985): 147–68.
ADE Bulletin. "News Notes: Memo Meltdown on Three Mile Island." No. 75 (1983): 53.
Brown, Robert L., Jr., and Carl G. Herndl. "An Ethnographic Study of Corporate Writing: Job Status as Reflected in Written Text." In *Functional Approaches*

Understanding Failures in Organizational Discourse

to *Writing: Research Perspectives*, ed. Barbara Couture, 11–28. Norwood, N.J.: Ablex, 1986.

Gouran, Dennis S., Randy Y. Hirokawa, and Amy E. Martz. "A Critical Analysis of Factors Related to Decisional Processes Involved in the Challenger Disaster." *Central States Speech Journal* 37 (1986): 119–35.

Levinson, Stephen C. *Pragmatics.* Cambridge: Cambridge University Press, 1983.

Lyons, John. *Semantics.* Vol. 2. Cambridge: Cambridge University Press, 1977.

Mathes, J. C. *Three Mile Island: The Management Communication Failure.* Ann Arbor: College of Engineering, University of Michigan, 1986.

Ochs, E., and B. B. Schieffelin. *Developmental Pragmatics.* New York: Academic Press, 1979.

Presidential Commission on the Space Shuttle Challenger Accident. *Report to the President.* 5 vols. Washington, D.C.: U.S. Government Printing Office, 1986.

Putnam, Linda L. "The Interpretive Perspective: An Alternative to Functionalism." In *Communication and Organizations: An Interpretive Approach,* ed. Linda L. Putnam and Michael E. Pacanowsky, 31–54. Beverly Hills, Calif.: Sage, 1983.

Redish, Janice C. "The Language of the Bureaucracy." In *Literacy for Life: The Demand for Reading and Writing,* ed. Richard W. Bailey and Robin Melanie Fosheim, 151–74. New York: Modern Language Association, 1983.

Rogovin, Mitchell, and George T. Frampton, Jr. *Three Mile Island: Report to the Commissioners and to the Public.* Vol. 2, Pt. 1. Washington, D.C.: Nuclear Regulatory Commission, 1980.

Toulmin, Stephen. *The Uses of Argument.* Cambridge: Cambridge University Press, 1958.

Toulmin, Stephen, Richard Rieke, and Allan Janik. *An Introduction to Reasoning.* New York: Macmillan, 1979.

White, James Boyd. "The Invisible Discourse of the Law: Reflections on Legal Literacy and General Education." In *Literacy for Life: The Demand for Reading and Writing,* ed. Richard W. Bailey and Robin Melanie Fosheim, 137–50. New York: Modern Language Association, 1983.

13

CREATING A TEXT /

CREATING A COMPANY

THE ROLE OF A TEXT

IN THE RISE AND DECLINE

OF A NEW ORGANIZATION

STEPHEN DOHENY-FARINA

In early 1982 a group of graduates and undergraduates from Northland State University, a highly respected Northeastern technological institution, founded Microware, Inc., a microcomputer software company.[1] Shortly thereafter, Microware became a member of the university's Start-Up Project, a program designed to incubate new, innovative, "start-up" companies. These companies were to develop business applications of the technologies being researched and developed at the university. As part of the process of applying for acceptance into the Start-Up Project, Microware's president, Bill Alexander, wrote a business plan. This document detailed Microware's business goals and the strategies that the company would employ to meet those goals. That is, the plan described the types of software that Microware would produce, the potential market for that software and the ways that the company would go about producing and selling that software.

As Bill described it, Microware's 1982 Business Plan was a powerful document:

> It was everything. Without a product, without money, without furniture, without machines, without anything, the Business Plan is it. That's your whole case for existence. That's what attracted money. That's what kept us in the (Start-Up) program. That's what

> got most of the Board (of Directors) into it. That's what got a
> lot of the employees into it. It did a lot of things (Interview, 18
> July 1983)

Microware was created in the writing of a business plan. The plan attracted investments and support, and it also gave direction to the fledgling organization during 1982.

In this chapter I will explore how the company arose from that plan and thus exemplify some of the ways that a text can shape an organization. I focus primarily on one text and one company, and do not wish to claim that I am exemplifying the typical way — or the best or worst way — that organizations are formed. One alternate way organizations can form is discussed in this chapter and compared to the way Microware developed. I do believe, however, that the case study of Microware and its 1982 Business Plan provides a particularly revealing glimpse of one way that a text can define and maintain an organization.

Microware's 1982 Business Plan defined the company by establishing its parameters. Before the company had tangible elements (employees, offices, equipment, products, bank accounts, organizational charts with names in the boxes, etc.), it was conceived in terms of three interrelated concepts: (1) a product, (2) a market for that product, and (3) a plan to bring that product to that market. Once established in the text, these concepts persuaded key individuals to act to create the physical, commercial, and interpersonal parameters that defined the organization. That is, the persuasive power of the plan encouraged individuals to take certain actions that brought the company from concept to reality. Thus, in one sense, the plan was an effective transactional document: it motivated individuals to act in ways that helped to establish the organization.

In another sense, however, the plan failed as a transactional document. It failed to give effective guidance to the continued operation of the company and was, therefore, deficient in the way it maintained the organization. As my analysis will show, the transactional quality of the business plan was the source of both constructive and destructive power.

Overall, this analysis reveals the ways that Microware's business plan both reflected and shaped the social and organizational environment. As such, this study is consistent with a growing body of research, some of which has explored how writers are influenced by social, organizational and disciplinary environments (e.g., Odell and Goswami; Selzer; Bazerman; Odell; Herrington; Larouche and Pearson; Broadhead and Freed; Spilka; Winsor). In these studies environmental factors are shown to affect the ways that writers construct their rhetorical situations.

Others have brought to light some of the ways that writing influences social, organizational, and disciplinary environments (e.g., Paradis,

Dobrin and Miller; Myers; Doheny-Farina). These case studies examine not only the ways that writers are affected by their perceptions of the communities in which they write, but also ways that their discourse, in turn, affects those communities. As Harrison states:

> Communities of thought render rhetoric comprehensible and meaningful. Conversely, however, rhetorical activity builds communities that subsequently give meaning to rhetorical action. (9)

The rhetorical activity that I investigated in this study clearly helped to build a community. At the same time that rhetorical activity was shaped by forces outside the newly forming community.

Thus, my analysis assumes what Cooper defines as an "ecological" view of writing — a view that places the writer in a fluid and reciprocal environment: a writer is not only influenced by but also influences his or her environment. That is, writing is an inherently social activity (Bazerman; Faigley; Bruffee, "Social Construction"; Lefevre) which involves (and often entangles) the writer in a range of interwoven social and organizational dimensions. Cooper's primary metaphor for writing is that of a web, "in which anything that affects one strand of the web vibrates throughout the whole" (370). Indeed, as this chapter will show, Microware's 1982 Business Plan was entangled in a web of institutional, commercial, technological, and interpersonal strands.

I begin with a brief review of my research methods and an overview of the history of Microware. The analysis that follows these sections will uncover the underlying arguments that made the plan persuasive, examine the effects that these arguments had on key participants, discuss the deficiencies in the plan and the effects that these deficiencies had on the company, and assess the transactional nature of the business plan.

Research Methods

Much of my data gathering was geared toward reconstructing the writing of the company's first business plan and observing the writing of the second plan (Doheny-Farina). To do these things, I (a) conducted open-ended interviews that explored the interviewee's perspective on the history of the company, (b) observed and recorded the participants' daily activities (Shatzman and Strauss), and (c) tape recorded meetings that captured the participants interacting as they discussed organizational and rhetorical issues.[2] I collected data at Microware for three to five days a week for eight months in 1983. Each visit lasted from one to eight hours and I typically collected data during formal and informal meetings in the offices and hallways of Microware's two buildings.

An Overview of Microware

From 1982 to 1986 Microware raised nearly $750,000 in investments, loans, and sales. While the typical microcomputer software company consisted of a few programmers and marketers, Microware was amply staffed and supported. The company employed approximately thirty-five programmers, engineers, managers, marketing specialists, and salespersons. The company was well-equipped with a range of advanced microcomputers, peripherals, and printers. From 1982 to 1984 the company enjoyed status as a member of the Northland State University Start-Up Project. In addition, the company had attracted as a principal financier and advisor, Ted Wilson, a senior partner for one of the Metro region's most successful and respected law firms. By 1984 the company had produced MicroMed, a business systems product designed to computerize a range of operations in small to mid-sized hospitals. This product, which received a favorable review in a health care industry trade publication, attracted approximately $340,000 in sales. Yet in 1986 the company went bankrupt. *While it undoubtedly failed for many reasons*, an examination of the role of the 1982 Business Plan can provide some insight into these events.

This plan played a significant role in the company's progress from January 1982 until the late summer of 1983 when Microware's executives began to write a new business plan (for a discussion of the collaborative process of writing this revised document, see Doheny-Farina). The executives decided to write a new plan because they were faced with the company's first major financial crisis. On 25 August 1983, the company's lawyer and principal financier, Ted Wilson, told the president and the other Microware executives that the company was in desperate financial trouble. "You are really a defunct corporation," he said. "You are bleeding to death. . . . You are not only looking at Chapter 11, you are there now." The executives agreed that writing a new business plan would be one of the first and most important steps in overcoming this crisis. As will be discussed later, the new plan was a better transactional document. That is, because key passages of the new plan were developed in far more detail, the plan provided much more specific and sophisticated operational guidance for the company's managers.

Even so, while the company continued on for three more years, the damage it had sustained in its first two years continued to burden the company until it finally went out of business in 1986. Even an improved operation could not overcome the deep debt into which Microware had sunk by 1983. Microware began with much promise and support and yet ultimately failed. The 1982 Business Plan played a central role in that rise and fall.

What follows is an analysis of the transactional function of the business plan. Because of my intense focus on the role of one document, this analysis may seem, at times, to attribute an unreal amount of influence to that document. With this danger of distortion in mind, I will conclude the chapter by briefly discussing an alternate interpretation of the function of Microware's 1982 Business Plan.

The Constructive Power of the 1982 Business Plan

In order to illustrate the plan's power, I will first show how it persuaded three key persons: (1) Paulo Abruzzi, one of the directors of the NSU Start-Up Project; (2) Edward Murphy, the NSU professor who helped the original founders launch the company through an independent study course; and (3) Ted Wilson, Microware's lawyer and principal financier. Although these three were not the only persons who were persuaded by the plan, they were among the most important participants in Microware's rise. By examining the persuasive power the plan had on these three individuals, I will illustrate Bill's claim, quoted above, that Microware arose because his business plan (1) enabled the company to join the Start-Up Project, (2) attracted participants (employees and members of the Board of Directors), and (3) attracted financial support.

JOINING THE START-UP PROJECT:
PAULO ABRUZZI AND THE GENERIC FORM

Most of what Bill learned about the genre of business plans came through his initial experiences with the Start-Up Project. Joining this project was one of Bill's first goals when he and his colleagues founded the company in early 1982. Start-Up Project companies were allowed low-rent office space in what was known as an "incubator building" on the NSU campus. In addition, the Start-Up committee offered business advice to member companies. Most important, the Start-Up Project helped member companies approach potential investors. As will be discussed later, it was crucial for Microware to be portrayed in its business plan as a product of NSU.

Gaining membership into the NSU Project, however, was not a simple task for Microware. The company's founders had to prove themselves before they were accepted. Paulo Abruzzi had made it clear that the Project Committee would give Microware a long, hard look before admitting the company. This heightened scrutiny can be attributed to the fact that Microware's origins were somewhat different from the other companies in the project. Microware grew out of an independent study course at NSU.

To enter the Start-Up Project, the first step for the founders of Microware — or for any potential candidate — was to write a business plan. Paulo Abruzzi placed great emphasis on such plans. Abruzzi, who had retired from General Electric Corporation before becoming a professor of technology management at NSU, was serving as a director of the Start-Up Project because his area of expertise was the management of technological innovations. While at NSU, Abruzzi had developed a new curriculum in the management of technological innovations for the university's MBA program. Abruzzi believed that business plans were important early steps in the development of companies that attempted to be technologically innovative. Abruzzi's emphasis on the importance of the business plan was reported in an NSU magazine article devoted to the Start-Up Project:[3]

> Right from the start, the Start-Up Project encourages you to develop a business plan. Paulo Abruzzi, Professor of Technology Management and Start-Up Project consultant says, "we have seen many companies that have prevented major problems simply by thinking out a business plan: they decide what they want and how they're going to get it." The Project board members want the entrepreneurs, technicians, and managers in each company to construct a short, concise explanation of just what product, procedure, or service that the company wants to sell; and how they want to go about selling it. "The business plan," says Abruzzi, "is like a road map that shows how you're going to get there from here."

According to Abruzzi, then, a business plan should be a plan of action for management to follow. However, in addition to serving as a plan of action, a business plan must also serve as a proposal directed to potential supporters of the company. A business plan outline (figure 13.1) which was given to Bill by the Start-Up Project Committee posited a general proposal structure: after a summary, the writer lays out the proposed financing that he or she is seeking from investors, including the amount of money sought, the terms of the financing, and the planned uses of that financing. This proposed financial deal is then followed by descriptions of the products and the marketing and production strategies, all of which serve as evidence to support the proposed deal.

Stephen Doheny-Farina

NORTHLAND STATE UNIVERSITY
SUGGESTED BUSINESS PLAN CONTENTS

A. Brief Summary
B. Proposed Financing
  1. Amount
  2. Terms
  3. Use of Proceeds
C. Product Description
D. Business Strategy and Five-year Milestones
E. Marketing Plan
  1. Summary
  2. Market Segmentation
  3. Channels of Distribution
  4. Sales Strategy and Plans
  5. Five-year Sales Forecast
  6. Competition
F. Operations Plan
  1. Engineering Program
  2. Manufacturing and Materials Programs
  3. Facilities Plan
  4. Incentive Program
G. Financial Statements and Projections
  1. Past and Present Financial Statements
  2. Existing Shareholders and Ownership Percentages
  3. Five-year Pro Forma Projections
    a. Items: Income statement, balance sheet, cash flow statement.
    b. Format: By month for first two years and then by year for next three years.
H. Management and Key Personnel
  1. Detailed Resumes
  2. Organization
  3. Staffing Plan
I. Appendices
10/81

Fig. 13.1. NSU business plan outline

Although this outline suggests that writers include financial information, such was not the most important information according to Paulo Abruzzi. He emphasized three components: the product, the market, and the plan to capture that market. In an NSU magazine interview, Abruzzi elaborated on these components:

> What we want in a business plan is first, a clear description of the product, process or service which this entrepreneur, this company intends to market. Second, what's the market for that

product, process or service — not how much, but who is the market going to be — the general public, some specialized companies, the government, lots of possibilities. In other words, who is going to buy this great innovation that they have in mind here?

Then (third), they have to delineate their strategy. What is their general strategy for going after this market? How are they going to get from here to there? What kind of resources do they need? Maybe human resources, maybe special equipment, computers. . . . Then maybe a timetable for the development, the manufacturing, and the marketing, if they are that far ahead.

By the end of the independent study course Bill Alexander had finished a draft of the business plan, and he and his fellow group members presented it to Abruzzi and the Start-Up Project Committee. In the plan Bill fulfilled the generic requirements in varying degrees of detail. The plan included sections that described the products, the market, and the production and sales strategies:

BUSINESS PLAN

Table of Contents

Stephen Doheny-Farina

Fig. 13.2. Table of contents for Microware's 1982 business plan

Microware's products. The company's software products included several games, a business graphics package, and MicroMed, the business systems package. All of these were described in sections 1.3 and 4.1 of the business plan (see figure 13.2). As will be discussed later, none of these products were completed in 1982 and those that were completed in 1983 were soon found to be deficient in one way or another and had to be revised. The one product that was the furthest developed in 1982 was MicroMed, the company's most sophisticated software package. The following is a segment of the product description of MicroMed:

> This system was designed to provide health care facilities with flexible, total control over their data processing requirements. The advantages of microcomputers in the business environment are just now being recognized. The ability to improve performance and, at the same time, decrease cost, is of the utmost importance to all facilities, including hospitals. The Microware system is designed for use by small and medium-sized hospitals, and is totally interactive and menu-driven. The users are able to manage all of their normal accounts, keep track of patients, perform their accounting and billing, print standard and custom reports, and perform a number of other vital functions. (7, sec. 1.3)

The most sophisticated — and unfinished — computer video game that the company had developed was named The Web:

> This is an original and fast action color video game designed for implementation on microcomputers, home video game systems and arcade systems. The Web features real-time animation, high-resolution color graphics, and several challenging game scenes from which to choose. Microware shall market the initial version for the new IBM Personal Computer. (6, sec. 1.3)

The only graphics package close to completion was Micrograph:

> This is a simple, low-cost ($59.95), full color business graphics system that allows the professional to design full color line charts,

graphs, and pie charts. All information and graphs are sorted in a database, which provides for additions, deletions and changes to the information. All functions are performed by the use of menus. (7, sec. 1.3)

In addition to describing this software, Bill had to discuss the market for the products.

The potential market for Microware's products. The consumer market for microcomputer software was spurred by the production of microcomputer hardware. In section 2 and sections 3.1 to 3.4 of his business plan, Bill discussed the software market as an outgrowth of the expanding hardware market; for example:

> 1982 sales for home computers are estimated to be $840 million, seven times the 1981 figures. By 1985, the home computer industry should have annual revenues of more than $3 billion, according to a study done by Future Computing, Inc., a Dallas consulting firm.
>
> The main reason for the rapid increase in sales of home computers is the rapid decreases by all hardware manufacturers, including the four leading home computer manufacturers, Atari (400), Tandy Corporation (TRS-80 Color Computer), Texas Instruments (99/4a), and Commodore International, Ltd. (12, sec. 2.1)

In addition, Bill also discussed the strategies necessary to produce the software and reach the markets.

Microware's production and sales strategies. The means to produce and sell software were outlined in sections 3.5, 4.1, 4.2. As will be discussed later, these sections were the least developed aspects of the plan. For example, the following passage describes the sales strategy:

> Microware has a goal of becoming a major software and service company in the computer industry. This strong industry position will be secured by:
> 1) Superior Products
> 2) Superior Documentation & Support
> 3) Full Financial, Managerial, & Technical Support
> 4) Establishment of a National Distribution Network
>
> (34, sec. 3.5)

The sales strategy, like the production strategy discussed in detail later in this chapter, was outlined in the broadest terms. In spite of these undeveloped "strategy" components, the Start-Up Committee reacted favorably to Bill's plan and, as Abruzzi recalled, he began to help Bill fine-tune the Plan.

> We required them to write a business plan. They wrote a first draft and I reviewed it and improved it and now (early 1983) it's a 70 page document. [Microware was accepted] once they met our requirements. (NSU magazine)

As reported in the NSU magazine: "Alexander worked with Abruzzi to develop the Plan and on June 14, 1982 Microware was accepted into the Start-Up Project."

The company officially became a member of the Start-Up Project after Bill and the other founders formally presented the business plan and fragments of working software to the Start-Up Committee. In their presentation they provided an overview of the business plan (presenting an outline of the plan via overhead projector) and demonstrated some of the unfinished software on a microcomputer. This same type of presentation was used when Bill and the other founders made formal presentations to others, such as potential investors and/or potential members of the company's board of directors.

In the business plan, Bill developed a powerful argument that emphasized how well Microware was positioned to take advantage of these possibilities. The major premise of the argument was that the total potential market for microcomputer software was extremely lucrative. The minor premise was that other companies, similar to Microware in that they were entrepreneurial start-up companies, have gained highly profitable shares of that potential market. The conclusion of the argument was that Microware is positioned to take a significant share of that market. Figures 13.3A, 13.3B, and 13.3C illustrate this argument with excerpts from the business plan.

Advertising Age estimates that the gross revenues for video games in 1982 will top $6 billion, and will approach $20 billion by 1985. (p. 3)

Today's computer revolution has been growing at a pace of well over 50 percent annually for the past several years. This growth, along with the expectation of future growth, has prompted several venture capital firms and public companies to invest significant amounts of money in recognized industry leaders, and in new start-ups such as Microware. (p. 10)

Video game mania is sweeping the country, and many consumers are finding that home computers, in addition to performing home tasks such as budgeting, finance, and education, are also very good game machines. (p. 12)

Only 10 percent of American homes have a video game system, which leaves 90 percent still to be conquered. (p. 13)

In 1981, Americans spent 20 billion quarters on video games, including arcades. That was more money than was spent on baseball, basketball, and football combined. That's quite substantial. (p. 14)

The release, in the summer of 1981, of IBM's new Personal Computer has brought significant attention to the microcomputer industry. The IBM Personal Computer is becoming the computer of the decade. By the end of 1982, less than a year after initial release, IBM will have 250,000 to 300,000 personal computers installed. Estimates place the number of IBM personal computers (to be) sold in 1983 at 3 million machines. (p. 19)

Figure 13.3A: Major Premise: Business Plan Excerpts That Illustrate the Lucrative Market for Microcomputer Software

Atari, owned by Warner Communications, has been the leader in the video games market since its humble beginning back in 1971 when Nolan Bushnell and Joe Keenan founded Atari. Warner Communications bought out Atari in 1976 for $32 million, and in 1981 Atari had gross revenue of $1.23 billion, with net profit of $286 million. 1981 figures estimate Atari's revenue to be $2.0 billion with net profit of $504 million. Atari was obviously a very profitable acquisition for Warner Communications.

Other home game system manufacturers are hot on the trail of Atari and Mattel, and a number of them released new products at the end of 1982. This competition in the home game systems and cartridges market has already placed Atari in a difficult position. Atari's share of the games systems hardware market has slipped from 75 percent last year to 65 percent this year, and from 85 percent to 60 percent for the game cartridges market, due to increasing number of independent companies providing cartridges for the Atari VCS. (p. 130)

Activision was founded on October 1, 1979 by its current President Jim Levy and 4 ex-Atari game designers. . . . in 1980 Activision's gross sales were $6 million. In 1981 gross sales were $66 million, an increase of 110 percent. . . . From the original 4 (game) designers, the Activision designers have grown to 31 at five separate design centers on the East and West Coasts. Activision, which is privately held, now has about 15 percent of the game cartridge market. (p. 15)

Figure 13.3B: Minor Premise: Business Plan Excerpts That Discuss the Success of Other Entrepreneurial, Start-Up Software Companies

Stephen Doheny-Farina

Microware's five year milestones include gross annual sales in 1987 of $100 million; complete product lines in video games and business systems; a state-of-the-art commercial graphics facility; complete development of a national customer base; and initial expansion into the international market. (p. 2)

Microware recognizes that the growing versatility of the technology opens up the opportunity to invent programs and games radically different from today's war-type games, or shoot-em-ups, as they are called in the industry. Peter Odak, past president of Atari's Consumer Products Division stated, "the heart of the market for shoot-em-up" comprises about 20 million homes out of the 83 million homes that have TV sets. This leaves a tremendous void in the market to be filled. A void of 63 million households. (p. 17)

Figure 13.3C: Conclusion: Business Plan Excerpts That Explain How Microware Is Positioned to Gain a Significant Market Share

Even though there were serious problems with this argument, it attracted people. The fact that by 1983 Microware had still not produced a finished, marketable piece of software still did not deter others' receptivity to this argument. The production problems that undercut this argument — as will be discussed in detail later — did not become crucial until the second half of 1983. In 1982 the partial pieces of software indicated that the company was headed in the right direction and many people were excited by the seemingly unlimited potential of the market. In an interview a year and a half after the independent study courses began, Murphy recalled why Bill and his colleagues were persuasive: "They were in the right business, at the right place, at the right time, with the right machine."

ATTRACTING FINANCES: TED WILSON AND THE
INSTITUTIONAL/ENTREPRENEURIAL MELD ARGUMENT

Once accepted into the Start-Up Project, Bill was able to add a significant argument to the plan. This argument was one of the most powerful of all because it attracted Microware's most powerful supporter, Ted Wilson, who, at 70 years of age, was a senior partner in a highly respected regional law firm. Ted first became interested in Microware when Bill was filing for both incorporation and for membership into the Start-Up Project.

From the time Ted became involved with Microware until the 1983 financial crisis that precipitated a new business plan, Microware survived primarily through the graces of Ted Wilson. He supported the company in four ways: (1) He afforded Microware hundreds of hours of legal advice without charge. (2) He helped Bill sell $50–100,000 worth of Microware stock. (3) He rented to Microware some of the company's equipment and its downtown offices, and collected very little rent. (4) Most important, Ted had cosigned and guaranteed a loan of $250,000 from the the Northland Bank to Microware. Thus, in the company's first two years, it existed not only on the fruits of its production, but on the fruits of Ted's confidence in Bill's vision.

What argument was so powerful that Ted would throw this much support behind a fledgling operation? First, Ted was impressed with many of the partially completed software products. He was especially impressed with MicroMed. But more significantly, Ted was persuaded by what I have labelled as the Institutional/Entrepreneurial Meld argument. This argument was built upon two visions: (1) university and city codevelopment, and (2) the entrepreneurial spirit of the Start-Up Project.

University/city codevelopment. As noted above, the purpose of the Start-Up Project was to help generate small, innovative companies that could develop commercial applications of the state-of-the-art technology being developed at the university. While the university offered office space, consulting advice, and technological resources, the Start-Up companies offered employment to university students and faculty as well as connections to the region's business community. This relationship was extolled by Michael Waller, one of the Start-Up Directors:

> Individual academic departments at NSU, with which the new companies often interact, receive valuable input from new high technology developments in the business sector. The new businesses also offer research and employment opportunities for students who want to apply their engineerinng studies directly in a competitive environment. "What we have here," says Waller, "is a truly synergistic relationship between the educational and industrial communities." (NSU magazine)

It was hoped that this relationship could help the Metro region develop a stronger, more diverse economy similar to that of California's Silicon Valley, or Boston's Rte. 128, high-technology region. As Paulo Abruzzi stated in the NSU magazine:

> The whole point of the program is to develop new markets and new businesses, to increase employment and to increase the wealth of this area.

Bill Alexander tapped this vision in his business plan and Ted Wilson was persuaded by it. Ted was also persuaded by entrepreneurial quality of these ventures.

The entrepreneurial spirit of the Start-Up Project. When the Start-Up Project began, it had fostered an unqualified success with its first entre-preneurial venture. In 1980, Macro Technologies was founded by two NSU graduates who had developed a potentially marketable computer graphics hardware project. Within a year, the company, through investments and sales, had raised enough money to move out of the Start-Up Project and go on its own. Shortly thereafter, to the disappointment of many in the region, Macro Technologies moved to new offices near Boston. Ted Wilson, whose law firm had worked for Macro, described his disappointment at the sudden loss:

> Macro got themselves positioned . . . to get a million dollar commitment from VenCap, a New York City venture capital group. VenCap insisted on a consultant coming on board, a business advisor. He came from Boston. He was competent, and he served the company well. But he picked up the whole operation when it got going and brought it over to Rte. 128. Now that was a heartbreaker. A young man came in from Dale and Darwin, a Boston law firm, and picked up the file from us one day and the client was gone. (Interview, 31 August 1983)

Macro Technologies had given the Start-Up Project a taste of entrepre-neurial success and then left.

Bill Alexander was another who had been excited by the entrepreneur-ial success of Macro Technologies. A year before he founded Microware, Bill offered his services to the company by proposing to analyze the com-puter graphics market, and the current and future position of Macro Tech-nologies in that market. The proposal was signed, "Bill Alexander, Presi-dent, Compu Advisors, Inc." Although nothing came of this proposal, Bill had clearly been interested in creating a vehicle for entering the microcomputer market in one way or another. When Microware was founded, Bill was twenty-one and possessed a strong entrepreneurial drive. From the beginning, he saw himself not as someone who had the techni-cal expertise to produce innovative and profitable products, but as some-one who could lead others who had the technical skills to build such products. This was one of the elements that the Start-Up committee was looking for in a company's leader. Abruzzi painted a picture of the kind of person he thought should head a Start-Up company:

Someone who is motivated, independent, who has the entrepreneurial spirit: they want to get somewhere, do something special. Self-reliant people who would rather be their own boss than rely on the company. This someone would show the profile of high-technology: the entrepreneur. (NSU magazine)

Bill's entrepreneurial ambition was clearly evident to Ted Wilson:

Did he sell me? He certainly did. He is a consummate entrepreneur. . . . He is entrepreneur from head to toe, and as I told him early on. . . . I bet on people. He impressed me. I knew he'd provide the entrepreneurial spirit, the driving force to get things done. (Interview, 31 August 1983)

As an entrepreneur, Bill expressed his vision in his business plan and much of this vision was based on three interrelated enthymemes: (1) the Silicon Valley enthymeme, (2) the NSU enthymeme, and (3) the Macro Technologies enthymeme. Although these arguments proved to be appealing, they masked a serious deficiency in the company's ability to produce software. That is, the structures of these arguments are based upon an unstated premise that I will later show to be invalid.

The Silicon Valley enthymeme equated the goals of the Start-Up project with the successes of other university/city alliances:

MAJOR PREMISE: Silicon Valley and Boston's Rte. 128 region developed an extensions of major technological universities;

MINOR PREMISE: the Start-Up project has developed as an extension of NSU;

CONCLUSION: the Metro region can develop like Silicon Valley and Rte. 128.

The NSU enthymeme equated the level of innovative technology which was being developed at NSU to the level of technology that Microware would develop:

MAJOR PREMISE: NSU represents state-of-the-art technology;

MINOR PREMISE: as a Start-Up company Microware is an extension of NSU;

Stephen Doheny-Farina

CONCLUSION: Microware will create state-of-the-art applications of that technology.

The Macro Technologies enthymeme equated the origins and successes of Macro Technologies to the origins and potential successes of Microware:

MAJOR PREMISE: Macro Technologies, a successful company, was begun by NSU graduates as the first Start-Up Project company; MINOR PREMISE: Microware was started by NSU graduates and undergraduates; CONCLUSION: Microware will succeed as did Macro Technologies.

Even though these three arguments masked an invalid unstated premise, they enabled Bill to argue that Microware represented a new kind of venture: a company driven by the young technological entrepreneurs arising out of prestigious technological institutions and reviving the local economy. In making these arguments Bill could show that the relative youth of most of the key employees was not a liability but a boon — as long as he made NSU prominent in his argument. Below are excerpts from the 1982 Business Plan that illustrate the enthymemes:

Northland State University President Lawrence M. Highland had developed a plan called *Northland 21st Century*, where "NSU is with bold, calculated strokes, being transformed into one of a small number of first-rank, internationally renowned technological universities." . . . The Metro Region, its steel and textile mills long empty, will rival the Silicon Valley as a boom town. Our Governor also envisions the Metro Region becoming the hub of a high technology belt similar to California's Silicon Valley or Boston's Rte. 128. . . . The final element for the Northland 21st Century plan is the development of the NSU Start-Up Project, of which Microware is a member. The companies involved have complete access to faculty, students, and NSU facilities and equipment. One of the most recent Start-Up companies was Macro Technologies, founded in March 1981 by . . . two 1979 NSU graduates. (8–9, sec. 1.5)

We offer the "cutting edge of technology" in the information revolution through our existing management team and employees. The Company, through its affiliation with the Start-Up Project at

Northland State University, will continue to offer state-of-the-art technology well into the future. (11, sec. 1.5)

Microware IS PEOPLE. In its people, Microware possesses youth, intelligence, creativity and, most importantly, the maturity to seek out professional advice and direction in choosing its partners for the future. Through its association with Northland State University, Microware will have continuing access to the research and development resources of an institution which is at the forefront of high technology. (11, sec. 1.5)

Microware is strategically positioned to enter the educational games market with its association with Northland State University. The Company's objectives are to design games that have an element of fun for the child or young adult as well as being highly educational. (17, sec. 2.1)

By having *highly talented students* working on projects, and by using NSU facilities for certain functions, Microware has been able to achieve drastic cost savings. (37, sec. 4.1)

Without completed products, Bill constructed an intoxicating, double-edged image of Microware. On the one hand he portrayed a company that was the youthful, innovative, fast-growing, entrepreneurial venture characteristic of other high-tech success stories made popular in the national media (e.g., Apple, Microsoft, Atari). On the other hand, he balanced this against the stable, rigorous, and eminently successful institution that could give birth and guidance to such ventures (NSU).

In 1982, with the country in the midst of a severe economic recession, this dual image offered new hope to a region debilitated by the decline of heavy industry. Ted Wilson was persuaded by this hope. Even during Microware's first major financial crisis in August 1983, Ted was still persuaded by Bill's vision. At that time he explained in an interview why he supported Microware:

I'm a third generation resident [of the Microware's city] on my father's side. And my progenitors lived to ripe old ages, so I'm going back to the middle of the last century. And I am very concerned about this city. It was the heart and soul of the industrial revolution. And during my lifetime, I'm now seventy years of age, I've seen it go downhill. . . . It's not the vibrant and creative driving force that it once was in our national economy. It's been in the backwater.

I had seen the possibility of its reemergence as a driving economic force in the American economy in the new high technology communications revolution with an unending stream of talent coming out of NSU, particularly in the computer science field. . . . I know of the university's efforts to develop that synergism between industry and university that has been spawned around Boston and out in Silicon Valley, and I want very much to play a role in developing that industrial complex for the new age.

It seems to me that we [the city] can again rise to a position of preeminence. It requires, however, more than just an intellectual resource. . . . If we're going to develop the way Silicon Valley has, and the way Rte. 128 has, we must have venture capital. We must have entrepreneurs. (Interview, 31 August 1983)

Accordingly, the 1982 Business Plan was written by Microware's entrepreneur to attract venture capital. Thus, the plan had a powerful impact on Ted Wilson.

The parts of the plan that persuaded Abruzzi, Murphy, and Wilson described a company that would be run by a young and ambitious staff and supported by a major technological institution, in order to produce a range of software products for wide-open markets that were projected to grow at very fast rates over the next five years. This image was Microware. This image enabled the company to join the Start-Up Project and attract initial investments. The investments then enabled the company to move into two fully equipped offices, hire more staff, and begin producing software. Unfortunately, this image was not enough to sustain the company in the long run.

The most significant unstated premise for all of the arguments described above was that Microware could design, build, and sell products. This unstated premise was the production strategy that the company would need to follow to capture that large market. Such a strategy was a key aspect of the "road-map" quality of a business plan that Abruzzi described. Therefore, while the plan created a company by attracting powerful supporters, the plan also created a company by setting goals and the strategies to meet those goals. However, because such strategies were not well-developed, the 1982 Business Plan proved to be a deficient road map and the company suffered because of it.

The Destructive Power of the
1982 Business Plan

By July 1983, more than a year after the independent study group incorporated, Microware was on the verge of bankruptcy even though the company was well-equipped with the resources it needed to produce marketable software. At that time Dr. Murphy observed, "Although there seem to be talented programmers working for the company, they have not produced marketable software." They had been able to generate outside support from investors, employees, the university, and a board of directors. The promotion of the primary arguments of the business plan attracted this support. The primary deficiency in that plan, however, inhibited the production of software. As I stated in a related report on this research, "the company achieved a tenuous existence: It was able to survive on outside investments, but unable to produce profit generating products" (Doheny-Farina, 170). Three issues help identify why the plan was deficient.

WRITING A BUSINESS PLAN VS. BUILDING A PRODUCT

Professor Murphy thought that Bill put the writing of a business plan ahead of producing marketable software. Although he was favorably impressed by the marketing goals set out by the business plan, Murphy thought that the group had to first establish that it could create the products that would grab a share of those markets. Murphy recognized that by starting the company via a business plan alone, Bill produced an organization before that organization produced marketable software.

In addition, Murphy felt that from the beginning of the course through to the establishment of the company, Microware had scattered its effort by following the prescribed path of the business plan. He believed that the independent study group should have concentrated on the production of a few well-defined products first, then formed an organization around the products that they created. As Murphy stated,

> During the school year they were focusing on the business plan. I urged them instead to get some programs written. My feeling was that if they had programs I could very quickly show them how to write a business plan and get investors on board. (Interview, 15 July 1983)

What Murphy thought they should have done was to follow the model of Macro Technologies. As he recounted, the Macro people actually built products, showed them at trade shows and then went on to form a company. Murphy believed that Macro answered the two big questions before they became a company: Can we produce a product? And will the market accept it? In contrast, Bill and his fellow founders put together, not products, but an image of an organization and eventually sold the promise of that image in a business plan to investors. Although the image was attractive, the plans behind the image were deficient.

THE PLAN'S LACK OF SYNERGY

Microware, as described in the business plan, was a unique entry into the largely undetermined personal computer software industry. At one point in the business plan — to highlight the newness of the industry — Bill quoted Jim Levy, the president of Activision, then one of the nation's largest personal computer software companies.

> "I feel that the personal computer is as fundamental a revolution in the way we entertain ourselves, live our lives, and educate ourselves, as television or any other development we have witnessed in this century, and therefore in all of history. We're in an industry that's only four or five years old. Many years of growth and change in the technology and the creative uses of it lie ahead." (15, sec. 2.1)

Microware was unique because it would go after three largely untapped markets: games, graphics, and business systems. No companies cited in the business plan had attempted to do that. If Microware gained shares of all three markets, the company would become a formidable presence in the software industry and would, in effect, redefine what a software company could be. This was an ambitious redefinition, but it belied a shaky foundation.

The heart of this deficiency was that the business plan did not explain how the three-way production goals related to each other. As Bill later recognized, he did not unify these three different directions with a common purpose. Instead, in the plan he created a company whose direction was diffused by too many unconnected goals. During an interview (5 October 1983) while he was writing the subsequent 1983 Business Plan, Bill admitted, "I didn't build a synergy in. So when a reader reads it he is confused as to what our direction is."

Bill's plan did not account for the relationship between product types.

That is, the plan did not state that the company develop products that were inherently integrated. Such products could proceed from an integrated production system out of which the fundamental elements of all the company's products could be produced. In the latter half of 1983 such a system was proposed. It would have at its center a group that produced "core" programs. These would then be used by an "applications" group — a group that would apply the core development in the company's products. Such a system was the "synergy" that Bill came to realize was missing from his plan and from the company's production sykstem. This new integrated system, however, was not implemented in time to keep the company from squandering much of its resources through the inadequate production system fostered by Bill's original plan.

In addition to establishing three unconnected goals, the business plan stipulated as its primary goal the creation of games and graphics, and deemphasized the creation of business application software. When the company's lack of production threatened its existence, Bill recognized this problem:

> In some cases I set my priorities wrong. In some cases I gave too much information on Graphics and not enough on the Business Applications products. (Interview, 5 October 1983)

This lack of focus came to a head in July 1983. Bill and the Microware's managers agreed that the company was trying to produce too many different kinds of software at the same time. They agreed that all of the company's production deadlines were continually being missed because the production effort for each type of software disrupted the production effort of the rest of the software. Bill was afraid that games in particular would "go down the tubes and pull the rest down." Overall, it had been very expensive for them to pursue three different types of software production. To do so, they had hired more and more employees during the company's first year and a half. When Microware had incorporated in the spring of 1982 it comprised approximately eleven employees. By July 1983, this number had risen to approximately thirty employees, who cost the company $50,000 a month on payroll alone. Also, in order for these employees to do their work, the company had purchased or rented thousands of dollars in computer equipment, office space, furniture, and supplies. The company was in debt to financiers, banks, and other companies.

THE PLAN'S UNDERDEVELOPED PRODUCTION STRATEGY

In addition to not creating a synergistic production process, the plan did not articulate a well-developed sequence of events that would lead the company to meet those goals. For example, the only page in the business plan that described the company's production process offered only a skeletal description of a linear production process:

> Microware defines a two phase process in the development of all software.
>
> *Alpha phase* — This includes the development of initial product concepts. Preliminary design and development is completed at this stage, with the full involvement of the Engineering Group and the Software Development Group.
>
> At the end of alpha phase, the Technical Services Group evaluates the potential product according to product specifications. These specifications indicate product function, components, quality standards, and other vital information. Once approved by the Technical Services Group, the potential product begins *Beta phase*.
>
> *Beta phase* — In the beta phase, products are completed to meet marketing requirements, including packaging and promotion. Products are then run through a series of tests by the Engineering, Software Development, Marketing, and Technical Services Groups to determine true marketability.
>
> Upon approval by the Vice Presidents of Engineering, Software Development, and Marketing, the new product is released for initial test marketing. Final approval for regional or national distribution will be given after successful test marketing. (38, sec. 4.2)

These five paragraphs represent the flimsy foundation upon which Bill's most powerful arguments were based. This passage reveals that the goals of those arguments were not supported by specific strategies that could be actually carried out by Microware employees. The description of the "alpha phase" of production offers a few broad generalizations (e.g., "preliminary design and development is completed at this stage . . .") that do not specify any particular actions. Likewise, the "beta phase" describes a production process in the most rudimentary terms: products will be completed and tested. With an underspecified system, Microware was beset by production problems for well over a year after the independent study was over and the company had incorporated. Managers had difficulty in articulating design goals and schedules as well as getting their programmers to finish the programs on time; programmers had trouble writing programs that worked as they were supposed to work; and once products were complete they were found to be unacceptable for sale.

Overall, Greg Jerling noted that most of these setbacks were the result of short-sightedness and poor planning. The need for crucial design changes in a product were sometimes discovered long after the product was conceived, designed, and, in some cases, manufactured in large numbers. Often programmers who had been writing a program so that it would perform certain tasks were told in midstream to stop doing that and write programs that did something different. There seemed to be little consistent production direction.

For quite a while there was very little direction given programmers from the management because the production system was not structured for this to happen. Greg Jerling characterized the company's production system as "one fluid mass." For example, in April 1983, nearly a year after the company incorporated, one of its programmers, Larry Williams, was asked if there was a system for deciding upon production project. "No, everyone just does what they want, what they have ideas on," he said. "Some games are developed totally by one person. It depends. Some people are very organization-minded. Others are not." The freedom for product developers to do "what they want" resulted in chaotic production.

After more than a year of work, Microware did not have one finished product to be sold. By August 1983 the company was beginning to sell an unfinished product: their business applications system, MicroMed. These sales, however, were not yet covering the costs of producing the system. By the end of August a loan of $110,000 from a major bank's venture capital arm was virtually all gone.

The company's executives needed to find a way out of this predicament. The only way out, they decided, was to completely revamp the company—the way it was run and what it produced. The first step in this process was to write a new business plan. The process of writing the new plan included the creation of an integrated production strategy. As a result, the new business plan outlined a more complex production system than that which was outlined in the original plan. The Appendix to this chapter contains this revised version.

Whereas the original version offered only a linear, two-stage production plan, the revised version describes a multilevel, multistage plan. In fact, the latter version incorporates the 1982 two-stage process as one part of the new process (under the heading "Quality Control").

Clearly, this overview of the improved production system (Appendix) was primarily directed toward potential investors and not the Microware production personnel. That is, this version merely describes the new system; if it had been directed toward production personnel, it would most likely be in the form of instructions on how to go about implementing the system. Even so, the new version attempts to delineate some actions that can be carried out. For example, the scheduling of the production of a new product is explained as a series of steps that "works its way backwards" from a conception of the product sitting on the shelf in a store to the beginning of the production process (see the Appendix, under the heading "Product Engineering").

Conclusion

The 1982 Business Plan had conflicting influences. On one hand, the writing of the plan played a major role in designing an organization and attracting supporters to make that organization a viable commercial entity. On the other hand, the deficiencies in the plan led to deficiencies in the company. Microware was never able to extricate itself from its debts—debts that the 1982 Business Plan enabled it to incur.

This case study thus illustrates an instance of the relationship of a text to action. Bill's promotional language was effective in that it motivated others to act; his production language was unable to effectively guide production. The 1982 Business Plan succeeded as a proposal but failed in what Abruzzi labeled as the "road-map" function. Thus, the instance of the genre failed to live up to the ideal of that genre. The burden that the generic business plan would carry was too weighty for an actual document.

To better understand this striving toward the ideal, it is useful to place in a larger context my analyses of the writing of both of Microware's business plans (1982 and 1983). If we look at the rise of Microware, the writing of the 1982 Business Plan, and the subsequent writing of the 1983 Business Plan (see Doheny-Farina), we get a glimpse of the creation of a community. We see the social conversation (Bruffee, "Collaborative Working") that sustained and altered (and ultimately destroyed) that community. That is, we see how the actions of individuals were influenced by the community. And, most important, we learn that striving to write the ideal business plan was at the center of these processes.

An alternate view.[4] Although it is tempting to paint the 1982 Business Plan as an extremely powerful document, it may seem quite implausible to place the company's failure squarely on the deficiencies of that plan. I have done this largely by presenting an uncritical depiction of Bill's and Abruzzi's claims that a business plan must serve as the complete "road map" for a company's operation and development. An alternate view indicates that the failure of Microware demonstrates not just the deficiencies of Bill's plan, but the failure of Bill and Abruzzi (and others) to understand the limitations of business plans. This interpretation suggests that the business plan *as a genre* is insufficient to serve the function that Bill and Abruzzi claimed it could serve.

Supporting this view is the seemingly obvious assumption that even a "start-up" company cannot be solely constituted by discourse but must be composed of significant nondiscursive reality as well. Clearly, in this case, those nondiscursive elements — the technical means to produce software — were deficient and *no matter how exacting* the business plan, those deficiencies could not be overcome. This view, while suggesting a generic limitation of business plans, does not undercut their potentially constructive power. Indeed, this case shows how an entrepreneurial vision expressed in a business plan drew the attention of, ironically, experts in the assessment of technology *away from* the problematic technology of the company. Thus, while it may have been a mistake to assume that such a document could give direction to an entire organization, in this case the organization was left with little else to give it that direction. Therefore, we are left with a picture of a text that played a very important but not exclusive role in the rise and decline of a new organization.

APPENDIX

The Engineering Group

The function of the Engineering Group of Microware can clearly be broken down into two distinct areas:
1) Product Engineering
2) Product Production

PRODUCT ENGINEERING

The function of the Engineering Group in the product engineering area is to coordinate the activities of both the Marketing and Software Development Groups in order to produce a finished product which can be taken to market. This job consists of many different elements which must be effectively coordinated to meet a product deadline.

This process begins when a new product concept is conceived by either the Marketing or Software Development Group. After conception, the first function performed by the Engineering Group is a feasibility study. This study consists of reviewing the product concept with both the Marketing and Development Group department heads to make sure it is consistent with the company's marketing and development strategies. Also, at this time it must be determined if the necessary resources (personnel, machine time, and financing) are available, or can be made available, to complete the project by a mutually determined product completion date.

If the new product concept fits in with these strategies and requirements, the Engineering Group then must begin working with the Software Development Group in the scheduling of the project.

In order to properly schedule a new product, the Engineering Group must, with the help of the Marketing Group, decide on what the product will look like when placed on the shelf. Once this is determined, the Engineering Group works its way backwards from a product completion date (determined by Engineering, Marketing, and Software Development Group department heads) and begins scheduling each individual task which will eventually form the finished product.

In general terms, this consists of working with technical writers to write documentation, artists to design the packaging, printers to do any necessary printing, software reproduction houses to schedule production runs and the Marketing and Software Development Groups in order to schedule all activities so they will culminate in a finished marketable product on a specific date.

PRODUCT PRODUCTION

There are five distinct task areas that the Engineering Group is responsible for within the overall area called Product Production. These are:

1) Production of Product,
2) Quality Control,
3) Inventory Control,
4) Purchasing, and
5) Shipping/Receiving.

Production of Product. Microware will use the services of outside firms which specialize in the manufacturing of the various components that will comprise the overall product. By using these speciality firms (professional printers, software duplication houses, etc.), the Company is able to produce a quality product with the economies of scale of a much larger firm, allowing for a greater profit margin for the firm.

Quality Control. Microware will continue in the future, as it has in the past, to do all final assembly work of their products. Doing this step in-house enables the Company to inspect all the components of the finished product before it is assembled, therefore guaranteeing a very high quality finished product.

Quality control is a very important consideration within our firm and for this reason we have developed a two-phase quality control process which is used during the development stage of our software products. These two phases are:

1) Alpha Phase, and
2) Beta Phase.

The Alpha Phase consists of the development of the initial product concepts into detailed design specifications, which then lead into the development of a prototype. During this stage, the Engineering Group coordinates the activities of both the Software Development and Marketing Groups to ensure that each is getting what resources it needs from the other group to efficiently develop a marketable product.

As the prototype is being developed, Engineering, Software Development and Marketing compare the prototype against the original product specification. This specification indicates product function, components, product attributes and other vital information. Once approved by the department heads of each of the three groups, the potential product begins the Beta Phase.

In the Beta Phase, the prototype product is completed to meet all marketing requirements, including all documentation and product packaging. The prototype product is then run through a series of tests by each of the three departments involved in its creation before it is released for test marketing.

By using this two-phase quality control process, the Company is able to make any needed product revisions at an early stage of the product's development, as well as guaranteeing that the Company will produce a high quality product.

Inventory Control. With the high cost of capital and the short shelf-life of some of the product components, inventory control is a very important issue for Microware. The Engineering Group is responsible for maintaining proper inventory levels on all product components, as well as for finished goods.

Since there are relatively few components that comprise the finished product, this task is not as difficult as it may appear. Also, by using speciality firms that have short lead times, the Company is able to keep its inventory and buffer stocks at a relatively low level, and therefore able to avoid having large amounts of money invested in inventory.

Purchasing. The Engineering Group also acts as the purchasing agent for the Company. This simplifies the purchasing process and allows the Engineering Group to build a good working relationship with its various vendors. This also helps maintain a high quality level.

Shipping/Receiving. The Engineering Group is also responsible for shipping and receiving of finished goods to dealers and distributors. As the volume and complexity of products shipped increases, this function will become a separate department.

NOTES

1. Pseudonyms are used for all individuals, organizations, programs, and products directly involved in this research.

2. Although my process of data analysis was somewhat intuitive and idiosyncratic, I generally followed the "Constant Comparison" method of data

analysis (Glaser and Strauss). For a discussion of the intuitive nature of data analysis in ethnography, see Doheny-Farina and Odell, 525–30. In addition to these research methods, I employed variations on the Discourse-Baed Interview methodology (Odell, Goswami, and Herrington). Those interviews provided data that I used in my previous report on writing at Microware (Doheny-Farina). Although those interviews do not play a direct role in the analysis in this chapter, they do play an indirect role in that the interviews increased my overall understanding of the participants and their writing.

3. To insure complete confidentiality, I have not identified the university magazine that I quote from a number of times in this chapter. The magazine issue that I used as a source contained three major articles about the Start-Up Project: an interview with Paulo Abruzzi, an article about Microware, and an article about all of the companies in the Start-Up Project. All of Abruzzi's quotes come from these articles.

4. I am indebted to the editors and the unnamed reviewers for suggesting the direction of this alternate view.

BIBLIOGRAPHY

Bazerman, Charles. "Scientific Writing as a Social Act: A Review of the Literature of the Sociology of Science." In *New Essays in Technical and Scientific Communication: Research, Theory, Practice*, ed. P. Anderson, R. Brockman, and C. Miller, 156–84. Farmingdale, N.Y.: Baywood, 1983.

Broadhead, Glenn, and Richard Freed. *The Variables of Composition: Process and Product in a Business Setting*. Carbondale, Ill.: Southern Illinois University Press, 1986.

Bruffee, Kenneth A. "Collaborative Learning and the Conversation of Mankind." *College English* 46 (November 1984): 635–52.

Bruffee, Kenneth A. "Social Construction, Language, and the Authority of Knowledge: A Bibliographic Essay." *College English* 48 (December 1986): 773–90.

Cooper, Marilyn M. "The Ecology of Writing." *College English* 48 (April 1986): 364–75.

Doheny-Farina, Stephen. "Writing in an Emerging Organization: An Ethnographic Study." *Written Communication* 3 (April 1986): 158–85.

Doheny-Farina, Stephen, and Lee Odell. "Ethnographic Research on Writing: Assumptions and Methods." In *Writing in Nonacademic Settings*, ed. Lee Odell and Dixie Goswami, 503–35. New York: Guilford Press, 1985.

Faigley, Lester. "Nonacademic Writing: The Social Perspective." In *Writing in Nonacademic Settings*, ed. Lee Odell and Dixie Goswami, 231–48. New York: Guilford Press, 1985.

Glaser, Barney, and Anselm Strauss. *The Discovery of Grounded Theory: Strategies for Qualitative Research*. New York: Aldine, 1967.

Harrison, Teresa. "Frameworks for the Study of Writing in Organizational Contexts." *Written Communication* 9 (January 1987): 3–23.

Herrington, Anne J. "Classrooms as Forums for Reasoning and Writing." *College Composition and Communication* 36 (December 1985): 404–13.

Larouche, Mary G., and Sheryl S. Pearson. "Rhetoric and Rational Enterprises: Reassessing Discourse in Organizations." *Written Communication* 2 (July 1985): 246–68.

Lefevre, Karen Burke. *Invention as a Social Act.* Carbondale: Southern Illinois University Press, 1987.

Myers, Greg. "The Social Construction of Two Biologists' Proposals." *Written Communication* 2 (July 1985): 219–45.

Odell, Lee. "Beyond the Text: Relations Between Writing and Social Context." In *Writing in Nonacademic Settings*, ed. Lee Odell and Dixie Goswami, 249–80. New York: Guilford Press, 1985.

Odell, Lee, and Dixie Goswami. "Writing in a Non-Academic Setting." *Research in the Teaching of English* 16 (October 1982): 201–23.

Odell, Lee, Dixie Goswami, and Anne Herrington. "The Discourse-Based Interview: A Procedure for Exploring Tacit Knowledge of Writers in Nonacademic Settings." In *Research on Writing: Principles and Methods*, ed. P. Mosenthal, L. Tamor, and S. Walmsley, 220–36. New York: Longman, 1983.

Paradis, James, David Dobrin, and Richard Miller. "Writing at Exxon ITD: Notes on the Writing Environment of an R&D Organization." In *Writing in Nonacademic Settings*, ed. Lee Odell and Dixie Goswami, 281–307. New York: Guilford Press, 1985.

Selzer, Jack. "The Composing Process of an Engineer." *College Composition and Communication* 34 (May 1983): 178–87.

Shatzman, Leonard, and Anselm Strauss. *Field Research.* Englewood Cliffs, N.J.: Prentice Hall, 1973.

Spilka, Rachel. "Studying Writer-Reader Interactions in the Workplace." *The Technical Writing Teacher* 3 (Fall 1988): 208–21.

Winsor, Dorothy A. "An Engineer's Writing and the Corporate Construction of Knowledge." *Written Communication* 6 (July 1989): 270–85.

14 INTERTEXTUALITY IN

TAX ACCOUNTING

GENERIC, REFERENTIAL,

AND FUNCTIONAL

AMY J. DEVITT

This article examines the definition and function of text in a single professional community, that of tax accountants.[1] Within a social constructivist perspective (e.g., Faigley; Bizzell; Bruffee), this study extends the many productive studies of single text-types (e.g., Miller and Selzer; Myers, "Text as Knowledge Claims") and of a discourse community's epistemology and values (e.g., studies by Bazerman and by Myers). It both describes the many different text-types in the tax accounting community and interprets these texts in terms of their social and epistemological functions for that community. Such description and interpretation should contribute to our developing understanding of how texts work in specific discourse communities. Because this study explores all of the text-types within a community, however, it explores not only how single texts function but also how texts interact. This chapter will try to sort out the complex set of relationships among texts within a single professional field. Examining the structured set of relationships among texts reveals a professional community that is highly intertextual as well as textual.

The tax accounting community is interwoven with texts: texts are the tax accountant's product, constituting and defining the accountant's work. These texts also interact within the community. They form a complex network of interaction, a structured set of relationships among texts, so that any text is best understood within the context of other texts. No text is single, as texts refer to one another, draw from one another, create the purpose for one another. These texts and their interaction are so integral to the community's work that they essentially constitute and govern the tax accounting community, defining and reflecting that community's epistemology and values.

Although my emphasis on textual interaction and the term "intertextuality" has its source in a concept from recent literary theory, this article's exploration of intertextuality is not attempting to apply the literary concept to nonliterary texts. This article's use of the term shares with literary theory the attempt to define how texts interact with past, present, and future texts, and it shares what Thais Morgan describes as an emphasis on "text/discourse/culture" (2). But the descriptive term "intertextuality" is used here more broadly to encapsulate the interaction of texts within a single discourse community, a single field of knowledge, and to enable the study of all types of relationships among texts, whether referential, generic, functional, or any other kind.

It is in this sense that this chapter will explore the highly textual and intertextual world of the tax accountant. It explores the range of texts written by members of that profession, how those texts serve the rhetorical needs of the community, how those texts interact, and how that interaction both reflects the values and constitutes the work of the profession. After describing the study's sources, this article will describe: the types of texts (or genres) written by tax accountants (generic intertextuality); how those types use other texts (referential intertextuality); and how those types interact in the particular community (functional intertextuality). Overall, this study shows that the profession exists within a rich intertextual environment, that the profession's texts weave an intricate web of intertextuality. The tax accountant's world is as much a world of texts as of numbers.

Methods: Sample Texts and Interviews

This study was designed to discover the kinds of texts written within a single professional community and how those texts function for the community. The sources of information in this study took primarily two forms: samples of texts, and interviews with accountants. In order to examine the range of written texts, I contacted the managing partner of a regional office of each of the "Big 8" accounting firms and asked him to send me at least three samples of every kind of writing done in his tax accounting department. Six of the eight firms responded by sending me samples of between five and seven different types of texts. These samples were examined primarily to define the kinds of writing they represented, the rhetorical situations they seemed to reflect, and the use they seemed to make of other texts. First, these texts were examined to determine the degree of overlap among the types established by the six firms, to determine whether the texts themselves confirmed the existence of these types, and to hypothesize reconciliations of any conflicts between the textual and expert evidence. Second, the texts were examined for evidence of the rhetorical situations to which they responded, paying special attention to a comparison of situations within and across the text-types. Third, all of the texts were examined for internal reference to other texts of any type, and selected references to published texts were compared to the original sources.

The hypotheses deriving from these textual analyses became the bases for interview questions. Interviews of at least one hour each were conducted with eight different accountants from the six firms, ranging in experience from two to eighteen years and ranging in rank from "Senior" accountants (one step up from "Staff" or entry-level accountants) to "Managers" and "Partners." Each interview included discourse-based (see Odell et al.) and open-ended questions, including questions about what is written in that firm's tax department, who writes and reviews what is written, and how the texts originate, are written, and are used. Those discoveries of the textual analyses and interviews most relevant to intertextuality are presented in the rest of this article. The next three sections explore three kinds of intertextuality, the forms and functions they take, and their relationships to the culture and its rhetorical situations.

Generic Intertextuality: Situation and Task from Intertextuality

Essentially, as Faigley and Miller have suggested for some other companies (564), texts are the accounting firm's product. In return for their fees, its clients receive texts—whether a tax return, a letter to the Internal Revenue Service (IRS), an opinion letter, or a verbal text over the phone[2] (then documented by a memorandum in the client's file). Seen as a corporate product, the accountant's text is designed to fulfill some corporate need; as a rhetorical product, a piece of discourse, the text is designed to respond to a rhetorical need. In Lloyd Bitzer's terms, the text responds to a rhetorical situation. The rhetorical situations to which the accountant's texts must respond, however, tend to be repeated because of the defining context of the professional community. Clients have recurring rhetorical needs for which they request the accountant's rhetorical products. As accountants repeatedly respond to these recurring rhetorical situations, common discourse forms tend also to recur (see Bitzer; Miller). Each text draws on previous texts written in response to similar situations. Through such interaction of texts, genres evolve as recurring forms in recurring rhetorical situations.[3] Whenever an accountant writes a text within a genre, he or she is making a connection to previous texts within the community.

As a corporate product, this generic intertextuality both defines and serves the needs of the tax accounting community. As a corporate product, too, the genres of tax accountants constitute "social actions," as defined by Miller in her "Genre As Social Action." Although how to define genre has been a controversial issue in several disciplines (see, for example, Campbell and Jamieson's 1978 collection of articles), the understanding of genre as social action requires that genre be defined by the genre's users, that the essence of genre be *recognition* by its users (see Bazerman, *Shaping Written Knowledge*). As Marie-Laure Ryan writes, "The significance of generic categories thus resides in their cognitive and cultural value, and the purpose of genre theory is to lay out the implicit knowledge of the users of genres" (112). Asking the users, the members of the community, to create their own categories, as this study did, thus enables a community definition of genres.

Although the labels given vary slightly, the tax accountants consulted in this study (henceforth referred to as "experts") generally agreed on the kinds of writing they produce. The thirteen genres of tax accounting are listed in table 14.1.[4]

Table 14.1. The Genres Written by Tax Accountants

Genres	No. of firms sending	No. of samples received
Nontechnical correspondence	3	5
Administrative memoranda	4	17
Transmittal letters	5	20
Engagement letters	2	4
Memoranda for the files	4	9
Research memoranda	5	18
Letters to clients: Promotional	2	6
Letters to clients: Opinion	6	11
Letters to clients: Response	4	10
Letters to taxing authorities	5	14
Tax protests	3	5
Tax provision reviews	2	6
Proposals	1	3

These thirteen genres form a set which reflects the professional activities and social relations of tax accountants. Each genre reflects a different rhetorical situation which in turn reflects a different combination of circumstances that the tax accountant repeatedly encounters. In the somewhat simplified terms of rhetorical audience, purpose, subject, and occasion, tax accountants are called on to write to clients or to IRS representatives or to each other; they are required to inform, persuade, or argue; they must deal with the subjects of tax returns, IRS notices, IRS documents, tax legislation, or audit workpapers; and they must be the first contact or a follow-up contact, making a legal statement or transmitting a legal statement, and so on. In general terms, the accountant's primary activity is to interpret the tax regulations for a client, involving subactivities ranging from completing tax forms to advocating the client's position to the taxing authorities. As middleman, the accountant establishes relationships with both the client and the taxing authorities (as well as with other accountants). These repeated, structured activities and relationships of the profession constitute the rhetorical situations to which the established genres respond.

Research memoranda, for example, respond to the need to support with evidence from IRS documents every important position taken by the firm on a tax question or issue involved in a client's taxes; thus a senior accountant typically asks a junior accountant to write a research memorandum summarizing the IRS statements on an issue. Letters to taxing authorities respond to notices or assessments sent to clients and attempt to negotiate a favorable action by an agent. A tax protest is written when negotiation has been unsuccessful; it is a legal and formal argument to a taxing authority for a client's position on an issue. Tax provision reviews, also legal documents, officially certify to both shareholders and taxing authorities the validity of a corporation's provisions for taxes, as part of a larger audit. The three kinds of letters to clients all explain tax regulations to clients: the promotional letter explains the relevance of a tax law to a client's situation in order to encourage effective tax planning and to generate new business; the opinion letter explains the firm's interpretation of the tax rules on a specific client issue, taking an official and legally liable stand on how a client's taxes should be treated; finally, a response letter explains what tax regulations say about a tax issue, summarizing general alternatives in response to a client's question but without taking a stand on how the regulations would apply to the client's specific case.

Together with oral genres and tax returns, these kinds of texts form the accountant's genre system, a set of genres interacting to accomplish the work of the tax department. In examining the genre set of a community, we are examining the community's situations, its recurring activities and relationships. The genre set accomplishes its work.

This genre set not only reflects the profession's situations; it may also help to define and stabilize those situations. The mere existence of an established genre may encourage its continued use, and hence the continuation of the activities and relations associated with that genre. Since a tax provision review has always been attached to an audit, for example, a review of the company's tax provisions is expected as part of the auditing activity; since a transmittal letter has always accompanied tax returns and literature, sending a return may require the establishment of some personal contact, whether or not any personal relationship exists.

The existence and stabilizing function of this intertextuality both within and across genres are demonstrated by the similarity of the genre sets and all instances of a genre across all of the accounting firms. A research memorandum or an opinion letter is essentially the same no matter which firm produces it. Originally, the similarity of "superstructure" (in "canonical form," see van Dijk and Kintsch) within texts of the same genre may have derived from choices made in response to a rhetorical situation. For example, a research memorandum typically states the tax question and the answer before discussing the IRS evidence for that answer; such an organization may have developed as the most effective response to the situation of a busy partner with a specific question who needs later to document his answer. Yet this organization eventually becomes an expectation of the genre: writers may organize in this way and readers may expect this organization not, any longer, because it is most effective rhetorically but because it is the way other texts responding to similar situations have been organized. Bazerman points out both the "constraints and opportunities" provided by these generic expectations, for:

> the individual writer in making decisions concerning persuasion, must write within a form that takes into account the audience's current expectation of what appropriate writing in the field is. These expectations provide resources as well as constraints, for they provide a guide as to how an argument should be formulated, and may suggest ways of presenting material that might not have occurred to the free play of imagination. . . . The conventions provide both the symbolic tools to be used and suggestions for their use. ("Modern Evolution," 165)

These shared conventions serve to stabilize the profession's activities also because they help the community to accomplish its work more efficiently. One accountant, for example, explained that, when he trusts the writer of a research memorandum, "if I were in a hurry to get back to a client, I could read his first page, and I'd feel very comfortable with being able to call the client with the answer. . . . but I know that if sometime I were ever pressed or the question came up on review, that [his] memo would have behind the initial answer the documentation to back up our position." The stabilizing power of genres, through the interaction of texts within the same genre, thus increases the efficiency of creating the firm's products.

In this way, genres both may restrict the profession's activities and relationships to those embodied in the genre system and may enable the most effective and efficient response to any recurring situation. Thus generic intertextuality serves the needs of the professional community within each genre as well as within a genre system. Both kinds of generic intertextuality reflect and serve the needs of tax accountants, the rhetorical situations to which they must respond in writing in order to accomplish the firm's work.

Referential Intertextuality: Intertextuality as Resource

A more precise understanding of tax accountants' activities and relationships is revealed by their use of other texts, by the reference within one text to another text. This internal reference to other texts, what I call "referential intertextuality," is the most obvious kind of interaction among texts. Its significance lies in the manner and function of such reference, for the patterns of reference reflect again the profession's activities and relationships. For tax accountants, texts serve as their primary resource, as both their subject and their authority. How they serve these functions depends in part on the genre being written, as a consequence of genre's embodiment of a rhetorical situation, and in part on the epistemology of the profession.

TEXTS AS SUBJECT

In addition to serving as the accounting firm's product, texts also serve as the accountant's subject matter. Most commonly, the tax accountant writes about other texts—about a client's tax return, about an IRS notice, or about an IRS regulation. Because each genre reflects a different rhetorical situation, each genre also reflects a typical subject, one component of the situation; and the subjects of the genres most specific to tax accounting tend to be other texts. The genres of nontechnical correspondence, administrative memoranda, engagement letters, and proposals take a variety of subjects, not necessarily text-based. Memoranda for the files are always about oral texts, the meetings and phone calls that they are designed to document. The remaining eight genres typically or even by definition have written texts as their primary subject matter. In some senses, not only does intertextuality help accountants to accomplish their work; intertextuality *is* their work.

Transmittal letters, of course, are basically references to enclosed documents (for tax accountants, those documents are usually tax returns; occasionally they are planning brochures or research memoranda). The tax provision review is explicitly a review of other documents: the audit's workpapers. Both tax protests and letters to taxing authorities are about the documents exchanged between a taxpayer and the IRS: the taxpayer's returns and associated schedules and forms, and the IRS' notices, assessments, and letters to the taxpayer in response to those documents. Finally, research memoranda and all three kinds of letters to clients are essentially about IRS publications. Though each may have an issue or question as its subject, that issue is essentially always a version of "What does the IRS say about this issue?" For example, one research memorandum asks "What is the appropriate tax treatment of [several specific business transactions] under the Tax Reform Act of 1986?"[5] Another considers "Does the annual lease value for an employer-provided automobile consider the value for fuel provided in kind by the employer?" In both cases, the answer is a review of what specific IRS documents say. Letters to clients may be less direct than research memoranda in the statement of their subjects; nonetheless, their subjects too are the IRS documents. Promotional letters, in fact, often originate in a new IRS text: the Tax Reform Act of 1986 produced a spate of promotional as well as other letters to clients. Opinion and response letters to clients may be responses to a client's question about S-corporation status or the deductibility of types of interest or the tax impact of a corporate gain or innumerable other topics. Again, each asks about IRS statements on the issue.

Thus each text — and each genre — in part derives its meaning from other texts, those that constitute its subject matter. Because each genre embodies a recurring typical situation, each genre has a typical subject matter; for tax accountants, that typical subject is a set of texts. Of course, each text refers explicitly to its typical subject, thereby creating a pattern of reference that reveals explicitly the text's professional purpose. The role of the accountant in this professional activity is more subtly revealed in the other use of intertextual reference: in the use of texts for authority.

TEXTS AS AUTHORITY

Two kinds of texts are most important as both subject and authority in tax accounting: client-specific documents and general tax publications. Client-specific documents include completed state and federal tax returns, schedules, and forms as well as IRS letters and notices to the individual client. There are many different general tax publications, applicable to all potential taxpayers. Most commonly used are the IRS Codes and Regulations, Revenue Rulings and Bulletins, Tax Court decisions, and tax legislation (such as the Tax Reform Act of 1986). Though not all equal in authority, all of these documents serve as a backdrop to most of the writing done by tax accountants. The IRS documents lie behind most texts in tax accounting as the Bible lies behind most texts written by Christian ministers.

Amount of explicit reference. Explicit reference to general tax publications, including citation and quotation, is thus prevalent in the texts of tax accountants. Table 14.2 summarizes how many such references to specific IRS documents occur for every 200 words. The nine genres included are those written by the tax department alone (thereby excluding engagement letters and proposals) and about tax matters (excluding administrative memoranda and nontechnical correspondence).

Table 14.2. Number of Explicit References to Specific IRS Publications per 200 Words, by Genre

Genre	No. of Texts	Average No. of References	Median No. of References	Range
Memoranda for files	9	.24	0	0/1.19
Transmittal letters	20	.35	0	0/2.74
Letters to taxing authorities	14	.38	0	0/3.08
Tax provision reviews	6	.47	.34	0/1.39
Letters to clients: Response	10	.86	.67	0/3.00
Letters to clients: Promotional	6	1.94	1.69	0/5.02
Letters to clients: Opinion	11	2.62	2.26	0/7.64
Research memoranda	18	3.72	2.32	0/10.67
Tax protests	5	2.47	2.54	.81/4.34
All texts	99	1.47	.50	0/10.67

Although the numbers are sometimes too few (and judgments of what constitutes a reference sometimes too ambiguous)[6] for these numbers to be statistically valid, they are suggestive of the differences among genres in terms of how often they refer to IRS documents. These differing amounts of reference relate again to the differing activities and relationships, the situations, embedded in each genre, especially to the roles that the accountant must serve in each genre.

Transmittal letters and memoranda for the files, of course, neither take the IRS regulations as their subject matter nor need them as evidence for an explanation or argument. They refer heavily instead to the client-specific documents, primarily the returns enclosed or discussed. (The six of these twenty-nine texts that do refer to the IRS documents do so when they incorporate or report discussion of a client's question or of the need to follow an IRS regulation.) The third genre with a median of zero references to IRS documents uses the general tax publications only, but significantly, as deep background. We might expect letters to the IRS which are requesting an agent's action to be full of IRS authority for taking that action. However, the texts and the interviews with the accountants reveal a different role for the accountant in such letters. At issue is not the tax law, but the facts of the case: whether the agent calculated correctly in her penalty assessment, whether the taxpayer has a required document, or whether the agent has implemented a previously agreed-upon adjustment, for example. One letter thus asks an agent to "investigate the discrepancy between the 1099-G issued to [the taxpayers] (copy enclosed) and the amount they have received"; another responds to a penalty notice with copies of the original return and forms which document the exception to the penalty. Thus, only the client-specific documents are cited explicitly. In this genre, the accountant acts as documenter of facts rather than interpreter of tax law, assuming that the agent will apply the tax law correctly once the correct facts are known. The general tax publications thus serve here as the unacknowledged, but pervasive, environment within which both accountant and agent operate.

The accountant does take on the role of interpreter of tax law (and hence uses frequent reference to IRS texts) in a tax protest, when the facts of a case have been settled in an audit but the agent and accountant disagree on how tax law applies to those facts. The accountant's protest of the agent's interpretation is then formally presented to higher authorities, to what one expert referred to as "fellow technicians," who will decide the issue based on the arguments of the written text. The accountant's role in such a protest is that of advocate for the client, but his or her advocacy will succeed only to the extent that he or she is successful in the role of interpreter of the tax law. Not surprisingly, then, these official protests use more reference to specific IRS documents than any other genre except perhaps the research memorandum. As one accountant said, "you really want to supply them with as much ammunition from your side as possible in hopes that they will just simply say, 'Well, there is an awful lot of support, and we're not going to pursue our side of the argument.' " The source of such ammunition is the general tax publications, the IRS authority.

Whether tax accountants are serving as documenters of facts or as interpreters of law, texts thus serve as the final authority for their work. When a genre requires the accountant merely to describe the facts — as in letters to taxing authorities or, to some extent, tax provision reviews — client-specific documents are sufficient authority. When a genre requires the accountant to interpret the law, the general tax publications must establish the authority. Thus the three genres with the highest rate of reference to IRS documents are tax protests, research memoranda, and opinion letters to clients — all three genres which embody situations demanding a precise stand on a debatable tax issue.

Type of reference. The rhetorical demands of each genre are reflected in the type as well as the number of references to general tax publications. More broadly, the manner of reference in accountants' texts reveals an underlying perspective of the profession, a set of beliefs about the source of knowledge, expertise, and authority that may influence other aspects of their rhetoric.[7] In essence, the accountant's authority and expertise reside in the general tax publications. This epistemology is so pervasive that virtually every text is at least implicitly and deeply tied to the tax publications. How explicitly the epistemology is acknowledged may correlate with the genre and its underlying situation, but all manner of reference to the general tax publications is predicated on this belief in the authority of the text.

As described above, those genres which require interpretation of the tax law also include the greatest number of references to the tax publications — a fact reflecting the belief that knowledge and authority reside in the IRS documents. These genres also cite those sources as specifically as possible. Citations in opinion letters, for example, include "I.R.C. Section 953(c)(3)(C)," "IRC section 1504(a)(4)," "Treasury Regulation 1.305-5 (b)(2)," and "The Conference Report to the Tax Reform Act of 1984"; or one encloses a copy of "Revenue Announcement 87-4." Such specific citations are much more common than references to, say, "Treasury Regulations" in general. Although written to a nonexpert audience, to a client rather than an accountant, the opinion letter must be as specific as possible to be precisely accurate and legally defensible. The costs of inaccuracy are high: if the IRS disagrees with any position in an opinion letter, as one expert said, "Our insurance premiums go up"; another partner defined the opinion letter as "anything we could be sued on." To establish the accuracy of their interpretation of the law, accountants depend not on extensive explanations of their logic but rather on frequent and specific citation of the tax codes and regulations, on citation of the authority. Such specific citation is even more true of tax protests and research memoranda, which are always written to tax experts and which always specify the precise authority.

In contrast, a response letter, with fewer than one explicit reference per 200 words on average, refers generally to "Section 401(k)" or "Code Section 7872," or even more commonly to the law without any precise reference, as in nonspecific references to "tax law" or "several specific requirements" or "5 sets of regulations" or "the new law" or "the rules and guidelines." One expert explained the lack of specific reference in response and promotional letters in terms of rhetorical strategy: "A lot of times when we're writing to clients, we're either answering a question to them or we're trying to get them to react. And if you're going to try and get the typical client to react, you have to make them understand what you're saying. And if you add citations, a lot of times they'll turn off to it." Even such general citations, of course, still lend documented authority to the accountant's explanation, but more of the authority comes from the reader's trust of the accountant. As one expert stated, "Typically, clients don't know about the Code and the Regs, and if they do know they don't care to know in detail. They just want the bottom-line answer. They don't want how you got there." Clients want the answer without the citations, but they still want the answer of an accountant, someone who can "get there" because of his or her knowledge of the IRS documents. While the client's trust is in the accountant's expertise (and hence explicit references to authoritative texts are generally unnecessary except as signs of that expertise), the *accountant's* trust is in the IRS texts, from which that expertise derives. To the accountant, therefore, a response letter may require few references but establishing an opinion requires specific reference to the authority of the texts, no matter who the audience. Accountants often even create research memoranda, with their frequent and specific citations, to be placed in the file of a client who just wanted "the bottom-line answer." The answer lies in the texts, so the source of the answer must be cited.

The pervasiveness of this textual authority appears even more powerfully in accounting texts' use of quotation. As accountants draw on the IRS texts for subject matter and authority, they may use those texts in four general ways: explicit quotation, unmarked quotation, paraphrase, or interpretation. But in the texts of tax accountants, the distinctions among these four methods blur. By far the most common method in all genres is unmarked quotation, what teachers might call "plagiarism." According to the experts interviewed, unmarked quotation often suits the rhetorical needs and especially the epistemological values of the accounting community. The most authoritative texts of the tax community (the IRS Codes and Regulations) must be taken literally, with Tax Court Decisions and Revenue Rulings and so on serving as interpretive guides. To change a word in the Code may be to change its meaning; thus quotation is always more accurate than paraphrase. (In fact, some accountants, for their files, attach to their research memoranda and letters photocopies of the actual code sections and other texts — the most extreme form of quotation.)

Most of the experts agreed that paraphrase may be used when the section needed is too long to quote or occasionally when it is too technical for the audience, especially in letters to clients (though only then if the clients would not act on the basis of the letter's instructions). But the experts preferred paraphrase much more often than they actually used it in the sample texts. One expert, a partner especially reluctant ever to paraphrase, echoed others when he said:

> If it's a memorandum to an [in-house] auditor, or an outside party that is not tax-knowledgeable, then paraphrasing is *probably* OK and appropriate unless you're writing a tax opinion, where someone is going to rely on that information. Then you need to make sure that either what you've paraphrased or what you're telling them is in fact what is. . . . In the tax rules and tax law, you can get into a lot of trouble missing an "and" or an "or" or a comma.

In essence, the acceptability of paraphrase depended on the level of knowledge of the primary audience and even more on the use to be made of the document. During interviews, the experts most often stated a preference for paraphrase over quotation when the audience had no technical background; but in the sample texts, including response letters to clients, paraphrase appeared much less often than did unmarked quotation.

With paraphrase often eliminated as potentially inaccurate, unmarked quotation appears to take the place of paraphrase as a rhetorical strategy. Although some of the experts seemed self-conscious about the potential "plagiarism" and several seemed unaware that they used unmarked quotation, most easily argued their rhetorical need for unmarked quotation. While choosing quotation for accuracy (and presumably also for ease, since even genres in which the experts preferred paraphrase showed more unmarked quotation), the writers often responded to the rhetorical situation of a lay audience by leaving the quotation unmarked. As one expert stated:

If it had the quote marks around it, the reader may think that, "Well, now I'm reading a Code section" — well, the reader *would* think that they're reading a Code section and that may scare them away. Whereas without the quotes, they may simply be saying, "Well, now I'm reading the writer's interpretation of the section, which ought to be more understandable because supposedly they're putting it in a more layman's language." Again, it depends on who the reader is.

The client, in other words, would interpret the unmarked quotation as paraphrase or interpretation. Again, the client wants the accountant's expertise based on his or her knowledge of the tax documents; the accountant's authority is not only sufficient but preferred. But for the accountant, only the text itself is sufficient. From the accountant's view, unmarked quotation satisfies the needs of both.

For the other audiences of the accountant, however, the tax regulators and colleagues, only the text itself has such authority. Paraphrasing in a tax protest is "diluting its effect." Explicit quotation may lend extra support to the argument:

I think the [quotation marks] help. . . . I really want the reader when he sees the quotes to *know* that this isn't *my personal* thinking, that this truly *is* a Revenue Ruling. The words here are not my words but the words of the Revenue Ruling. . . . When I'm writing to the agent I want him to believe that I'm quoting what he *has* to follow, namely the Revenue Rulings.

Yet, in texts other than tax protests, most of the experts said that using quotation marks was unimportant. Unless explicit quotation supported a rhetorical argument, as in tax protests, quotation marks often seemed to them unnecessary. Perhaps with fellow technicians as audience, the quotations contain the authority of the text's original words whether marked explicitly or not. Most revealing, perhaps, may be one accountant's comment when asked about using quotation marks:

I guess in my mind I'm not sure I'm citing it verbatim. . . . If a *person* had said it, maybe it's different, because I would give credit to that person. But the Internal Revenue Code is essentially a text to be utilized by practitioners as a guide, essentially, and what's right and what's wrong according to tax law. And I don't even think about quoting them sometimes. It doesn't lend anything more to it.

The words of the texts *are* the tax law.

Amy J. Devitt

The last quotation also reveals how pervasive the reliance on the tax publications is. Since the general tax publications are the tax law, governing and regulating the entire profession, virtually any statement made about taxes by a tax accountant is tied to those documents. Since the accountant's expertise derives from his or her knowledge of the tax code and regulations, the distinction between accounting's textual knowledge and professional knowledge breaks down. The tax publications are so deeply and implicitly embedded in the accountant's work that they often leave few explicit markers and are virtually invisible to the textual analyst. The tax codes, how to work with them, and how to apply them to cases *are* the tacit knowledge of the profession.

Because the tax codes and regulations constitute the accountant's work in so many ways and because they are the source of the accountant's expertise, the education of aspiring accountants emphasizes learning what these documents contain and how to use them. The students are being trained in the profession's epistemological assumptions, that these documents are the source of all knowledge and authority. However, beginning accountants must also learn how that epistemology translates into their own texts. They must learn that different types of reference to the tax codes are appropriate in different genres, that quotation is generally preferable to paraphrase, that unmarked quotation may be used in most genres. Most of all, they must learn that those tax publications are the highest authority for anything they might write. Perhaps the centrality of this epistemology is why entry-level accountants in all of the firms begin by writing research memoranda. As the simplest and most explicit form of translation from tax publications into other texts, research memoranda require new accountants to begin learning how to translate while keeping them tied to the authoritative texts. The structure of this genre also reinforces the profession's epistemology most explicitly: focus on the issue, state the answer, then spend most of the pages citing sources and quoting passages from the tax code to support that answer. As central as referential intertextuality appears to be to the work of the accountant, learning the translations of this epistemology to other texts, learning the techniques of reference for different genres and rhetorical situations, may well be a major learning task of the junior accountant and a crucial mark of membership in that professional community.

Functional Intertextuality: Community Consequences of Intertextuality

The authority of text and the interactions among texts (both generic and referential) may be seen in many ways as what defines the community of tax accountants. All members of the community share a deep knowledge of the general tax publications; all members use a single set of genres; all members learn the appropriate techniques of translating the tax publications into the different genres; and all members acknowledge the authority of these tax publications. All members also acknowledge the authority of specific past texts over future texts. Every text written in an accounting firm consequently has a residual life within the firm. These texts — and the belief in the authority of these texts — also help to define membership in the more particular community of the specific accounting firm.

Ideally, every bit of work done for a client is documented on paper, and, ideally, every one of those documents is placed in the client's file. Each text thus becomes part of a larger macrotext, the macrotext of that client's "tax situation" or "fact pattern." Ideally, every accountant who ever does work for a client reviews that client's file, that macrotext. In practice, accountants sometimes forget to document a meeting or decide that it is too costly to create a memorandum about a simple phone call. In practice, some busy accountants often perform work for a client without taking the time to check the client's file. In spite of the discrepancy between the ideal and the real, all of the accountants interviewed held strongly to the importance of the ideal. Even an accountant with only two years' experience had learned its importance: "The longer you're here the more you learn that you *have* to document. . . . So that's something that, as I progress here, I'm trying to impress on people below me: 'Write it down. Write it down. I don't care how silly it seems, make a note of it.' "

This same accountant always pulls the file on a client before doing any work for the client: "One thing could affect another thing. Even though you wouldn't off the top of your head think they would be related, unless you go through and look at everything, your recommendation may change based on other things that have happened." The complete set of facts about the client, represented by the file's macrotext, creates the unique situation to which they must respond. A slight change in the fact pattern can produce a change in the treatment of the client's taxes. As another expert noted:

> The hardest part about getting anybody's return done correctly is not the [tax] law; it is the facts. But the reason that's hard is because the law has become so complicated, and there's so many different variations of facts and so many specific little details you have to know about each item in order to make sure you're complying with the law. . . . We struggle more with getting the facts than we do deciding what to do with the facts once we have them.

Thus, every memorandum for the files, every opinion letter, every letter to the IRS, and every research memorandum potentially affects every future text written for that client. Combined, they constitute the client's situation, the text to which, in some part, all future texts must respond. These past texts thus to some extent have authority over any future text.

Every one of the texts written by tax accountants thus has a residual life in the macrotext of the client's file. As part of this larger text, it may influence future texts. Texts also may have residual lives if they become incorporated into other texts or if they prompt the writing of other texts. Accountants sometimes use the "cut and paste" method of composition: they may create letters to clients or occasionally tax protests out of research memoranda; they may modify form letters and explanations sent by the national office to create promotional or response letters; and they typically create transmittal and engagement letters (and some proposals) out of standard form letters.

In addition to such incorporation of one text into another, past texts may influence future texts by creating the need for those future texts. Of course, no accounting text stands alone in that virtually every text written by an accountant is prompted by another text — audit workpapers produce a tax provision review; a request for proposals produces a proposal; a tax notice produces a letter to the IRS; or a written or verbal request from a client produces an opinion or response letter. Yet some of the texts written within the firm may also serve as prompts for other texts. A successful proposal, for example, produces an engagement letter; a letter to the IRS may prompt a transmittal letter for a copy to the client; a successful promotional letter may lead to a response or opinion letter. A few samples received from the firms suggested a more complex cycle of texts: a call from a client prompted two memoranda for the files (documenting the call and requesting help), which prompted a research memorandum, which resulted in another memorandum for the files (reporting the call to answer the client and the client's request for a written response), which in turn prompted an opinion letter to the client. In fact, however, such traces are often hard to follow or to separate. One piece of work for a client may often result in other pieces, without the effect becoming explicit. Since the product of the accountant's work is a text, every text would seem to have some influence on the request for another text, if only through the client's satisfaction with the previous text.

All of these instances of the residual life of texts suggest the centrality of text to the accounting profession's work, and the role of each text in constituting a client's macrotext reveals again the profession's belief in the authority of text. The existence of a higher-level macrotext, the macrotext of the entire firm's work, also helps to define the narrower community of a particular firm within the larger community of accountants.

The use of texts to distinguish the accounting firm community depends on the interaction of texts at the firm level. At this level, texts both establish the firm's hierarchy and draw together all of the higher-level accountants. The firm's hierarchy is reflected in its review procedures, in its policies about who may sign and especially who must review different types of texts. Policies vary across firms, ranging from one in which review is used at the partner's discretion to one in which every document must be reviewed by a single partner; typically, however, review policies require that documents of specific genres be reviewed by any tax partner. Explicitly, the purpose of review procedures is what one firm calls "quality control," for ensuring the technical accuracy of all the firm's documents. Since technical accuracy rests in knowledge of the general tax publications, these review procedures use texts doubly to reinforce the firm's hierarchy (and its epistemology): texts are too important for junior accountants to produce on their own, and only tax partners have sufficient knowledge of the authoritative tax texts to ensure the accuracy of important answers.

These review procedures also help to inform the higher-level accountants of all of the firm's work. Although junior accountants may work from project to project, with their only sense of the firm's work coming from their examination of texts in a client's file, higher-level accountants see much of the work of their subordinates and can use these texts to create a picture of the entire firm's work, across clients. Because texts constitute so much of the accounting firm's work, all of the firm's documents together — its complete set of files, if you will — in important ways constitute a larger macrotext, the text of that firm's work. The use of review procedures to establish a firm-wide text is made explicit in one firm: a tax partner relatively new to the firm requires temporarily that he review every text of any genre; the reason, he says, is that "I'm still uncomfortable with the situation" and he needs to learn more about the firm — he needs to read the firm's text. In another firm, the constitution of a firm's text is literal: all texts written by all accountants in the department are periodically copied, stapled into a single text, and routed to every manager and partner, so that, though described as cumbersome and inefficient, an actual and literal text of the firm is created. Within the specific accounting firm as within the profession as a whole, text constitutes and governs the community.

Conclusion

This examination of the role and interaction of texts within tax accounting has revealed how essential texts are to the constitution and accomplishment of this professional community. Each text functions to accomplish some of the firm's work; together the texts describe a genre system which both delimits and enables its work; particular in-

Amy J. Devitt

stances of the genres together constitute a macrotext for each client and for the firm as a whole, which in turn influences future texts. All of these texts, and the entire profession, rest on another set of texts: the general tax publications which govern and constitute the need for the profession. Acknowledging the authority of these texts is a prerequisite for membership in the accounting community. The profession's epistemology — the implicit belief that these texts are the source of all knowledge and expertise — reveals itself in how these texts are translated into other texts. The interaction of texts within a particular text, within a particular firm, and within the profession at large reveals a profession ultimately dependent on texts in a way essential to understanding writing in that profession.

Such an intricate web of texts may exist in other professions; both law and academe seem obvious instances of professions bound and enabled by texts. To discover such webs, however, we must examine the role of all texts and their interactions in a community — their genre systems and their rhetorical situations, their intertextual references and their underlying epistemologies, their uses and their community functions. Even though tax accountants would appear to work in a world of numbers and of meetings, the source and product of that work appear in texts, resulting in a profession both highly textual and highly intertextual. For tax accountants — and perhaps for other professionals — texts are so interwoven with and deeply embedded in the community that texts constitute its products and its resources, its expertise and its evidence, its needs and its values.

NOTES

This investigation was supported by the University of Kansas General Research Allocation #38120038. I am grateful to the following firms and individuals for their time and generosity: Marci A. Flanery and Kim Mace of Arthur Andersen & Co.; Paul Tyson and Terry L. Gerrond of Arthur Young & Co.; Joseph R. Sims and Jim Nelson of Coopers & Lybrand; W. Rodger Marsh, Jr., of Ernst & Whinney; Christopher A. Cipriano of Price Waterhouse; and Frank Friedman of Touche Ross. I also wish to thank my colleagues in the School of Business, Professors Chester Vanatta and Allen Ford, for sharing their advice and expertise.

1. Because this study examined texts from the regional offices of Big 8 firms only, it does not necessarily apply to the tax accounting profession at large, which includes regional and local accounting firms. I will, however, talk about writing by tax accountants in this article, though more precisely my statements will be about writing by tax accountants in regional offices of Big 8 firms. Based on my information from a variety of sources, I suspect that the

main differences concentrate in who writes different texts rather than in the types of texts written or the rhetorical situations which prompt those texts.

2. Because this section attempts to describe the larger roles of texts, I am here using the broader linguistic definition of texts as either oral or written (see, for example, Halliday). The main concern of this study, however, is with written texts only, and future sections will discriminate between the two media.

3. The relationship among genre, form, and situation is discussed more fully in my *Standardizing Written English: The Case of Scotland 1520–1659* (Cambridge University Press, 1989).

4. Establishment of these thirteen genres is not as clear-cut as table 14.1 implies. Five of these genres served unambiguously as distinct recognition categories for all of the experts (even though some were not considered important enough to send in the original samples). Tax provision reviews were not written as separate documents by two of the six firms. Other genres are potentially troublesome because some experts grouped them into more general categories — i.e., a single category including memoranda for the files and research memoranda, one including letters to taxing authorities and tax protests, and one including all letters to clients. Although raising the issue of distinguishing genres from subgenres, the first two groups are divisible into separate genres based on their recognition as separate categories by the experts in interviews. Letters to clients are subdivided based largely on textual and functional differences, with only partial support from the experts; hence, letters to clients are listed as subgenres.

5. To maintain confidentiality, all identifying information will be removed from cited texts.

6. Table 14.2 includes any references to specific IRS documents and any explicit quotations. The judgments that had to be made were held constant across all texts, yet they do complicate this apparently simple table. For example, a reference to "the new law" was counted if the specific document (i.e., "the Tax Reform Act of 1986") had already been cited in that text, allowing context then to make "the new law" as explicit a reference as "this regulation" after citing a specific regulation; yet the phrase "the new law" occurs in other texts when no specific citation has been given and hence was not counted as a specific reference. This example is, however, the most troublesome of the judgments made. More common were judgments not to count adjectival use of Code section numbers (e.g., "401(k) plan") when they appeared to be merely the name of the concept, or to distinguish between words in quotation marks as quoted terms from a text or as informal expressions. Because of such judgments and the low number of samples of some genres, table 14.2 should be viewed as suggestive only.

7. That tax accountants' dependence on the literal wording of the tax publications has a broader epistemological significance occurred to me as I read the draft of an article about legal writing by Philip C. Kissam, Professor in the School of Law at the University of Kansas. I am indebted to his discussion of "unreflective positivism," embodied in literal adherence to legal texts, and its implications for law school knowledge.

BIBLIOGRAPHY

Bazerman, Charles. "Modern Evolution of the Experimental Report in Physics: Spectroscopic Articles in *Physical Review*, 1893–1980." *Social Studies of Science* 4 (1984): 163–96.

Bazerman, Charles. "Physicists Reading Physics: Schema-Laden Purposes and Purpose-Laden Schema." *Written Communication* 2 (1985): 3–23.

Bazerman, Charles. "Scientific Writing as a Social Act: A Review of the Literature of the Sociology of Science." In *New Essays in Technical and Scientific Communication: Research, Theory, Practice*, ed. Paul V. Anderson, R. John Brockmann, and Carolyn R. Miller, 156–84. Baywood's Technical Communication Series, vol. 2. Farmingdale, N.Y.: Baywood, 1983.

Bazerman, Charles. *Shaping Written Knowledge*. Madison: University of Wisconsin Press, 1988.

Bazerman, Charles. "What Written Knowledge Does: Three Examples of Academic Discourse." *Philosophy of the Social Sciences* 11 (1981): 361–87.

Bazerman, Charles. "The Writing of Scientific Non-Fiction: Contexts, Choices, Constraints." *Pre/Text* 5 (1984): 39–74.

Bitzer, Lloyd. "The Rhetorical Situation." *Philosophy and Rhetoric* 1 (1968): 1–14.

Bizzell, Patricia. "Cognition, Convention, and Certainty: What We Need to Know about Writing." *Pre/Text* 3 (1982): 213–43.

Bruffee, Kenneth A. "Social Construction, Language, and the Authority of Knowledge: A Bibliographical Essay." *College English* 48 (1986): 773–90.

Campbell, Karlyn Kohrs, and Kathleen Hall Jamieson, eds. *Form and Genre: Shaping Rhetorical Action*. Falls Church, Va.: Speech Communication Association, 1978.

Dijk, Teun A. van, and Walter Kintsch. *Strategies of Discourse Comprehension*. New York & London: Academic Press, 1983.

Faigley, Lester. "Nonacademic Writing: The Social Perspective." In *Writing in Nonacademic Settings*, ed. Lee Odell and Dixie Goswami, 231–48. New York: Guilford Press, 1985.

Faigley, Lester, and Thomas P. Miller. "What We Learn from Writing on the Job." *College English* 44 (1982): 557–69.

Freed, Richard C., and Glenn J. Broadhead. "Discourse Communities, Sacred Texts, and Institutional Norms." *College Composition and Communication* 38 (1987): 154–65.

Halliday, M. A. K. *Language as Social Semiotic: The Social Interpretation of Language and Meaning*. Baltimore: University Park Press, 1978.

Miller, Carolyn R. "Genre As Social Action." *Quarterly Journal of Speech* 70 (1984): 151–67.

Miller, Carolyn R., and Jack Selzer. "Special Topics of Argument in Engineering Reports." In *Writing in Nonacademic Settings*, ed. Lee Odell and Dixie Goswami, 309–41. New York: Guilford Press, 1985.

Morgan, Thais E. "Is There an Intertext in This Text?: Literary and Interdisciplinary Approaches to Intertextuality." *American Journal of Semiotics* (special issue) 3, 4 (1985): 1–40.

Myers, Greg. "The Social Construction of Two Biologists' Proposals." *Written Communication* 2 (1985): 219–45.

Myers, Greg. "Text as Knowledge Claims: The Social Construction of Two Biology Articles." *Social Studies of Science* 15 (1985): 593–630.

Odell, Lee, Dixie Goswami, and Anne Herrington. "The Discourse-Based Interview: A Procedure for Exploring the Tacit Knowledge of Writers in Nonacademic Settings." In *Research On Writing: Principles and Methods*, ed. Peter Mosenthal, Lynne Tamor, and Sean A. Walmsley, 221–36. New York: Longman, 1983.

Paradis, James, David Dobrin, and Richard Miller. "Writing at Exxon ITD: Notes on the Writing Environment of an R & D Organization." In *Writing in Nonacademic Settings*, ed. Lee Odell and Dixie Goswami, 281–307. New York: Guilford Press, 1985.

Ryan, Marie-Laure. "Introduction: On the Why, What and How of Generic Taxonomy." *Poetics* 10 (1981): 109–26.

15 A PSYCHIATRIST USING *DSM-III*

THE INFLUENCE OF A CHARTER

DOCUMENT IN PSYCHIATRY

LUCILLE PARKINSON McCARTHY

In 1979, the 34,000 members of the American Psychiatric Association voted to approve the third edition of its *Diagnostic and Statistical Manual of Mental Disorders*. In this 500-page book, referred to as *DSM-III*, some 200 mental disorders are named, described, and defined with specific operational criteria. This classification system differs from its predecessors in fundamental ways and has been called a landmark achievement in the history of American psychiatry (Rutter and Shaffer) and the central document of the new scientific psychiatry (Maxmen). In the seven years following its publication in 1980 *DSM-III* sold 600,000 copies worldwide, and it is now used not only by psychiatrists but also by professionals in related health care fields, and in government, insurance, and legal agencies.

DSM-III was developed between 1974 and 1979 by a 130-member task force of the American Psychiatric Association in response to a concern in psychiatry about the lack of diagnostic reliability (Klerman). Before the publication of this manual there were no standardized definitions of mental disorders, and thus schizophrenia, for example, meant something different in New York than it did in Baltimore or London. In essence, psychiatrists used a variety of definitions of mental disorders, and this made research and clinical conversations very difficult. This concern about the absence of an objective and reliable system of diagnosis arose in large part because of the development in the 1950s of drugs that acted specifically on particular mental disorders. Before the advent of such drugs, when treatment for all disorders was either talk-based psychotherapy or institutionalization, the patient's diagnosis mattered very little. However, these medications required accurate description of the patient's symptoms and accurate diagnoses, both for treatment planning and for studying treatment results.

The *DSM-III* descriptions of 200 mental disorders which were created to meet these needs of the profession are not considered final. That is, most of *DSM-III*'s diagnostic categories are not fully validated by research. In fact, the definitions of many of the disorders were established on the basis of the developers' clinical experience and thus are controversial and have been called arbitrary and incomplete. The developers of *DSM-III* concede that these allegations are true (Spitzer, Williams, and Skodol), and the manual is being revised as research adds to what is now known. The first revision of *DSM-III* appeared in 1987, and *DSM-IV* is expected in the mid-1990s.

In this essay, I will explore the influence of *DSM-III* in a very limited sphere: the rhetorical universe of a single child psychiatrist, Dr. Joan Page. Put differently, I will examine how this 500-page classification system of psychiatric disorders shapes reality for Dr. Page, that is, shapes what she knows about mental illness and how she communicates that knowledge. I will limit my study to an exploration of the influence of this text on Dr. Page's diagnostic work; I will not examine how *DSM-III* influences her therapy, research, or teaching. More specifically, I focus on Dr. Page's diagnostic evaluation reports, five-page documents that she writes for each child admitted to her unit in the hospital. In her diagnostic evaluations, Dr. Page creates a full pictiure of the child's psychosocial adjustment, and she then diagnoses any mental illnesses that are present. My central question in this essay is how does the *DSM-III* manual shape Dr. Page's diagnostic work: her information gathering, her analyses, and her writing? That is, what are the epistemological and textual consequences of *DSM-III*? How is it linked to what Dr. Page knows about mental illness and how she writes about it?

The metaphor of a charter document has proven useful in looking at the meaning of *DSM-III* for Dr. Page. The charter document of a social or political group establishes an organizing framework that specifies what is significant and draws people's attention to certain rules and relationships. In other words, the charter defines as authoritative certain ways of seeing and deflects attention from other ways. It thus stabilizes a particular reality and sets the terms for future discussions. *DSM-III* is a charter document is psychiatry, and the particular reality that it stabilizes is the biomedical conceptual model of mental illness. More specifically, *DSM-III* provides a diagnostic framework for psychiatry, and diagnosis is central in modern medicine. As Feinstein says, "Diagnosis is the focal point of thought in the treatment of a patient. From diagnosis, which gives a name to the patient's ailment, thinking goes chronologically backward to

Lucille Parkinson McCarthy

explore the mechanisms and causes of the ailment . . . and chronologically forward to predict prognosis and choose therapy. . . . *The taxonomy used for diagnosis will inevitably establish the patterns in which clinicians observe, think, remember, and act"* (73, emphasis mine). How the *DSM-III* charter document influences the ways in which Dr. Page observes, thinks, and writes about mental disorder is what I will explore in this essay.

Models of Mental Illness

In order to understand the nature of the *DSM-III* charter framework and the view of mental illness that underlies it, it is necessary to sketch the two independent and competing conceptual models that dominate contemporary psychiatry. The first of these, the one that is invoked in *DSM-III*, is the biomedical model. The second is the interpretation of meaning model (McHugh and Slavney).

The biomedical model in psychiatry is familiar to us from medicine where it so dominates theory and practice that it is, as Mishler argues, "often treated as *the* representation or picture of reality rather than understood as *a* representation" (Mishler et al., 1). Two assumptions from the biomedical model underlie *DSM-III*. The first concerns the nature of mental disorders. This assumption is that there are real, discrete entities to which disease labels such as "schizophrenia" or "major depressive episode" or "attention deficit disorder" ought properly to be applied. These disorders are seen as generic and universal across cultures.

A second assumption of the biomedical model, found in modified form in psychiatry, relates to the causation of disease. It is what Dubos calls the doctrine of specific etiology. In medicine it is widely assumed that diseases are caused by a single specific biological factor and can be cured or prevented with chemical drugs. This is an assumption that developed in the nineteenth and twentieth centuries from work with the infectious diseases, diseases such as pneumonia, tuberculosis, typhoid fever, and syphilis. However, the notion of specific etiology has had to be modified in psychiatry for most (but not all) mental disorders. The assumption of specific etiology has been replaced in psychiatry with the assumption of multiple, interacting etiological factors: biological, psychological, genetic, environmental, and/or social. In fact, it is widely acknowledged in psychiatry that there is not yet much known about the actual causes of most disorders. Further, though there are some drugs that do act specifically on particular disorders, the treatment for most psychiatric disorders is still not "one diagnosis-one drug," as it is for many physical disorders, and it may never be (Rapoport and Ismond, 33). Rather, psychiatric treatment generally consists of some combination of drugs and individual or family psychotherapy and is likely to vary from case to case, even among patients with the same *DSM-III* diagnosis.

Just as the assumptions of the biomedical model about the nature and causation of mental disorders are familiar to us from medicine, so is its mode of reasoning: identification and then explanation. Patients are first identified by their reported or observed symptoms. Their symptoms are clustered and a disorder then is diagnosed by the psychiatrist. A disease may be known for centuries before its mechanisms and etiology, the how and why of the disease, are explained. In the biomedical model explanation is a cumulative affair, with later research building on earlier. Explanation begins with a search for correlations in populations of patieints with the same diagnosis, and the discovery of a correlation can be the first step toward a hypothesis, theory, or law. This familiar hypothetico-deductive approach of medical science, with its stages of identification and explanation, underlies the biomedical perspective in psychiatry and its charter document, *DSM-III*.

The *DSM-III* taxonomy of mental disorders reflects, as I have said, biomedical assumptions, defining mental disorders as real, generic entities which cause distress or impairment in functioning. Further, there is an implication of underlying behavioral, psychological, or biological dysfunction; that is, the disturbance is not just in the relationship between the individual and society (*DSM-III*, 6). However, in defining psychiatric disorders, *DSM-III* avoids speculation about etiology because so little is yet actually known about the causes of most disorders. Rather, *DSM-III* adopts a fully descriptive approach: each of the 200 *DSM-III* disorders is defined with specific operational criteria which are either observable or verifiable clinical findings. The operational criteria for the disorders include such clinical features as type and quantity of symptoms, age of onset, quality of onset (abrupt or gradual), course, impairment, familial patterns of transmission, sex ratio, and complications. The diagnostic criteria for mental disorders do not yet include lab tests, treatment response, or autopsy findings, the biologic criteria which are commonly used to verify diagnoses of physical diseases. Neither does *DSM-III* recommend treatment. Rather, it attempts to describe comprehensively the *manifestations* of mental disorders. It is, then, *DSM-III* categories of mental disorder which control diagnosis, the identification stage of the identification-explanation process of reasoning in the biomedical model.

By contrast, the second conceptual model in contemporary psychiatry, interpretation of meaning, represents a very different set of assumptions about mental illness. The interpretation of meaning model reflects the tradition in which each mentally ill patient is seen as an individual whose symptoms have meaning particular to him or her. Interpretation is usually guided by the comprehensive constructs of intrapsychic workings and theories of etiology developed by Freud, Adler, or Jung. Generally, symptoms are interpreted as symbolic attempts to express and resolve unconscious conflicts. That is, a patient's unconscious conflicts result in the symptoms. The attitude toward diagnosis in the interpretation of meaning perspective is very different than that in the biomedical perspective. The focus is less on distinguishing, describing, and classifying symptoms than it is on what lies behind these superficial manifestations, that is, on the meaning of the symptoms to the individual patient. Generalizations are less certain in this perspective because insights are drawn from a small number of particular life stories rather than from population samples. In fact, psychiatrists who share this perspective have made little effort to derive refutable principles, because their all-inclusive theoretical constructs of unconscious mechanisms are not susceptible to disproof. Rather, because this type of knowing is based on intuition and empathy, effort has been expended in developing skills in communication and persuasion for use with individual patients (Frank, 173–78).

In summary, those psychiatrists who work within the interpretation of meaning perspective understand the patient as an individual with a story to tell. Those who work within the biomedical perspective see the patient as a member of a group with impairments to be explained. For psychiatrists in the interpretation of meaning perspective each patient presents "an exercise in hermeneutics: a reading of the books of consciousness and behavior for their hidden meanings" (McHugh and Slavney, 133). For psychiatrists who share the biomedical perspective each patient exhibits a form of human activity which can be correlated with biological, psychological, and sociological variables (15). (For more detailed discussions of concepts of mental and physical disease, see Caplan, Engelhardt, and McCartney; Dixon; Fleck; Grob; and Szasz.)

A psychiatrist's choice of perspective, which is often unacknowledged, is the result of his or her personality, education, interests, and particular work situation. And there may be some switching between perspectives as when, for example, a psychiatrist whose perspective is interpretation of meaning must designate a *DSM-III* diagnosis for insurance purposes. Or a psychiatrist whose perspective is biomedical may at times during therapy interpret a patient's symptoms in psychoanalytic terms. However, it is certain that the dominant perspective of virtually all of the 130 members of the American Psychiatric Association task force which developed *DSM-III* was biomedical. These people were chosen on the basis of their clinical and research experience, and most had made "significant contributions" to the literature in diagnosis (*DSM-III*, 2).

Research Methods

To answer my questions about the epistemological and textual consequences of *DSM-III* for the diagnostic work of one child psychiatrist, I used a triangulated approach, examining Dr. Page's writing activities and texts from several angles (Denzin). First, in order to illuminate *DSM-III*'s role in shaping Dr. Page's understanding of what constitutes significant information and how to collect that information, I observed her in the hospital and interviewed her frequently over a two year period (1984–1986). I was guided in my procedures and analyses by the work of Spradley and Odell, Goswami, and Herrington. I also had Dr. Page keep a log in which she recorded all her data-gathering activities as she prepared to write one of her diagnostic evaluations.

Second, in order to illuminate *DSM-III*'s role in shaping Dr. Page's analysis of her patient data, I audiotaped her as she composed and dictated the diagnostic evaluations of four patients. I also studied the resulting evaluation texts, paying special attention to the ways Dr. Page analyzed the data to reach her diagnosis.

Finally, in order to elucidate the role *DSM-III* played in the social functioning of Dr. Page's evaluation texts, I interviewed her readers, that is, her colleagues on the hospital unit. I asked them how they perceived and used Dr. Page's evaluations and what for them were the evaluations' sources of authority and persuasion. I also questioned Dr. Page in this regard.

These multiple data sources worked together, adding to, refining, and cross-checking each other, as I worked to establish the influence of the *DSM-III* charter document on Dr. Page's knowing and writing. The role I played as I observed and interviewed Dr. Page and her colleagues was that of Dr. Page's friend and coresearcher. Thus, as I began my research in the hospital, Dr. Page introduced me to various informants, and because she is a person who is respected and trusted, I was granted immediate access to that setting.

THE SETTING AND THE PARTICIPANTS

The hospital in which Dr. Page works is a large, university-affiliated, evaluation, research, and treatment hospital for handicapped children. She is the child psychiatrist member of the rehabilitation team, a group of eighteen professionals from ten disciplines. This team runs an eight-bed rehabilitation unit for children who have suffered brain injuries from accidents or illnesses.

The rehabilitation ward is comprised of two large adjoining rooms, each with four beds. At the end of one of the rooms is a glass-enclosed nursing station with three desks, medicine cabinets, and a shelf where patients' notebook-like charts stand side by side. At the time I observed the ward, there were four children in the first room, two of whom were still in their beds in coma. A third child was walking unsteadily with a cane, and the fourth was in a wheel chair. Three of these children had been struck by cars while on foot or bicycle, and one was thrown from a three-wheel motor bike. On the wall beside each child's bed was a bulletin board covered with get well cards and posters. Also on each bulletin board was a recent school photograph of the child. According to Dr. Page, the photograph of the pre-injury child is useful to parents and staff. The healthy child in the photograph looks very different than the injured one, the healthy child's face animated and vital, eyes focused on the viewer, muscles relaxed. The photo reminds staff and parents of the goal of rehabilitation, a goal that at times seems terribly remote.

The child in the wheel chair was five-year-old Eddie Farnham who, the nurse told me, was responding to simple commands, saying a few words, and beginning to regain muscle control. Eddie was hit by a car when he ran into the street, and he suffered severe closed head trauma and was in a coma for six weeks. At the end of four weeks, as he was emerging from coma, he was admitted to the rehab unit from a neighboring hospital's intensive care unit. In the two months since Eddie's admission to the rehab unit, he had been evaluated and/or treated by all of the eighteen specialists on the rehabilitation team, and his family had been counselled about accepting and managing what were certain to be permanent disabilities and long-term care needs. It is on Dr. Page's diagnostic evaluation of Eddie, conducted and written during his first two weeks on the unit, that I will focus in this essay.

In Dr. Page's diagnostic evaluations she constructs a full picture of the child's behavior and functioning before the accident and diagnoses any mental disorders that were present at that time. These psychiatric evaluation documents help the team plan treatment and deliver care because it is known that the emotional and behavior problems that children have before such disabling accidents are likely to reappear in exaggerated form during the long recovery period. When Dr. Page completes her diagnostic evaluation text, she gives one copy to the rehab unit director and one to the unit social worker. A third copy goes into the patient's chart for other team members to read. Dr. Page keeps the original for her own clinical and research needs and for patients' future therapists and school personnel who may request it.

Dr. Page's workplace, the rehabilitation unit, is, obviously, medically rather than psychiatrically oriented. And because the hospital is university-affiliated, it is also research oriented. In fact, this institution is well known for its research on the correlation of biologic factors and particular psychiatric disorders and on the effects of drug therapies: types of research commonly conducted within the biomedical model. Thus, the biomedical perspective, rather than the interpretation of meaning perspective, is likely to be adopted by psychiatrists working in this setting. This is the case with Dr. Page. In addition, she told me, her training influenced her biomedical understanding of mental illness. She spent four years after medical school learning a medical specialty, pediatrics, before she decided to enter a five-year training program in psychiatry. Although she was, during her training in psychiatry, exposed to psychoanalytic interpretation, she chose not to undergo analysis herself, and she never really abandoned her medical ways of thinking. Eight years ago she came to this university medical center where she now does both clinical and research work. It is not surprising then that the rehab unit director, Dr. John Van Zante, a surgeon/rehabilitation specialist, described Dr. Page's evaluation as taking "the standard medical approach to illness." He explained, "Joan takes a complete history. She examines the symptoms and then groups them to see if mental disorder is present. We must know the sort of thing that Joan finds: the emotional and social factors of the case. We need to know these if we're to help our patients and their families reconstruct their lives. The challenge of rehabilitation is not just physical. Relieving pain and suffering on this unit requires both physical *and* emotional work."

Results and Discussion

The *DSM-III* charter document had epistemological and textual consequences for Dr. Page's diagnostic work in two general areas. The first is *DSM-III selectivity*. That is, the *DSM-III* diagnostic classification system determined the type and amount of information that Dr. Page gathered about her patients. Put differently, this manual defined what Dr. Page chose, tacitly and explicitly, to observe and to know. *DSM-III* selectivity was particularly evident in Dr. Page's interview with the parent, an extremely important source of information for the child psychiatrist (Rapoport and Ismond, 37). And because *DSM-III* selectivity controlled what Dr. Page chose to find out about her patients, it is also evident in her final evaluation text.

The second area in which *DSM-III* influenced Dr. Page's diagnostic evaluations was in her analysis of the information she gathered about her patients. *DSM-III* controlled not only the information Dr. Page selected as significant, but also how she analyzed that information, how she reasoned from her data to reach a diagnosis. The source of Dr. Page's confidence in her diagnostic judgments lies in her *DSM-III-backed analysis* of the appropriate information. *DSM-III*-backed analysis is particularly evident in the two final sections of her evaluation text, "Summary and Recommendations" and "*DSM-III* Diagnoses."

DSM-III SELECTIVITY: THE PARENT INTERVIEW

Underlying Dr. Page's interview with Eddie Farnham's mother was the *DSM-III* assumption that mental disorders are real, discrete entities that can be identified in patients by their clinical features. Dr. Page spent one and a half hours with Mrs. Farnham eliciting information about the clinical features designated by *DSM-III* as constituting criteria for various disorders. Dr. Page did not attempt to interpret the underlying meaning of Eddie's symptoms nor to speculate about the etiology of those symptoms.

Dr. Page structured her questioning of Mrs. Farnham with an interview schedule, a set of questions based on *DSM-III* diagnostic categories. This interview schedule, the "Kiddie/SADS" (the Children's Schedule of Affective Disorders and Schizophrenia), is designed to lead directly to a *DSM-III* diagnosis of mental disorder. The Kiddie/SADS moves from one diagnosis to the next, with each question referring to one of the operational criteria defining a disorder. If, during her questioning of Mrs. Farnham about Eddie, Dr. Page found no symptoms for a particular disorder, she moved on quickly. However, when her questioning revealed the presence of some of the diagnostic criteria for a disorder, she questioned Mrs. Farnham further. If Dr. Page found all of the required criteria for a disorder to be present, she made a diagnosis. In Eddie's case, as we'll see below, criteria were partially fulfilled for one disorder (attention deficit disorder with hyperactivity) and completely fulfilled for another (delirium).

Mrs. Farnham cooperated fully during the interview, answering Dr. Page's questions calmly and thoughtfully. Many diagnoses were passed over quickly when no symptoms were found. For example, Eddie manifested no evidence of such disorders as depression, mania, thought disorder, autism, eating disorder, or panic disorder. Movement through the interview schedule slowed down, however, when Dr. Page reached the questions concerning the clinical features of the *DSM-III* disorder, attention deficit disorder with hyperactivity (ADD). These questions concerned Eddie's behavior, activities, attention span at home and school, his sleep patterns, his interactions with others, and the age of onset and duration of various behaviors. The *DSM-III* criteria for attention deficit disorder with hyperactivity are reproduced in table 15.1. The manual requires that eleven of the nineteen criteria be present if a diagnosis of ADD is to be made.

Diagnostic Criteria for Attention Deficit Disorder with Hyperactivity

The child displays, for his or her mental and chronological age, signs of developmentally inappropriate inattention, impulsivity, and hyperactivity. The signs must be reported by adults in the child's environment, such as parents and teachers. Because the symptoms are typically variable, they may not be observed directly by the clinician. When the reports of teachers and parents conflict, primary consideration should be given to the teacher reports becaue of greater familiarity with age-appropriate norms. Symptoms typically worsen in situations that require self-application, as in the classroom. Signs of the disorder may be absent when the child is in a new or a one-to-one situation.

The number of symptoms specified is for children between the ages of eight and ten, the peak age range for referral. In younger children, more severe forms of the symptoms and a greater number of symptoms are usually present. The opposite is true of older children.

A. **Inattention.** At least three of the following:
 (1) often fails to finish things he or she starts
 (2) often doesn't seem to listen
 (3) easily distracted
 (4) has difficulty concentrating on schoolwork or other tasks requiring sustained attention
 (5) has difficulty sticking to a play activity
B. **Impulsivity.** At least three of the following:
 (1) often acts before thinking
 (2) shifts excessively from one activity to another
 (3) has difficulty organizing work (this not being due to cognitive impairment)
 (4) needs a lot of supervision
 (5) frequently calls out in class
 (6) has difficulty awaiting turn in games or group situations
C. **Hyperactivity.** At least two of the following:
 (1) runs about or climbs on things excessively
 (2) has difficulty sitting still or fidgets excessively
 (3) has difficulty staying seated
 (4) moves about excessively during sleep
 (5) is always "on the go" or acts as if "driven by a motor"
D. Onset before the age of seven.
E. Duration of at least six months.
F. Not due to Schizophrenia, Affective Disorder, or Severe or Profound Mental Retardation.

Table 15.1.
Reprinted with permission from the *Diagnostic and Statistical Manual of Mental Disorders, (Third Edition).* Copyright 1980 American Psychiatric Association.

In 1987, one year after the present study was completed, revised criteria for ADD were published in *DSM-III-R*(evised). The revised criteria for this disorder, which was renamed attention-deficit hyperactivity disorder (ADHD), are appended at the end of this chapter.

Lucille Parkinson McCarthy

In her interview with Mrs. Farnham, Dr. Page elicited a large amount of information about Eddie's emotions, behaviors, impairments, family history, and patterns of interaction. These verifiable clinical features constitute the operational criteria required for a diagnosis of mental disorder. Although the large amount of information that Dr. Page elicited with her *DSM-III*-based interview schedule will serve her clinical and research endeavors very well, she said that at times she feels frustrated by what the manual selects to *leave out*. Her *DSM-III*-based interview schedule, she said, requires her to structure the parent interview more tightly than she used to do, more tightly, in fact, than she considers ideal. "Time is the problem," she said. "I just can't let the parent go off on tangents. Which is too bad, because sometimes by following the parent's lead you get the richest material. Now I go in and get lots of information as quickly as possible. The hour and a half it takes me to get all that information and the diagnosis is really very quick. But at times I feel like a parent might tell me that her husband committed suicide last week by walking in front of a truck, and I'd go to the next question on the schedule and ask, 'What's your place of employment?' "

Thus, for Dr. Page *DSM-III* selectivity is not wholly satisfying. But apparently its limitation, the fact that it permits no time to "let people ramble on about their situations," is compensated for by Dr. Page's certainty that she has elicited the type and amount of information she needs to make an accurate *DSM-III* diagnosis. (For an analysis of physician-patient discourse that examines the issues of structure and control in medical interviews, see Mishler.)

DSM-III SELECTIVITY: THE EVALUATION TEXT

Bazerman argues that certain textual features reveal the writer as a "statement-maker coming to terms with reality from a distinctive perspective" (363). Features of Dr. Page's texts which reveal her biomedical orientation and, more particularly, her *DSM-III* selectivity are her headings, her citations of her data sources, and her patterns of reporting and organizing her data.

Six of Dr. Page's eight headings in her evaluation of Eddie Farnham reflect *DSM-III* assumptions about what counts as relevant knowledge in defining mental disorder. These six headings all focus on the clinical features of the case and Dr. Page's sources of information about these features. Because *DSM-III* takes a descriptive approach to mental illness, the clinical features of the case are, as I have said, the *sine qua non* of diagnosis. And Dr. Page's focus on the sources of her data reflects the assumption that psychiatric disorders are generic and universal and are known by objective signs and symptoms. Knowledge lies in verifiable data, not in the individual psychiatrist's interpretation of particular cases. Moreover, Dr. Page's focus on the sources of her data emphasizes the reliability of her diagnoses, the concern which initiated the development of *DSM-III*, as I explained earlier. The first six headings in Dr. Page's diagnostic evaluation text are:

1. "Identifying Information" (Basic facts about the patient)
2. "Information Sources"
3. "History" (of the present physical illness)
4. "Kiddie/SADS" (review of psychiatric symptoms)
5. "Observation of Patient"
6. "Information about Family"

Like the headings of Dr. Page's text, her patterns of reporting and organizing of her data also reveal her biomedical perspective and *DSM-III* selectivity. In the evaluation's central section, "Kiddie/SADS," found on pages 2–4 of the five-page evaluation, Dr. Page presents the clinical data from the parent interview. She reports her clinical findings at the lowest possible level of inference, presenting them in the same order in which she elicited them in the interview: first, the facts about the child's psychosocial adjustment and, second, the child's psychiatric symptoms organized by *DSM-III* categories of mental disorder. This *DSM-III*-based review of psychiatric symptoms is modelled on the review of symptoms (or systems) which forms an essential part of the medical history. Dr. Page's Kiddie/SADS review of psychiatric symptoms forms the core of her evaluation and provides the grounds for her subsequent analysis and diagnostic conclusions.

The assumptions about knowledge which underlie Dr. Page's reporting and organizing of her data are very different than those which underlie the psychoanalytic case study, the best-known written form of the interpretation of meaning perspective. Unlike Dr. Page's evaluation text which describes and classifies clinical findings, the psychoanalytic case study presents a narrative which attempts to explain them. The aim of the psychoanalytic case study is to construct the most coherent, plausible, and therapeutic story of the patient's symptoms and their relationship to his or her unconscious conflicts. As Spence puts it, the psychoanalytic case study is less interested in "historical" events than it is in "narrative" events. In fact the psychoanalytic narrative may leave out, and eventually take the place of, the patient's original "raw" data and the analyst's original "basic" observations. And clinical findings which don't fit the prevailing narrative order of the psychoanalytic case story may receive no attention at all (Spence, 23–24). By contrast, Dr. Page avoids interpreting the meaning or etiology of the patient's symptoms with psychoanalytic constructs. Rather, she describes all of the clinical facts that she has elicited or observed, facts generated and organized by the biomedical constructs of *DSM-III*.

In addition to reporting all of her clinical findings at the lowest possible level of inference, Dr. Page reports the source of nearly every one of her findings. The sources she cites in Eddie's evaluation include his mother, his teacher, the social worker, the nurse, the hospital chart, and the Achenbach Child Behavior Checklist that Eddie's mother filled out. In the following quote, taken from the middle of the "Kiddie/SADS" section's review of symptoms, Dr. Page rules out several *DSM-III* diagnoses because no symptoms are present. She then reports the symptoms that Eddie exhibits which fulfill some (but not all) of the operational criteria for a *DSM-III* diagnosis of attention deficit disorder with hyperactivity. This section of Dr. Page's evaluation text illustrates her patterns of reporting and organizing her data and her citing of her information sources. These are all shaped by *DSM-III* selectivity.

> Mrs. Farnham denies any symptoms suggestive of depression or mania. Symptoms of psychosis are also denied. Since age 4, Eddie has had an imaginary companion whose name is Edward. Since age 4, his occupation with the imaginary companion has lessened and is now only an occasional thing. Symptoms of delusions are denied. Symptoms of thought disorder are denied. Autistic behavior is denied. Symptoms of eating disorder are denied.
>
> The teacher complains that Eddie does not listen in the classroom. He has difficulty paying attention and keeping his mind on school work. The mother denies symptoms of impulsivity; however, it is important to note that the school is holding the child back for a very short attention span.
>
> It is difficult for Eddie to sit still. He appears always on the go. He likes to run about and climb about on things a lot. His mother states that he enjoys doing the busier things.

DSM-III selectivity, then, determines the type, amount, and sources of data that Dr. Page gathers during the evaluation process, and it shapes her presentation of that data. That *DSM-III* selectivity plays a central role in Dr. Page's confidence in her diagnostic conclusions is suggested by her response to a question in a text-based interview. I asked her if she would be willing to delete the second section of the evaluation, "Information Sources," where she lists all her data sources before she begins her presentation. She said she would not and offered this explanation: "In the 'Information Sources' section I show how reliable the evaluation is, if it's based on enough data from the right sources to make an accurate diagnosis, a diagnosis that other psychiatrists will agree with."

DSM-III selectivity, then, shapes several features of Dr. Page's evaluation text. These textual features include her headings, which focus on the clinical features established by the manual as defining mental disorders, her careful citing of the sources of her information, her reporting of her data at the lowest level of inference, and her organizing of the patient data according to *DSM-III* diagnostic categories.

DSM-III-BACKED ANALYSIS: "SUMMARY AND RECOMMENDATIONS"

In Dr. Page's "Summary and Recommendations" near the end of her evaluation text, we see the second way in which *DSM-III* influences her work: *DSM-III*-backed analysis. In this section of her evaluation Dr. Page's analysis of her data is shaped by rules of diagnosis outlined in *DSM-III*. As she works with the information she gathered on Eddie Farnham, she applies the rules of diagnosis specified by the manual for attention deficit disorder with hyperactivity. She is aware, of course, of *DSM-III*'s stipulation that a patient, in order to be diagnosed ADD, must fulfill eleven of the nineteen diagnostic criteria for that disorder.

Dr. Page told me in an interview following her dictation of Eddie's evaluation, "In planning my Summary and Recommendations I summarize the criteria I've identified that suggest a possible diagnosis in the patient. I then ask myself, 'What do I have here? Can I make this claim?' " In the first paragraph of her "Summary and Recommendations," which is quoted below, Dr. Page makes a limited "claim," explaining that though many of the criteria for a diagnosis of ADD are present in Eddie's case, some of the required criteria — those providing evidence for impulsivity — are not. The mother did not report impulsivity, and the teacher's report, always an important source of information for the child psychiatrist, had not yet arrived.

> Eddie is a 5 and ½ year old white child with a history of prematurity, rocking, head banging, and bruxism. From the mother's account, he fulfills many diagnostic criteria for attention deficit disorder with hyperactivity. The mother, however, does not describe impulsivity. So a school report of observation from the teacher would be helpful in conclusively making the *DSM-III* diagnosis. Because of this prior behavioral problem, Eddie is at high risk for the development of a post-traumatic psychiatric disorder.

Because Dr. Page did not have the evidence of impulsivity required for a diagnosis of ADD, she recorded in the final section of Eddie's evaluation, "*DSM-III* Diagnoses": "Rule out attention deficit disorder with hyperactivity." This statement both alerts her readers that it is a likely diagnosis and works to control future diagnostic discussions of this patient.

Dr. Page's *DSM-III*-backed analysis of her data also resulted in a second diagnosis. Principles outlined in the manual for reasoning from clinical data to diagnosic conclusions state that more than one disorder may be diagnosed in a patient if the required criteria are met. In the second paragraph of Dr. Page's "Summary and Recommendations" she diagnoses in one sentence the obvious second diagnosis of delirium. "Being still comatose, Eddie fulfills diagnostic criteria for delirium." Delirium is one of ten *DSM-III* disorders in which psychological or behavioral abnormality is due to brain dysfunction of known cause. The diagnostic criteria for delirium are reproduced in table 15.2.

Diagnostic Criteria for Delirium
A. Clouding of consciousness (reduced clarity of awareness of the environment), with reduced capacity to shift, focus, and sustain attention to environmental stimuli.
B. At least two of the following:
    (1) perceptual disturbance: misinterpretations, illusions, or hallucinations
    (2) speech that is at times incoherent
    (3) disturbance of sleep-wakefulness cycle, with insomnia or daytime drowsiness
    (4) increased or decreased psychomotor activity
C. Disorientation and memory impairment (if testable).
D. Clinical features that develop over a short period of time (usually hours to days) and tend to fluctuate over the course of a day.
E. Evidence, from the history, physical examination, or laboratory tests, of a specific organic factor judged to be etiologically related to the disturbance.

Table 15.2.
Reprinted with permission from the *Diagnostic and Statistical Manual of Mental Disorders, (Third Edition)*. Copyright 1980 American Psychiatric Association.

In her "Summary and Recommendations" Dr. Page refers briefly to "diagnostic criteria" and "*DSM-III* diagnosis," making no effort to explain them. She assumes that her readers know and value this way of defining and reasoning about mental illness. And she is right. The interviews with the readers of Dr. Page's evaluation texts revealed that *DSM-III* is indeed a powerful source of persuasion for them. All three of her audiences — rehab unit clinicians, mental health researchers, and insurance/legal personnel — expect, indeed require, *DSM-III* diagnostic analysis in Dr. Page's evaluations. However, a full exploration of the manual's role in the social functioning of Dr. Page's texts (and in enhancing her own professional self-esteem) lies beyond the scope of this essay. The point to be made here is that Dr. Page's clinical and diagnostic judgments in her "Summary and Recommendations" are those of a professional speaking authoritatively, a professional confident of her conclusions. The evidence on which her claims are grounded and the analysis that produces them are shaped by *DSM-III*.

DSM-III-BACKED ANALYSIS: "DSM-III DIAGNOSES"

In the final section of Eddie Farnham's evaluation text, "*DSM-III* Diagnoses," Dr. Page lists her diagnostic conclusions. Here, in addition to ADD and delirium, the two disorders that she argues for in her "Summary and Recommendations," Dr. Page makes the four other diagnostic statements required by *DSM-III*'s "multiaxial" framework.

The developers of *DSM-III* departed from earlier, unitary diagnostic systems in order to include as much information about the patient as possible. It was argued that several types of information are needed in order to understand the complexity of individual patients. Thus a psychiatrist makes diagnostic statements about the patient on five "axes," each of which records a different kind of information. On Axis I are recorded the diagnoses of mental disorders such as those discussed above, delirium and attention deficit disorder, as well as schizophrenia, paranoia, manic depressive illness, major depression, the anxiety disorders, and many more. Fewer diagnoses are recorded on Axis II: only the adult personality disorders and the specific childhood developmental disorders of language, reading, math, and articulation. The reason for separating out these Axis II diagnoses was to highlight them; they tend to be overlooked when attention is paid to the more obvious Axis I disorders. Multiple diagnoses may be made on both axes. On Axis III the psychiatrist describes any physical illness the patient may have, and on Axis IV he or she judges the severity of psychological stressors in the patient's environment. Finally, on Axis V, the psychiatrist records a judgment about the patient's highest level of functioning in the past year. The first three axes, the mental and physical diagnoses, are typological, and require statements involving categories. Axes IV and V, levels of stressors and functioning, require dimensional judgments. Dr. Page's diagnostic judgments about Eddie Farnham conclude her evaluation:

DSM-III Diagnoses

Axis I: 293.00 Delirium
          314.01 Rule out attention deficit disorder with
          hyperactivity.
Axis II: 799.90 Diagnosis deferred on Axis II.
Axis III: History of severe closed head injury on 3/13/86 with

multiple skull fractures and cerebral contusion, followed
by persistent coma.

Axis IV: Severity of psychosocial stressor — unspecified.

Axis V: Highest level of adaptive functioning in past year — fair.
Moderate impairment in school functioning necessitating
being held back for a second year.

The diagnostic conclusions about Eddie that Dr. Page makes on Axes
II–V, like those on Axis I, are based on the clinical data reported in the
evaluation and are controlled by *DSM-III*-backed rules of analysis. Dr.
Page made these latter diagnostic statements quickly as she dictated,
without pausing to study her notes and her manual as she did during her
formulation of the diagnoses on Axis I. This relative speed is explained
by the fact that she decided to put off making statements on Axes II and
IV because of inadequate information and lack of immediate relevance
to treatment planning. And on Axes III and V she briefly summarizes the
evaluation's clinical data and makes the judgment that Eddie's functioning during the preceding year was fair.

DSM-III's multiaxial diagnostic system thus provides several kinds of
information about the patient — physical, socio-familial, and behavioral —
without implying that these are the causes of the mental disorders diagnosed on Axes I and II. In this way, *DSM-III* has satisfied the need of
clinicians and researchers for a full picture of the patient while keeping
the psychiatric diagnoses free from unproven theories of etiology. For
example, the patient's physical condition and social situation, recorded
on Axes III and IV, are important pieces of information for treatment planning. But the role these play in causing most mental disorders is not yet
known.

DSM-III-backed analysis, then, shapes Dr. Page's reasoning as she moves
from clinical data to diagnostic conclusions. That is, *DSM-III* provides
the diagnostic principles she uses, principles such as numbers of criteria
required for a diagnosis and ways of splitting the data into discrete parts,
the five "axes." *DSM-III*-backed analysis is most obvious in the final two
sections of the evaluation, "Summary and Recommendations" and "*DSM-III*
Diagnoses," where Dr. Page refers specifically to it in her text and final
heading.

Conclusion

To summarize, in this essay I have argued that the Amer-
ican Psychiatric Association's third edition of the *Diagnostic and Statistical
Manual of Mental Disorders* (1980) can be understood as a charter document for contemporary psychiatry. That is, it provides a framework for
diagnosing mental illness that has epistemological and textual consequences

for the discipline. The *DSM-III* diagnostic taxonomy is based on the assumptions of the biomedical model about what disease is and how it can be known.

To examine the epistemological and textual consequences of the *DSM-III* charter document for psychiatrists, I studied the diagnostic processes and texts of one child psychiatrist, Dr. Joan Page, a staff psychiatrist in a large university hospital. I found that her diagnostic thinking and writing is profoundly influenced by *DSM-III*. First, this manual shapes Dr. Page's understanding of what counts as relevant information about her patients and thus controls her gathering of data. Second, its diagnostic principles control her analysis of that information. In its role as charter document, the *DSM-III* manual of mental disorders is closely linked to what Dr. Page knows about mental illness and how she writes about it.

DSM-III is, then, an extremely important document in Dr. Page's diagnostic work, work which lies at the heart of both her clinical and research endeavors. *DSM-III* is also an important document in the history of American psychiatry and has, apparently, resulted in one of the main purposes for which it was developed, achieving "a noticeable increase in the reliability of diagnostic judgments and a facilitation of communication among clinicians and researchers" (Klerman, 18). The manual's specific operational definitions of mental disorders have also played an important role in suggesting the questions that psychiatric researchers are now asking. Because so many of the statements made in *DSM-III* about the various disorders are not based on research data, this text has spotlighted the gaps in factual information in psychiatry. That is, it has pointed to areas of needed research. As Maxmen explains, before *DSM-III*, when mental disorders were only vaguely defined, "the profession could conceal its ignorance" (58). However, in *DSM-III* "areas of ignorance" are now clear, and, according to Robert Spitzer, the manual's chief developer, *DSM-III* has resulted in an "explosion" of research (pers. com., February 1987). Some 2000 articles were published between 1980 and 1987 reporting research that used or directly investigated the manual's diagnostic categories and criteria. By providing a matrix and forms for discourse, the *DSM-III* text has proven to be a powerful heuristic for psychiatric inquiry and writing, generating a large number of additional texts.

Besides informing the work of psychiatric researchers and clinicians, *DSM-III* now plays an important role in the education of most young psychiatrists. Students read and learn *DSM-III*, and the manual's diagnostic categories provide the organizing framework for most textbooks of psychiatry. Moreover, *DSM-III*-based activities inform at least part of students' clinical training. This text thus shapes students' knowledge and articulation of mental disorder from the beginning. The implications of this are clear. Various kinds of *DSM-III*-based documents produced for these students, and eventually by them, will proliferate, further increas-

Lucille Parkinson McCarthy

ing the web of this discourse system. The influence of the *DSM-III* charter document on thinking and writing in psychiatry is thus likely to become more and more pervasive.

APPENDIX

Diagnostic criteria for 314.01 Attention-deficit Hyperactivity Disorder

Note: Consider a criterion met only if the behavior is considerably more frequent than that of most people of the same mental age.

A. A disturbance of at least six months during which at least eight of the following are present:

    (1) often fidgets with hands or feet or squirms in seat (in adolescents, may be limited to subjective feelings of restlessness)

    (2) has difficulty remaining seated when required to do so

    (3) is easily distracted by extraneous stimuli

    (4) has difficulty awaiting turn in games or group situations

    (5) often blurts out answers to questions before they have been completed

    (6) has difficulty following through on instructions from others (not due to oppositional behavior or failure of comprehension), e.g., fails to finish chores

    (7) has difficulty sustaining attention in tasks or play activities

    (8) often shifts from one uncompleted activity to another

    (9) has difficulty playing quietly

    (10) often talks excessively

    (11) often interrupts or intrudes on others, e.g., butts into other children's games

    (12) often does not seem to listen to what is being said to him or her

    (13) often loses things necessary for tasks or activities at school or at home (e.g., toys, pencils, books, assignments)

    (14) often engages in physically dangerous activities without considering possible consequences (not for the purpose of thrill-seeking), e.g., runs into street without looking

Note: The above items are listed in descending order of discriminating power based on data from a national field trial of the DSM-III-R criteria for Disruptive Behavior Disorders.

B. Onset before the age of seven.

C. Does not meet the criteria for a Pervasive Developmental Disorder.

Criteria for severity of Attention-deficit Hyperactivity Disorder:

Mild: Few, if any, symptoms in excess of those required to make the diagnosis **and** only minimal or no impairment in school and social functioning.

Moderate: Symptoms or functional impairment intermediate between "mild" and "severe."

Severe: Many symptoms in excess of those required to make the diagnosis **and** significant and pervasive impairment in functioning at home and school and with peers.

Reprinted with permission from the *Diagnostic and Statistical Manual of Mental Disorders (Third Edition Revised).* Copyright 1987 American Psychiatric Association.

BIBLIOGRAPHY

Bazerman, Charles. "What Written Knowledge Does: Three Examples of Academic Discourse." *Philosophy of the Social Sciences* 11 (1981): 361–87.
Caplan, Arthur L., H. Tristram Engelhardt, Jr., and James J. McCartney. *Concepts of Health and Disease: Interdisciplinary Perspectives.* London: Addison-Wesley, 1981.
Denzin, Norman K. *Sociological Methods.* New York: McGraw-Hill, 1978.
Dixon, Bernard. *Beyond the Magic Bullet.* New York: Harper & Row, 1978.
Diagnostic and Statistical Manual of Mental Disorders. 3d ed. Washington, D.C.: American Psychiatric Association, 1980.
Dubos, René. *Mirage of Health.* New York: Anchor Books, 1961.
Feinstein, A. R. *Clinical Judgment.* Baltimore: Williams & Wilkins, 1967.
Fleck, Ludwik. *Genesis and Development of a Scientific Fact.* Chicago: University of Chicago Press, 1979.
Frank, Jerome. *Persuasion and Healing: A Comparative Study of Psychotherapy.* Baltimore: Johns Hopkins University Press, 1961.
Grob, Gerald N. *Mental Illness and American Society, 1875–1940.* Princeton: Princeton University Press, 1983.
Klerman, Gerald L. "The Significance of DSM-III in American Psychiatry." In *International Perspectives on DSM-III,* ed. Robert Spitzer, Janet Williams, and Andrew Skodol, 3–25. Washington, D.C.: American Psychiatric Press, 1983.
McHugh, Paul R., and Phillip R. Slavney. *The Perspectives of Psychiatry.* Baltimore: Johns Hopkins University Press, 1983.
Maxmen, Jerrold S. *The New Psychiatry.* New York: William Morrow, 1985.
Mishler, Elliot G. *The Discourse of Medicine: Dialectics of Medical Interviews.* Norwood, N.J.: Ablex, 1984.
Mishler, Elliot G., et al. *Social Contexts of Health, Illness, and Patient Care.* Cambridge: Cambridge University Press, 1981.
Odell, Lee, Dixie Goswami, and Anne Herrington. "The Discourse Based Interview." In *Research on Writing: Principles and Methods,* ed. Peter Mosenthal, Lynn Tamor, and Sean Walmsley, 220–35. New York: Longman, 1983.
Rapoport, Judith L., and Deborah R. Ismond. *DSM-III Training Guide for Diagnosis of Childhood Disorders.* New York: Brunner/Mazel, 1984.
Rutter, Michael, and David Shaffer. "DSM-III: A Step Forward or Back in Terms of the Classification of Child Psychiatric Disorders?" *Journal of the American Academy of Child Psychiatry* 19 (1980): 371–94.
Spence, Donald P. *Narrative Truth and Historical Truth: Meaning and Interpretation in Psychoanalysis.* New York: Norton, 1982.
Spitzer, Robert, Janet Williams, and Andrew Skodol. "International Perspectives: Summary and Commentary." In *International Perspectives on DSM-III,* ed. Robert Spitzer, Janet Williams, and Andrew Skodol, 339–54. Washington, D.C.: American Psychiatric Press, 1983.
Spradley, James. *The Ethnographic Interview.* New York: Holt, Rinehart and Winston, 1979.

Lucille Parkinson McCarthy

Spradley, James. *Participant Observation*. New York: Holt, Rinehart and Winston, 1980.

Szasz, Thomas. *Insanity: The Idea and Its Consequences*. New York: John Wiley, 1987.

INDEX

INDEX

Abelson, John, 66
Abruzzi, Paulo, 310–23 *passim*, 331
Ackerman, John, 7, 191–215
Adams, Henry, 158
Adler, Alfred, 361
Agar, Michael, 280, 304
Alberic of Monte Cassino, 100, 103–6;
  Flowers of Rhetoric, 103–4, 105; "The
  Outline of Composition," 105
Albert of Morra, 101–2
Alexander, Bill, 306–31 *passim*
Ambassadors, The (James), 89
American Psychiatric Association, 9–10,
  357, 361
Anomalies, significance of, 25, 26, 27
Anyon, Paul, 123
Appearance/reality topos, 85–87, 91, 95
Archetypes, 89
Archimedes, 19
Arguments, 9, 302, 304; and letter writing,
  103–4, 109, 113, 115; and speeches,
  103–4; and the theory of *status*, 104,
  109; and proofs, 109, 150, 151; use of,
  in business plans, 318–19, 320, 326,
  329 — literary, 9, 76–95; as means of
  persuasion, 77; and stases, 78–80, 84;
  causal arguments, 79, 263; for categorical
  propositions, 80, 81–82; and common
  topoi, 84–91, 94; and complexity,
  90–91, 94, 95; ethos of, 91–93; in the
  ceremonial mode, 94; and the pleasure
  principle, 94; and *evidentiary* functions,
  226; closing, in legal discourse, 242,
  243, 246; analysis, of organizational
  discourse, 290–95, 299
Aristotle, 19, 78, 87, 194, 202; special topoi
  in, 84; speaker, subject and audience
  in, triad of, 104, 107–8; on narration,
  126, 131; on rhetoric, logic and politics,
  relationship of, 145, 146, 148–49; and
  Whateley's *Rhetoric*, 150, 151
Ars dictaminis (letter writing), 6, 98–119;
  and the legal profession, 98, 99, 101,

103, 104, 108; and collections of
formulae, 99, 101, 114; development
of, 99–107; and Caroline Minuscule
(imperial court hand), 100; and *dictamen*,
100; and the Roman Curial hand, 100,
101; and the *cursus*, 101–2; and
Mandamenta (Letters of Justice), 101;
and *privileges*, 101, 105; and *Tituli*
(Letters of Grace), 101; and the *Froman
Dictandi*, 102; and social rank, 102,
106, 107, 112; and Ciceronian rhetoric,
103, 104, 105, 106, 107–16; and the
conclusio, 103–5; and the *exordium*,
103–5, 107, 110, 111; and Isadore of
Seville's four-part division of speeches,
103–5; and narration, 103–5, 109–10,
111–12, 114, 115; and salutations,
104–5, 106, 110–11, 114, 115; and the
Bolognese "Approved Format," 107,
108–9, 110, 111, 114–15; and
dictaminal phatic rhetoric, 107; and
ephodos, 111; and classes of petitions,
112, 114
Ars poetriae (the Art of Poetry), 113
Ars praedicandi (the Art of Preaching), 113
Audience, 203–6: for literary arguments,
84; /reader, and the stage of real history,
the text and, 86; and letter writing, 103,
104; speaker, and subject, Aristotelian
triad of, 104, 107–8; — speaker relation,
and temporality, 126. *See also* Author-
reader relation
Author: —ial purpose, and texts, 3; —s,
life of particular, unresolved tensions
in, and complexity, 90; —ship, construct
of, and literacy, 176, 181, 182; —reader
relation, 46, 112; and *ethos, logos* and
pathos, 103, 104, 108; and letter writing,
103, 104, 108, 113; and case study
reports, 126, 129, 134–39, 144; and
Whateley's *Rhetoric*, 150, 151; Geisler
on, 171; and legal texts, 234–35. *See
also* Audience

Index

John Lyne, Donald N. McCloskey, and John S. Nelson
General Editors

Lying Down Together: Law, Metaphor, and Theology
Milner S. Ball

Shaping Written Knowledge: The Genre and Activity of the
Experimental Article in Science
Charles Bazerman

Textual Dynamics of the Professions: Historical and Contemporary
Studies of Writing in Professional Communities
Charles Bazerman and James Paradis, ed.

Politics and Ambiguity
William E. Connolly

Machiavelli and the History of Prudence
Eugene Garver

Language and Historical Representation: Getting the Story Crooked
Hans Kellner

The Rhetoric of Economics
Donald N. McCloskey

Therapeutic Discourse and Socratic Dialogue: A Cultural Critique
Tullio Maranhao

The Rhetoric of the Human Sciences: Language and Argument in
Scholarship and Public Affairs
John S. Nelson, Allan Megill, and Donald N. McClosley, ed.

What's Left? The Ecole Normale Supérieure and the Right
Diane Rubenstein

The Politics of Representation: Writing Practices in Biography,
Photography, and Policy Analysis
Michael J. Shapiro

The Legacy of Kenneth Burke
Herbert Simons and Trevor Melia, ed.

The Unspeakable: Discourse, Dialogue, and Rhetoric in the
Postmodern World
Stephen A. Tyler

Heracles' Bow: Essays on the Rhetoric and the Poetics of the Law
James Boyd White